"*A truly Catholic president will come in the nineteenth century, a man of character, to whom Our Lord God will give the palm of martyrdom in the plaza where this convent of mine is. He will consecrate the republic to the Divine Heart of my Blessed Son. This consecration will uphold the Catholic religion in the subsequent years, which will be tragic for the Church.*"
(Prediction of Our Lady of Good Success of January 16, 1599)

Severo Gomezjurado, S. J.

# The Consecration of Ecuador to the Sacred Heart of Jesus

*October 18, 1873*
*March 25, 1874*

Translated by Mrs. Joan Mart

*Dolorosa Press*
2013

*All rights reserved. No part of this book may be reproduced or transmitted in any form or by any means, electronic or mechanical, including photocopying, or by any information storage and retrieval system, without permission in writing from the publisher, except by a reviewer who may quote brief passages in a review.*

*Imprimatur*
*Ambrosio Cruz, S. J.*
Provincial — Ecuador

*Imprimatur*
Quito, May 15, 1972
† *Juan Larrea H.,*
Auxiliary Bishop and Vicar General.

Copyright © 2013 Paul M. Kimball
ISBN: 978-0-9883723-3-7

To order additional copies, please contact:

*Dolorosa Press*
www.dolorosapress.com
Email: avemaria@dolorosapress.com

# Table of Contents

*Page*

Introduction ..................................................................................i

1. "Steady, Manuel, steady!" ............................................................1
2. Consecration by Legislative Decree ...........................................7
3. Ratified by Church, State and the People ...............................27
4. Garcia Moreno Seals It with His Blood ...................................43
5. Monsignor Checa Seals the National Consecration with His Blood..................................................................................81
6. June 21, 1886, The Consecration is Renewed.........................89
7. January 1890, The Heart of Jesus from the Consecration goes to Chile ...............................................................................121
8. The Name "Garcia Moreno's Heart of Jesus" Conquers the Homes of the World ...........................................................137
9. Heads of State Who Followed Garcia Moreno's Example .....149
10. Division among Catholics Ruined the Catholic Regime .....163
11. October 21, 1900: De-consecration...........................................177
12. The Mason, Alfaro, and Six of his Minions Are Lynched .....209
13. Fiftieth Anniversary of the Consecration ...........................247
14. The Return of the Heart of Jesus of Garcia Moreno, January 29, 1942 ..............................................................................279

Appendices .............................................................................322

# Introduction

On May 13, 1931, in a solemn and public ceremony at Fatima, the bishops of Portugal consecrated their entire country to the Immaculate Heart of Mary. This consecration, attended by three hundred thousand faithful, was done specifically to place Portugal formally under the protection of the Blessed Virgin Mary. What had Portugal to be concerned about in 1931? The diabolical scourge of Communism, which had spread from Russia into Europe, ravaging all in its path, was practically on Portugal's doorstep. Only five years later, under the lying mask of a "civil war" in Spain, this infernal and atheistic ideology wrought devastation as horrific as any war. Most agreed that it was only a matter of time before the Communist carnage in Spain would spread into the defenseless neighboring country of Portugal.

But shortly after the outbreak of the war in Spain in 1936, the Portuguese bishops vowed to the Blessed Virgin, that if she would preserve their nation from the barbarities of the Communist invasion in Spain, then they would renew the national consecration as a public gesture of their gratitude. On May 13, 1938, they once again gathered publicly — this time to renew the consecration of Portugal to the Immaculate Heart of Mary. They kept their part of the agreement, for Mary had kept hers.

In addition, Portugal would later be spared the horrors of an even larger conflict — World War II. In a letter dated February 6, 1939, Sister Lucy of Fatima explained to Bishop da Silva that "In this horrible war, Portugal would be spared because of the national consecration to the Immaculate Heart of Mary made by the bishops." And in a letter to Pope Pius XII on December 2, 1940, she further explained that "Our Lord promises special protection to our country in this war, due to the consecration of the nation by the Portuguese prelates to the Immaculate Heart of Mary, as proof of the graces *that would have been granted to other nations, had they also consecrated themselves to Her.*" [emphasis added]

It should also be emphasized that, even in the heat of the gruesome Spanish "civil war," Our Lady's power would still shine forth. Of the one and a half million Catholics who were slaughtered in that vicious anti-Catholic invasion, not a single death occurred within the Diocese of Seville — because the Archbishop of Seville had formally consecrated his diocese to Mary's Immaculate Heart.

And in 1945, yet another example proves the powerful protection which our Heavenly Mother bestows on those who trustfully invoke her protection. At eight fifteen in the morning on August 6, 1945, the atom bomb was detonated above the city of Hiroshima, Japan. History has already recorded the unprecedented annihilation — over seventy thousand people were killed instantaneously and almost as many more would die from burns and radiation sickness. And yet, only eight blocks from the epicenter of the blast, the Jesuit rectory and church of Our Lady's Assumption, though damaged, remained standing. And in even greater defiance of the laws of science, the four Jesuit priests assigned to the church were still alive. Not only did they miraculously survive the searing explosion, but they would live the rest of their lives without ever suffering any effects from the nuclear radiation. More than two hundred scientists examined the survivors over time, and yet they were unable to explain scientifically why these Jesuits continued to live unscathed. The explanation comes to us in the words of one of the survivors, Father Hubert Shiffner: "In that house, the Rosary was prayed every day. In that house, we were living the message of Fatima." Praying the Rosary daily and making acts of reparation to the Immaculate Heart of Mary are an integral part of living the message of Fatima.[1]

At Rianjo, Spain, in 1931, Our Lord Himself told Sister Lucy: "Make it known to My ministers, that since they follow the example of the King of France in delaying the execution of My command, they will follow him into misfortune."

What was the example of the King of France? He failed to consecrate France to the Sacred Heart as Our Lord had commanded in His apparition to St. Margaret Mary Alacoque on June 17, 1689 — another apparition approved by the Church as worthy of belief. A succession of subsequent French kings also failed to execute this command. One hundred years to the day after that apparition, on June 17, 1789, King Louis XVI of France was stripped of his power by the Third Estate and four years later he was guillotined. His attempt to consecrate France in his jail cell while he awaited execution was too little, too late; it was not the solemn public act that Our Lord had commanded so that the whole world would know that His power had saved France.[2]

The first nation to consecrate itself to the Sacred Heart, however, was Ecuador. The Archbishop of Quito, His Grace Jose Ignacio Checa y Barba, and President Gabriel Garcia Moreno jointly and solemnly consecrated Ecuador to the Sacred Heart on March 25, 1874. The importance of this national consecration can be surmised as it was foretold by Our Lady of Good Success two hundred seventy four years in advance when she said, "A truly Catholic president will come in the nineteenth century, a man of character, to whom Our Lord God will give the palm of martyrdom in the plaza where this convent of mine is. He will consecrate the republic to the Divine Heart of my Blessed Son. This consecration will uphold the Catholic religion in subsequent years, which will be tragic for the Church."[3] Both President Garcia Moreno and Archbishop Checa y Barba later sealed their covenant with God by shedding their own blood as martyrs in the same Cathedral where the consecration was made. The assassins were hired by Freemasonry, which felt threatened by this noble act of publicly restoring the Kingship of Christ in one small nation. Formerly, Christ's reign had universally flourished in Europe as the cornerstone of Christendom and the antithesis of the diabolic, Masonic New World Order.

The Kingship of Christ requires both the union and indirect subordination of the State to the Church in mixed matters, i. e. matters that are both spiritual and temporal, such as marriage and education. The Church has solemnly condemned the proposition, "The Church ought to be separated from the State, and the State from the Church."[4] Pope Leo XIII condemned the secular state model, saying that the Church without the State is a soul without a body, and the State without the Church is a body without a soul.[5] He likewise condemned the religious indifference of secular states which follows as a necessary consequence. "Justice and reason forbid a state to be atheistic, or to be what amounts to the same thing as being atheistic, to have the same attitude towards various, so-called 'religions' and to grant the same rights to all of them indifferently."[6]

Pope Saint Pius X echoed this critical teaching of Catholic Social doctrine in his encyclical, *Vehementer nos*, written on February 11, 1906: "That the State should be separated from the Church is an absolutely false and most pernicious thesis. For first, since it is based on the principle that religion should be of no concern to the State, it does a grave injury to God, He Who is the founder and conserver of human society no less than He is of individual men, for which reason He should be worshipped not only privately but also publicly."

Since the Second Vatican Council, the current Catholic hierarchy has treacherously abandoned the Kingship of Christ as the necessary cornerstone of peace in the world. See for example Pope Paul VI's address to rulers given on December 8, 1965, at the close of Vatican II:

In your earthly and temporal city, God constructs mysteriously His spiritual and eternal city, His Church. And what does this Church ask of you after close to two thousand years of experiences of all kinds in her relations with you, the powers of the earth? What does the Church ask of you today? She tells you in one of the major documents of this Council [the one on religious liberty]. She asks you only liberty, the liberty to believe and to preach her faith, the freedom to love her God and serve Him, the freedom to live and to bring to men her message of life. Do not fear her.

According to Archbishop Marcel Lefebvre, "This position is false and inadequate: the State should help the Church. Otherwise, it might divest itself of all interest in the Church's affairs, maintenance of buildings, and compensation for priests ..."[7]

Archbishop Lefebvre more fully illustrated this abandonment of the Kingship of Christ in his famous sermon at Lille on August 29, 1976, as follows:

... they [modern Catholic Churchmen] reject the social reign of our Lord Jesus Christ under the pretext that it is no longer feasible. I have heard this from the mouth of the Nuncio of Berne; I have heard it from the mouth of the Vatican ambassador Fr. Dhanis, former Rector of the Gregorian University, who came in the name of the Holy See to ask me not to perform the ordinations of June twenty-ninth. It was June twenty-seventh at Flavigny, and I was preaching the retreat to the seminarians. He said to me, "Why are you against the Council?" I answered, "Is it possible to accept the Council, while in the name of the Council you say that all the Catholic States must be destroyed, that there must be no Catholic States left, and thus no more States where our Lord Jesus Christ reigns? Such a state is no longer possible." But it is one thing for something to be no longer possible, and another to accept that as a principle, and consequently, no longer to seek the social reign of our Lord Jesus Christ. But what do we say every day in the Our Father? "Thy kingdom come, Thy will be done on earth as it is in heaven." What is this reign? A little while ago you sang in the Gloria "You alone are Lord, You alone are the Most High, Jesus Christ." And are we to sing these words, and then go out and say, "No, Jesus Christ must not reign over us any longer." Are we living illogically? Are we Catholics or not?

# Introduction

There will be no peace on earth except under the reign of our Lord Jesus Christ. Nations are in conflict. Every day we have page after page in the newspapers about it, we have it on radio and television; and now with the change of prime minister: What are we going to do to improve the economy? What are we going to do to help the currency? What are we going to do so that manufacturing prospers, etc.? All the newspapers in the world are full of such questions. Well, even from an economic standpoint, our Lord Jesus Christ must reign, because the reign of our Lord Jesus Christ is the reign of the principles of love and of the Commandments of God, which establish equilibrium in society, and which make justice and peace reign. It is only with order, justice, and peace in society that the economy can thrive…

It is the reign of our Lord Jesus Christ that we want; and we profess our faith, saying that our Lord Jesus Christ is God.[8]

The author of this book, Father Severo Gomezjurado, does not give any indication of his agreement in this particular work about the opposition between traditional Church teaching regarding the necessity of a public profession of faith by Catholic nations and the Masonic religious liberty for all religions promoted by Vatican II. But there are a couple of headings which seem to have escaped censorship in his *magnum opus*, *Vida de Garcia Moreno*, where we find some such indications. There we find two enlightening headings, but not the corresponding text. Here are the two headings that could have come from the mouth of Archbishop Lefebvre: "Laxity Camouflaged under the Garb of *Aggiornamento*" and "Novelties and Suppression of the Old, under the Guise of Being Up-to-Date and a Sign of the Times."[9]

Garcia Moreno's Consecration of Ecuador to the Sacred Heart is in stark contrast to the modern Catholic policy of encouraging nations to abandon their public profession of Catholicism as the state religion. The *Syllabus of Errors* condemned such *aggiornamento* by condemning the following proposition: "The Roman Pontiff can, and ought to, reconcile himself and come to terms with progress, Liberalism and modern civilization."[10] Archbishop Lefebvre comments on this condemned proposition, "That is to say, come to terms with the civilization that is molded by all the principles that issued from the Revolution of 1789: liberty, equality, fraternity. 'Progress' is used here in the modernist sense of evolution. Modern civilization is the fruit of this evolution, of this Liberalism in every domain."[11]

As will be seen in this book, before Vatican II the Catholic world enthusiastically promoted the beatification of Garcia Moreno, whom Our Lady of Good Success had heralded as "a truly Catholic president." The history of his little known beatification process in Quito has been added in Appendix I; favors attributed to his intercession in Appendix II; and the story of the discovery of his mortal remains in Appendix III.

Allow us to give a summary here of the reasons why the President-martyr of Ecuador, Gabriel Garcia Moreno, who was assassinated by order of Freemasonry for being a model Catholic statesman, ought to be raised to the altars:

1. *Such was the explicit desire of Pope St. Pius X.*
    In Rome on November 1, 1907, Monsignor Manuel Maria Polit heard these words from His Holiness Pope Pius X:
    *You ought to introduce Garcia Moreno's cause of beatification. Take advantage of my Pontificate. You Ecuadorians will never find a Pope like me, so desirous of placing your Hero on the altars, nor a College of Cardinals like the present one, so eager to contribute to the glorification of such an exalted person.*[12]

2. *Venerable Pope Pius IX spoke of him as a martyr worthy of public honor by the Church:*
    *In the midst of all this, the Republic of Ecuador was miraculously distinguished by the spirit of justice and the unshakeable faith of its President, who showed himself ever the submissive son of the Church, full of devotion for the Holy See and of zeal to maintain religion and piety throughout his nation. And now the impious, in their blind fury, look upon, as an insult to their pretended modern civilization, the existence of a Government, which, while concerning itself with the material well-being of the people, strives at the same time to assure its moral and spiritual progress. Then, in the councils of darkness organized by the sects, these villains decreed the murder of the illustrious President. He fell under the steel of an assassin, as a victim of his faith and Christian charity.* (Address of Pope Pius IX to the pilgrims of Laval on September 20, 1875)
    Pope Pius IX did not limit himself to words. A few days later he had a magnificent funeral service celebrated for the soul of Garcia Moreno in the Basilica of Our Lady in Trastevere, as Pontiffs do when God has taken away one of the most eminent children of the

Church; and when certain Italian Catholics determined to erect a statue in his honor, Pius IX generously contributed to it, and placed it in the South American College in Rome.[13]

3. Pope Pius XII publicly supported the canonization of Garcia Moreno. *One of the causes of canonization that I would most willingly like to see in Rome is that of Garcia Moreno.*[14]

4. In Rome, the renowned theologian, Cardinal Luis Billot (+1931), strongly supported his canonization:
    *[Bishop Carlos Maria de la Torre's] allocution about the great… renowned martyr, Garcia Moreno has awakened in my soul such a lively joy that I cannot find words to express it…. Oh, what a beautiful figure, truly worthy of being placed on the altars; worthy of being proposed as an example to our modern Catholics…*[15]

5. The Ecuadorian bishops likewise supported his canonization:
    a) His Excellency Bishop Heredia, Bishop of Guayaquil, has said, "*I have always maintained my opinion that God is asking two equally obligatory things of us: firstly, the construction of the National Basilica, so that national and perpetual worship may be given there; and secondly, the glorification, as far as possible on our part, of the Martyr of God and of country amongst us.*"[16]
    b) The Bishop of Riobamba, Monsignor Andres Machado, said, "*The day will come when Garcia Moreno will be exalted on the altars.*"[17]
    c) Monsignor Polit, on January 22, 1922, referred to "*the Ecuadorian Hero whom I firmly hope will rise one day to the altars as a martyr of Jesus Christ.*"[18]
    d) The words of His Excellency Carlos Maria de la Torre, Bishop of Riobamba [subsequent Cardinal Archbishop of Quito]: "*The moral greatness of Garcia Moreno had soared to such a height that without the glorious martyrdom that was its worthy conclusion, God's work would have been unfinished and imperfect…*"[19]

6. The Bishops of France added their support to the canonization of Garcia Moreno:
    His Grace, Archbishop Manuel Maria Polit of Quito gave the following discourse on August 6, the anniversary of the death of Garcia Moreno:

> *In Paris, while conversing with some eminent bishops, ...those French prelates opposed me with these words: "Put these Causes aside for now* [for a certain bishop and a brother, both of Ecuador, that he came to personally present in Rome], *and undertake the Cause of Beatification of Garcia Moreno. Bishops and religious of eminent virtue abound on the altars; whereas the exaltation of someone like Garcia Moreno would be the first and sensational case of a president of a republic haloed with such honors. Commission Ecuadorians to collect all the documents that exist in your country regarding the death of Garcia Moreno, and all the rest will be done by the French Episcopate."*[20]

7. Father Mateo Crawley, the founder of the practice of the home enthronement of the Sacred Heart, longed for his canonization:

    > *... how happy I would consider myself to be if one day it were given to me to contribute in some way to his* [Garcia Moreno's] *exaltation on the altars...! If then, one day the Church renders such glory to the President-martyr, the Congregation of the Sacred Hearts should request that Rome would assign him to us as Patron of the Enthronement Crusade, since I made my debut in the shadow of his standard.*[21]

Wherefore, it is the aim of the publisher in making known this rare and valuable book to the English speaking world not merely to promote the beatification of Gabriel Garcia Moreno, but to make known his importance as a model for the Catholic restoration of nations at the "hour" foretold by Our Lady of Good Success, who said:

> In order to dispel this black cloud, which prevents the Church from enjoying the clear day of liberty, there will be a tremendous and frightful war in which the blood will flow of citizens and foreigners, of secular and religious priests, and also of religious. That night will be most horrifying, because, to human eyes, evil will seem to triumph. Then my hour shall have arrived, in which I, in an astonishing manner, will destroy the proud and accursed Satan, placing him under my feet and burying him in the infernal abyss, while the Church and country finally shall be free of his cruel tyranny.[22]

When this long awaited day finally arrives and the Immaculate Heart of Mary triumphs over her enemies, may "the prelate who shall restore the spirit of his priests," Archbishop Marcel Lefebvre, and the "truly Catholic president," Gabriel Garcia Moreno, thus prophetically foretold by Our Lady of Good Success, be then both recognized as the "two sons of oil who stand before the Lord of the whole earth" [23] as model heads of Church and State for the upcoming restoration of all things in Christ and the triumphant Marian Age.

Reverend Paul M. Kimball
Priest of the Society of Saint Pius X
Bristol, England
April 30, 2013

# Endnotes

[1] "Consecration to the Immaculate Heart of Mary," http://www.catholickingdom.com (accessed April 10, 2013).
[2] "Fatima Essentials: What you can do," www.fatima.org (accessed April 10, 2013).
[3] Rev. Fr. Manuel Sousa Pereira, *Vida admirable de la Madre Mariana* (Quito, Jesus de la Misericordia, 2008), vol. I, p. 159.
[4,5] Blessed Pius IX, *Syllabus of Errors*, n. 55.
[6] *Libertas*, §18.
[7] *Libertas*, §21.
[8] *Against the Heresies* (Kansas City, Angelus Press, 1997), p. 159.
[9] *A Bishop Speaks: Writings and Addresses, 1963-1976* (Kansas City, Angelus Press, 2007), pp. 269-271.
[10] "Relajacion camuflada con el ropaje de agiornamento.— Novelerias y supresion de lo antiguo, bajo el senuelo de nueva ola y signo de los tiempos. (Gomezjurado, vol. 12, p. 348).
[11] Pius IX, *Syllabus of Errors*, n. 80.
[12] *Against the Heresies*, p. 240.
[13] Fr. Severo Gomezjurado, *Vida de Garcia Moreno*, vol. 11, p. 268 and *La Consagracion*, pp. 278-279.
[14] Augustine Berthe, C. Ss. R., *Garcia Moreno* (Dolorosa Press, 2006), p. 334.
[15] Gomezjurado, *Vida de Garcia Moreno*, vol. 12, p. 407.
[16] *Boletin Eclesiastico de la Archidiocesis de Quito* (1921), p. 508. Gomezjurado, *¿Martir Garcia Moreno?* (*Is Garcia Moreno a Martyr?*), p. 151, *Vida de Garcia Moreno*, vol. 11, p.385, and *La Consagracion*, p. 319.
[17] *Boletin Eclesiastico de la Archidiocesis de Quito* (1921), p. 508. Gomezjurado, *¿Martir Garcia Moreno?* (*Is Garcia Moreno a Martyr?*), p. 151, *Vida de Garcia Moreno*, vol. 11, p.385, and *La Consecracion*, p. 319.
[18] Gomerjurado, vol. 11, p. 308.
[19] *Ibid.*, p. 376.
[20] *Ibid.*, p. 385.
[21] Gomezjurado, vol. 12, pp. 181-182.
[22] Gomezjurado, vol. 11, p. 129.
[23] Manuel Sousa Pereira, O. F. M., *Vida admirable de la Madre Mariana* (Quito, *Jesus de Misericordia*, 2008), pp. 32-33.
[24] Zacharias 4, 14. According to the meaning of the original passage in Zacharias, the "two sons of oil" are the anointed ones of the Lord; viz., Jesus the high priest, and Zorobabel the prince.

# Acknowledgements

Grateful thanks are hereby given to the Jesuits of the Province of Ecuador who kindly gave permission for the publication of this book in English, to Joan Mart for her untiring work of translation of these pages, to Mrs. Patti Petersen, Mrs. Cheryl Hadley, and Mrs. Grace Kimball for their meticulous editing, and lastly to Mr. Stephen McNulty for translating the last Appendix from French.

# Chapter 1
## "Steady, Manuel, Steady!"

It was eleven thirty on the night of November 21, 1852. A torrential downpour unfurled over the city of Quito. Nevertheless, millions of men and women were out on the streets shouting, "The Jesuit fathers are leaving! Let us ask for their final blessing!" Gabriel Garcia Moreno, a young man, thirty-one years old, suffered from a wound in one leg. Even so, clenching his crutches, he also went out into the street and headed for the Jesuit Rectory. Several battalions, armed with rifles and bayonets, had formed a kind of wall around the Rectory to stop the approach of the multitude. Undoubtedly Garcia Moreno displayed his aptitude for command bordering on magic, to prevail over the "Tauras"[1] and managed to station himself on one side of the main door. The clocks struck midnight when the Rector, Pablo de Blas, crossed the threshold and emerged on the way to ostracism. The kneeling multitude shouted, "Father, your last blessing!" In turn, Garcia Moreno, whose voice trembling from the emotion of sorrow, but simultaneously robust and sonorous, exclaimed, "Father Superior, now you leave this unhappy soil. But you shall return in ten years and we will chant the *Te Deum* in the Cathedral!"

The other Jesuits were emerging behind Father Blas. One of the last ones to leave was Manuel Proano, a sixteen year old novice from Quito. But his mother, Mercedes Vega de Proano, blocked his way saying, "My son, do not go. You are not under any obligation since you have not yet pronounced your religious vows!"

"My dear mother," answered the energetic novice, "I want to be faithful to my vocation, even though it means going into exile!"

His mother replied, "My son, you will not leave; and in case you do, you will have to tread on your mother's body!" No sooner said, she threw herself to the ground and stretched out the length of the threshold. Faced with such an expedient, the novice was perplexed and doubted for a minute. The people were in suspense in expectation of the outcome. Garcia Moreno decided it quickly. He fixed his vigorous gaze on the novice and said energetically, "Steady, Manuel; steady!" With that, the inexperienced Jesuit recovered unusual courage. He knelt by his mother and said to her, "My mother, God is first and then my affectionate parents. I will leave without touching you with my feet." No sooner said than done, he took a fast running start, leaped and landed on the other side of his mother. She got up from the ground and, turning her sorrow into heroic sacrifice, shouted to him, "My son, now I know clearly that

God is calling you. Receive my blessing and set off in the direction of your exile!"[2]

Garcia Moreno soon abandoned his crutches and took up the steel of his pen. The written word! The blade of his sharp, cutting words have been pondered by Doctor Antonio Borrero: "Garcia Moreno kills with bullets as well as with words." Listen to these verses by Garcia against Dictator Urbina, the main agent of Jesuit ostracism:

> There hides the infamous prostitute
> Under martial adornment, and his timid
> Hand holds the glaring steel
> Never reddened in battle.
> Printed on his yellow forehead:
> Loathsome wrinkles, the signs
> Accumulated in a dishonest bed.
> Not one of all the vices invented by man
> In long centuries of evil, does he ignore:
> Treason, perjury, robbery, fraud,
> Lewd licentiousness, the frenzy
> Of barbaric oppression. His impure life,
> Enclosed in articles, is found
> In the severe statutes that inspire
> Salutary terror in the perverse.
> Yet he, of total and horrible corruption,
> A monster that would even dishonor the scaffold:
> Triumphs, dominates, tyrannizes,
> And breathes tranquilly..."[3]

A month later Garcia Moreno founded his fourth newspaper, which he distinguished with the name of *The Nation*. Urbina's regime addressed this communication to the newspaperman: "If you publish a second edition of your newspaper, you will be exiled." Garcia Moreno replied to him, "Together with the many reasons I have for publishing the newspaper, from now on I add that of not dishonoring myself by yielding to your intimations."

The next edition of *The Nation* appeared to the public, and Garcia Moreno was seized and driven into exile. It lasted more than three years. Our hero managed to slip away. He left for Paris and entered the Sorbonne. He studied sixteen hours a day. Extremely absorbed by the desire to learn, he dodged his religious practices. But he never rejected his esteem for the Catholic Faith. Based on this, one day he understood that religious practices should hold first place in his enthusiasm and concerns. At once he sought a priest and went to Confession. The next morning he went to Communion. That afternoon he prayed the Holy Rosary. He firmly maintained this program.

Garcia Moreno was living in this atmosphere of love for study and for religion in the City of Light when he learned that the French bishops, gathered in Synod, had requested the Holy Pontiff Pius IX for the Feast of the Most Holy Heart of Jesus to be celebrated obligatorily in the Universal Church. Here is a fact that Gabriel could hardly avoid turning into a matter for speculation and food for his fervent Christian soul. He recalled that in his homeland, Ecuador, the same as in all of Spanish America, that feast had been celebrated for the past forty years, thanks to a privilege conceded by the Vicar of Christ, Pius VII, in the year 1815. He also began to learn that our Lord Jesus Christ, through Saint Margaret Mary Alacoque, had requested King Louis XIV to consecrate France officially to His Divine Heart, and promised him spiritual as well as material favors if such an act were carried out. To the disgrace of the French monarchy, that consecration did not take place.

What was Pius IX's answer to the French bishops? He granted the Feast of the Heart of Jesus to be celebrated obligatorily in the whole world. Pope Pius IX signed the document on August 23, 1856. Two months later Garcia Moreno left France and returned to Ecuador, thanks to a decree of amnesty granted by the new President of the Republic, General Francisco Robles.[4]

That new President was not the fruit of free elections by the people of Ecuador, but rather a fraudulent imposition by his predecessor, General Jose Maria Urbina. The result was a more or less identical regime to the previous one, with its embezzlements and outrages. A Masonic Lodge was installed in Ecuador for the first time, in Guayaquil. Of necessity, rupture and war had to arise with Garcia Moreno. But he was now a more powerful leader than before. He was slender of stature with an authoritarian bearing. He was oval headed and he had black hair with a bit of grey, along with a dense, black moustache. He had large, brilliant, dark brown eyes, wider-set than normal. In polemic cases his gaze magnetized and overwhelmed the adversary. His voice, a bit high-pitched, ordinarily acquired vigor and resonance when needed to strengthen his authority and intimidate the enemy.

He was an athlete in physical strength. On his long trips by horseback, he surpassed everyone in speed and resistance. He was an acrobat. If he ran up against a mule train that blocked the passage, Garcia Moreno leaped over the heads, necks, shoulders and haunches of the beasts of burden and went on his way. He was a genius, and even seething with genius, according to Aparicio Ortega. Therefore he found a thousand means to get out of a fix and to triumph. He was thirty five years old when he started the crusade for the salvation and exaltation of his native land. He fought with the pen and with the sword. He knew how to transmit his patriotism to those around him. He suffered defeat, but did not quit; on the contrary, he returned to the contest with greater daring. At the end of four years of standing out as a champion in battle, he had defeated, exterminated and thrown the enemies out of his Fatherland.[5]

# Endnotes

[1] "The 'Tauras,' a guard of mamelukes whom Urbina called his 'canons,' armed with daggers, went up and down the country, attacking inoffensive men, insulting women, and assassinating all who would not be robbed without a struggle" (Rev. Fr. Augustine Berthe, *Garcia Moreno* (Dolorosa Press, 2006), pg. 102).

[2] Severo Gomezjurado, S. J., *Vida de Garcia Moreno* (Imprenta ARPI, Quito, 1979), vol. 2, pp. 147 ff.

[3] Here is the original Spanish poem:
"Allá se esconde prostituta infame, / Bajo adornos marciales; y su mano / Tímida empuña el relumbrante acero / Jamás enrojecido en las batallas. / Impresos lleva en su amarillo rostro / los asquerosos surcos, las señales / que en lecho torpe atesoró. Ninguno / de cuantos vicios inventara el hombre / En largos siglos de maldad, ignora: / Traición, perjuicio, latrocinio, estafa, / Libertinaje impúdico, furores / De bárbara opresión. Su vida impura / Encerrada en artículos se encuentra / En el severo código que inspira / Saludable terror a los perversos. / ¡I este de corrupción conjunto horrible; / Monstruo que hasta el patíbulo infamara: / Éste triunfa, domina, tiraniza, / Y respira tranquilo"…

[4] *Ibid.* p. 165 ff. Cf. 351 ff.

[5] *Idem.* vol. 3, p. 251 ff.

*Manuel Proano, who initiated and promoted the Consecration*

# Chapter 2
# Consecration by Legislative Decree

The Jesuit, Manuel Proano Vega, also returned from exile to Ecuador. A young priest, he visited President Garcia Moreno and reminded him of his words: "In ten years you will return," and of the other ones: "Steady, Manuel; steady!" His Excellency, also remembering with what assurance he had pronounced that prediction, said, "It was Hannibal's oath. To a large extent, to carry it out is why I decided to intervene in politics."

It was the year 1873 when Father Manuel Proano, at that time in Riobamba, received the following news:

In the German city of Ratibor[1] there was a feast day in honor of the Most Sacred Heart of Jesus, which aroused the fury of the Protestants. Supported by the National Police, they entered the Catholic Church, seized the faithful and started the task of reducing them to imprisonment. Some, who succeeded in slipping away, chose to leave their native soil and even their country.

Having read this news, the above-mentioned Jesuit felt very sorry, since he was an apostle of the devotion to the Heart of Jesus. How could that sacrilege be repaired? In a way unheard of until then... There is a reason why Ecuador had the good fortune to be governed by the most Catholic President in the contemporary world. So he wrote to Garcia Moreno as follows:

> The time seems to have come when Your Excellency, as a Catholic magistrate and fervent son of the Church, interpreting the almost unanimous faith of the people of Ecuador, should strengthen the bonds of love that have united Ecuadorians to God, by means of a decree to officially consecrate the Republic to the Divine Heart of Jesus. The world is lost due to the Naturalism which, at present, has invaded the high regions of power almost everywhere and has pathetically led people's ideas astray. Your Excellency is the Head of Ecuador, a country that is a most outstanding exception nowadays, largely due to the sincere piety and heroic fearlessness of him who governs her destiny.
>
> But, alas! Your Excellency is a man...who will leave this earth in the future...; and then..., what will Ecuador's fate be? ... Your Excellency is used to saying frequently: "No man is necessary in the world... God does not die." Then let us entrust ourselves to that true God, the constant object of your humble adoration. Let Ecuador rec-

ognize the Divine Heart of Jesus Christ as its eternal and absolute Sovereign and Protector. And the volleys of the Republic in greeting the radiant dawn of its national feast day will be sufficient to deafen the intimidated ears of impiety, and to drive the bold hordes from Hell far from the borders of our Fatherland.

Unfortunately the exact date of the above letter was not recorded. The month is calculated as being in March.

The extremely Christian Chief of State's reply unfolds in the following paragraphs:

> A more commendable idea cannot be conceived, consistent with the sentiments that encourage me to promote in every way the prosperity and happiness of the country whose government Divine Providence has entrusted to me, than by giving it the foundation of the highest moral and religious perfection to which the practical profession of Catholicism calls us. I acknowledge the faith of the people of Ecuador. And that faith imposes on me the sacred duty of preserving its deposit intact, even if it is at the price of my life. I do not fear men, because God is higher. And if it were at any time the unavoidable duty of every sincere child of the Church to confirm the faith of his heart with the most explicit, reiterated and solemn profession of his lips, it is undoubtedly at the present time, when, even among believing nations, this century's chronic malady is weakness of character.
>
> I am hated, I am detested. But in deference to Our Lord Jesus Christ, I acknowledge myself unworthy of such great glory. Therefore, I do not fear men; but I ask, "Is Ecuador a worthy offering to the Heart of the God-Man?" ... This Heart is holy, immaculate. Have we already improved the people's ethical standards enough? ... Have we sanctified the domestic home? ... Does justice prevail in the Court, peace in our families, harmony among citizens, fervor at church?
>
> The Heart of Jesus is the throne of Wisdom. Do the people of Ecuador accept all His teachings? Are they docile and submissive to His divine doctrine? Do they receive and welcome His inspirations with love, reject practically all the world's errors, and overcome all current perversion of ideas? ...I do not fear men. But I fear that this country is not yet a worthy offering to the Heart of Jesus Christ. Let us implore the Lord in fervent prayer to send us holy missionaries,

untiring apostles. May at least fifty zealous, charitable priests come to cover the entire territory, visit our villages, and not overlook a single nook. Let them teach and preach the Gospel and convert, if possible, all sinners. Then, with pure hands, we can consecrate to the God of purity, a people purified with the divine blood. Then we will raise a new temple to the Divine Heart.

It is pleasant to find in Garcia Moreno the first idea for the construction of a temple as an architectural testimony of the projected Consecration. Such an idea could easily have sprung from contact with Parisian newspapers, which spoke of raising a national church on the hill of Montmartre as the monument of France's consecration to the Divine Heart.

Father Manuel Proano answered the President. The substance of his concepts was the following:

> The consecration of an entire people to the Heart of Jesus Christ certainly requires moral purity, not only in individuals and families, but also in the whole of society. But it is no less certain that such purity is inconceivable without the supernatural, divine grace which would be copiously poured out on Ecuador if she gives public, solemn witness to her religious Faith, contrary to the almost universal apostasy of nations. To reward such an act, the Lord will open the wings of his protection over us. And turning His compassionate eyes aside from our miseries, He will take pleasure in what, on our part, somehow repairs our outrages and renders Him honor and glory.

Garcia Moreno's acceptance is perceptible in his reply. He asked only for the realization of a requisite contained in these words quoted from the Commander in chief:

> I am a son of the Church and she imposes the duty on me of acknowledging the most sacred authority and the surest teaching in her prelates. I am a son of the Church, and I deeply respect good souls whose criteria are all the wiser, the more immediate their communication with God in prayer.[2]

In reading this reply, the Jesuit saw that the undertaking was on the right track, although it took a new direction. This new direction presaged complete success, since the Third Provincial Council of Quito had been summoned, whose tasks were to begin June 1, 1873, which happened to be Pentecost Sunday that year.

The bishops or their representatives came from the various dioceses, except from the diocese of Cuenca. Why? Because their bishop, the Illustrious Esteves Toral, was in kind of a rift with Garcia Moreno. How did that happen? Well, this bishop had excommunicated the Governor of Cuenca, Carlos Ordonez, who was innocent, or, at the most, guilty only of venial faults. Learning of such an abuse, Gabriel Garcia Moreno had recourse to the Roman Pontiff, informing him of that unjust and violent conduct, and asking him to apply the corresponding remedy. Pius IX did so through a Papal Brief addressed to the impulsive prelate dated July 21, 1873. Let us listen to it:

> With sadness we have heard that your very Catholic country has been disturbed by the enemies of legitimate authority, and that the most insolent ones dwell in your diocese. But with greater displeasure we have received the news that not only do you not withdraw from the rebels' deceit and friendship, but on the contrary that you have made a kind of alliance with them and their snares. It is true that, by means of a pastoral letter, you have established harmony between the antagonistic groups. But, agreement being impossible between irreproachable subjects and the adversaries of the legitimate Power, the Bishop should have suppressed the impudence of the latter above all, making the precept from Exodus reach their ears: "Thou shalt not speak ill of the gods, and the prince of thy people;"[3] and the Apostle's commandment: "Obey your prelates, and be subject to them."[4] "Let every soul be subject to higher powers. For there is no power but from God... Therefore, he that resisteth the power resisteth the ordinance of God. And they that resist purchase to themselves damnation."[5]
>
> These teachings would have united the subjects from both jurisdictions against common enemies; they would have increased harmony, stimulated good souls, and restrained the insolence of evil ones, and finally would have removed the suspicion that you had taken sides with an evil party. Consequently your Pastoral letter was a mistake, by attempting to bring about a league between rebels and loyal subjects, forcing the latter to submit to the opinion of the former. All the more so since your words seemed to blame the whole tumult on the officials of the Republic, and you position yourself on the revolutionaries' side and stimulate their audacity.

In this conflict, the Provincial Governor, desiring to extinguish the flare-up of minds, judged it necessary to publish some objections to the Pastoral Letter, which he did. On that occasion, you could have mitigated the harshness of your previous assertions, and skillfully adapted them to an upright criterion. Far from that, pushed by malicious advisors, you increased the seriousness of your error. For, through a public ecclesiastical summons, you threatened major excommunication of the Governor and those who were on his side. By such rash means, you opened the door to schism with the Catholics faithful to the Civil Government. You simultaneously encouraged the rebels, and helped them to increase the number of their gullible followers. On the other hand, even supposing that there had been an exaggeration or abuse on the part of the civil power, it did not go beyond a slight fault, given the respectful way it was expressed, in no way worthy of being sanctioned with what is usually the greatest punishment used by the Church. Therefore, very serious complaints and reproaches have reached us against you. Their justice, once the reasons have been well weighed, cannot be doubted.

It is therefore appropriate for you make complete satisfaction, not only by more prudent and cautious behavior in the future, but also by positive demonstrations, with a view to expiating the fault, publicly showing your friendly disposition of spirit, and giving a sign of future harmony between ecclesiastical and civil powers. We desire, venerable Brother, for you to do whatever might be necessary on this point to appease the indignation of the civil authority and gain his good disposition. That way you will avoid forcing us to take another type of measure, for the sake of public tranquility and the spiritual good of your diocesans... In testimony of our benevolence, we impart our apostolic blessing to you as well as to your entire diocese with the greatest affection.

While the above Pontifical Brief sailed the Atlantic towards Ecuador, Father Manuel Proano addressed his letters and prayers to the Fathers of the Third Provincial Council of Quito, entreating them to issue a decree to consecrate the Ecuadorian Church to the Divine Heart of Jesus. And he exhorted President Garcia Moreno to cooperate in that act. Expectation grew as the date approached for opening the National Political Congress on the tenth of August, thanks to the eminently religious paragraphs of the message pronounced by the Head of State. Let us listen to them:

> Our rapid progress would be useless to us if the Republic did not advance, day by day, in morality. As morals are reformed through the free and saving action of the Catholic Church...
>
> Since we are so fortunate as to be Catholic, let us be so logically and openly. Let us be so in our private lives and in our political existence. And let us confirm the truth of our sentiments and of our words with the public witness of our works. Do not be satisfied, therefore, with carrying out all that we have just indicated to you. Let us erase even the least trace of hostility against the Church from our laws. For, some provisions still remain in them from the ancient and oppressive Spanish Regalism. Their tolerance from now on would be a shameful contradiction and miserable inconsistency.
>
> This should always be the conduct of a Catholic nation. But more so now, in the times of an appalling and universal war waged against our most holy religion, now when the apostates' blasphemy denies even the Divinity of Jesus, our God and Lord, now when everything unites, everything conspires, everything turns against God and His Anointed One. A torrent of evil and furor against the Church and against society itself rises from the depths of a disturbed society. As in the earth's tremendous upheavals, formidable rivers of putrid slime gush from unknown depths. Now consequent, resolute, lively conduct is doubly obligatory for us. For, inaction in combat is treason or cowardliness.
>
> Let us then proceed like sincere Catholics with unshakeable loyalty, basing our hope not on our insignificant power, but rather on the omnipotent protection of the Most High. We will be happy a thousand times over if Heaven continues to lavish its blessings on our dear Country as a reward; and I would be happier yet if, besides hate, I should deserve slander and insults from the enemies of our God and of our Faith.

There is no need to ponder the enthusiasm this caused in the Legislators, the people and the Council Fathers. The latter had grown in number, with the presence of two representatives from the diocese of Cuenca: Canons Mariano Borja and Jose Antonio Piedra. On the memorable day of August 31, 1873, the Synod issued a decree whose most important clauses follow:

Considering:

That the greatest good that a people can enjoy is the pure preservation of the Roman, Catholic, Apostolic Faith, a precious gift not obtained by merits but rather by the merciful grace of the Lord.

That they eagerly desire, therefore, to obtain this special grace from God for the Republic; being intimately convinced that they will gain it, if prostrate with humility, they offer the Nation to the Most Sacred and most loving Heart of Jesus.

Decree:

The Third Provincial Council of Quito offers and solemnly consecrates the Republic of Ecuador to the Most Sacred Heart of Jesus. And with all possible faith, humility and urgency, they implore that from now and forever, He will be her Protector, guide and helper, so that her inhabitants may conform their ways to this Faith, the only one that can make them happy in time and eternity.

The solemnities corresponding to the Consecration will be celebrated in all the Cathedrals and parish Churches during the upcoming Lent.

For the first time, the Church of an entire Sovereign State was consecrated to the Divine Heart of Jesus. Three days later, her most outstanding representative, Monsignor Ignacio Checa, directed the following official letter to Doctor Francisco Javier Leon, Minister of the Interior of the Supreme Civil Government:

My intimate conviction of the Chief of State's pure Catholicism gives me hope that on his part he will contribute to the holy end that the Council Fathers proposed when they issued the indicated decree, whether by supporting it before the Holy See in his position as legitimate Patron of the Church of Ecuador; or by giving it, as well, all the official increment that he sees fit, assured of receiving the most distinguished favors from that Sacred Heart in compensation, together with the gratitude of the Prelates and faithful of the Republic.

On his part, the above-mentioned Minister of the Government addressed the following official letter to the Honorable Senate:

I forward to you the original official letter from the Illustrious Reverend Archbishop of the Archdiocese to this Office, and the original decree issued by the Third Provincial Council of Quito, consecrating the Republic to the Sacred Heart of Jesus and placing it under His guardianship and protection, so that Your Honorable Chamber, taking those documents into consideration, would deign to second that Council's intentions, since the Government promises, on its part, to lend its cooperation, so that what was agreed upon will be made effective.

Manuel Proano, referring to the members of the Senate, printed these words, which I quote:

> Everyone said that a project of this nature was not even worth discussion or debate. They said that it should pass unanimously and be acclaimed enthusiastically, since everyone desired the glorious honor of signing that project. And this they effectively did, beginning with our good General Saenz.

The Church Business Commission, headed by Monsignor Ignacio Ordonez, was inspired by France's efforts to build a national church dedicated to the Heart of Jesus on Montmartre hill. They wanted to give their country an analogous monument and fixed the sum of one hundred thousand pesos in the name of the exchequer. Before proposing the project to the Senate, the Committee requested Garcia Moreno's opinion in an interview. The President answered:

> One hundred thousand pesos are not enough for this project. God will give me three hundred thousand to build the best church in the Republic in honor of the Exalted Heart. However, structures of this nature require many years to carry out and run the risk of ending up as a dead letter. Maybe the present Government will begin the job, and the next one will paralyze it. In that case such a beginning would give occasion for ridicule and protest against the country. It is best then for the Senate to be satisfied for now with the Official Consecration.

The text of the Consecration, written by the Church Business Commission, was discussed and approved unanimously in the Senate on September 16 and 17, 1873. Meanwhile, Garcia Moreno pressed for missionaries to come to prepare the people. He remembered article five of the conciliar decree: "The solemnities corresponding to the Consecration will be celebrated in all Cathedrals and parish churches during the upcoming season of Lent."

"Oh, if only a month before next Lent a great number of missionaries would arrive from Europe!" That was the Head of State's yearning, who in order not to shirk the means for bringing it about, on that very day, September seventeenth, wrote the following letter to General Francisco Javier Salazar, the Representative of Ecuador in Paris:

> By reason of the expulsion of the Redemptorists from Germany, there is a considerable number of those excellent Fathers who could come to Ecuador. Please go personally, if possible, to come to an understanding with the Provincial, whose address you will find on the attached letter. Upon agreement with him, you will easily obtain permission from the Father General at Rome for up to fifty religious to come. May they arrive in Guayaquil before the end of the year to establish houses in Guayaquil, Manabi, Ambato, Latacunga and Loja, and even in Quito, if their number permits. If fifty cannot come, obtain at least the number that is closest to it.
>
> In the name of the Government you can offer:
>
> 1. Travel expenses; 2. a monthly pension to sustain each one, until they have other means of sufficient sustenance; 3. effective help for repairing or building the houses and churches that they need. Only in Manabi does everything have to be done. There are churches and houses in the other cities that will be in good, serviceable condition with few expenses.
>
> Ask Anibal Gonzalez for the necessary funds to defray the cost of the Fathers' trip, and give it to Fourquet, so he will understand everything relative to the trip. Please present this letter to Anibal, to whom I have written today and cannot manage to write again now. This letter will serve as a letter of credit, since Anibal knows that I am a good payer.
>
> Yours faithfully,
> G. Garcia Moreno.
>
> P.S. The greatest good you could do for our beautiful country is to send us those good apostles, who will bring us morals and virtues, and through them civilization and prosperity.

Two days later, on September nineteenth, the Senate definitely approved the above-mentioned Decree of Consecration, and sent it to the House of Representatives. It was studied there in the sessions on the twenty-third and twenty-fifth of that same month, and approved without the slightest change. However, in the session on the twenty-seventh, Jose Justiniano Estupinan, the Representative from Manabi, decided that this deprecatory phrase should be eliminated: "humbly imploring Him that by this act of the people of Ecuador, making honorable ostentation of their Christian virtues, from now on it may be the bulwark of their institutions and source of their prosperity." What reasons did the Honorable member put forth? That the nature of a decree is to command or forbid, but not to raise prayers even though it is to the Almighty. The objection was discussed and voted on. The majority deemed it reasonable and so the deprecatory phrase was deleted.

Juan Leon Mera, a famous man of letters and Representative from the Province of Tungurahua, influenced the final form of the text. Let us hear him:

> The Senate and House of Representatives of Ecuador, assembled in Congress, considering:
> 1. That the Third Provincial Council of Quito by special decree has consecrated the Republic of Ecuador to the Most Sacred Heart of Jesus, placing her under His protection and help, and
> 2. That it corresponds to the Legislature to contribute, in the name of the Nation, to an act that, being so conformed to her sentiments of eminent Catholicism, is also the most effective means of preserving the Faith and attaining the progress and temporal well-being of the State
>
> Decree:
>
> Article 1. That the Republic of Ecuador be consecrated to the Most Sacred Heart of Jesus, declaring Him her Patron and Protector.
>
> Article 2. The Feast of the Most Sacred Heart of Jesus be declared a civil holiday with first class attendance, which will be celebrated in all the Cathedrals of the Republic by the Diocesan Prelates with the greatest possible solemnity.
>
> Article 3. An altar dedicated to the Heart of Jesus will be raised in every Cathedral; may the zeal and piety of the diocesans be aroused for this purpose.

Article 4. A memorial stone with the inscription of this decree will be placed in the facade of each altar mentioned in the above article and paid for by national incomes.

Transmit to the Executive Branch for implementation and compliance.

In Quito, Capital of the Republic, October 8, 1873.
The President of the Senate: R. de Ascasubi.
The President of the House of Representatives: Vicente Lucio Salazar.
The Secretary of the Senate: Carlos Casares.
The Secretary of the House of Representatives: Pedro Jose Cevallos.

Ten days later, that legislative decree was executed and signed in the Presidential Office, in the Chief of State's handwriting, with the following words:

Government Palace in Quito, October 18, 1873.
Let this be published and enforced.
G. Garcia Moreno.
Minister of the Interior: Francisco Javier Leon.

What a truly unique decree, unequalled and never prefigured in previous centuries! Six days later, on October twenty-fourth, it appeared on the first page of the government newspaper, *The National*, printed not with ordinary ink, but in gold letters. It is moving to see, in spite of the wear and discoloration caused by the slow but constant action of time over one hundred years.

"Something entirely singular and very worthy of perpetual memory" were the words the Austrian Jesuit, Nicolas Nilles, used to manifest his joy and admiration in his work entitled *De rationibus festorum Sacratissimi Cordis Jesu.*

The text of the decree was reproduced in the Italian magazine *Unita Catolica* three months after being published in Quito, and in the fourth month, in the French magazine *Le Messager du Coeur de Jesus*. It is impossible not to recall the tribute pronounced by Cardinal Gasparri, Secretary of State to Pope Benedict XV: "A man of solid piety, Garcia Moreno had the merit of being the first one officially to consecrate the

*Decree of Consecration of Ecuador to the Sacred Heart*

*executed on October 18, 1873, by President Garcia Moreno.*

*Roberto de Azcasubi Matheu*
*From an oil painting by Antonio Salas in the year 1830.*

*Vicente Lucio Salazar Cabal*

*Garcia Moreno holding the Decree of the Consecration.*

nation he governed to the Sacred Heart of Jesus, thus endowing her with glorious primacy."[6]

It is worth noting that on the same date, October 18, 1873, when Garcia Moreno signed the decree of Consecration, this ruler addressed a severe, scathing letter to Monsignor Esteves Toral as follows:

> Quito, October 18, 1873.
> His Excellency, Bishop Remigio Toral, MD
> My most respected Bishop:
> I would have received your letter of the fourth of the present month with great pleasure if I could have believed in the desire your Excellency expresses to renew the friendly relations that united us in times past. But, unfortunately, Your Excellency's conduct manifests the lack of truth and sincerity with which that letter was written, perhaps with the exclusive aim of forging a supporting document to be sent to Rome.
> It is not true to affirm that Your Excellency had been presented erroneously to me with calumnious reports, Your Excellency, unless Your Excellency calls your very notorious deeds calumnious reports, such as your infamous pastoral letter, excommunication, etc., and, above all, your union with the enemies of the previous Governor Ordonez, that is to say, with the enemies of the Government and of public order, since they abhorred Ordonez for being a government agent. And they wounded him with three bullets attempting to assassinate him, when they thought that I was going to be the victim of other assassins.
> There is no sincerity, Your Excellency, in your friendly words. For, not only does Your Excellency continue united to the same men as before, but also you have just given two most serious, scandalous proofs of the ill will that you harbor. The first consists of having disobeyed the Supreme Pontiff's forthright command, refusing to revoke the unjust censorship that you fulminated against the authors and editors of the answer to Your Excellency's pastoral letter. The second amounts to having assigned the infamous Doctor Carrasco, a priest from Tixan, to the parish of Azogues as an interim priest, although Your Excellency is perfectly well aware of the part he played in the rebellion of Tambo and of Cannar in 1864, towns near Azogues where, as in Azogues, that liberal priest has many relatives.

Your Excellency will recall that the revolutionary laws of Machala and Santa Rosa in the year 1864, written with the approval of the enemy leader at that time, the former General Jose Maria Urbina, rationalized rebellion against the government because of the celebration of the Concordat and the introduction of the Company of Jesus and other religious Orders, etc. Your Excellency will also remember that the blood shed in the assassination of the national guards in Tambo Viejo, in the rebel attacks on Cuenca and in the torture and execution of the fierce traitor, Campoverde, fell back on the contemptible Doctor Carrasco, author and stimulator of the above-mentioned rebellion whose object was to help Urbina's invasion that year. And finally, Your Excellency will not have forgotten that for these reasons, that priest was separated from Tambo, whom you now place on a more visible stage for the consummation of new crimes.

The Minister has officially protested the placement of this clergyman, who in the tiny village of Tixan could do nothing important against public order. But I cannot expect anything from a bishop who has disobeyed the Holy See. And from now on, I make Your Excellency responsible for the blood that may be shed and the evil of all kinds that the Republic may suffer.

Concluding, I remind you that Your Excellency has had no cause for complaint against the government or against me, just as none of your brother bishops have had. And Your Excellency is the only one in the Church of Ecuador who has obliged me to complain before the Holy See. If only Your Excellency would return to the right path, by obeying the Vicar of Jesus Christ and being separated from the enemies of the government before the Holy Father has to take sorrowful measures!

Your Excellency's obliging, humble servant who kisses your hands,
G. Garcia Moreno.

During those same days the President also wrote to the painter from Quito, Rafael Salas, then on a government scholarship to Rome to perfect his pictorial art. He asked him to make a painting of the Heart of Jesus with these characteristics:

Let the divine eyes be raised to Heaven in an attitude of prayer to our Heavenly Father. Let Christ's right hand hold the royal scepter. His left hand should bear the globe of the world where the nation of Ecuador is obvious. Finally let the Divine Heart shed its outpouring of warmth and light over the world, and especially over Ecuador. If only this image would reach Quito in about three months, so it can preside over the Consecration that will be made with the greatest solemnity, when the Church and the State will be united!

A little philosophy is fitting here as regards Garcia Moreno and the Divine Love.

It was none other than the National Congress on August 16, 1875, who defined Garcia Moreno in these terms: "He was a genius tormented by two divine passions: love for Catholicism and love for his country." Let us develop these ideas.

Through love of country he sought to increase its territory, economy, science, art, morals and religion. Out of love for Catholicism, he undertook what constitutes her fifth essence and compendium, that is, devotion to the Heart of Jesus. Now then, the Heart of Jesus is a symbol of Divine Love, which the Catholic Church recognizes and to whom she offers hymns as Creator of the heavens, oceans and continents; rich to those who invoke Him; source of wisdom; charity toward His Heavenly Father and the Human Race. It is understood that such Divine Love is the impulse of progress and advancement for all works, therefore, to whatever is great, strong, rich, prosperous, virtuous, heroic, saintly, and finally to the imitation and correspondence of His creatures to His love. Of course the genius tormented by love for Catholicism and Country would have to receive and be delighted with such a religion!

# Endnotes

[1] Ratibor, Germany is today Raciborz, Poland.
[2] Severo Gomezjurado S. J., *Vida de Garcia Moreno* (Imprenta ARPI, Quito, 1979), vol. 9, p. 118 ff.
[3] Exodus 22, 28.
[4] Hebrews 13, 17.
[5] Romans 13, 1-2.
[6] *Idem*. p. 121 ff. Also p. 139 ff. And finally, p. 125 ff.

# Chapter 3
# Ratified by Church, State and the People

According to Garcia Moreno's letter, the Illustrious Bishop of Cuenca delayed for two months his retraction, which he wrote on November 13, 1873. Here are his words:

> We, although unworthy, who were made Bishop and Prince of the Church, should edify and evangelize our diocesans with our actions and words. We are pleased, therefore, to tell the whole world that We have just now submitted promptly and humbly to the voice of our Superior, the august Vicar of Jesus Christ, who, because of the Pastoral letter that We sent you on April twenty-third of this year, and due to the censure[1] which we inflicted in reaction to a published article, "The Pastoral Letter of the Bishop of Cuenca," decided to send Us a respectful letter on July twenty-first. Describing that Pastoral letter as imprudent, and as slight the faults that the printed article contained against Us, he disapproved of Our conduct. This disapproval, to which We have already said We have humbly submitted, has caused very deep affliction in our spirit, especially since, without expecting it and much less desiring it, We have perhaps shed a drop of bitter aloes in the afflicted heart of the Holy Father...[2]

Bishop Toral also made a change in the Secretariat of the Curia. He assigned Canon Antonio Piedra to Doctor Antonio Borrero's position. And he wrote to Pius IX, giving an account of having corrected his conduct. The Pope replied on February 5, 1874, in the following tenor:

> With supreme approval, We have received your letter full of filial love, and especially your Pastoral letter of last November, in which the spirit of Christ's humility and meekness is evident... Certainly, since you have confessed your own errors and have obeyed the Apostolic See, no one who has been unjustly reprimanded by you will find any excuse to deny you his obedience. And your conduct, conformed to the Gospel, will consolidate your authority in the Flock of Christ, and extinguish past discord between ecclesiastical and secular powers; and through a reciprocal reconciliation, unite your efforts for the benefit of the people. Those benefits are of such importance that all insistence must be

applied to promote and extend them, and not hinder their salutary influence under the pretext of doing good.

Be most careful, then, not to allow anything that could disturb the harmony obtained, and to abstain from cooperation and advice from those who, although on the other hand may be suitable and honest, display nonetheless partiality and hostility toward the Civil Powers. Avoid giving occasion to suspicion against you again due to such friendship and dealings with them. Through such a course of action you will attain peace and harmony between both powers; your authority will grow; the people will make progress; your apostolate will be more fruitful; and your soul will enjoy greater tranquility.

Many lustrums[3] later, another Bishop from Cuenca, Monsignor Daniel Hermida, characterized the subsequent times. Opening his arms, he exclaimed, "What tranquility, what peace! ... I was a boy of ten or eleven years old."

Placid bonanza reigned then, when Garcia Moreno received a moving letter from the reigning Pontiff, Pope Pius IX:

With great pleasure We have seen, beloved and venerable son, your relationship to that Congress about public affairs. And We do not know whether you deserve greater congratulations on our part for your sincere piety that shines through it, or for the abundance of heavenly favors that have rewarded it. It would certainly be difficult to understand, without special help from God, how it has been possible in such a short time, to pay part of the debt, double the income, simultaneously abolish the most burdensome taxes, promote the public education of youth, open new roads, and endow hospitals and asylums.

But although the happiness of these results should be referred to God, from whom we receive every good thing, not for this reason is your prudence and activity less recommended, even more so when, in the midst of all these attentions, you have also managed the reformation of laws, the prompt administration of justice, the luster of the magistracy, the regulation of harbors and of the army, and finally all that leads to the increase and prosperity of the nation.

Nevertheless, your faith greatly exceeds all this since you give God the glory for this successful advancement; and you affirm that optimal fruit should be expected from the observance of the Divine law. You wisely warn that true progress cannot be attained without good moral habits, which only the Catholic religion can obtain and preserve. Rightly then you advised promoting attention to Divine worship and obtaining a sufficient number of sacred ministers, supplying them with honest support so that they could devote themselves entirely to the moralization of the people. And to show the utility of these works plainly, you mentioned the progress in the missions of the East.

Moreover, by disseminating life and vigor to the Church in general through this Holy See, center of unity, you very expediently converted the souls of your listeners to Her; against whom a cruel persecution has arisen, precisely because of this. They preserved filial love toward Us, while you confirmed them in the intention and desire to meet Our needs.

Therefore, if everyone makes an effort, as you counseled them with Christian liberty, to prove with their works the faith that they profess with their mouths, and to abolish everything that opposes the rights and free action of the Church and of religion in your laws and institutions: the protection that you and the Republic have experienced at other times will increase: which with Heaven's blessings will be received together with those on earth as is written: "Blessed is the nation whose God is the Lord."[4]

We beg these graces with all our heart for you, Our beloved, illustrious and honorable son, and for the Republic you govern. Meanwhile, as a sign of heavenly gifts and pledge of Our paternal benevolence, We lovingly concede Our apostolic blessing to you and to your entire Republic.

Given in St. Peter's at Rome, October 20, 1873, in the twenty-eighth year of Our Pontificate, Pope Pius IX.[5]

Garcia Moreno's reply was expressed in the following terms:

> Most Holy Father:
> I am incapable of explaining to Your Holiness the profound impression of gratitude caused me by reading Your paternal and affectionate letter of last October twentieth. The approval that Your Holiness deigns to give my poor efforts is the greatest reward that I could receive on earth. And no matter how much those

efforts are worth, Your approval is certainly superior to anything that I could merit.

But in justice I must confess that we owe it all to God: not only the growing prosperity of this tiny Republic, but also all the means I use, and even the desire He inspires in me to work for His glory. I am not worthy, then, of any compensation whatsoever. And I greatly fear that on the last day He will charge me for the good that I could have done with the help of His grace and which I did not do.

Please, then, Your Holiness, be so kind as to obtain that He forgive and save me, and that He enlighten and direct me in all things, and grant that I may die for the defense of the faith and the Church.

It is most gratifying for me to let Your Holiness know that the Congress deigned to accept all the indications that I made in my address on August tenth; and consequently have reformed civil and penal law, in accordance with the observations of our Most Illustrious Bishops. Funds have been designated to sponsor the arrival of zealous priests during the next biennium; to increase the endowment for rural priests; to contribute to the reconstruction of destroyed churches, and promote the missions. To help the Holy See, they have also assigned what I proposed to them. In fulfillment of this disposition and counting on a larger sum, I had the small quantity of ten thousand pesos of our currency delivered to the Apostolic Delegate. Finally, they crowned their work by consecrating this Republic to the Divine Heart of Jesus, our God and Lord.

In the midst of the unspeakable sufferings that surround Your Holiness in these unhappy times of persecution and abandonment, may it serve as a consolation to know that although we are nothing and can do nothing in the world, we have the great honor and the greatest happiness of manifesting ourselves as children of the Catholic Church.

Now, may Your Holiness forgive the liberty that I take in asking you a great favor. Please send us from there your Apostolic Blessing for this Republic, my wife and family and myself every day. For, the more Your Holiness blesses us, the more I feel that my trust in God grows, the only source of all courage and all fortitude. While Your Holiness blesses us, God will protect us. This is all your obedient, loving and humble son desires.[6]

Perhaps also approximately during these days is when Garcia Moreno addressed a special letter to Europe, probably to Italy, commissioning large marble plaques to be made for placing in the front piece of the altars to the Heart of Jesus in the Cathedrals, with the following inscription conceived and written by the Commander in Chief himself:

> Divine Heart of Jesus, help, enlighten, and guide the people and the government of Ecuador which has been consecrated to Thee.
> Legislative decree of October 18, 1873

At the beginning of the year 1874, missions were given in cities and villages in preparation for the great religious feast. In February and March, Lent contributed to an increase in fervor. Eager to outdo himself, the Illustrious Archbishop Ignacio Checa, on February 12, 1874, issued the order presented below:

1. In the Metropolitan Church and in the parishes and regulars of the Archdiocese, there will be a novena in honor of the Heart of Jesus, with the morning Mass; and with the praying or singing of the Trisagion[7] of the same Most Sacred Heart in the afternoon. Besides, in the afternoon after the Trisagion a priest will preach exhorting the people to do penance, making them understand how pleased God will be that the entire Republic will be consecrated to the most pious Heart of Jesus, and what great spiritual benefit will redound to each individual that comprises it.
2. On the day after the novena there will be a General Communion, together with the most solemn possible feast day. And the Act of Consecration will be read clearly, distinctly and slowly from the pulpit, so that all present can repeat it easily.
3. His Excellency, the President of the Republic, will ask all public officials to attend that feast day in this capital, in the provincial capitals and in the parishes, so that, as representatives of the Republic, they can execute the Act of Consecration.
4. An indulgence of eighty days will be conceded on each day of the novena to all who assemble to hear Mass or the preaching or to pray the Trisagion. A plenary indulgence will be conceded to those who, having received Communion on any day of the month of March, have pronounced the Act of Consecration.

The text of the novena to be used was composed by Father Manuel Proano and edited in Riobamba with this title: "Novena to the Divine Heart of Jesus Christ, for the Republic of Ecuador, which, by reason of two decrees, conciliar and legislative, has been placed under the protection and help of that same Divine Heart." On the first day of those Divine services mainly Ecuadorian children and youth were to act; on the second day, fathers and mothers of families; on the third, craftsmen; on the fourth, the army and all its members; on the fifth, legislators; on the sixth, the Judicial Branch and its members; on the seventh, the Chiefs of State; lastly, on the eighth and ninth days, secular and regular clergy with their prelates and bishops.

The oleograph of the Heart of Jesus had arrived that was to preside. The French magazine *Regne Social du Sacre Coeur* of June 1923 formulated these concepts about it:

> This picture represents Christ the King, with the scepter and globe. So in His hands Jesus has power, empire and complete sovereignty. His Heart, just as was manifested to Saint Margaret Mary, is shown with all the insignias of love and sorrow.

In turn Monsignor Jose Felix Heredia, S. J., later Bishop of Guayaquil, added the following details to this description:

> It is sufficient to contemplate the picture a bit thoroughly to feel deeply stirred. The lovingly majestic figure of our Divine Savior stands out against the purest blue background, like the clear Ecuadorian sky. As the God of purity, He is wearing a tunic as white as snow and gracefully belted by a golden chain. The intense scarlet royal cloak hangs on His left shoulder with elegant grace... Our Lord holds the royal scepter in His right hand, extended gently downward. Meanwhile He holds the terrestrial globe in His left hand, as if drawing it near to His Divine Heart. The latter is shown encircled with brilliant rays, surrounded by a crown of thorns, and emitting a considerable bundle of burning flames from the top. Our Divine Lord's face reflects winning goodness and overawing majesty in admirable combination. His gaze tenderly directed toward Heaven, and as if bathed in waves of merciful compassion, somewhat uncovers the treasures of holiness and the oceans of goodness that are enclosed within that Divine Heart. An intelligent observer cannot help but admire the marvelously beau-

tiful expression of the Redeemer's features: that tender face, where endearment, joy, compassion, goodness, and the serene tranquility of incomparable royalty are gently mixed. Those fine, unaffected details! That body bent forward clearly shows the innate propensity of His Heart toward us creatures. Absolutely everything makes the image a faithful portrayal of Jesus' immense charity and the regal nobility of His august person. In all justice, that picture of Christ the King has been greatly admired in French worship and the following words have been written about it: "It would be a venture bordering on folly to try to give a statue all the fineness and delicacy of detail characteristic to that canvas, a true masterpiece of religious painting in our times."

From our own observation, we point out that the rays of light from of the Divine Heart shine principally on the Republic of Ecuador, bounded on the South by the Amazon River. Furthermore, two names are written there: Ecuador and Quito. The Divine eyes gazing on high show that Jesus is imploring His Heavenly Father for the world and especially for Ecuador.

In Riobamba, in May of 1933, one of Rafael Salas' descendants told the author of these pages that the precious image had been blessed by Pope Pius IX, whom the painter from Quito had interviewed and to whom he had also shown an oleograph of the Andean landscapes.

Finally the memorable day of Wednesday, March 25, 1874, dawned in Quito. The tricolor national flag was raised on all public and nearly all private buildings. And the report of the cannon reverberated on the nearby Yavirac hill.[8] This was according to the current Military Code for any first class attendance of the Government at religious feast days.

At eight o'clock in the morning, the spacious naves of the Cathedral proved too narrow to hold the immense, variegated multitude: clergy and religious communities, State members, Court of Justice personnel, army, police, professional groups, elegant ladies, humble daughters of the people, gentlemen and workers. The center of all eyes was the oleograph of the Heart of Jesus. The second target of everyone's gaze was Garcia Moreno, of tall and elegant physique, wearing the Presidential band across his chest, and dressed as the Supreme General of the Army. He was in the presbytery, to one side of the main altar.

Mass was celebrated by the Illustrious Archbishop Ignacio Checa. The cannon thundered every five minutes and reminded everyone how Jehovah, encircled by clouds on Mount Sinai and applauded by a volley of electric thunder and lightning, made an alliance with the people of Israel. Now in the Andes Mountains that same Jehovah, but under a loving, human figure, was making an alliance with the Republic of Ecuador.

After the holy Epistle, the Canon Rafael Gonzalez Calixto ascended the pulpit and spoke of the meaning of the consecration to be made within the hour, and of its transcendental importance. The Mass resumed. Communion was given to the Most Excellent President and to the compact multitude.

When the Holy Sacrifice had finished, there was Benediction of the Most Holy Sacrament. The above-mentioned prebendary[9] ascended the pulpit again, carrying a page in his hands printed with the Act of Consecration written by Father Manuel Proano. Practically the entire assembly also had a copy of that page in their hands and could easily pronounce its contents well. The Canon pronounced two or three words and immediately the people repeated them. A sea of voices, with the President's standing out more strongly, which is not fiction, but reality! In fact, the Jesuit Manuel Proano himself, in his funeral oration eleven years later, referred to Garcia Moreno's voice in public worship, saying, "In a louder and more perceptible voice than that of the vast nation." Let us listen to the text of that historic prayer:

> We are Thy People, O Lord. My Jesus, we will always recognize Thee as our God. Our eyes will not turn to any star other than this one of love and mercy that shines in the center of Thy breast, sanctuary of the Divinity, ark of Thy Heart. Behold, Our God! Powerful peoples and nations pierce the sweetest bosom of Thy mercy with most sharp lances. Our enemies insult our Faith and mock our hopes, because we have placed them in Thee. Nevertheless, this Thy People, its Leader, its legislators and its pontiffs, console Thy Vicar, dry the tears of the Church, and putting the world's impiety and apostasy to shame, run to be submerged in the ocean of love and charity that Thy most gentle Heart uncovers for them.
>
> Our God! May Thy Heart then be the shining beacon of our Faith, the sure anchor of our hope, the emblem on our flags, the impenetrable shield against our weakness, the beautiful dawn of imperturbable peace, the intimate bond of holy harmony, the cloud that makes our fields fertile, the sun that brightens our horizons, finally the most rich stream of prosperity and abundance such as

*Archbishop Ignacio Checa and President Garcia Moreno*

we need to raise churches and altars where Thy holy and magnificent glory will shine with eternal and pacific radiance.

And since we are unreservedly consecrated and submitted to Thy Divine Heart, multiply our unending years of religious peace; exile impiety and corruption, calamity and misery from the bounds of our country. May Thy Faith dictate our laws; Thy justice govern our courts; Thy clemency and fortitude sustain and direct our leaders; Thy wisdom, holiness and zeal perfect our priests; Thy grace convert all the children of Ecuador and Thy glory crown them in eternity: so that all peoples and nations on earth, contemplating with holy envy the true happiness and good fortune of our nation, may resort in turn to Thy loving Heart, and rest in the tranquil sleep of peace that this pure Fount and perfect Symbol of love and charity offers the world. Amen.

Next, the Illustrious Archbishop blessed the faithful with the Most Holy Sacrament. And the ringing of the bells and the tremendous roar of the cannon, and the festive music, without a doubt the notes of the National Anthem played by one of the military bands, announced to the world that the Republic of Ecuador had just been consecrated by plebiscite to the Divine Heart of Jesus. For, more or less at that same hour, the ecclesiastical and civil authorities and the people in the provincial capitals and rural parishes recited the above Act of Consecration.

The following prayers complemented the epic achievement we have recorded, composed as well by the above-mentioned Jesuit for the private use of Ecuadorians:

> Sweetest Heart of my Jesus, King of love and Universal Monarch of nations, as a child of the nation consecrated to Thee, I most truly offer and submit myself to the refuge of mercy that Thou hast opened to my Catholic country. In return, preserve Ecuador's faith, secure our hope, inflame our charity, defend us from our enemies, and grant us peace and abundance in time and glory in eternity. And may the world know that the nation Thou dost protect and help is truly happy. Amen.
>
> Ejaculation: Divine Heart of Jesus, since we are consecrated to Thee, forgive, convert and sanctify all the children of Thy nation, and establish in them the kingdom of charity.

The oleograph that presided over the national consecration remained enthroned in the Metropolitan Church for one or two days. Then it was removed by its owner, President Garcia Moreno, and displayed with honors in the main drawing-room of his private dwelling. This was located in the *Plaza de la Independencia*, next to the Archbishop's Palace.[10] However, the following year, that picture was moved to the building that was already Garcia Moreno's property in *the Plaza de Santo Domingo*.[11] Undoubtedly, it was the first time that an image of the Heart of Jesus was enthroned in the house of a Head of State.

What is more, Garcia Moreno wanted to carry out an international apostolate in that religious field. And to that end, he sent a facsimile of the historical painting to the Most Excellent President of France, Major General Patrice MacMahon, who publicly manifested his Catholicism. When presenting him with this image, Garcia Moreno suggested that he consecrate France to the Heart of Jesus, for which he could make use of this oleograph. This most beautiful gesture of Garcia Moreno attained publicity due to the exposition of the cited facsimile in the crypt of the Heart of Jesus Basilica on Montmartre, Paris. That copy was seen there by the distinguished gentleman from Quito, Cristobal Bonifaz Jijon, one day in November of 1961. To one side of the painting, its origin and Garcia Moreno's purpose[12] was displayed on a tripod, just as we have recorded in the previous lines.

Since Mr. Bonifaz held the office of Ambassador, he had to pronounce a speech about the friendly and beneficial relations that had always existed between noble France and Ecuador. One of the paragraphs of that oratorical piece said the following:

> There is a witnessed fact in the very heart of this capital city, a testimony that I am going to recall. After the war of 1870, President MacMahon wanted to consecrate the French people to the Sacred Heart of Jesus, following the example of the President of Ecuador, Gabriel Garcia Moreno. The latter, then, donated a copy of the image to France that had been used for the Consecration of Ecuador and that is now displayed here in Paris, in the crypt of the Basilica of the Heart of Jesus of Montmartre.

Mr. Bonifaz also said the following words to the author of these pages:

*Cristobal Bonifaz Jijon,
Ambassador of Ecuador in Paris*

It was probably my testimony that influenced the Director of the newspaper *La Renaissance*, edited at Paray le Monial on November 2, 1963, to print these lines: "President Garcia Moreno gave Major General MacMahon, President of France, the painting in which Our Lord Jesus Christ radiates rays of light. At the same time, he addressed a letter to him asking him to consecrate the French Republic to the Heart of Jesus."[13]

As an *ex-voto* of his convictions, the pious Head of State sent the Sanctuary of Paray le Monial a white silk flag on which was written this inscription in authentic gold metal: "Glory and honor to the Divine Heart. Republic of Ecuador—1874." The cloth fell to pieces with time and then the Mother Superior of the Convent of the Visitation disposed that the gold from the letters be used to make an artifact destined to divine worship. There is a divergence of opinion as to whether the precious metal was made into a chalice for Holy Mass or one of the lamps for the Most Holy Sacrament.

Mr. Bonifaz heard the following from one of the nuns from Paray: "The Garcia Moreno family from Chile visited the Sanctuary. When they learned that the flag sent by the President had fallen apart, they put an oriflamme[14] in its place."

Our Christian hero also wrote to the Father Director of the Confraternity of Our Lady of the Sacred Heart, established in the French city of Issoudun, requesting to be inscribed in their association. Needless to say, he received an affirmative answer by return mail. The purpose of that confraternity is to obtain, through Mary Most Holy, the most perfect worship of the Heart of Jesus.

Finding out about that step taken by Garcia Moreno, the Director of the Archconfraternity of Our Lady of Lourdes, France, wrote in turn to the distinguished President, asking him to give his name as well to that pious entity. Garcia Moreno's immediate reply was affirmative. Then the Director sent him the corresponding medal and certificate of admission.

If he was inscribed in foreign associations, how much more in those of his own country! It is said that Garcia Moreno was a member of all the confraternities in Quito.[15] Of course, that includes the classically Jesuit Apostolate of Prayer, the objective of which is consecration to the Heart of Jesus and reparation for the offenses He receives. Also of the *Bona Mors*[16] Confraternity, as is evident from the documents of the Confraternity's church, seen by the author. Of the "School of Poor

Christ" whose prayers or office he read in front of his brothers, sometimes making a small commentary, "with a penetrating, sonorous voice," according to the quote of a witness, a relative of Garcia Moreno himself. He was a member of the Third Franciscan Order, according to the testimony of Friar Jose Maria Aguirre, who said so in Garcia Moreno's funeral speech on the thirteenth anniversary of his victimization. In Guayaquil he had an interview with the members from the meeting of the Saint Vincent de Paul Society, who begged him to obtain a pecuniary subsidy from the National Congress in favor of that entity. Garcia Moreno interrogated them, "Where does the Congress get such a subsidy?"

"From a slight tax on merchandise," they answered.

"Consequently, it will go up in price," replied the President, "which cannot be tolerated. Rather, I promise to collaborate with twenty-five pesos a month from my pocket." And so he did, starting from the first days of the year 1871, and he complied faithfully, as is clear from the acts of the above-mentioned meeting.

Another indication of his Catholic asceticism was the religious objects he always wore over his chest. His scapular of the Heart of Jesus with this inscription: "Cease! The Heart of Jesus is with me" is kept in the Provincial Hall of the Franciscan Fathers of Quito. Garcia Moreno also wore the Scapular of the Missions, a rosary, a medal with the portrait of Pius IX on the front and a symbol of the First Vatican Council on the back, and a reliquary with a diminutive cross inside made with a fragment of the true cross of Jesus Christ. The medal as well as the reliquary had been sent to him by the above-mentioned Pontiff. These tokens are now kept in the Jesuit Museum at Cotocollao.

In the author's hands there is a holy card of the Heart of Jesus, four and a half inches high by almost three inches wide. Below it is this ejaculation: "Heart of Jesus, I trust in Thee." On the back the following is handwritten: "President Garcia Moreno had this holy card on his chest at the time of his assassination. It was given to Father Lopez, a Redemptorist, who in turn entrusted it to the signer who guarantees and witnesses it, Daniel Barona C. Ss. R.[17] (Here is his signature.) *El Espino* (Burgos, Spain). 10-VII-1952." One of the Redemptorist priests, probably Father Alarcon Falconi, gave it to the author in Cuenca, Ecuador.

It is credible that this holy card came to the hands of the Redemptorist Father Lopez, since that religious, through his oratory, stimulated Garcia Moreno to take up the cross in a procession. He was an enthusiastic panegyrist of the President-martyr. But for it to have been on García Moreno's chest is only conceivable on the condition that it was found in the interior of the booklet of the *Imitation of Christ*, which he for certain had in the inside pocket of his frock coat when he was assassinated. Notice that the referred holy card has no traces of having been damaged.

Above the left shoulder of Christ there is an inscription with these words: "Julia Beck – Paris 1715 – Picpus."[18] The eyes of Our Lord are looking at Heaven. Rays of light flow from His chest, or better yet, from His heart. But they do not appear on the holy card, whose dimensions prevent it. If this image really belonged to García Moreno, one might surmise that the details inspired him, which would be evident in the canvas that would preside over the consecration by plebiscite.

# Endnotes

[1] Bishop Remigio Esteves Toral of Cuenca had excommunicated the Governor Carlos Ordonez, who was innocent, or at the most, was guilty of small faults. Garcia Moreno was informed of the abuse and had recourse to the Roman Pontiff, informing him of such unjust and violent conduct, asking him to apply a suitable remedy (Severo Gomezjurado, S.J., *Vida de Garcia Moreno*, vol. 9, p. 121).

[2] Severo Gomezjurado, S. J., *Vida de Garcia Moreno* (Imprenta ARPI, Quito, 1979), vol. 9, p. 139ff.

[3] A lustrum was a term for a five-year period in Ancient Rome.

[4] Ps. 32, 12.

[5] Severo Gomezjurado, S. J., *Vida de Garcia Moreno* (Imprenta ARPI, Quito, 1979), vol. 7, p. 373 ff.

[6] *Ibid.*, p. 375 ff.

[7] "The Trisagion ('O Holy God, holy and strong, holy and immortal, have mercy on us') is said in Greek and Latin by the celebrant at the veneration of the Cross on Good Friday, and is used in the prayers at Prime in the Divine Office on penitential days. It has been adopted into the Western Church from the Greek liturgy, and is traceable back to the fifth century" (Msgr. John F. Sullivan, *Externals of the Catholic Church* (London; Longmans, Green, 1955), pg. 367).

[8] Yavirac hill is now known as El Panecillo hill, although its original name by the aboriginal inhabitants of Quito was Yavirac.

[9] I.e. an honorary canon in a cathedral.

[10] *Ibid.* vol. 6, p. 373.

[11] *Ibid.* vol. 5, p. 330.

[12] I.e. an explanation of the origin and the reason why Garcia Moreno had given the picture to the French president was displayed upon a tripod next to the picture.

[13] These words from the above-mentioned periodical were translated from French to Spanish, and now to English. (Cf. *Ibid.* vol. 5, p. 155).

[14] The Oriflamme (from Latin *aurea flamma*, "golden flame") was the battle standard of the King of France.

[15] *Anales de los Padres Lazaristas* [Annals of the Lazarist Fathers], vol. 40, p. 620.

[16] "Happy Death" in Latin.

[17] C.Ss.R (*Congregatio Sanctissimi Redemptoris*) is the abbreviation for the official name of the Redemptorists, "the Congregation of the Most Holy Redeemer."

[18] "Picpus," is the name used in some countries for the Congregation of the Sacred Hearts of Jesus and Mary, and is derived from rue de Picpus, the street where their central house was established shortly after the community's foundation.

# Chapter 4
# Garcia Moreno Seals It with His Blood

It was the year 1689 when our Lord Jesus Christ appeared to Saint Margaret Mary Alacoque and told her:

> Make known to the eldest son[1] of My Sacred Heart that the Eternal Father, desiring to make amends for the bitterness and the sufferings which the adorable Heart of His Divine Son received in the house of the princes of the earth, amid the humiliations and ill-treatment of His Passion, wishes to establish His kingdom in the heart of our great monarch, whom He desires to use for the fulfillment of His design. He wishes then, as it seems to me, to enter with pomp and splendor into the house of princes. He wishes to establish His kingdom in the heart of our great monarch, by his consecration to My adorable Heart, which desires to conquer his. It desires to reign in his palace. He has chosen him to make amends before men for the bitterness and humiliations that this Divine Heart received in the houses of princes and kings. This will happen by rendering and securing to Him the honors, love and glory that He hopes to receive. He has therefore chosen him to obtain permission from the Holy Apostolic See for the Mass in His honor, and to obtain all the other privileges which ought to accompany the devotion to this Divine Heart. Through him He wants to triumph in the hearts of the powerful of the world. Let him erect an edifice where the image of the Divine Heart is shown, to receive the consecration and homage of the king and all the court there. He desires to be painted on the King's standard and engraved on his arms. This unique love of our hearts will be a powerful protection for France. The Sacred Heart wants to be made the protector and defender of the sacred person of the King, against his visible and invisible foes. He will abundantly pour out His blessings on all this monarch's undertakings and make them prosper to His glory…[2]

Did this divine message reach the ears of the Sun King?[3] It is not known. If perhaps it did, it is a fact that it was not obeyed.

One hundred eighty-four years passed and Garcia Moreno amended that frustration as best he could. His example has influenced the governments of other nations such as Colombia, Peru, Bolivia, Spain, etc., which have consecrated their countries to the Heart of Jesus.

Then, did the promises made to Louis XIV and his monarchy transfer to Garcia Moreno and his Republic? It does not follow, at least not literally. God lavishes diverse measures on different persons and times. Still, it must be considered that munificence is proper to Christ, and therefore He must have disposed something great and special in favor of the most distinguished President of Ecuador. Besides, there are promises from the Heart of Jesus that refer to His devotees in general, for example:

> I will abundantly bless their undertakings that redound to My glory. Fervent Christians will rise quickly to sanctity. I will bless the houses where the image of My Heart is exposed and honored. The persons who propagate My worship will have their names written on My Heart. I will be their safe refuge in life and especially at the hour of their deaths.[4]

Who is not aware that these promises especially concerned Garcia Moreno? Let us recall also what Father Manuel Proano said one year earlier: "Divine grace will be copiously poured out over Ecuador, if it gives public and solemn witness to its religious faith, as opposed to the practically general apostasy of nations." This was spectacularly fulfilled, especially in Quito, thanks to a mission preached by the Redemptorist Fathers Pedro Lopez, Luis Lopez, Bibona and Rodrigo.[5]

Garcia Moreno presided with his good example, attending morning and evening conferences. He arrived at the latter an hour and a half beforehand with his little son Gabriel of only four years and three months of age. Monsignor Serafin Vannutelli, the Apostolic Delegate, and Monsignor Ignacio Checa, Archbishop of Quito, also attended. With such good examples, the people overran the church, in spite of the torrential downpours characteristic of April. Since the multitude did not fit into the Cathedral, a parallel mission was required in the Church of San Francisco, which filled in a minute, with no noticeable diminishment in the Metropolitan Church. There were days when four churches were insufficient to hold the thousands of listeners. Here are the impressions from the May 4, 1874, edition of Quito's newspaper, *La Verdad*:[6]

> In the pulpit, with the insignia of the cross on their chest and the eloquent exposition of the Gospel morals on their lips, they have attracted an innumerable crowd, and have won the respect and admiration that the human spirit pays to priests endowed with sublime intelligence and the faithful observance of God's pre-

cepts. Father Luis Lopez preached the doctrinal conferences in the morning, giving proofs of varied instruction and that his eagerness to spread Christian truths is equal to his other virtues. The afternoons were occupied with sacred hymns admirably sung in a melodious, sonorous voice. The more than ten thousand people gathered there could hear the harmonious accents of the plain chant that greatly increased the fervor of souls.

Fathers Ribona and Rodrigo, selected for the missions in San Francisco, had an extraordinary attendance at each of their deliveries.

In his various recitations Father Pedro Lopez changed his voice with admirable appropriateness. First it was terrifying with the announcement of eternal punishment, or tender with Jesus' love; then mild as the recitation of some example or historical passage required; or sad as in the situation when he depicted man in enmity with God. His eloquence, his interesting aspect, his oratorical delivery, all gave his discourses unction and amenity.

Blessed Quito that honors your God and your Lord as much as possible! Together with the rest of the nation, you are on a sea of rough waves like the ark of the Deluge. Impiety and Liberalism flood the entire globe. The spirit of Satan hovers over the hearts of men. Do not faint! Keep your eyes fixed on Heaven. The Dove of the Vatican will announce a bonanza. Other nations with a sneer on their lips and scorn in their hearts, point with their fingers to the lines in our Constitution and laws assigned in honor of the most holy religion of the Crucified.

On Friday, April twenty-fourth, there was General Communion for the women. The next day, Saturday, thousands of men poured into the churches to go to confession. Garcia Moreno went to the Cathedral. Wrapped in his cloak, he knelt behind the last penitent. Father Luis Lopez saw him, left his confessional and walked straight toward the exemplary Head of State.

"Your Excellency, Sir, undoubtedly Your Excellency has urgent government business. I can attend to your confession immediately."

"Father Lopez," answered the Head of State, "I must give my nation a good example. Therefore I should wait my turn."

The missionary, edified and full of admiration, returned to his confessional; and the Supreme Leader patiently waited until it was his turn.[7]

The next day, Garcia Moreno could not keep back his tears of joy when he saw a compact multitude of men approach the Communion rail, not a few after many years of not having done so. He euphorically left his home that afternoon to preside over the closing ceremony of the mission. Its culmination was to consist of the procession of the Holy Cross, which had been purposely made for this act, together with its respective portable platform with carrying poles. It had cost one hundred eighty pesos since its dimensions were enormous.

The Head of State did not have in mind to carry the sacred wood, not because he suffered from human respect, which he had trodden on innumerable occasions, but on this occasion, he did not wish to encourage the talk and commentaries of those who said they were members of the Liberal Party. Let them be disappointed! However, very much to the contrary, the Redemptorist Priest, Father Pedro Lopez, had resolved to preach in such a way as to oblige the President to change his intention so that Sunday, April 26, 1874, would be forever memorable.

The Head of State presided in the Cathedral presbytery, accompanied by his entire cabinet. In the center of the church the Holy Cross was horizontally laid over the bier. Both were adorned with flowers, an honor rendered by the ladies of the city. The multitude occupied all three wide naves and were so packed together that Father Lopez said you could not even breathe there. Certainly not a few faithful had to be content to attend from the vestibule or railings, especially the music bands.

The most poignant paragraphs of the sermon were later consigned to a book entitled ¿España es Catolica?[8] written by the Redemptorist, Father Ramon Saravia, and published in the year 1939. Saravia said that Father Pedro Lopez was one of the most eminent orators in Spain. He bordered on forty years old when he came to Ecuador. He got on admirably well with Garcia Moreno: two good hearts and two strong wills.

In his exhortation before the procession, he evoked the deed of the Emperor Heraclius with the Cross of Christ on his shoulders on his way to Mount Calvary. Suddenly the Emperor's feet could not continue the walk, as if they were nailed to the ground. Then Bishop Zacharias, inspired by the Holy Ghost, told him: "The reason for such an unexpected case can well be that you, O Emperor, do not wear the humble, degraded clothes with which Christ shouldered this sacred wood to Calvary." Heraclitus hardly heard these words when he took off his shoes and instead of his purple cloak, covered himself with coarse clothing. He tried to continue walking and did so with the greatest ease. Then the missionary turned toward the place where Garcia Moreno was sitting and in a solemn and deliberate voice, said:

> Kings and emperors of ancient times were like that, fervent believers. They respected the Divine laws and were not ashamed of their God, even though He was a crucified God. But there is no longer even a shadow of such magistrates. In their place we have kings from a deck of cards and paper presidents of republics...

The orator could not continue speaking, for his sentence was interrupted immediately by Garcia Moreno's intervention, who, standing up and extending his arm towards the preacher, with a loud, sonorous voice told him, "Father Lopez, you are lying! I, the President of this Republic, am not ashamed of Christ Crucified. I will also bear the cross on my shoulders."

In the book quoted, *¿Espana es Catolica?*, it is noted that Garcia Moreno almost never missed extending his arm in a gesture of authority.

The President's unexpected reply was the best epilogue to the sermon, which did not take the triumphant missionary long to finish.

The Head of State gave his baton to the aide-de-camp, walked straight to the place of the cross and took the front position at the bier. At once the ministers of state and other high government officials, enthusiastic because of the example of their President, also approached the bier. A military musical band led the procession, playing lugubrious marches. Next the male devotees came in two lines, at whose end was the bier of the Holy Cross; then a second band of musicians. Next was the women's representation and at the end was the float of Our Lady of Sorrows carried by the ladies. Then a multitude of people came in a compact mass. Lastly, there was a third band of musicians, and behind them, the infantry battalion. The extended lines [of devotees carrying] lit candles enhanced the splendor of the procession, and at its sides were the buildings adorned with flags, flowers and drapery.

Those carrying the bier were frequently substituted, for the numerous devotees also insisted on the honor of carrying the sacred weight on their shoulders. Only Garcia Moreno refused to yield the glorious burden to others and pronounced these words, "I do not want what I do to be just a ceremony." Without exchanging places with anyone, he supported the bier and the holy wood until it returned to the cathedral, after an hour and a half long procession. Father Lopez says that the President's collar bone almost broke and that he must have suffered a painful wound. This historical cross remained and still remains in that church.

Commentaries: the newspaper *La Voz del Clero*[9] expressed its judgment in the following terms: "Let the impious and philosophers of today think and say what they like. The sight was worthy of God, the angels and men."

In a letter, Garcia Moreno himself said:

> The good God blesses us, and our country truly makes progress. Improvement in customs is seen everywhere, thanks to the Jesuits, Dominicans, Observants, Redemptorists, Carmelites, etc., who zealously help the priests in this country. The number is incalculable of those who have been regenerated through Penance during Lent. When young we counted those who obeyed their religious duties; now we count those who refuse to obey them. It can be truly said that God leads us by the hand, just like a tender father does with his little child who starts to take his first steps.

In turn, Monsignor Pedro Schumaker, Bishop of Portoviejo, wrote these lines:

> When I was in Paris in 1878, I found a work dealing with South American republics in a public library. Moved by curiosity I skimmed through it. Immediately I recognized that it was a Masonic book. Speaking about Garcia Moreno, it said the following, "When we learned that this man had carried a cross in procession through the streets of Quito, we found that the measure was full and we decreed his death."[10]

In September, 1874, Father Manuel Proano returned to Quito where he hastened to pay a visit to Garcia Moreno. The chat did not take long to change to the cherished project of building a votive church of the Consecration. The President endorsed it by pronouncing these words full of great meaning:

> It is necessary to build a new and magnificent church in the capital to perpetuate the memory of our official Consecration for

future generations. Let it also be the center of religious restoration, at least for the republics of Spanish America.

At the same time, a Spanish newspaper called the *Revista Franciscana*[11] reproduced the following assertions, written by a Capuchin priest from Ibarra: "Religion is most respected. Churches are raised everywhere. Roads are opened in all places. Everything breathes religion in this country."

Here are some other characteristics about the social environment:

In November, 1874, there was a drought in Quito and the surrounding area. The Virgin of Quinche[12] was brought to the capital and invoked with intense fervor. At once there were downpours, the countryside turned green again and the sown fields made abundant harvests foreseeable. During the festival days of the Holy Innocents, Francisco Rossa, Director of the Conservatory of Music, left Quito with his entire orchestra and went to other towns to conduct the folk dances. Replacing them, the military bands and the jubilee orchestra enlivened the squares and streets of the capital, occupied by dancers, people in costumes and spectators. The newspaper *El Nacional* noted that even so, this did not decrease the attendance for paying homage to the Virgin of Quinche.

It was marvelous that Garcia Moreno also disguised himself to amuse his beloved people and dance with the women of the modest social class. This event has been narrated by an immediate eyewitness, Doctor Aparicio Ortega, who at that time was a university student at the Polytechnic School. Later he recorded it in his booklet titled *Boceto de Garcia Moreno.*[13] Ortega adds that the embittered enemies of the President commented, "He is old and even so is the idol of the women. He disguises himself to discover conspiracies from feminine lips." The true age of Garcia Moreno was fifty three.

In turn, the biographer, Luis Robalino Davila, on page five hundred seventy-eight of the first edition, points out these details:

> In December of 1874, during the Innocents Folk Festivals,[14] Garcia Moreno acceded to his friends' requests that he take part, disguising himself and getting into the swing of things in an ostentatious party of masked people. His height, majestic bearing and the rapid pace that was so like him, all revealed him. Passing in front of the Cathedral Square street doors, all the social classes

acclaimed him, shouting with true affection, "Long live Garcia Moreno!" The children rushed at him and hugged his legs. One individual shouted, "Thanks to this great man, there is work, there is much money, great abundance of everything, and total freedom for everything except crime." Garcia Moreno had danced that night like when he was young. He had toasted to the happiness of the people. And all those present had hugged him, acclaiming him as Father and Savior of the Nation.

Masonry became furious in the presence of the man who had made his people happy at the prompting of, and based on, an ardent, integral Catholicism.

In his pamphlet entitled *La Dictadura Perpetua*[15] the author, Juan Montalvo, said, "When the New World has still not finished laughing from seeing that ingenious Caius, by solemn act, dedicate the Republic to the Sacred Heart of Jesus..."[16]

Ten years after Garcia Moreno's assassination, the French ex-Mason, Leo Taxil, wrote, "Is the assassination of Garcia Moreno, President of the Republic of Ecuador, also not per chance the work of Freemasonry? Who would be capable of doubting it?"[17]

Two years had elapsed when Ramon Nocedal, Director of the Madrid newspaper, *El Siglo Futuro*,[18] gave a speech about the crimes perpetrated through the influence of Masonry. There were gentlemen in the auditorium famous for their erudition, and also two outstanding Freemasons, Miguel Moraita, Grand Master of the Madrid Orient, and N. Dualde, Leader of the Lodges in the city of Valencia. Well then, Ramon expressed the following to them right to their faces:

> Mr. Moraita knows the very glorious history of the distinguished President that brought the Republic of Ecuador out of the clutches of anarchy and barbarity by defeating and eradicating Freemasonry from its soil. All the newspapers of the sect in America and Europe overwhelmed him with calumny and unceasingly incited the people of Ecuador to free themselves from that monster who, in addition to defending their Faith, has given them peace, covered them with roads, schools and all sciences and arts, pious institutes, industry and wealth, and has considerably reduced taxes and sacrifices. Moreover, as the grateful people loved him and abhorred his calumniators, the Lodges decreed his death three times in vain. There were more or less veiled announcements

about the three attempts in the European Masonic and Jewish newspapers. Only an unexpected, providential event could free him and did free him from one of them. Newspapers from Nueva Granada reported the news when they thought that it had been consummated, telling all the details as having happened, which had been devised and prepared.

The fourth time he was condemned to die by the high Masonic powers that then resided in Germany. *L'Independence Belge*[19] announced one day with admirable precision that in three or four months, things would happen in Ecuador that the whole world would talk about. The news of the Lodge's decree spread throughout all Europe. In Ecuador nothing else was talked about months before the event; and it was known in which treacherous and perfidious Legation the assassins were assembled.[20]

It is noteworthy that Moraita and Dualde did not contradict Nocedal in reference to Garcia Moreno.

In Belgium itself, there was a second repercussion of the edict given by the Berlin Masonry. One of the March, 1875, editions of the *Gaceta Internacional*[21] published in Brussels said: "A revolution is currently being plotted against Ecuador that, when it explodes, will leave deep marks on the country."[22]

Nocedal's statement regarding the news spread throughout Europe about an alleged assassination of Garcia Moreno is endorsed through this assertion by Monsignor Manuel Maria Polit, "I was a boy of twelve and was in Paris. One day we went to see the newspaper headlines and we read one that said: 'President Garcia Moreno has been assassinated.' It was written on a blood-red background. My father was tremendously shocked, giving him a stomach ache. Fortunately, a few days later, a denial of that news was published." This item was uttered by the Monsignor himself in Pelileo about the year 1926. Among others, it was heard by Father Francisco de los Reyes, who passed it on to the author.

The part about "the fourth time he was condemned to die by the high Masonic powers that then resided in Germany" was reinforced in this paragraph written by Jose Quignard in his biography on Father Didier:

> Who does not already know it? This great man, justly called ***the Charlemagne of the nineteenth century***, was viewed unfa-

vorably by Freemasonry. Bismarck was annoyed that he alone among all rulers, the president of a tiny Republic, should have dared protest officially against the capture of Rome, and publicly consoled the Holy Father. Grieved by this assault and that of *Kulturkampf*, Bismarck entrusted the South American lodges to take care of freeing the world of ***this inopportune critic of his great works***. The decree of assassination, signed in Berlin at the beginning of 1875, was executed in Quito on August sixth by outlaws hired with gold from Peru.

It must be advised that the words "this inopportune critic of his great works" are written in italics, to show that they were uttered literally by the Iron Chancellor. It would be well to research and weigh the documents that Father Quignard used for recording that expression of Bismarck's.

If the sentence pronounced by Bismarck was fulminated in January of 1875, it could have easily reached the lodges of Lima two months later, that is, in March. It began to be commented on and studied by radical Peruvian Masons in that republic. What is certain is that the following month, that is, in April, one of those three-dotted ones,[23] Antonio Urizar Garfias, in his pamphlet titled *EL Gobierno de la Republica del Ecuador en presencia de America,*[24] predicted the fall of our Hero as soon and irreparable. Those textual words "soon and irreparable fall," showed that Urizar was informed. The event proved that he was right.

In plenty of time Masonry in Lima could have sent their agents at the end of the month, that is, in April. They landed in Guayaquil at the beginning of May. In that city an international plot was disclosed among some enemies of Garcia's regime. One of them wrote to Quito, reporting that conspiracy to a friend. The mail took six days. The friend from Quito read the letter and then departed for the neighborhood of Perucho, a day's journey. He attended, doubtlessly out of pure curiosity, the talks by some Franciscan missionaries. One of these, Friar Baltasar Moner, in his old age, had the following paragraphs recorded in writing:

> During that mission, in which I occupied the role of catechist, one of those listening came to me proposing a meeting with me before going to confession and I answered him in the affirmative. In this meeting he told me that he was plotting with his person and dagger to assassinate Garcia Moreno, for this reason and that and the other, etc., etc.

I made him see the enormity of his determination, before God as well as before men, and that at the same time he was committing a crime of treachery against his country, so that the entire Republic would catch fire with flames of hate against one another. And besides all this, a fine thanks this would be to President Garcia Moreno, who had just given a scholarship to one of this man's daughters to the School of the Sacred Hearts! Fully convinced by my weighty reasons that this gentleman had just heard, he desisted from that undertaking which he had embraced at an evil hour. And not only did he yield to the truth, but he read me a letter that he had received from Guayaquil, whose contents, substantially, were the following:

That the German Lodge, in joint agreement with the one in Lima, had sent six thousand pesos to Guayaquil to be distributed among those dissatisfied with Garcia Moreno; so that by all means possible they would secure his assassination; and that he was one of the many who had entered into this wretched conspiracy. He repented of all of it, and at the same time authorized me to reveal that whole sinister secret to Garcia Moreno on the condition, however, that I would never, ever reveal his name.

When the mission ended, we went to Quito and I immediately went to give an account of all of it (without revealing the man's name, that is), to our very Reverend Father Commissioner General Jose Maria, who ordered me to go inform Garcia Moreno of all that I knew without losing any time. I immediately appeared in person at his palace. I found him there conversing with one of the principal ladies of Quito, a distinguished benefactress of ours named Virginia Villacis. Deferring to the insinuation that I made to President Garcia Moreno that I had to deal with him about a matter privately, she ended the interview at once. The President stood up immediately and we both went to another reserved room. He bolted the door himself and there alone and without witnesses, I disclosed everything I knew to him. He listened to me very attentively. He stood up from the sofa and began to cross the drawing room and said to me, "And can I not know the origin of all this that you have just revealed?" I said it could not be in any way since it was confided to me under the secrecy of the confessional. He answered that I did very well in keeping silence and added that he knew that he had many petty lawyers and petty doctors without clients who for some time were scheming his death. I added that on May fourth of the previous year four Negroes were posted in the little square of *Santo Domingo* to assassinate him as soon as he left the church. But they desisted then because of the multitude that passed by there.

I also stated that his predecessor in the presidency, General Flores, was very courageous. And even so, when possible, he took both aides-de-camp that the Republic conceded the President. But his Excellency takes only one, named Pallares, and he is so far behind him that there are over two hundred feet between the two of them...

He also told me that his monthly salary was one thousand pesos; and that during the twelve years that he had governed, he had invested it all in charitable works; and that in the end his life was in the hands of God, and to let come what might. I answered that God says, help yourself and I will help you and that we must not be reckless, as I would be if instead of leaving this, his palace, by way of the door, I would insist on going out the window; or if from some balcony or around some corner or treacherously, they would shoot him and leave him dead, as happened...

After observing him so greatly impressed and mysterious for a long time, I took leave of him, by making him realize that I had now finished my task, and that what I most desired was that he, of course, would take some precautions, since these things are not to be looked at contemptuously. He thanked me very much and accompanied me to the door and we said good-bye to each other...

So things stood. I calculate that after what has just been told, about two months passed, a little more or a little less. During that time the Reverend Father confessor of Garcia Moreno had to go... to the province of Cantabria, where he later became Provincial Commissary. I think that his illustrious penitent, Garcia Moreno, continued going to confession at the same school to another priest of great fame and prestige called Father Martinez. And so the sixth of August arrived, a fatal and disastrous day not only for Ecuador but also for all Christianity...[25]

In December of 1879, that is four years and five months after the assassination of Garcia Moreno, Peru was at war with Chile and lost a series of battles. Mariano Prado, President of Peru, incapable of saving the situation, was ousted by Nicolas Pierola who proclaimed himself

Dictator. In such circumstances, a writer under the pseudonym of Stobeo, who seems to be Peruvian, recorded the following note:

> Peru has just been dealt a mortal blow with the revolution of Lima. But a better man can rise from this revolution. Pierola is a hope that can turn that mortal blow into a saving act. But is the measure of the punishment filled to overflowing for the people from whose lodges, obedient to European lodges, the order was dispatched to assassinate the renowned Garcia Moreno?[26]

On June 16, 1875, Garcia Moreno himself wrote in these terms to his friend Juan Aguierre who was in Paris:

> They have written from Germany, to a Redemptorist priest, that the lodges there have ordered the ones in America to do everything possible to overthrow the government of Ecuador. It could be that the Grand Master Bismarck had a part in this. But God protects us. And confiding in Him, I fear no one, although we are nothing, and of our own power are equal to zero, compared to the power of that Colossus with feet of clay.[27]

A valuable testimony about the influence of Masonry in Lima is also established by what Mr. J. M. Vela Jaramillo circulated in his pamphlet entitled *El Liberalismo Futuro.*[28] According to the History of Ecuador written by the Jesuit Legohuir,[29] this Mr. Vela Jaramillo lived many years in the intimacy of the Masons from Lima, and participated in all their opinions. But afterward he rectified many of them. Let us hear that testimony:

> Although [Garcia Moreno] had stopped being [a tyrant] and was merely concerned with the progress of the Republic, to raise it to the highest degree of morality, making it famous in the world, Montalvo was being praised for being the author of Garcia Moreno's death, when it was the work of a conspiracy promoted by Masonry in Lima, which was not fully informed of the change in Garcia Moreno, or rather, because it saw in him a religious paladin and an obstacle to its aims, as was public and well-known. The agents were known who vanished without a trace shortly before the crime was consummated; one of them had been

employed by the Southern Railway. The newspapers of the day echoed this truth, which had no relation at all to Montalvo.[30]

Undoubtedly, Mr. J. M. Vela Jaramillo knew the names of the emissaries who came from Lima. It is a pity they were not recorded. There is hope that the name of the Southern Railway employee will be discovered in the vast sea of the Ecuadorian press.

Surely one of the emissaries was that man whose last name was Cortes. Born in Guatemala, but living in Peru, he arrived in Quito in May of 1875. He turned up in the appearance of a poor man. He did not take long to frequent the Peruvian Minister's assembly rooms, strike up friendships with the customary attendants at that embassy, passing his time in singing hymns to freedom and in speaking out against despots. One day his outrages and insolent objectives went so far that Garcia Moreno ordered him to leave the Republic immediately. Manuel Cornejo Astorga, who nurtured not only friendship but also familiarity with Garcia Moreno, took an interest in the revocation of the order, or at least the postponement of Cortes' departure until he obtained the indispensible money. Don[31] Gabriel answered, "Let him return with the money he brought."[32]

On July thirteenth of the same year of 1875, the Jesuit priest, Father Perez Barba, who at that time resided in Riobamba, wrote to the Father Superior at Poyanne, France, in these terms:

> What is certain and positive is that paid assassins came from Peru not long ago to finish off the President. One of our priests, Father Lopez himself, found it out and informed the President, who said to Father Lopez that he believed it and asked Father to entrust him to God.[33]

A new argument is the abundance of money in the hands of the ringleaders starting from the end of May, 1875.

One day the harness maker, Faustino Rayo, saw a servant approach him from the family whose last name was Bueno.

"What do you want?"

"My boss wants to speak with you about an interesting matter."

"When and at what time?"

"Perhaps tonight, at about seven."

"Very well, I will do it that way."

After the routine greeting, Mr. Bueno said to Rayo, "Why don't you take revenge on the Tyrant who removed you from the Amazon region in the East?"

"This is not the time, Mr. Bueno. To take revenge, I would have had to do it three years ago when my rage was fresh."

"But your financial situation is not good, Faustino. Kill the Tyrant, go back to the East and remake your fortune."

"I kill the Tyrant and at once I am executed by an army firing squad. That is no way to regain my fortune."

"Oh! But the death of the Tyrant will be accompanied by a change of government and regime, since we revolutionaries have the army on our side."

"Ah, if it is like that, it is worth considering. I will think about it."

"Faustino, serve yourself a drink and take these few coins that will serve to help you."

Rayo drank the liquor and took the coins with a show of gratitude. Mr. Bueno concluded, "Come here, Faustino, every night to continue conferring."

"That I will. Good night."[34]

An individual who held the job of coachman for Mr. Bueno had listened to these meetings, since only a thin partition separated the parlor from the poor little room where that employee used to sleep. The latter came in person to the famous Jesuit, Manuel Proano Vega, years later and told him:

> What I am going to narrate could be of use to history. At first Faustino Rayo did not want to intervene in the assassination of Garcia Moreno. But in subsequent interviews that he had at my boss's house, by virtue of the talk he heard, the liquor he drank, and the banknotes he received, he finally agreed to kill the President.[35]

Note that the Bueno family were in-laws of the lawyer Manuel Polanco, ringleader of the plot against Garcia Moreno.

According to the report entitled *"Criminales. Contra el Doctor Polanco Tribunal Marcial. Corte Suprema"*[36] it is clear that the above-mentioned syndicate was giving money to Sergeant Major Campuzano, urging him to go to Guayaquil to stir up a riot in the barracks. On the other hand, in the inquiry made by Jorge Villavicencio, Director of Police, it was discovered that Polanco gave ten pesos to Campuzano on a first occasion and twenty pesos on the second one. A short time later he put in his hands a letter addressed to General Uraga and Doctor Yerovi, who were in Guayaquil. "How can I arrange for that letter to reach those gentlemen?" Doctor Polanco answered him, "Come to an agreement with their friend, Captain Faustino Rayo." And so it was done. Captain Rayo committed to it, availing himself of a fellow countryman, a Columbian, who performed the job of mail delivery marvelously. But the latter, of course, did not carry out that long round trip save being well paid in money.[37]

Besides, in the report, *"Primer Cuerpo. Criminal de Oficio para descubrir a los autores y complices del asesinato de Garcia Moreno,"*[38] it appears that the sum of five hundred pesos was given to an officer of the Guayaquil Artillery Brigade. That military man did not want to accept it, undoubtedly being God-fearing and also frightened by the executions that could ensue in an unsuccessful case. Consequently the officer returned that large quantity, although not completely but with a decrease of twenty pesos.

Having returned from Guayaquil, the aforesaid "mailman" gave this news, "Neither General Uraga nor Doctor Yerovi accept the risk of instigating a military uprising."[39] When he heard this, Doctor Polanco became very irate, even against Sergeant Campuzano who was not to blame for the fiasco. Campuzano, angry in turn, replied to him, "I withdraw forever from these foolhardy attempts and revolutions." In order not to lose the Campuzano contingent, Doctor Polanco made use of Mr. Jose Maria Estrada, an expert in finances and banking.

Estrada approached the Sergeant Major and told him amicably, "Don't worry about the losses that you say you have undergone for having collaborated in this revolutionary commotion. You will be absolutely compensated for the twenty thousand pesos that you affirm you have lost. In exchange you will lend your help, being placed at the head of brave young men who will be enlisted by Doctor Polanco." As a result of that interview, Major Campuzano and Jose Maria Estrada became friends. The former began to frequent the latter's house every day, speaking with him for long periods of time as is evident in the *"Juicio Penal seguido contra el Sargento Major Gregorio Campuzano."*[40] These interviews began during the first days of June.

Suspecting the existence of a secret revolutionary meeting, the Director of Police, Jorge Villavicencio, approached Garcia Moreno. He informed him of those unexpected meetings and asked him whether Estrada was an enemy of his Excellency or not. The President answered,

"Estrada has no reason to be my enemy. We have never had the slightest unpleasantness between the two of us." Truly, we have seen that Don Gabriel, in a letter he addressed to Jose Maria Estrada, closed with "Your most affectionate and assured servant."[41] This was an old friendship as was evident five lustrums[42] before when Garcia Moreno, writing from Paris to Roberto Ascasubi, wrote these words on the back of the envelope, "Confided to Mr. Jose Maria Estrada." This same gentleman served as intermediary for the transportation of some packages of books from Babahoyo to Quito to the Ministry of Exterior Relations in June of 1872, as is clear in *El Nacional* on July 5, 1872. On December 29, 1858, Don Gabriel wrote in these terms from Guayaquil:

> Pedro Pablo has involved me in accompanying him to Lima to liquidate the Estrada Country House and to proceed immediately to Chile by myself to conclude a very important matter that Estrada had commissioned to his brother, Jose Maria, who returned without finishing it.

On January 5, 1859:
> I spoke to Jose Maria Estrada who arrived on the night of the thirty-first and I resolved not to go because of the following:

> The Estrada House lawsuit was already in the hands of a lawyer from Valparaiso, to whom five hundred pesos had been paid in advance. If I went, either the case would be taken away from the lawyer, with the loss of the sum already paid, or I would be reduced to taking the role of a mere representative or attorney. The former would cause financial loss, with a burden to my conscience. The latter would involve making a fool of myself and proving them right who were already saying that I was taking a vacation and the cost was defrayed. The Estrada widow and children are still very determined to have me go and take charge of the case. The former even wept to get Pedro Pablo to implicate me. But I have refused and will continue to refuse for the above-mentioned reasons.

The preceding paragraphs are sufficient to persuade us that Garcia Moreno's relations with Jose Maria Estrada were of an old and constant friendship. This contrasts with the proposals made by that financier to Campuzano, inducing him to subvert Garcia Moreno's government. And this was but the beginning. Jose Maria Estrada went in person to Captain Faustino Rayo's house, where he conferred with Mr. N. Galarza regarding the overthrow of Garcia Moreno's government.[43] And Jose Maria Estrada notified Campuzano that Garcia Moreno and his Ministers would be taken prisoners on August sixth, and that the troops from the First Battalion would abstain from hindering it.[44]

It came out in the *"Juicio Penal contra el Mayor Campuzano"*[45] that at the beginning of June, that same Mr. Estrada also began to have a friendship and frequent interviews with Doctor Manuel Polanco, the main inciter and organizer of the Garcia Moreno tragedy.

In the booklet *Defensa del Doctor Polanco*,[46] it is pointed out that this ringleader was in the tiny secluded La Loma Square on August fifth, in the company of the conspirator Abelardo Moncayo; and that Jose Maria Estrada was walking toward that same place.

In the *"Juicio Penal contra Campuzano"*[47] it is clear that, after the revolution failed, Mr. Estrada was very careful not to appear in public. He concealed and hid himself. Therefore, his conscience bothered him. He feared being captured.

If Estrada, far from having motives for annoyance, rather had cause for friendship with Garcia Moreno, what powerful reasons did he harbor to intervene in the assassination of his friend? This interrogation of Doctor Polanco is in the *"Juzgado Fiscal Militar de Oficiales Generales"*[48] held on August 25, 1875:

> 3. Is it true that Campuzano said that Doctor Polanco had been the defending counsel in the above-mentioned Campuzano's lawsuits and of one pertaining to his children, worth I do not know how many thousands, which had been won; and whether later he told them that Mr. Estrada had been the treasurer of the revolution and gave I do not know how many thousands to the above-mentioned Campuzano as well as to Faustino Rayo; and 4. whether that same Campuzano in other meetings that he had with His Honorable Excellency, the Vice President of the Republic, retracted the imputations that he had made about the above-mentioned Doctor Polanco in the beginning?[49]

The Judge, Francisco Javier Salazar, answered those questions in these terms: "The content of the third one is false; and that instead of

Campuzano retracting his assertions regarding Doctor Polanco, he maintained them till the end."

Therefore, according to Salazar, it is false, based on what Campuzano said, that Polanco had been the defense attorney in lawsuits for the aforesaid Campuzano and for one of his children. Consequently those thousands of pesos were not the earnings from a lawsuit but rather came from somewhere else. Note that at the time of this trial, Campuzano had already been executed by a firing squad.

At another time the Judge, Secundino Darquea, said to Polanco:

> The origin of the five thousand pesos was not a lawsuit that you won. Rather, as Campuzano has already declared, the treasurer of the Revolution was Estrada and he gave Campuzano five thousand pesos and ten thousand to Rayo.

In his own defense, Polanco interrogated Darquea whether it was true or not that he had stuck in that clause. The Judge answered, "It is true, but without referring to Campuzano but rather to what is said by the common people."

So, according to Salazar, the money given by Estrada was not the earnings from lawsuits but a stipend contributed to Campuzano in payment for his revolutionary activities. According to Darquea, the preceding assertion was hearsay among the people.

Other evidence that Mr. Estrada certainly was the treasurer of the revolution:

Campuzano, because of his criminal comings and goings, was compelled to stay within the confines of Quito. Desiring to take a trip to the city of Ambato, he feigned attempting to go only to the province of Cotopaxi to buy fattened cattle there and then sell them for a better price. He asked for the corresponding permission from the Government, which obliged him to present written proof that his intention was that business. Campuzano gave more than a thousand pesos to Mr. Vilacis, the owner of the cattle, obtained the receipt and presented it to the government, which issued the requested permission.

Two months later, the courts examined Campuzano:

"Where did you get so much money?"

"Well, from a maternal inheritance from the children by my first marriage. That is why, with the government's permission, I left for Ambato to collect the inheritance"

But when he had a thousand and some pesos in his hands, he had not yet gone to Ambato. That means that he acquired them from another person, and so he was convicted of lying.

On the other hand, when Campuzano reached the farm where he had to buy the cattle, he was intoxicated and full of insults for the government. Besides he demanded an excessive number of animals; and he did not take long to declare that his purpose was not to buy them but to continue his trip to Ambato, which he actually did. When he returned to the capital, he recovered about a thousand pesos and went to deposit them... Where? Well, where Jose Maria Estrada was. From that it can be inferred that he had obtained them from that same gentleman. This individual had handed over that quantity to a revolutionary. He was at the risk of not recovering it, for the failure of the revolution was possible. It is difficult to believe that Jose Maria Estrada would have been resigned to such a great loss. It is rather understood that this amount had not been taken from his bank account, but from another one, whose trustee he was.

Campuzano was caught by surprise in an attempt to violate his confinement, for the second time, by trying to go to Ambato again without permission. Consequently he was sent to prison. But, after a few days passed, he heard an advantageous proposal: "You can leave jail if a solvent citizen guarantees that you will strictly observe your confinement in Quito for six months."

"I accept. Can Mr. Estrada be my guarantor?"

That question was transmitted to Garcia Moreno, and he gave his acquiescence. Here is another sign of the esteem that Don Gabriel had for that character. The latter accepted being guarantor, but he did not take long to desist. Having reflected on it a little, he understood that his very person would be investigated and persecuted in the very possible case that the revolution failed. This evasion is another indication that Jose Maria Estrada knew about the scheme and was an accomplice.

Then Campuzano proposed a bond in money. The government accepted it by means of the consignment of one thousand pesos in the Public Treasury. Where did the prisoner get that quantity? From Jose Maria's bank account. The deposit was made at three in the afternoon on August fifth, the eve of Garcia Moreno's assassination. Campuzano was freed and at once had an interview with his compatriot, Faustino Rayo, and the next morning, two more interviews. For sure they spoke of Estrada's words to Campuzano: "Today the President will be taken prisoner with his Ministers, and the First Battalion will abstain from hindering it."

Did Estrada confer with the accomplice, Commander Sanchez, head of the First Battalion? It is not known. But without the shadow of a doubt, Estrada knew about it from the lips of the ringleader Polanco. Did he receive a cut from the offer of money to the armed forces? Very likely he did.

In the *"Primer Cuerpo. Criminal de Oficio. Para descubrir autores, complices, etc."*[50] it is clearly seen that Polanco said, "I am going to offer ten thousand pesos to a military man who was raised in my house." Manuel Cornejo objected: "One must offer only what he can give." Polanco replied, "What are ten thousand pesos compared to saving the country?" Cornejo replied, "I do not note the aim but rather what cannot be carried out due to the enormous quantity offered." Let us listen to these words written by Abelardo Moncayo, referring to the years we are recording: "Ten thousand pesos in capital was enough so that we would consider the one who possessed them as a Rothschild."[51]

Who was this military man that was brought up in Polanco's house? In the booklet *Defensa del Doctor Planco*[52] it is seen that this military man was an officer of the Second Artillery Battalion. But it is unlikely that Polanco would think seriously about giving such a large quantity to a mere officer, lacking powerful influence in his barracks, when he could do so to Francisco Sanchez, who acted as the First Officer in Command on August sixth, at the head of the First Battalion, the highest superior in Quito and who, besides, as Officer in Command of Night Patrol, was also in command of the Artillery.

Cornejo himself considered this second alternative as a fact when conversing with Doctor Jose Antonio Correa, who referred to it under oath in the presence of the Tribunal established to discover the authors and accomplices of Garcia Moreno's assassination.[53] Here it is textually:

> Manuel Cornejo referred, with regard to Doctor Polanco and Commander Sanchez, about whom that same Mr. Cornejo had said that Polanco had told him that he was implicated, and had offered to give him ten thousand pesos... That the same Mr. Cornejo also told him that on the day that the crime was committed, they had desisted in doing it, leaving it for another day, but that a message from Sanchez forced the revolutionary plan; and they substantiated this fact.[54]

Nineteen days after the parricide, Canon Vicente Cuesta was in Quito and wrote as follows:

> He (that is, Manuel Cornejo) suspected that the agreement was also false that Manuel Polanco told him existed with Sanchez, the Officer in Command of the First Battalion. To get rid of these doubts, one afternoon Polanco took Sanchez by the arm and strolled and conversed with Sanchez for about an hour in the balustrade of the Cathedral, in sight of the conspirators in the square. At night Polanco told them that Sanchez was committed at the meeting they held in Moncayo's house, and that they would give him ten thousand pesos, (I do not know where they would get them); and that on Friday, August sixth, he would be the Officer in Command on Day Patrol, and that they should take advantage of this circumstance.[55]

Let Mr. Eloy Proano's assertion serve as proof. He was highly authorized, because that citizen was then the editor in chief of the government newspaper *El Nacional*.

> One of those (implicated) was Commander Francisco Sanchez, who, according to the accusations and evidence exhibited before the court-martial, was the basis and support upon which the revolutionary plan rested. This corrupt and ill-fated military man was bribed by Doctor Manuel Polanco.[56]

It can be understood that Sanchez, to secure rich gain, became the most decisive factor for the perpetration of the parricide. Furthermore this was testified by the above-mentioned Cornejo in the presence of Mr. Mariano Aviles who declared in these terms:

> It is clear to me that Mr. Cornejo places all the blame on Commander Sanchez, saying that he had shown them disrespect and betrayed them, besides being the whole of the revolution, and that he had made the revolutionaries rush to the President's death, which that Commander had insisted on at every moment of that day and previously. He ended by saying that, before killing him or anyone, they should execute Commander Sanchez by firing squad as the cause of everything. Mr. Cornejo said many things in this sense, as is clear, to the entire bodyguard and the people.

Therefore it happened later that everyone had such revenge against Commander Sanchez, and that everyone demanded his death, having seen that he had been to blame for everything.

Also these statements of Manuel Polanco's:

> Finally, I no longer looked for Sanchez. Rather Sanchez looked for me. Three meetings took place with me. The first one in the street of the coaches and the new butcher shop from seven until eight thirty at night; the second, at home and in the presence of Doctor Jorge Bueno, who Sanchez said was an intimate friend and had been a fellow student, from seven until midnight; and the third in my house from seven until nine... I told him that if he wished, or if he did not trust some soldiers and an officer, I would place a group of young men to guard the small house of that commander's headquarters, to block Salazar's and Saenz's way to the barracks. He answered that no, I should not weaken and distract my people from taking the main barracks which was the Tyrant; and that everything else was secondary and the rest was up to him. Finally, until the last moment he ordered us to say on repeated occasions that once the Tyrant's head was cut off, we should fear nothing. We should come confidently to the barracks and he would even answer for Saenz; he would tie him up...[57]

Sanchez had no reason to loathe Garcia Moreno, as is obvious and no one doubts it. He was an instrument. It is deduced that the temptation was a powerful external factor that he could not resist: ten thousand pesos! Who does not know the power of money for the purchase of consciences and perpetration of crimes! A second attraction could be promotion to the rank of Colonel. A third, perhaps, was a public, peaceful concubinage with Juana Terrazas, with whom he had secret relations.

It is worth considering that the quantity denounced by Father Moner's penitent, six thousand pesos, must have been but one of Masonry's installments. Making an inventory, the outlays or promises to Rayo, Campuzano, Sanchez, and the five hundred pesos given to an officer of the Guayaquil Artillery Brigade, come to a total of twenty-five thousand five hundred pesos. Add small quantities spent on negotiations, and coming and goings. The Jesuit historian, Jose Legohuir, annotates that a few years later, Roberto Andrade claimed the pecuniary quota from the Lima Masonry that they had promised him and had not given him. After Faustino Rayo was lynched, his pockets were searched and around four thousand sols were found, between minted silver and thousand sol bills from the Bank of Peru.[58] This item appeared in a Spanish magazine by the name of *La Cruz* in October 1875.[59] That magazine says they had copied it from a Quito newspaper sent to their press spokesman. Unfortunately, the author has not found the newspaper from Quito.

What is certain is that the monetary purchase of Rayo's arm was known everywhere in Ecuador and in the world. The wise priest, Father Gonzalez Suarez, in his funeral oration on August 25, 1875, pronounced in Cuenca, said, "The man who was, we will not say a criminal but rather so unfortunate as to receive a price for shedding the blood of the President of the Republic, when perhaps he meditated on peacefully enjoying the reward from his barbarous act, was suddenly snatched away to eternity."[60]

Immediately after the assassination on the sixth of August, the Chilean magazine, *El Independiente* contained this paragraph: "An officer, and a beloved officer he was, who immolated the Chilean Minister (Portales): these were precisely the headlines that, according to the news received by telegraph, adorned, to its great shame, Garcia Moreno's assassination. Florin himself, we recall, when executing his crime, perhaps did not carry the infamous price of it in the pockets of his jacket. Mr. Garcia Moreno was ordered to be assassinated from afar, probably from foreign shores."

And the article entitled *"Luto en el Ecuador,"*[61] published in Buenos Aires, said, "This great man, this great figure who majestically towers over the most eminent men in America, has perished, the victim of the treachery of an infamous man, paid, as is believed, with four thousand sols..."

Over in Paris, the Redemptorist, Augusto Berthe, sketched Don Gabriel's biography. Data was furnished to him by Doctor Pablo Herrera, Juan Leon Mera, the Most Illustrious Bishop Ordonez Lazo and others who were in Quito as a result of the assassination to participate in the Congress that inaugurated sessions on August tenth. Twelve years after the horrendous crime, the biography appeared in public. Its prologue stated, "The greatest part of the facts consigned to this work have been narrated to us to the least detail by eyewitnesses, members of the clergy, the magistrate, the parliament and the army: Garcia Moreno's friends and enemies." He establishes this proposition:

Peruvian bank checks found in the assassin's pockets demonstrated to everyone that the venerable and virtuous Freemasonry, just like the Jewish Sanhedrin, does not economize its denarii to pay the Judases who have been their instruments.[62]

The Redemptorist's work was read in Quito. The following judgment was made by the magazine entitled *La Republica del Sagrado Corazon*:[63]

This work is the fruit of ten years of research, a book of momentous importance due to its scholarship. It suffers only from an unimportant defect, its insignificant inaccuracies, since the author had not visited our country. But they will undoubtedly disappear in another edition.

The French author requested competent Ecuadorians to point out those inaccuracies. He received a satisfactory answer and according to the corrections sent from Quito, published a fourth, enlarged, improved edition. Anyway, what relates to the Peruvian bank checks appeared unchanged, since the correctors found nothing to refute in it.

Father Berthe requested his Ecuadorian helpers to correct him even more for the sixth edition presented now in the language of Cervantes. He obtained new data and details and with them and the stupendous pen of the Spanish translator, Navarro Villoslada, obtained an even greater success. At any rate, what referred to the bills from Lima turned out written the way we quote it below:

Checks against the Bank of Peru, found in the assassin's pockets, proved to everyone that the venerable and virtuous Masonry, just like the Jewish Synagogue, does not dispense with the thirty coins for the Judases whom they hire.

According to the Jesuit historian, Jose Legohuir, one of the witnesses of the Peruvian bills in Rayo's pockets was Doctor Pablo Herrera, who as President of the Supreme Court of Justice, intervened in the trials relating to the tragic sixth of August. Nevertheless, the author confesses that he has not found Pablo Herrera's testimony in writing. However, it is certain that Father Virgilio Herrera, Pablo Herrera's son, never ceased stating that Peruvian bills were found in Rayo's pockets. Father Virgilio Herrera was a Jesuit and as such lived for many years under the same roof as Legohuir. During his adolescence, the author even heard that from Father Virgilio Herrera's lips, who seemed to be especially determined to tell about it.

It can be assured that there is historical certainty about the Peruvian money, provided that the numerous pieces of evidence and suppositions are considered regarding what Father Moner's penitent affirmed, "That the German Lodge, in agreement with the one in Lima, had sent six thousand pesos to Guayaquil, to be distributed among those dissatisfied with Garcia Moreno, and by all means possible to secure his assassination."

Doctor Antonio Borrero has objected in the following way, "If Peruvian bills were found in Rayo's pockets, why were they not taken by the government and exhibited at the trials? So then, it is nothing more than a street rumor." Father Virgilio Herrera answered:

> Those bills could have had no utility in a trial against Faustino Rayo, because there was none. The hired assassin died even before Garcia Moreno did. The government's determination was feverishly devoted to capturing the fugitive assassins and hindering any attempt of a revolution. According to written testimony by General Venancio Rueda, the Columbian Ambassador in Quito, a throng of common people approached Rayo's corpse and stripped him of his wallet, papers and everything he had on him. It is an easy thing to look for bank documents, take them and distribute them. It is noted that there were no arguments, which shows that what was taken stimulated but little greed, without a doubt precisely because they were checks from another nation.

Certainly the assassins were paid in small quantities, with promises to complete payment after the perpetration of the crime. The latter was thwarted due to the failure of the revolution, the flight of the evildoers, capture of the ringleader Polanco, and finally, the concealment of Jose Maria Estrada. The latter was undoubtedly assigned a large percentage as a reward for his job as administrator and distributer.

It is now time to ask what mental attitude Garcia Moreno maintained once he was the target of the assassins' snares? At least he was not afraid of death. The following paragraph, written by Juan Leon Mera, fits in here, "A friend once spoke to him of how much his courage and contempt of death surprised him. 'In order not to fear it,' Garcia Moreno answered, 'there is an excellent solution and it is to live like a

Christian and always be prepared to receive it when God sends it to us.' But, as he began to see the happiness of martyrdom, his tranquility turned into a longing to die." Let us listen to the expressions he addressed to Pius IX twenty days before the tragic sixth of August:

> Most Holy Father, I implore your blessing, having been chosen again, without any merit on my part, to rule this Catholic republic during the coming six years. The new presidential term does not commence until August thirtieth, when I take the oath to the Constitution, and then I shall dutifully inform Your Holiness officially of the fact; but I wish to obtain your blessing before that day, so that I may have the strength and the light which I need so much in order to be unto the end a faithful son of our Redeemer, and a loyal and obedient servant of His infallible Vicar. Now that the Masonic lodges of the neighboring countries, instigated by Germany, are vomiting against me all sorts of atrocious insults and horrible calumnies; now, also, that the lodges are secretly arranging for my assassination; I have more need than ever of the Divine protection, so that I may live and die in defense of our holy religion, and for the dear republic, which I am called once more to rule. What happiness can be mine, Most Holy Father, so great as that of being hated and calumniated for the sake of our Divine Redeemer? And how great a happiness Your blessing will be to me if it procures for me from heaven the privilege of shedding my blood for the God who shed His own for us on the Cross![64]

During these days he also addressed letters to Father Pedro de Blas. The latter had written to him regarding some Bethlemite[65] nuns from Guatemala, persecuted by the Masonic government there. Garcia Moreno answered him more or less in the following manner:

> Let those nuns come to Ecuador to run schools for girls in the city and province where they see fit. The whole territory of Ecuador is at their command. If they suffer persecution in Guatemala on the part of the Masonic government, in this equinoctial country the government will receive them with open arms like an affectionate father.

He also wrote in similar terms to their Founder and Superior, Sister Encarnacion Rosales. This distinguished religious nun was very pleased with the reading of that letter, so much the more since she had heard that the Republic of Ecuador was officially consecrated to the Heart of Jesus. The Bethlemite Congregation ardently appreciated the worship of the Deified Heart of the God-Man. They were making preparations for the trip when lo, it happened that their ears were wounded by the stampede of the horrendous news: "President Garcia Moreno died riddled with machete blows and bullet wounds." Sister Encarnacion, who desired to die in the Republic of the Heart of Jesus, could do no more than surrender to the dispositions of Divine Providence and wait for God's time and hour. This came at the end of eleven years, when the Foundress was in the Colombian city of Pasto at the head of a group of novices, the hope of the Congregation. She was visited by Father Valentin Carpio, an Ecuadorian, who was provided with powers conferred by Monsignor Gonzalez Calixto with a view to founding a Bethlemite school in Tulcan. "Is the political atmosphere good in Ecuador?" they asked. "It is magnificent," responded the envoy. "We have Jose Maria Placido Caamano as President, who follows in the footsteps of Garcia Moreno." The holy Foundress exclaimed jubilantly, "I accept the foundation in Tulcan. We will gladly go. I want to die in the Republic of the Heart of Jesus."

It was August 14, 1886, when the cavalcade arrived at the Rumichaca Bridge, the border between Colombia and Ecuador. She hardly had crossed the line when Sister Encarnacion broke out in these words, "Oh, Ecuador! In you I deliver my soul into the hands of the Lord." She had them lower her from her horse, bent her knees and kissed the ground. The entry into Tulcan was tremendous. A procession of horseback riders, triumphal arches along the way, festive musical pieces, cascades of flowers from the balconies, and lastly speeches and poetry. It was the prelude for her entrance into Heaven. In fact, ten days later Sister Encarnacion flew to receive her eternal reward. Tulcan dressed its buildings in mourning. The municipal musical band played funeral marches. One woman took the flowers that covered the venerable corpse and applied them to her eyes. She immediately recovered her sight. Due to such a prodigy the people surged forward with rosaries, medals and crosses to touch them to the miraculous mortal remains.

Returning to mid-July, 1875, we find Father Manuel Proano conversing with Garcia Moreno. Since rumors were public and insistent about the Head of State's assassination at an early date, that matter together with the distressing future of the country, affected their conversation. That was when the President pronounced this memorable prediction:

> After my death the Antichristian Revolution will again take over the government of the country and will govern it tyrannically, despotically, under the deceitful name of Liberalism. But the Heart of Jesus, to whom I have consecrated it, will wrest it from their claws once again, to make it live free and upright under the protection of the great Catholic principles.

The Jesuit told the Head of State, "If it happens as your Excellency predicts, we Jesuits will again be exiled from the country." At that Garcia Moreno caught his interlocutor's wrist and closing his eyes a bit as if making out something far away, he exclaimed, "Father, that will not happen. The impious will not dare expel you again." In later chapters it will be made clear that this prediction has been fulfilled up to the present time.

The Jesuit historian, Jose Legohuir, states that in the final years of his life Garcia Moreno received Communion almost every day. This is significant at a time when even those in religious communities received Communion only once every eight days, and during the week when they attended a special religious solemnity. As a member of the Apostolate of Prayer, His Excellency had a particular obligation to receive Communion on the First Friday of the month in satisfaction for the offenses inflicted against Christ in the Most Holy Sacrament. Since Don Gabriel was a member of that confraternity, these Communions are explicitly specified in the Annals of the Lazarist priests.[66] However, those Annals did no more than reproduce the letters dispatched from Quito. There are two insignificant errors in that correspondence. First, that Garcia Moreno was a member of the Congregation of the Heart of Jesus. That name, Congregation, had existed six years previously under the regency of Father Francisco Hernaez, S. J. But afterward, under the regency of Fathers Antonio Garces and Manuel Proano, it was changed to Apostolate of Prayer. One of its statutes requests its members to receive Communion on the First Friday of the month. The second error lies in stating that Garcia Moreno, as a member of that confraternity, received Communion on the eve of the first Friday of August. It has already been said that the statutes prescribed Communion on the day of that Friday.

At dawn on that memorable August sixth, Garcia Moreno wrote the following ejaculation on his identity card, "My Jesus, Jesus Christ, grant me love and humility, and indicate to me what I ought to do today in Thy service."

At about seven in the morning, he left the church of Santo Domingo with his wife, Mariana del Alcazar. The university student Jose Maria Banderas also left, whose mind was concerned with the exams he would take that morning. Finally, an ordinary number of faithful left. Banderas testified that Faustino Rayo, who was in the vestibule of the church, greeted the President, "Good morning, Your Excellency." The greeting was answered and the harness maker added, "Has Your Excellency heard the Mass of Our Lord of the Agony?"

"I do practice that devotion," was the President's answer.

Around the year 1940, the author consulted Father Jervis, a scholarly Dominican, regarding that devotion to Our Lord. The answer was that, in truth, the people on Friday paid private homage to a statue of Christ Crucified, but that its name was not "of the Agony" but rather "of the Expiration."

More or less at one fifteen in the afternoon, Garcia Moreno directed his steps toward the Government Palace. On the way he entered the Cathedral and knelt before the Most Holy Sacrament, which was solemnly exposed, since that day was the First Friday of the month. There are at least three declarations that Garcia Moreno made that visit minutes before being assassinated. The first is by Doctor Ignacio Salazar, an eyewitness, quoted by the Jesuit historian Legohuir. The second is by Mrs. Ana Chiriboga de Davalos and Miss Maria Chiriboga Delgado, who were also visiting the Most Holy Sacrament and who prayed for Don Gabriel as well, impressed by the rumors that his victimization was being plotted. The third declaration was that of the Mercedarian Friar, Domingo Cabezas Moncayo, who as a child observed that his uncle, Abelardo Moncayo Jijon, went out of his house suddenly and shouted, "Bull, bull!" The boy went out into the street also, turned his eyes toward the Cathedral, and noted that Garcia Moreno entered that church. Later he told it to the above-mentioned prelate who told it to the author.

Ten minutes later, Mrs. Margarita Carrera left one of the small shops beneath the Government Palace and ran into President Garcia Moreno fallen on the ground, riddled with machete blows and bullet wounds. Days later that woman was interrogated by Eloy Proano Vega, the Director of *El Nacional,* who published her testimony literally as follows:

> When the President was pushed from the Palace arcade to the Square, he made an effort to get up. And leaning on his arm, he straightened out, with her helping him. Then Rayo, who had turned around at the next corner, again rushed toward the place where Mr. Garcia Moreno lay and ordered that woman to move away if she didn't want to die at his hands. He finished dealing the frenzied machete blows onto the fallen body of the President, which triturated his skull. Each blow was accompanied by the drone of insults, saying to him, "Die, hypocrite! Die, villain! Jesuit in a frock coat! Tyrant!" And then Garcia Moreno, making a supreme effort said, "God does not die!"

The preceding narration, given by the exemplary gentleman, Eloy Proano, thirteen years after Garcia Moreno's assassination, was published in the magazine that had as a title *La Republica del Corazon de Jesus.*[67] In the preface, Eloy asserts that his historical study is consistent in all things with the most austere truth. And in the epilogue, he printed the following quoted words:

> I am able to state, on my word of honor, that all I have related is the authentic account of the events connected to the bloody catastrophe of August 6, 1875; without arguing to the contrary, others better-informed about the event may point out some details that they were able to know. I relate what is clear to me.[68]

It is revolting to suspect that Proano Vega invented the words: God does not die. Margarita Camera would have invented them even less, being humble, illiterate, of the Negro race, a wet nurse in her shop. Simple people tell things the way they saw and heard them.

Contrary to what has been said, the following objection militates:

Garcia Moreno, approximately six and a half feet tall, having just fallen, was wounded with around seven machete blows and four bullet wounds. An individual named Vicente Montero came to him to lift him from the ground, who exclaimed, "On my life! They killed him." The victim answered with poorly articulated or babbling words that Vicente Montero did not understand. If then Garcia Moreno could not utter words with perfection, all the less could he clearly utter his "God does not die" some three minutes later, after receiving more machete blows on his head. I respond: He could clearly utter his "God does not die," by making a supreme effort, according to Margarita Carrera's expression and Proano Vega's. And he did make such an effort, stimulated by the insults: "Die, hypocrite! Die, villain! Jesuit in a frock coat! Tyrant!" Under the circumstances his answer fits even better, "God does not die."

A few moments later, the dying man received absolution for his sins, imparted by the Catalonian priest, Father Masampero, who by chance passed by there. Shortly afterward he was transported to the Cathedral in the arms of six men, and attended by the Canons Vicente Pastor, Ignacio Vera and Arsenio Andrade, kneeling on the floor and remaining silent, restrained by emotion. The prebendary Ignacio Vera livened up and spoke, "Most Excellent Sir, forgive your assassins before receiving absolution and the holy oils." To these words the dying man made two slight bows of his head accompanied by a death rattle. Then the prebendary Arsenio Andrade added, "Most Excellent Sir, I want a clearer sign. Since your Excellency cannot speak, raise your hand and take hold of mine, if you forgive your assassins." At once the dying man, with his left hand that only had one slight wound, took hold of the priest's hand. Ignacio Vera gave the dying man absolution and anointed him with the holy oils. Moments later the martyr expired.

According to the sworn testimony of the three surgeons that performed the autopsy on Garcia's cadaver, he should have expired at the very place where he fell from the Palace, therefore a few moments after having suffered Rayo's final "cintarazos,"[69] of which eight were essentially mortal. However, he lasted some twenty-five minutes more, so that he could die inside the Cathedral, where the Most Holy Sacrament was exposed, at the foot of the altar of Our Sorrowful Lady, next to the cross that he had carried a year and three months earlier in procession, and finally aided by the sacraments for the dying. That promise by the Heart of Jesus was prodigiously fulfilled in him: "Those who receive Communion nine consecutive First Fridays of the month will not die without the last sacraments." [70]

The above-mentioned surgeons extracted Garcia Moreno's heart from his corpse and enclosed it in a crystal jar. This precious relic is kept in a sacred place. [71]

A kind of panegyric was pronounced by Father Clemente Faller to the Jesuits of Quito. What did this religious say, who was President of the community at that time and had been the Provincial in Germany? "If dealing," he said, "with the beatification of Garcia Moreno, I could affirm under oath that this man possessed, to a heroic degree, the theological and moral virtues of his state. Since it would be too long for me to refer each and every one of Garcia Moreno's virtues that Father Faller praised by citing circumstantial deeds, I will conclude as that Father concluded one day, stating that he had seen and observed in Garcia Moreno all the virtues that are told of Saint Ferdinand, Saint Edward, and Saint Louis, King of France, much to his admiration." This declaration was published in *El Mensajero del Corazon de Jesus.*[72]

He was honored not only in Ecuador but in the whole Catholic world with splendid funeral rites. The press sounded his achievements. Naturally many spokesmen extolled the associations of the martyr to the Heart of Jesus. This is what the Colombian magazine, *El Mensajero del Corazon de Jesus* wrote:

> Victim of the Sacred Heart of Jesus! Not for a moment do we hesitate to place this new martyr, mourned by the entire Church, in the gallery of the Friends of the Heart of Jesus. After the Sovereign Pontiff, few men in our days have done so much as he did for the reign of Jesus Christ and the worship of His Divine Heart. That is why the Revolution condemned him to the hired assassin's dagger...[73]

A printed page in Lima expressed it this way:

> It was the sixth of August, the First Friday of the month, when according to his refined devotion to the Sacred Heart of Jesus he had received Communion in the morning: a presage of his eternal predestination. For, he broke his morning fast with the most Holy Body of Our Lord Jesus Christ, which would serve him as Viaticum for his passage into eternity...[74]

*El Siglo Futuro,*[75] a Madrid newspaper, came out in defense of the great Ecuadorian:

> The charge of tyranny made about the Catholic President, can have no other origin except a revolutionary one. When has it been a tyrannical act to place a State under the protection of the Virgin Mary and the Sacred Heart of Jesus? And what we say about this most noble deed of Garcia Moreno's can be applied to the others who are enumerated in the above paragraph...

Here we also have some verses published in France:

> Oh, what name will I give you? Prince, Apostle, Martyr? You who knew how to die with such greatness! Oh noble Moreno! Immense is your merit for having ascended to such a high peak in your love for the Divine Heart...
>
> Issoudum![76] Yes, this name, crossing the Atlantic, came to the hearing of the Hero-friend of the Heart of Christ. Because, full of love for God, this ardent Catholic was also an energetic servant of Mary. He consequently requested to be united to our brothers who by the thousands ascend to the Divine Heart through the intermediary of Mary...
>
> Come, kneel at the most holy altar! Jesus waits for you in His Tabernacle. Come to be sustained with the Bread of the predestined, and begin your departure. It is your exit from the Cenacle to the agony. It is now time to die for the Heart of Jesus...
>
> But what strikes our souls in the greatest degree is not so much your heroic virtues as having given your nation to Jesus, and Jesus to your nation...

# Endnotes

[1] Referring to the King of France, Louis XIV.
[2] Severo Gomezjurado, S. J., *Vida de Garcia Moreno* (Imprenta ARPI, Quito, 1979), vol. 9, p. 159 ff. where it is said that this passage is a "conjunct of clauses."
[3] I.e. King Louis XIV.
[4] Gomezjurado, p. 161.
[5] *Misions. Idem.* p. 178 ff.; cf. Gomezjurado, p. 178.
[6] "The Truth."
[7] Gomezjurado, p. 181.
[8] "Is Spain Catholic?"
[9] "The Voice of the Clergy."
[10] Gomezjurado, *op. cit.*, vol. 9, p. 186 & 310.
[11] "Franciscan Magazine."
[12] The miraculous statue of Our Lady of Quinche is a small wooden statue carved by Diego de Robles in the sixteenth century to resemble Our Lady of Guadalupe (Mexico). She is venerated in a large church in the town of Quinche as the Protectress of Ecuador. Her feast is celebrated on November 21.
[13] "Sketch of Garcia Moreno."
[14] Following a long-time tradition for the feast of the Holy Innocents, jokes and tricks are played from December 28$^{th}$ to January 6$^{th}$ and festivals are celebrated with dances and masquerades, lightened with music from typical bands in the streets and with the participation of neighbors and families.
[15] "The Perpetual Dictatorship."
[16] Gomezjurado, *Vida de Garcia Moreno*, vol. 9, p. 361.
[17] Martyrdom. *Idem.* p. 292 ff. The sentence "In order not to fear death, we should live like Christians and be ready to appear before God at any time" was related by Juan Leon Mera in his posthumous book on Garcia Moreno, page 222. Gomezjurado, *Vida de Garcia Moreno*, vol. 9, p. 311.
[18] "The Future Century."
[19] "The Belgian Independence."
[20] Gomezjurado, *Vida de Garcia Moreno*, vol. 9, pp. 312-313.
[21] "International Gazette."
[22] Gomezjurado, *Vida de Garcia Moreno*, vol. 9, p. 314.
[23] Masons often place three dots in the form of a pyramid after writing their name to show that they belong to Freemasonry.
[24] "The Government of the Republic of Ecuador in the presence of America."
[25] Gomezjurado, *op. cit.*, vol. 7, pp. 436-440.
[26] *Ibid.* p. 449.
[27] *Ibid.* p. 441.
[28] *The Future Liberalism,* printed in Guayaquil in 1909.
[29] Vol. 2, p. 627.
[30] Gomezjurado, vol. 7, p. 440.

[31] *Don* (or *Dona*) are honorific titles widely used in Spanish speaking countries.
[32] *Ibid.* pp. 441-442.
[33] *Ibid.* p. 441. "No one could disguise the imminence of the danger, and a prelate, who was devoted to Garcia Moreno, said to him: "It is a matter of public notoriety that the sects have publicly condemned you, and that their assassins are sharpening their poniards. For the love of God, take some precautions!"
"And what precautions do you suggest?" replied the President.
"Never to go out without an escort."
"And who will defend me against the escort, if they, too, should be corrupted? I would rather place my trust in God." And he added the words of the Psalmist: *Nisi Dominus custodierit civitatem, frustra vigilat qui custodit eam.* ("Unless the Lord keep the city, he watcheth in vain that keepeth it" (Ps. 126, 1). (Rev. Fr. Augustine Berthe, *Garcia Moreno* (Dolorosa Press, 2006) pp. 217-218.)
[34] Gomezjurado, vol. 7, p. 454.
[35] *Ibid.* p. 455.
[36] "Criminal Investigation. Supreme Court, Martial Tribunal: Against Doctor Polanco," p. 146.
[37] Gomezjurado, vol. 9, p. 444.
[38] "First Volume, Criminal Process, at the Magistrate's Initiative, to discover the authors and accomplices in the assassination of Garcia Moreno," p. 114.
[39] Gomezjurado, vol. 9, p. 445.
[40] "Criminal Process against Major Sergeant Gregorio Campuzano," p. 120.
[41] A formal way of ending letters in Spanish, something like "Yours truly" or "Yours faithfully" in English, but in Spanish it seems much more endearing.
[42] I.e. Approximately twenty-five years.
[43] Gomezjurado, S. J., *op. cit.*, vol. 7, p. 462.
[44] *Ibid.* p. 468.
[45] Criminal Procedure against Major Campuzano, p. 119.
[46] "Defense of Doctor Polanco", p. 121.
[47] Criminal Process against Campuzano, on the reverse side of p. 42 and on p. 44.
[48] Military Prosecutor's Court for General Officers.
[49] Gomezjurado, vol. 9, p. 448.
[50] "First volume. Criminal Procedure, at the Magistrate's Initiative, to discover the authors and accomplices, etc.," p. 127.
[51] Gomezjurado, vol. 9, p. 451.
[52] "Defense of Doctor Polanco," p. 88.
[53] Cf. p. 135 of the trial.
[54] Gomezjurado, vol. 9, p. 452.
[55] *Ibid.* pp. 452-453.
[56] *The Republic of the Heart of Jesus*, p. 510 ff.
[57] Gomezjurado, vol. 9, p. 454.
[58] *Ibid.* p. 455.
[59] "The Cross," p. 101. Cf. Gomezjurado, vol.7, p. 476.

[60] Gomezjurado, vol. 7, p. 477.
[61] "Mourning in Ecuador"
[62] P. 732 of Augusto Berthe's biography; cf. Gomezjurado, vol. 7, p. 478.
[63] "The Republic of the Sacred Heart," August, 1887 issue.
[64] Rev. Reuben Parsons, D. D., *Studies in Church History* (Philadelphia, John Joseph McVey, 1900), vol. 6, pp. 71-72.
[65] About the Bethlemites, see Severo Gomezjurado, S. J., (*op., cit.*, 1979), vol. 9, p. 112.
[66] Vol. 40, p. 620.
[67] "The Republic of the Heart of Jesus"
[68] Gomezjurado, vol. 9, p. 168.
[69] I.e. blows with the flat of a sword, or in this case, of a machete.
[70] "The spirit which animated Garcia Moreno is indicated in the message which he had prepared for the Congress as he was about to enter on his third term of office, when the Masonic assassins sent him to his reward in heaven: 'Only a few years have elapsed since Ecuador repeated every day the lament which the Liberator, Bolivar, expressed in his last message to the Congress of 1830: I must say, and with the blush of shame on my brow, that while we have won our independence, it has been won at the expense of every other blessing. But since that time, having placed our trust in God, and having abandoned the course of impiety and apostasy which entices the world in this epoch of blindness, we have reorganized ourselves into a thoroughly Catholic nation, and therefore each day has beheld an increase of happiness and prosperity in our beloved country. Once Ecuador was a body from which life was departing; it was being already devoured, just as a corpse is devoured by a multitude of those hideous insects which the license of putrefaction allows to develop in the darkness of the grave. But today, obeying the Sovereign Voice which commanded Lazarus to issue from his tomb, Ecuador returns to new life, although she still retains the winding-sheet of death, that is, some remnants of the misery and corruption in which she was once wrapped. In order to justify my words, I need only render an account of our progress during the last two years, referring you to the special reports of each ministerial department for documents and details; and, in order that you may perceive the extent of our progress during this period of regeneration, I shall compare the present conditions with those which were once obtained. And I shall institute this comparison, not for our self-glorification, but in order to glorify Him to whom we owe everything, and whom we adore as our Redeemer, Father, Protector, God... To the perfect liberty which the Church now enjoys among us, and to the apostolic zeal of our virtuous pastors, we owe a reformation of the clergy, an improvement in morals, and so great a diminution in the number of crimes that in our population of more than a million there are not enough criminals to fill our penitentiary. To the Church we owe those religious organizations which constantly produce such happy results in the education of the young, and in the care of the sick and the poor... If I have committed any errors, I ask your pardon a thousand times; but I am sure that my will has not been at fault. But if, on the contrary, you find

that I have succeeded in my endeavors, attribute all the merit, firstly, to God and the Immaculate Dispenser of the inexhaustible treasures of God's mercies; and, secondly, to yourselves, to the people, to the army, and to all the members of the administration who have seconded my efforts so admirably.'
"A strange document, truly, in the closing years of the nineteenth century—a document which could never have emanated from a Cavour or a Bismarck, a Gambetta or a Thiers, a Metternich or a Von Beust, a Palmerston or a Gladstone." (Rev. Reuben Parsons, D. D., *Studies in Church History* (Philadelphia, John Joseph McVey, 1900), vol. 6, pp. 65-66.)

[71] Gomezjurado, vol. 9, p. 170.

[72] "Messenger of the Heart of Jesus," Bilbao, October 1887.

[73] Garcia Moreno praised as a martyr of the Heart of Jesus, Gomezjurado, S. J., *op. cit.*, vol. 10, pp. 245 – 300. This passage may be found on page 245.

[74] Gomezjurado, vol. 10, pg. 262.

[75] "The Future Century"

[76] The Missionaries of the Sacred Heart of Jesus of Issoudun are a religious congregation founded at Issoudun, archdiocese of Bourges, France, in 1854, by Jules Chevalier. It is composed of priests and lay brothers, with the object of promoting the knowledge and practice of devotion to the Sacred Heart of Jesus, as embodied in the revelations of Our Lord to Saint Margaret Mary Alacoque, and of offering personal reparation to the Divine Heart.

# Chapter 5

# Monsignor Checa Seals the National Consecration with His Blood

The arrival of the following document meant special rejoicing for Ecuadorian Catholics:

> Decree by which the Sacred Heart of Jesus is declared the Principal Patron of the Republic:
> The Most Reverend Jose Ignacio Checa, Archbishop of Quito, in agreement with the second decree of the Third Provincial Council of Quito, humbly requested from the Holy See, in his own name as well as his fellow bishops' and all the faithful of the Republic of Ecuador, that the Most Holy Heart of Jesus would be declared the Principal Patron of that Republic. Those supplications were transmitted by the Council's Sacred Congregation to this Sacred Congregation of Rites, which deemed it well to answer: "Nothing prevents satisfying the desires of the Reverend Archbishop of Quito, if it pleases the Holy Father." Then, the below-signed Secretary gave an accurate account of the above to our Most Holy Father, Pius IX. His Holiness chose the Most Holy Heart of Jesus as the Principal Patron of the Republic of Ecuador; and ordered that His feast day be celebrated by both the secular and regular clergies in that entire Republic, as a double of the first class and with an octave. Given on December 17, 1875.
> Plac. Ralli, Secretary of the Congregation of Sacred Rites.[1]

At this same time, the Legislative Chambers wrote to the Pope on December 14, 1875. They expressed themselves in the following manner with regard to the protagonist of this book:

> We began our legislative tasks overwhelmed with sorrow. And our first act was to honor and bless the memory of the Great Catholic Head of State wrested from Our Fatherland by impiety and crime. And today we do not want the Chambers to close without proving to be worthy of the political, moral and religious school that he established among us, and of Garcia Moreno's elevated and most brilliant character...
> The deluge of evil ideas and impious iniquity grows and spreads over all the earth. Mr. Garcia Moreno, a providential and

great man, as the impartial opinion of Europe and America has justly recognized and proclaimed, employed all the strength of his character in defending Ecuador against that calamity. Today this sublime, untiring worker of good has disappeared; and who knows whether the waves of that deluge will not invade our unhappy country in the end! Before the sixth of August, joyous light briefly glimmered in the future of our Republic; but the blood shed on that dreadful day eclipsed it and today only sad shadows are descried.

Could the blood of the Martyr be sterile for the good? Could his blessed spirit, at the foot of God's throne forget Ecuadorians? Impossible![2]

The Pope replied on March 9, 1876. Let us listen to the allusive expressions about our Hero:

> And so, you weep in private for a truly eminent man, who, penetrated with the Catholic spirit, assumed the government of a disrupted Republic, exhausted and oppressed with taxes. He joined firmness with gentleness and prudence with courage in such a way that he suppressed rebels, pacified souls, re-established order, tried to aggrandize the country through missions, promoted divine worship and the instruction of the people, organized the military, ports, commerce, laws: all this without increasing but rather decreasing taxes.
>
> Certainly he would have benefited his country even more had he lived longer. But do not ignore that such a great man has been wrested from you, more through hate for Religion than through envy of your happiness... That sect which has been so detrimental to you, wherever it bitterly fights the Catholic Religion is accustomed to gaining access to the rulers of the people and the highest assemblies in order to prepare for the destruction of religious and civil order, managing to execute cunningly through its own powers what it cannot accomplish through civil power; for which it lays snares, so that civil power itself will undermine its own foundations which rest upon Religion...[3]

A year had not passed since the death of Garcia Moreno when his memory electrified the inhabitants of Quito to celebrate the feast of the Heart of Jesus with exceptional solemnity. This dealt with making reparation to the Divinity for the insults and attacks on Religion by the impious press of Quito and Guayaquil, which had gotten out of control, taking advantage of the "Silk Reined" government installed by President Antonio Borrero.

For the sake of brevity the description of the religious functions concerning the Novena will be passed over which preceded the feast on Sunday, July sixteenth.

The procession began at four o'clock in the afternoon, led by hundreds of artisans with the statue of their Patron, Saint Joseph, carried on a float followed by a musical band playing triumphant songs. Next was a cortege of women, carrying the statue of Our Lady of Loreto on their shoulders. Then the contingent of matronly aristocrats and ladies from the Congregation of the Daughters of Mary carried on high the relics of Blessed Mariana de Jesus, enclosed in her golden bronze urn, and also the statue of that holy heroine from Quito. A choir of girls dressed in white walked in front of the urn, throwing handfuls of flowers along the way. Next a second band of musicians and the dashing squadron of masculine youths, with the statue of their patron and model Saint Louis Gonzaga. The large number of inhabitants of Quito was noteworthy, that had overrun the sidewalks along the streets where the procession passed. And a kind of bouquet of pious people occupied the balconies from which a shower of petals fell on each of the sacred images. In addition, the buildings were adorned with the tricolor national flag and luxurious draperies.

The second part of the procession was led by hundreds of gentlemen and gallant young men who surrounded and pulled an imperial float on which Christ the King, displaying His Divine Heart, was the main object of all eyes. The most fervent talks were addressed to Him, imploring His forgiveness for the abuses of the press and pleading for His People of Ecuador. Behind the float was the Illustrious Archbishop, Monsignor Checa, the Ecclesiastical Chapter, the secular and regular clergy, and the religious communities. There was a third musical band and at the end, an army battalion.

In the semidarkness of dusk, the spectacle was fascinating with four thousand lighted candles oscillating in the hands of those present as they walked at a stroll. The illumination on the fronts of the churches and private buildings was most enchanting.

The religious procession ended when the immense crowd entered the naves of the Church of the Society of Jesus,[4] where the act of consecration of the Republic to the Heart of Jesus was recited. It is superfluous to ponder how the beloved memory of Garcia Moreno palpitated in the souls and on the lips of the multitude.

Three more months passed and President Borrero, with his silk reins in his hands, was brought down by a military coup that proclaimed General Ignacio Veintimilla the Supreme Head of the nation. A political regime frankly hostile to the Church was installed. Impious reporters exceeded the limits. Bishops, naturally including Monsignor Checa, protested bravely.[5] The Masonic sect wanted to make a show of power and hate toward Catholicism. It was March 30, 1877, Good Friday. In the morning the Illustrious Archbishop began the liturgical services for the Parasceve. When the large gathering of the faithful had their most intense attention on the sacred ceremonies, someone poured an enormous dose of strychnine into the wine that would be used for the ablutions. When it came time for them, at about eleven thirty in the morning, Monsignor consumed that wine and at once said to the deacon, "This wine has quinine; it cannot be used to celebrate." The divine services ended at twelve noon.

When His Grace reached the Archbishop's Palace, he felt very nauseated. Seized by tetanic convulsions, he exclaimed, "I have been poisoned." Later he said to Canon Vicente Pastor, "Absolve me from my sins." As soon as he had the practitioner, Doctor Miguel Egas, beside him, he said to him, "I have been poisoned. I drank a wine more bitter than quinine from the chalice and I feel like a dreadful fire burns my insides." When the vomit rose near his lips, the tetanic contractions got worse. In a dying voice he exclaimed, "I am suffocating. I am dying." A livid color covered the semblance of the victim and a bit of foam appeared between his lips. Seconds later the Prelate expired. It was about one in the afternoon. When his corpse was examined, a hair shirt was found: a wire chain mail with somewhat pointed ends: an instrument of mortification and penance. It is not necessary to ponder Quito's consternation.

Gentle and of a good character, Monsignor Checa had no enemies. Therefore his assassination is considered a crime of a purely religious aspect; consequently, the victimization of such a Prelate, martyrdom. He and Garcia Moreno were the leaders for the consecration of Ecuador to the Heart of Jesus. Both perished enhanced with the splendor of martyrdom.[6]

Seven years of a dictatorial, obstinate government had pretensions to continue. The people of Ecuador were inflamed and rose in arms on all sides, fought in bloody expeditions, and expelled the Despot bedecked with military decorations.

# Endnotes

[1] Severo Gomezjurado, S. J., *Vida de Garcia Moreno* (Imprenta ARPI, Quito, 1971), vol. 10, p. 385.
[2] *Ibid.* pp. 380-381.
[3] *Ibid.* p. 383.
[4] I.e. *La Iglesia de la Compania de Jesus.*
[5] "Freemasonry did not attain to power immediately after it had murdered Garcia Moreno; Borrero, the successor of the martyr, was a Liberal, but nevertheless a good Catholic. But in 1877 a creature of the Lodges, a drunken soldier named Veintemilla, was raised to a dictatorship, and a carnival of Masonry was initiated. A decree for the secularization of education, that is, for an atheistic training of the young, was issued immediately; and when the pastors, with the Bishop of Riobamba at their head, protested against the iniquity, another decree pronounced the penalty of banishment against 'ecclesiastics who alarmed consciences.' Monsignor Checa, the Archbishop of Quito, announced to the government: 'Come what may, I shall continue to resist the propagation of error. Such is my duty, and with the grace of God I shall be faithful to it.' Fifteen days after this protest, on Good Friday, March thirtieth, the Archbishop officiated at the Mass of the Presanctified in the cathedral. He had scarcely taken the wine of ablution when he was attacked by horrible convulsions, and died within an hour. The autopsy showed that twelve grains of strychnine had been given to the Prelate. Of course, the assassins were never punished. The remains of the Archbishop had scarcely been placed in the tomb, when Veintemilla ordered all the pastors in the republic to celebrate, on April nineteenth, Masses of Requiem for the souls of 'all the martyrs of holy Liberalism who had fallen since March 19, 1869'—this date being that of a famous insurrection against Moreno. To this decree the bishops opposed an order forbidding 'a scandal to the Catholic people'; and as nearly all the Ecuadorians applauded the action of the prelates, the dictator perforce contented himself with an oath of revenge. In quick succession came a revocation of the Concordat which had guaranteed the liberty of the Catholic religion, a suppression of all the ecclesiastical salaries, and the exile of many pastors. The Bishop of Guayaquil died with all the symptoms of poisoning, and the Bishop of Riobamba escaped assassination by fleeing to the mountains. The people of Ecuador were on the verge of revolution, when Veintemilla resolved to change his policy. The exiled priests were recalled, and the bishops were made to understand that the government desired peace. This 'treachery' on the part of their creature enraged the Masons; the Catholics could not rely on the sincerity of their recent enemy, and in 1883 a revolution, in which both Liberals and Conservatives took part, overthrew Veintemilla. From that time until the Masonic eruption under Alfaro, the sequels of which still persevere in the form of nearly every conceivable kind of persecution of the Church, the Brethren of the Three Points allowed Ecuador

to rest in comparative peace." (Rev. Reuben Parsons, D. D., *Studies in Church History* (Philadelphia, John Joseph McVey, 1900), vol. 6, pp. 75-76).
[6] Gomezjurado, vol. p. 380 ff. Also p. 457 ff.

*Julio Matovelle, the driving force behind the building of the Basilica of the National Vow*

## Chapter 6
## June 21, 1886, The Consecration is Renewed

A Provisional Government of five members was constituted, a Pentaverate. At the same time the priest, Father Julio Matovelle, began to stand out as a prime apostle, destined by God for two lofty purposes: 1) to found an appropriate religious institute for the nation as the first one in the world to be officially consecrated to the Heart of Jesus; and 2) to promote the construction of a magnificent votive church to be the tangible stone monument to the Consecration. Matovelle wondered whether all this could be a divine inspiration, or a simple human caprice. In order to find out, he recurred to this stratagem:

"I'm going to write Doctor Luis Cordero, a member of the Pentaverate, requesting that Government to decree the erection of a church dedicated to the Most Sacred Heart of Jesus in recognition of our gratitude to God for giving the Restoration Army victory and initiating an era of peace and prosperity." Could a favorable answer be predicted? Hardly probable humanly speaking, since the majority of the Pentaverate was composed of individuals slack in their Catholicism, and even liberals, although moderate. He who offered the best omen was Luis Cordero, who, in spite of his hostility to Garcia's system, nevertheless was proud of being Catholic. Matovelle made this reflection: "If I am successful in my request, in spite of the slim hope in the natural way of things, it is a sign that God also wants me to found the Institute." Let's get to work![1]

The all-powerful Divine Providence who handles persons and things disposed that two people, not only Catholics but also Garcia's supporters, entered the Pentaverate in those days as replacements. They were Doctor Pablo Herrera and Doctor Modesto Espinosa. The result was:

> The Provisional Government of the Republic, considering:
> That the recent victories, of which the nation boasts, are due to the manifest protection of the Almighty, to whom it is necessary to consecrate an imperishable monument to accredit the gratitude of the people of Ecuador,
> Decrees:
> Article 1. At the expense of the State and with the help of private donations, the construction is ordered of a sumptuous

Basilica dedicated to the Sacred Heart of Jesus, to whom the Republic was previously consecrated.

Article 2. The new church will be raised on public land in the capital city and will occupy the place that the government and the ecclesiastical authority unanimously designate.

Article 3. On the tenth day of next August, the auspicious anniversary of the Independence of Ecuador, the first stone of the above-mentioned Basilica will be laid with all solemnity.

Given in Quito, Capital of the Republic, on July 23, 1883.
Agustin Guerrero,
Luis Cordero,
Rafael Perez,
Pablo Herrera.
Minister of the Interior: J. Modesto Espinosa.

Doctor Pablo Herrera wrote Matovelle, "The Heart of Jesus has saved us and will save the Republic. He is our Fortress, our Protector, our Monarch. The nation is officially consecrated to Him and we should place our trust in Him."

The Most Illustrious Jose Ignacio Ordones was then the Archbishop of Quito, who knew well that the erection of a church with the nature of a Basilica is not a simple matter. Hence, these expressions addressed to the Pentaverate:

> It would be good for us to be happy for now with a memorial church, leaving the matter of a basilica for when the church is finished, which will take not a few generations. Then the Holy See would be asked to raise the church that has been built to a basilica. In this way the Basilica of the Sacred Heart would be, with time, the Metropolitan Church of Quito.[2]

The prudent Bishop noted as well that the first stone could not be placed without a previous study of the site regarding social function and type of architecture. This is what delayed the ceremony.[3]

Two months passed and the Pentaverate awarded a hectare of land in the place called *Belen*,[4] for the construction of the Votive Church and on October 5, 1883, the first stone was solemnly laid. Doctor Luis Cordero gave prominence to his Christian soul in a speech from which these paragraphs were selected:

See how, by the mysterious action of Providence in the face of which human efforts are paltry and derisory, the once pitiful situation of our beloved country has unexpectedly changed. Where desolation had been established, eradicating, so to speak, even the roots of hope from our afflicted hearts, the dawn of the future begins to shine today. And the dejection of good men gives way to a noble and justified aspiration of arriving at more fortunate times.

Peace now beats her snow-white wings over Ecuadorian counties, purified by the blood of the patriotic holocaust. The Republic rises from the bier where she lay. Her best children come with solicitous eagerness to heal the wounds of the outraged mother... This is the most adequate moment to reaffirm our thanksgiving to the Almighty by manifesting, or better yet, publicly and solemnly flaunting the religious faith that, superior to political faith, has saved us from shipwreck... Therefore, today our Provisional Government, faithful interpreter of the sentiments that enliven you, designates the area for the erection of a monument to testify to this free Republic's gratefulness to the Greatest and Loftiest of her Liberators...[5]

Needless to say all the towns in Ecuador applauded the Pentaverate's epic religious achievement. The foreign press joined forces. Here are some expressions from the *Messager du Coeur de Jesus*[6] from Toulouse, France, in November of 1883:

> The Republic of Ecuador had given us the beautiful example of a Christian State, affirming the rights of God in its laws and making them respected in all institutions. In 1873, under the initiative of Garcia Moreno, the entire Nation was officially consecrated to the Sacred Heart. Two years later, Garcia Moreno fell under the assassin's dagger. But when dying, that man of faith said to his weeping friends, "Take courage! God does not die." Garcia Moreno was a prophet. One of the acts of this Restorative Government [the Pentaverate], has been to issue the following decree ... [The decree of July twenty-third of the same year was then copied.][7]

The *Eco de Cordoba*[8] in Argentina commented on the act in these terms: "The Provisional Government, barely having defeated the dictatorship, which was an opprobrium and a disgrace to Garcia Moreno's native land, is determined to erect a Basilica with the purpose of dedicating it to the Sacred Heart of Jesus," etc. For the sake of brevity, ovations from other foreign newspapers are omitted.

The new Legislative Convention was installed in Quito, composed of a majority of Catholics. They wanted to issue a decree renewing the consecration made by the legislators in the year 1873. But they were afraid of provoking outrages and insults to the Catholic Church on the part of the few antireligious delegates. Consequently, that renovation was disposed to be done privately on February 4, 1884, in the Church of the Sacred Hearts.

The students, girls from the School, sang the *Veni Creator Spiritus*. Then the priest, Father Matovelle, had the consecration renewed through the following formula. The words were first pronounced by that priest and then repeated in unison by the Catholic Representatives of the Republic:

> Adorable Heart of Jesus, King of kings and Lord of lords, by whom and for whom all the peoples and nations of the earth have been created! In deference to Thy most lovable and infinite sovereignty, as much as we are able from this day forward, we offer and consecrate the Republic of Ecuador as Thy exclusive possession and property...[9] Grant, Lord, to take this nation as Thy inheritance. Receive her under Thy sovereign protection. Free her from all her enemies. Manifest to all nations that Ecuador is Thine. Prove to the world that the nation which chooses Thee as Lord and God is blessed. And make the glory of Thy Most Holy Name shine always in our Republic. Amen.[10]

Holy Mass was celebrated immediately by the above-mentioned minister of the altar. The students finalized the act with harmonious hymns in honor of the Heart of Jesus. All present had a joyful semblance of trust in God.

The campaign for the erection of the Votive Church came later. A few liberals tried to annul the decree regarding this building, but Julio Matovelle confronted them with this courageous harangue:

> The great crime of contemporary history is the cowardly apostasy of all nations on earth. All governments of the world, precisely as governments, have plotted against Christ and His

Church. And if they have not blasphemed the adorable Person of the Divine Savior, at least they deny Him and protest that they do not know Him. Well then, what the Government of Ecuador intends through the decree that is to be sanctioned is to proclaim loud and clear before nations that it recognizes Our Lord Jesus Christ as God and King, and that it obeys and adores the social sovereignty corresponding to the Savior over all nations on earth as King of kings and Lord of lords.

This we desire, this we intend, those of us who have formed the project under discussion: that the Convention of 1884 will bend its knees before the Divine and Supreme Monarch of all nations; renew the act of solemn subjection and consecration owed Him; and raise a permanent monument to remind coming generations that Ecuador is the Republic of the Most Holy Heart of Jesus. That is to say, Ecuador adores not the ideal god of the pantheists, but rather the true and living God, the Word Incarnate, Our Lord Jesus Christ.

The great evil of modern societies is political Naturalism, that disastrous error which assures that nations as nations, governments as governments, have nothing to do with God or with the supernatural order; that they owe everything to their own efforts; and that a government does not need to pray, nor do the people have to implore grace from on high... Well then, the erection of the National Ecuadorian Basilica, dedicated to the Most Holy Heart of Jesus, is a protest against such doctrines, and is a sincere confession of the greatest truths of our faith. Ecuador is going to raise that church, to bear witness through it that our people, just like all those on earth, are God's creatures; to ask the Lord forgiveness for the crimes she has committed against His Divine Majesty; to show thanksgiving for the benefits that have been given her from His Fatherly right hand; to ask for them in greater abundance in the future; and to remember perpetually that Ecuador is a nation consecrated to the Most Holy Heart of Jesus.

It is true that Ecuador is a small, poor nation; but for that reason, God will make a display of His power and His glory in her. Let us make Ecuador a solidly Christian nation and we will have raised her to the height of the greatest destinies. In spite of her littleness she will know how to obtain by conquest a place of distinguished glory among her American sisters. I am not a prophet, but with the common intuition that Catholic philosophy gives us all, I see the veils of the future drawn back before my eyes. And it seems to me that great and glorious destinies are prepared for our beloved homeland as a reward for her unswerving faith and generous courage with which she knows how to confess it in the presence of the whole world.

Ecuador is the only nation that has energetically protested against the sacrilegious usurpation of the Pontifical States. Ecuador, the Republic that has had one of the most profoundly Catholic heads of state in the Americas! Ecuador is the first nation that has been solemnly consecrated to the Most Holy Heart of Jesus since 1873. And now it is also going to be the first nation on earth to dedicate a church officially to this same Most Holy Heart. What more legitimate titles of glory or what more solid foundations than these for a great and blessed future? Those who look at no more than the appearance of things, call the people happy who abound in material wealth, even though it is decayed by corruption and unbelief. But we, following the testimony of our Holy Books, do not consider any other nation great or blessed than the one that has chosen God as Lord and King, because all other things will come to this people in addition.

For, I, with unswerving certainty, do not doubt but rather believe that our Republic will walk the way of solid progress if we direct her along the path of the faith. In that decree which we are going to sanction—in it is written our true Constitution. That decree is the anchor which we are going to throw into the stormy seas of the future, and which will maintain our native land firm in the midst of all storms.

The Basilica of the Sacred Heart of Jesus will be the Paladin of Ecuador. The sudden attacks of revolutions and the impact of envy and treason will impotently crash against the walls of that church. While the Most Holy Heart of Jesus is the Protector of our Republic, in spite of our littleness, we will have nothing to fear from all the powers on earth. There, in that decree, is enclosed the source of our happiness. Until now our politicians have built on thin air. Now we are going to build on the stone of God's temple, which is always the cornerstone of any civilization. Let us not doubt it; this decree, yes, this decree so attacked by some Honorable Members, will be the greatest title of glory from the Convention of 1884. The rest of the laws that it may dictate will probably pass away like the dry leaves of summer to be buried much later in oblivion. But this decree on the Basilica of the Sacred Heart of Jesus will not die. It will remain written in stone to bear witness to the faith of Ecuador to coming generations.[11]

Around the intrepid champion for the defense were grouped the Honorable Luis Salazar, Francisco Javier Salazar, Luis Cordero, Honorato Vazquez, and the Corral, Freire, Ojeda and Enriquez families. Able polemists, each in their own way made the apology for the project through solid arguments. It was refuted by the Honorable Luis Felipe Borja, A. M. Borja, Adriano Montalvo, Eloy Alfaro, and the Cardenas, Andrade Marin, Fernandez, Martinez, Pallares, Moreira, Venegas, Vargas Torres and Franco families. But these opponents were unsuccessful because their reasoning was easily convicted of sophisms. Alfaro's intervention was conceived in these terms:

> I have faith, and as much faith as the Honorable Matovelle has. But I am against the project for a lack of the necessary funds in the national Treasury. Our wars need to be forgotten rather than Basilicas in thanksgiving for victories of fratricidal struggles. I also have faith in the effectiveness of civilization in the future. And I do not think the erection of the Basilica is necessary.

The debate was closed and a vote by name requested. The project won by thirty-three affirmative votes against twelve negative ones. Let us listen to the text of the decree:

> The National Assembly of Ecuador, considering:
> 1. That it is necessary to show thanksgiving to the Almighty for the benefits that He has so manifestly granted to the Nation, especially in recent times; and
> 2. That, since the Republic is consecrated to the Sacred Heart of Jesus, it should raise a national monument to bear witness to this solemn consecration and to assure Ecuador of heavenly benefits,
>
> Decrees:
>
> Article 1. The decree of July twenty-third is approved by which the Provisional Government disposes the erection of a Basilica dedicated to the Heart of Jesus, as well as that of October

fourth which designates the place where the church must be raised.

Article 2. In order to carry out this work successfully, and until it is finished, the annual quantity of twelve thousand pesos from the Treasury will be approved by vote in the budget, which will be paid at one thousand pesos per month.

Article 3. The Executive Branch will fulfill the present decree, proceeding in everything relative to the building of the church in agreement with the ecclesiastical authority.

Article 4. Materials preferentially from this nation will be used in the construction. And the work of painting and sculpture in wood to decorate the Basilica will be carried out by Ecuadorian artists.

Given in Quito, Capital of the Republic, on February 29, 1884.

The President: Francisco Javier Salazar.
Vice-Secretary: Honorato Vasquez.
Vice-Secretary: Jose Maria Flor de las Banderas.
Secretary: Aparicio Ribadeneira.

Palace of the Government, in Quito on March 5, 1884.

Let this be published and enforced: Jose Maria Placido Caamano.

Minister of the Interior: J. Modesto Espinosa.[12]

Such a decree was accepted with acclaim by all the Catholics of Ecuador. The Vicar Capitular of Cuenca, Miguel Leon, wrote, "Ecuador publicy confesses her faith before the rest of the nations; and in the midst of the cowardly apostasy of nearly all governments, she appears, however small, in the vanguard of Christian countries by recognizing through her legislators the sovereignty of our Lord Jesus Christ."

The Franciscan Jose Maria Aguirre said:

> The Lord, angered with this people for crimes about which only He knows, sent the angel of death on August 6, 1875, to punish the Republic. And the exterminator, standing on the summit of the Andes, on Mount Pichincha,[13] unsheathed the avenging sword and shook it furiously over the nation for the space of eight years... The political parricides, the sacrilegious poisonings, the treacherous assassinations of illustrious citizens that took place

during that time, as well as the persecution of the Church, the decline of public morals, the infringement on national sovereignty, was the blood of our homeland that dripped from the edges of the angel's sword...

The Lord, appeased by the blood of so many innocent victims, at last sympathized with our misfortunes and, on the morning of July 9, 1883, ordered the angel to stop the slaughter. And the exterminator, spreading his wings, returned to heaven. And then our calamities ceased... On that day the arms of the Republic, against all human hope, triumphed over the infamous dictator. Young men, still inexperienced in the fortunes of war, snatched the laurels of victory from the hands of old men and tough captains. When the nation after this glorious battle again placed the diadem of her sovereignty on her head, she raised her eyes to Heaven. And depositing those laurels at the feet of the Lord of Hosts, she made a vow of gratitude to the Most High, promising Him to raise a magnificent national church at the foot of Pichincha in honor of the Sacred Heart of Jesus...[14]

A short time later, in June of the same 1884, the first issue of the monthly magazine entitled *La Republica del Corazon de Jesus*[15] saw the light of day. Its director was Father Julio Matovelle. Its writer and editor was the young Manuel Maria Polit Laso.[16]

On August tenth, a first class national holiday, Father Manuel Proano in his discourse pronounced in the Cathedral, mentioned Garcia Moreno in these terms:

> It is sufficient for me to remind you that in the days of the living, we have seen "the Man who honored man," the Benjamin of the Church in the nineteenth century, the greatest of Ecuadorians, carry the cross of the Redeemer in triumph through streets and squares, saying to the people he governed shortly before being sacrificed, "*Salva cruce liber esto, salva cruce libertatem et gloriam consequito*": Hail O Cross, be free; hail O Cross, obtain freedom and glory.[17] It is sufficient for me to remind you that the Ecuadorian Hero, not content with inspiring love of the Cross in us through his example, searched with faith the opulent breast of the God-Man. And in exercising the national sovereignty represented by him, left the Republic upheld by one of the sinews of the Divine Heart... And all this in the nineteenth century, in the midst of the

universal failure of beliefs, against the devastating flood of enraged passions, and despite the disagreeable and perfidious apostasy of modern civilization! **Digitus Dei est hic**: The finger of God is here...[18]

In June of 1885, the Fourth Provincial Council of Quito was established. One of its decrees organized the pecuniary collections from all the parishes for the construction of the Church of the National Vow, which would be a Sanctuary for pilgrimages proceeding from the entire Republic.

Two months later the Canon Juan de Dios Campuzano pronounced the following proclamation:

> May the People of Ecuador, gathered at the foot of the Most Holy Heart of Jesus, always and forever proclaim the greatness of the name of the Lord! United in charity, may they be a people of brothers where there are neither persecuted nor persecutors. May their magistrates be magnanimous like David, intrepid like Jonathan, patriotic like the Machabees; republicans, yes, but frank and decided Catholics. To fear the derision of the wicked is to become unworthy of the love of the good. May our prelates form a single body among them and be one with each other and one with their flocks. May the latter feel their spirits move with Christian love for each one of their pastors, and be docile to their teaching and pass through the abundant pastures of virtue until they reach the summit where the Lamb dwells. In short, we desire our Republic to be a group of heroes, patriots, and Catholics; a prosperous and happy city of brothers.[19]

June 21, 1886, is in the annals of history. Two hundred years previously on a day like this the Church had authorized the public worship of the Sacred Heart of Jesus. To celebrate this anniversary, bishops, personages of distinction and active Catholics met in Quito at the National Eucharistic Congress. Two days earlier the State had intervened with the following agreement:

> The Senate of the Republic of Ecuador, taking into consideration that the law of October 18, 1873, had consecrated the Republic of Ecuador to the Most Holy Heart of Jesus, declaring Him their Patron and Protector; that on June twenty-first of the

present year the second centenary of the public worship paid to this Divine Heart will be celebrated; that it is just and fitting for the Representatives of the Nation to bear witness to their Catholic Faith on such a solemn occasion: resolves to make an offering out of gratitude and praise to the Most Holy Heart of Jesus, Patron of the Republic of Ecuador, and not to hold any session on the day indicated as a sign of adhesion to popular sentiment.[20]

On the eve, June twentieth, the Capital was transformed at night as if by magic. The facades of the churches, the Government Palace, the Municipal Palace, and nearly all private buildings were profusely illuminated. The image of the Heart of Jesus stood out on the balconies of numerous houses as if on a brilliant altar. Fifty thousand men full of joy and enthusiasm traversed the streets and squares. Aerostatic balloons, displaying the tricolor national flag and the picture of the Heart of Jesus presented inscriptions like these: "Ecuador to her Divine Protector," "Long live the Republic of the Heart of Jesus!" Everywhere there were festive assemblies of musical bands and orchestras, and songs to the Divine Heart performed by children in choirs spread here and there and everywhere.

If it is taken into account that at the same time, the use of lights and festivities took place at all points of the Republic, without excluding the poorest, most desolate shantytowns, it will be understood that the religious movement of the Eucharistic Congress was truly national in the highest sense of these expressions.[21]

At the break of dawn the next day, salvos on Yavirac Hill woke the population, who did their utmost to get to the Cathedral. On the high altar, over a throne of white clouds, a magnificent statue of the Heart of Jesus stood out, carved by an Ecuadorian sculptor in 1876 in remembrance of the national Consecration of 1873. The Divine King wore a luxurious tunic of white satin, with a purple mantle on His shoulder. Surrounding Him at His feet appeared a group of seraphim, of whom some were as though in an ecstasy of admiration; others offered hearts burning in flames of love to the Monarch of the Heavens and Earth. Underneath there were four richly dressed statues that represented the four continents: America, Europe, Asia and Africa. Over each one of them descended a ray of light issuing from the hands of Christ. And above Ecuador's Coat of Arms was a triple yellow, blue, and red stream that flowed from the very Heart of Jesus.

Mass was officiated by the Most Illustrious Archbishop Jose Ordonez. The supreme act constituted the Eucharistic Banquet to which ten thousand Catholics approached and seventy thousand in the rest of Ecuador. This is the moral fiber and strength of a State that had only a million and a half inhabitants.

At twelve noon the first session of the Eucharistic Congress took place in the spacious Cathedral naves with the attendance of His Excellency the Constitutional President Jose Maria Caamano. The reports discussed the reasons why Ecuador should throw herself into the construction of a memorial church of enormous proportions.[22]

Benediction of the Most Holy Sacrament followed immediately. The innumerable people attending all fell on their knees. At their head was the President of the Republic, the Episcopate, the Supreme Court of Justice and the Legislature. And the consecration of Ecuador to the Heart of Jesus was renewed, using the following prayer:

> Adorable Heart of Jesus, King of kings and Lord of lords, by Whom and for Whom all peoples and nations on earth were created: out of respect for Thy most lovable and infinite sovereignty, all the Public Powers of the Church and State are prostrate in Thy Divine presence, we offer Thee and consecrate to Thee the Republic of Ecuador, today and forever, as Thy exclusive possession and property. Deign to take this people as Thy inheritance. Reign perpetually over her. Welcome her under Thy sovereign protection. Free her from all her enemies. Show all nations that Ecuador is Thine. Prove to the world that the nation which chooses Thee as Lord and God is blessed. And make the glory of Thy Most Holy Name shine always in our Republic. Amen.

The final act was prayers of atonement for the sins and crimes of Ecuador, through the following formula:

> Divine Heart of Jesus, Creator of Heaven and Earth, universal King of nations and absolute master of all things: Thou art Holy, Thou art Lord, Thou art the Most High, Thou art our only God, from Whom emanates all power, authority and sovereignty. Thee, through Whom kings reign and legislators dictate what is just. May all nations and peoples praise Thee, and all creatures extol Thee forever and ever.

> We give Thee thanks, Lord, for all Thy benefits, and especially because in the excesses of Thy goodness, Thou hast deigned to choose Ecuador as Thy inheritance. Thou hast defended her from her enemies and showered her with Thy gifts. But, oh! Instead of corresponding with gratitude to such generosity, we have sinned, Lord. We have worked iniquity. We have behaved wickedly, and have departed from Thy judgments and commandments. But do not look on our iniquities, O Most Kind God, but only at Thy mercy. Take Thy wrath away from us; remove Thy punishments from this people. [23]

Next a dialogue took place that made people cry. The Minister of the altar enumerated sins, and the multitude answered, "Forgive us, O Lord, forgive us!"

"For the sins of our priests," "Forgive us, O Lord, forgive us."

"For the misconduct of our Legislators," "Forgive us, O Lord, forgive us."

"For the faults of our Magistrates," "Forgive us, O Lord, forgive us."

"For the offences of fathers of families, for impiety and blasphemy, for perjuries and sacrileges, for revolutions and fratricidal wars, for the crimes of August sixth and March thirtieth," "Forgive us, O Lord, forgive us," etc. And that is how the twenty-first of June, 1886, ended.

Three days later, on Thursday, June twenty-fourth, the Feast of Corpus Christi, the procession of the Blessed Sacrament took place between salvos of the cannon situated on Yavirac hill and the assembly of military bands. With lit candles in their hands, the Ministers of State and the Most Excellent President of the Republic, Jose Maria Placido Caamano, stood honor guard to the Holy Host. The procession ended with the marching of a dashing battalion.[24]

Five more days elapsed and the First National Eucharistic Congress of Ecuador raised its voice as follows:

> Considering that the Republic of Ecuador is solemnly and officially consecrated to the Most Sacred Heart of Our Lord Jesus Christ, whom it has chosen as its Patron. That, as a reward for this consecration she has received very distinct benefits that oblige her to give public signs of her love and gratitude, resolves:
>
> To request humbly that the Ecuadorian Episcopate raise its prayers collectively to His Holiness Leo XIII so that he may deign

to declare the day when the Church celebrates the Feast of the Most Holy Heart of Jesus as a Holy Day of obligation in the Republic.
>Given in the Session Hall, in Quito, on June 29, 1886.
>President: Jose Ignacio, Archbishop of Quito.
>Secretary: Ramon Calvo.[25]

The resolution did not produce any results. Our Mother the Church observes wise reservation about increasing Holy Days of obligation.

The second session took place on July second, Feast of the Heart of Jesus. These expressions alluding to Garcia Moreno were in the discourse pronounced by Belisario Pena:

>Ecuador, in the midst of the universal apostasy, has preserved the integrity of her faith immaculate. This is a benefit that we are unable to fathom, because, just as we become acclimatized to the brightness of the sun, we can hardly conceive the misfortune of the blind man who is groping his way in the dark right in the light of day.
>And if the reward given to the Ecuadorian Republic for her consecration to Our Lord Jesus Christ had been limited only to this notable benefit of maintaining the gift of faith unharmed, the reward for such an act would already be adequate and even superabundant. But the munificent Heart of Jesus is pleased in recompensing as Who He is; and so I do not marvel at the great number of favors that I have seen descend upon you, among which the ones that I am going to propose for your reflection certainly are not small:
>Serene and happy were those times when sublime Christian virtues sat on the throne of supreme power with an extraordinary man, more worthy of glory than glorious, harmonized by providential consonance with the virtues of an eminent Head of State and of an energetic commander. Then this Nation blossomed, embellished with order, cheered with harmony, honored with good faith, tranquil with peace, graced with courtesy, supplied not only with what is necessary but also even with what is superfluous. He was the counsel for resolutions and the arm that executed them. He was... Imagine that Garcia Moreno had not existed. Take away the good morality and the material works for which you are

indebted to him, and tell me with noble loyalty to the truth, what would Ecuador be today? Perhaps when someone answers me, he would remember his mistakes. I will not be the one to insist on denying them. But I will reply that the dark spaces of the sun are two thousand times brighter than the light of the moon.

Ah, gentlemen! Let us at least be fair with the dead. And while the soul reigns unharmed there where glory does not look for an increase of earthly praise or fear a decrease from insults, may we here let the lacerated, bloody mortal remains of the Great Man enjoy the peace of thankless oblivion in his hidden tomb. I will only add, not without sorrow, and I say so because it fits my intention, that when we saw in this sacred enclosure and in this very place, the faded brow that would have worn the world's crown, the lightning intelligence extinguished that quickly, lively, instantaneously penetrated everything, the brilliance of those eyes dead in which flashed the nobility of command and the flames of courage and patriotism: I knew that an indefinable passion seized souls and I tasted it also, a passion without a name, a mixture of wrath, despair and terror. Who would not have feared that the order and peace of the Republic, linked to the life of her Great Man, would disappear forever from this soil? Who did not think then that the crime had vacated the throne so that impiety would sit there? And nevertheless, against human previsions, against the presentiments of the good and despite the sinister schemes of the wicked: Garcia Moreno's murderers have had to deplore with tears—oh! If only they were of repentance!—with tears of rage, the uselessness of their crime. Do not attribute the salvation of the Republic to the efficacy of human means. Do not take from God the glory of having freed us, even in spite of ourselves and of all we have done to become lost...[26]

The Most Holy Sacrament was exposed, President Caamano fell to his knees as did the entire, immense multitude in order to renew the consecration once again. Father Manuel Proano directed the recitations:

> Come today, Catholic Leader of our new Israel. Come to render subjection to the immortal King of the centuries, to Whom alone is due honor and glory... Come, Shepherds and Pontiffs of the House of Israel... Come, those who judge the Lord's land... Come those who enact laws!

The prayers that follow were repeated by everyone in a loud voice:

> Oh most loving Heart of our only Pontiff, King, Judge, Legislator and Father! We are overwhelmed by the immense weight of Thy glory and the singular benefits that Thou hast made and makes for the nation of Ecuador. We prostrate ourselves today in Thy sovereign presence. And we recognize before Heaven and Earth the fullness of power and social sovereignty conferred on Thee by the Eternal Father... We proclaim Thee our King and confess ourselves forever Thy most faithful vassals...[27]

Those attending vacated the naves of the Metropolitan Church to give preferential place to fathers and mothers of families, who by a special formula renewed the consecration. Then children and young people entered, later the members of the army, and lastly the artisans. This is a true social consecration. This was also done by a large number of people and with pomp, in all the other cities and neighborhoods in the Republic.

American and European periodicals filled Catholic Ecuador with acclaim. For example, the Chilean magazine, *El Estandarte Catolico*[28] printed these expressions:

> This happy Republic has just given the world a new testimony of her profound love of Religion and an example of Christian courage that will have a widespread effect, by celebrating with indescribable pomp the second centenary of the establishment of public worship of the Sacred Heart of Jesus on June twenty-first of this year. With deep emotion and very gratifying surprise we have read the series of manifestations of faith and piety that our readers will find in other columns... When reading them, our imagination has transported us to those fortunate times when Catholicism was the prime law of nations.[29]

The Madrid magazine, *La Cruz,*[30] wrote:

> The Republic of Ecuador, model of all States in the world, even Catholic monarchies... Ecuador saw, not many years ago, President Garcia Moreno, her highest temporal authority, and the Archbishop of Quito, her highest spiritual authority, fall under Masonic lead and poison. Faced with those two horrendous crimes

that revealed the power of Masonry and its abominable intentions, we Catholics shuddered for the future of the only truly Catholic State in the world; while liberals conceived the hope of seeing that living protest against the liberal spirit of our times disappear, to whose pattern all modern nations today are conformed. But God, who watches over Ecuador, received the holocaust of the lives of those two illustrious victims; and the tiny Republic continues more and more passionately on the way traced by her unforgettable President Garcia Moreno. This is proved by both of the beautiful acts conducted in a body by that fortunate nation, by which the chief of state, his ministers, the congress, the episcopate and the clergy, the army, the courts of justice, all public servants and the entire nation have just made a sublime profession of their beliefs and their unbreakable adhesion to our mother the Church.[31]

There was another approval at this time, no longer from a periodical, but from a distinguished foreign priest who came to Quito to extol the epic religious deeds of Ecuador by his presence. It was Monsignor Mariano Soler, Vicar General of Montevideo, Uruguay, who spoke to the magazine *La Republica del Corazon de Jesus*[32] in these terms:

> I wanted to offer the tribute of my sincere Christian admiration to the nation which saw the noble cradle rock and which possesses the glorious tomb of the Christian Hero, of the incomparable Ruler, of the great Catholic Head of State, a man of Jesus Christ in public life, and a leader of such a sort that it does not seem worthy for nations to have any longer: Garcia Moreno, martyr of Religion and Nation...
> As a Catholic and an American, I have a greater admiration than what I can express for the most heroic nation of modern times in the defense and practice of the sublime doctrines of Catholicism. Small among nations, she knows that "moral greatness is the honor of nations."
> I began to admire her and also to love her almost from my earliest years, from my youth. I was still a student of the South American College in Rome when the echo of her name reached the Eternal City, glorious and radiant due to the incomparable firmness of her faith, proclaimed without beating around the bush and without human respect. She officially and solemnly confronted the entire world in the days of cowardly and universal apostasy. I will

never forget this memory because it is indelible in all hearts that know how to be enthusiastic about what is heroic in the moral order.

The Common Father of the faithful had just been deprived of his temporal crown and was reduced to captivity in the Vatican. The silence of moral cowardliness had made all governments lose their voice in the face of the perpetration of such great iniquity. But only the one represented by the illustrious Garcia Moreno with unequalled nobility dared to protest "in the presence of God and of the world, in the name of outraged justice and especially in the name of the Ecuadorian Catholic nation, against the iniquitous invasion of Rome and against the false liberty to which the Venerable and Sovereign Pontiff was reduced..."

And to increase the heroism of such a noble protest, the heroic president wanted to communicate his intrepid zeal to all the governments of Latin America; and he had the magnanimous courage to urge them "not to imitate the silence of the kings of the Old World, and to protest against that inexcusable assault which, committed against the Supreme Pastor of Catholicism, directly wounded Catholics of the whole universe."

The name of the Catholic nation of Ecuador gloriously traversed the face of the earth. The Catholic world admiringly and enthusiastically acclaimed and repeated that noble cry of holy indignation against the triumphant iniquity. But the sublime greatness of that act—it seems unbelievable!—did not find a single echo in official regions. And cowards tried to cover such heroism with the most despicable contempt for the most heroic nation and government of the present times. No! Scorn cannot spoil such high honor. And Catholic Ecuador does not share that glorious page with any other nation, not even with those that in venerable Europe continue to be adorned with the honorary titles of **Catholic, most faithful, most Christian.**[33]

Those noble titles have passed on to the exemplary Republic... No nation has imitated it; no nation can rival her glory... And what good fortune for other Catholic nations if they would have had rulers like Garcia Moreno, a rival of Charlemagne and of St. Louis!

... The heroism that would break the silence with which fear and complicity had sealed all official lips was greatly increased by another singular glory of Ecuador which clearly deserves our highest admiration. It was the exceptional glory of having moreover a unique government among all the governments of the world, which was in fact and officially Catholic. And it was also the renowned Garcia Moreno who, in his Speech to the Congress of 1873, quite loudly proclaimed that distinguished privilege of the Ecuadorian nation.

He said, "Since we have the glory of being Catholic, let us be so logically and openly, let us be so in our private lives and in our political existence; and let us conform the truth of our sentiments and words to the public testimony of our works." And moreover, he took this solemn declaration to its legitimate consequence, which was "to erase from our laws even the least trace of hostility against the Church. For some provisions still remain in them from the old, oppressive Spanish regalism, whose tolerance would be from now on a shameful contradiction and a miserable inconsistency..."

Nor has any ruler in his speeches made the valiant and heroic confession that Garcia Moreno made! Having fulfilled his duties as Catholic Ruler, this great Christian exclaimed, "Happy am I if I deserve hate, calumnies, and the insults of the enemies of our God and our faith." He attained the glory of martyrdom for defending the religion of his nation. And he deserved the honor that his confession be qualified as **unheard of in government, even under the rule of the Constantines and Theodosiuses...**

But none the less glorious is the beautiful example that Ecuador has given the whole world, and that is a brilliant entitlement that justly merits the name of **Most Christian Nation.** That example is the consecration of the Republic to the Sacred Heart of Jesus, sanctioned through solemn decrees not only by the Third Provincial Council of Quito, but also by the Congress of 1873, and a Basilica with the same title,[34] as a **national monument,** making it possible for the great Garcia Moreno to have the honor of being the first President of the **Republic of the Sacred Heart.** And he deserved it by his illustrious virtues and famous deeds to the point of achieving the supreme honor of dying "Victim of his Christian faith and charity for the Nation," as the immortal Pius IX has said.

Garcia Moreno! What a man! What a Christian! What a Ruler! He is the joint glory of the Ecuadorian nation and of

Catholic rulership. To satisfy my own admiration, I make mine the funeral eulogy that the greatest of newspapermen, Louis Veuillot, paid him, and which history and the Catholic world have ratified to the glory of Ecuador:

> Garcia Moreno "was of quite a different order, and posterity will recognize it. He was admired by his people; he shunned criminal activity, vulgarity, remorse, oblivion, and would even have avoided hatred itself, if God had permitted it that virtue should not attract hatred. We might suggest that he was the most ancient of the moderns, 'a man who gave honor to man.'"[35]

What will not be Ecuador's glory on the day when the nations come, one after another, and they will come to pay homage to the Social Reign of Christ? For, this happy republic was the first to lead that triumphal march of nations. What an enviable privilege! Yes, we will say with an eloquent orator of the Eucharistic Congress, "Jesus Christ, King of nations, has placed the cornerstone of His social sovereignty in this fortunate Republic, transferring to her as to Jacob the primogeniture of his future reign over peoples and nations. Such magnificent glory, by a mysterious secret was stored up for Ecuador, which like another Bethlehem of Ephrata, is a little one among nations... The primacy of the social reign of Jesus Christ was conceded to you, and no one can dispossess you of this glory, enviable above all glory, which will pass on resplendently to coming ages... Even though many victims succumb in defense of the holy cause, **God does not die**... Quito, August 26, 1886. Mariano Soler."[36]

On February 8, 1887, His Holiness Pope Leo XIII decorated President Caamano with the title of "First Class Knight of the Order of Pius IX"[37] The Head of State in return placed his signature on the following agreement of the National Congress on July 28, 1887:

> Article 1. The Congress of the Republic of Ecuador respectfully presents its congratulations to His Holiness Pope Leo XIII, on the fiftieth anniversary of his first Mass...
> Article 2. In its own name and in that of the Nation that it represents, it reiterates the declaration that the Nation has already made, to be faithful to the teachings of the Holy See...

Article 3. In the budget of expenses, ten thousand sucres will be voted to contribute to the alms that the Catholic world ought to give to his Holiness for the Mass that he will celebrate on the above-mentioned day of his anniversary...

Article 4. Next December thirty-first will be a civil holiday for the nation; and the executive power will order a solemn Mass to be celebrated with the *Te Deum* in all the cathedrals where there will be first class attendance.[38]

On their part, the Eucharistic Congress that was mentioned on previous pages, determined to send the gift to the Pope of Garcia Moreno's last speech splattered with his blood. This most precious document, placed in the hands of Mr. Eloy Proano, was nonetheless the inherited property of Mariana del Alcazar, widow of the martyred President. That gentleman came to this matron and begged her to make a gift of those esteemed pages. Having obtained this favor, Eloy Proano was besieged by Pedro Pablo Garcia Moreno, brother of the exalted victim, with petitions for the relic. His attempts through simple requests were frustrated, so Pedro Pablo recurred to its purchase with money. This factor did even less in the heart of Proano, who continued to keep those sheets during the lapse of three years, at the end of which he had to undergo another siege of requests, this time on the part of Doctor Antonio Flores, who appealed to much more powerful reasons: "I am leaving to go abroad," he repeated insistently. "I am going to New York, Paris and Rome where that handwritten and bloodstained speech will redound in immense glory to Garcia Moreno." These reasons made a decisive impact on the heart of the possessor.[39]

Doctor Flores had this relic with him for nine years until, as plenipotentiary in Paris, he received a letter in which Pablo Herrera, President of the above-mentioned Eucharistic Congress, wrote him, "We trust in your patriotism that in the name of Ecuador you will make the gift of that document to his Holiness Pope Leo XIII for the golden anniversary of his priesthood." He agreed with pleasure to the Ambassador's request and with part of the sum of money destined by the national Congress for the donation to the Holy Father, he had a splendid little chest made, placed the speech inside, and presented it to the Roman Pontiff. Let us listen to the description made by the Parisian newspaper, *Le Nouveau Monde*[40]:

The gift offered by the Republic of Ecuador to the Holy Father is a marvelous little eight-sided chest of rock crystal, mounted on gilded silver, enriched with enamel and precious stones mounted on thick scalloped settings. It is one of the most remarkable works of art that has been given us to admire for a long time. A kind of thick perforated button serves as a finishing touch, also embossed with precious stones, and presents the arms of the nation in enamel on its face. On the opposite side, an inscription reveals it is a gift to the Holy Father. In the interior of the little chest is a rich crimson satin pillow, on which rests President Garcia Moreno's speech. The case that encloses this object of art is all of white morocco leather, lined inside with crimson velvet. On the lid is the coat of arms of the Holy Father. The key is also a silversmith's masterpiece. Its exquisiteness is increased by ten large diamonds of the purest clarity.

The admiration that we have experienced upon seeing this precious treasure, that will stand out among the most beautiful gifts offered to Pope Leo XIII, will seem natural, when it is known that this splendid little chest comes from the Froment-Maurice workshop, whose reputation is so well earned that it is unrivaled in the world.[41]

It was January 20, 1888, when Doctor Antonio Flores, as an Extraordinary Envoy to his Holiness, delivered Garcia Moreno's speech and thirty thousand sucres, that is, one hundred and fifty thousand francs, donated by the government and the people of Ecuador.

"Most Holy Father!" he said, "I very much recognize the high honor that Your Holiness confers on me, by allowing me to present my homage, as well as the modest offering that my government adds to the humble contribution that I have already placed in the hands of the Very Eminent Cardinal Secretary of State. In this urn of rock crystal I have deposited the handwritten speech that the lamented President Garcia Moreno carried in his hand on the day of his cruel immolation and which is sealed with his heroic blood. I beg Your Holiness to accept this offering benignly that I have the honor to make you in my name and that of the Catholic writer Eloy Proano Vega, who picked up that document on the very scene of the crime, and sent it to me in a far-away land where I have carefully preserved it for the space of nine years."

Pope Leo XIII answered in these terms:

We make the most ardent good wishes for the prosperity of Ecuador and her President, to whom we again recommend the interests of the Catholic Religion, which are those of the nation whose happiness they insure. Besides, we accept with pleasure the precious offering that you have been kind enough to make us, Mr. Minister, on this happy anniversary. We will preserve that autographed speech, which the illustrious Garcia Moreno intended to read in the Congress when he was immolated, as a moving remembrance of the man who is the champion of the Catholic Faith, and to whom are applied, by a just title, the words which the Church uses to celebrate the memory of the holy martyrs Thomas of Canterbury and Stanislaus of Poland: "*Pro Ecclesia gládiis impiorum occúbuit*: He fell for the Church under the knife of the impious."[42]

His Excellency Mr. Flores communicated to President Caamano some more of the details of that audience. Speaking of the acceptance of the speech, he summarized the words of Leo XIII as follows: "He appreciated this document in all its worth, sealed with the blood of the man who had fulfilled his duty. He will place it in the Vatican Library or in his private chapel. Garcia Moreno could say like Saint Thomas of Canterbury, "*Et ego pro Ecclesia Dei libenter mortem subibo*: and I, for the Church of God, will receive death willingly." And it could also be said of him what was said of that same saint and of Saint Stanislaus, King of Poland, "He died for justice and the faith. Through his death he bequeathed an example that he hoped would be imitated by his successors."

The following commentary was made by the Most Illustrious Archbishop Manuel Maria Polit:

> And so, there in the Vatican is the autographed bloodstained speech of the great Catholic President. It is good that it is there, lovingly guarded by the Church of Christ which has done justice to his heroic virtues. Meanwhile, among us his fellow citizens—what a shame!—bitter criticism is still heard from obdurate and loathed Liberalism. And the bold and shameless cry of the assassins who survived him still resounds. And obstacles are placed to raising a glorious monument of national gratitude. At least his last lines, the testament, some of the blood of the Martyr of the Catholic Faith, repose there in a place of honor near the confession of the Apostles; while in this his beloved city of Quito, his mortal remains lie hidden, extracted from the profanation of infernal hate

and revenge and reserved for the respect and affection of coming generations.

It is obvious that Caamano's Presidency was similar to Garcia Moreno's regime. And he rightfully brought to mind our biographee's prophecy: "After my death, the Republic will fall again in the hands of the revolution which will govern despotically under the deceitful name of Liberalism. But the Sacred Heart of Jesus, to whom I consecrated my homeland, will wrest her once again from its claws to make her live freely and honored, under the protection of the great Catholic principles." For their part, the liberals called Caamano's government the "government of Garcia Moreno's bones."[43]

Another donation to Leo XIII was a portrait of Garcia Moreno, oil painted by the insigne artist Rafael Salas. It was Mariana Alcazar, Garcia Moreno's widow, together with her sisters, who paid for that oleograph and made a gift of it to the Vicar of Christ. There our hero appears standing full-length and life-sized. He is dressed as a civilian but wears the presidential sash diagonally across his chest. He holds a roll of paper in his right hand on which is recorded his courageous declaration against the usurpation of the Papal States.

The precious canvas was taken to Rome by the holy Brother Miguel Febres Cordero, who left for that city to attend the beatification of his Founder John Baptist de la Salle. The monk arrived there during the early days of February 1888. Therefore delivery into the hands of Leo XIII had to have happened towards the fifteenth of that same February. The Pope placed and displayed the painting with Constantine the Great. It was of great significance and honor for Garcia Moreno to be on a par in a certain way with that Emperor who gave peace to the Church in the immense Roman Empire. And it is, in turn, the Ecuadorian Head of State who spoke, by his speeches and spectacular examples, to the whole world in praise and defense of the Church.[44]

The Archbishop of Quito, Monsignor Ignacio Ordonez was not left behind. He made the following gift to the Pope: The future Basilica of the National Vow in reduced proportions and solid silver. In the interior was a relic of the Blessed Mariana de Jesus. On one side was the symbolic statue of Ecuador, holding the holy Cross in its right hand and with the left, Leo XIII's coat of arms. At its feet a condor holds the blazon of the Republic in its claws. The sun of Ecuador sends its rays from the summit of the Andes. At the base is Our Lord Jesus Christ with open arms and a blazing heart. Near Him, to the right is a medallion of

*It was stolen in the early hours of November 26, 1965. Thanks to the Interpol, it has been discovered that this document ended in the hands of a collector in one of the Greater Colombian countries.*

President Garcia Moreno; and at the left, the coat of arms of the above-mentioned Archbishop of Quito.[45]

On August sixth of that same year, 1888, in the eulogy that Friar Jose Maria Aguirre preached, was this paragraph regarding our topic:

> What immense horizons of prosperity are left open for the nation in the fields of the future, ever since it is under the guardianship and care of the Divine Heart of the Prince of Eternity! Yes, our illustrious President with this official act of his government raised the rod of command and pierced the eternal and unshakeable rock that is Christ, and opened in it an inexhaustible fountain of happiness for the Republic. O great Head of State! You can now sleep in peace, because there is a Heart that watches over your nation. "I sleep but my Heart watches." Now you can say in your agony, "God does not die!"[46]

# Endnotes

[1] Monsignor Jose Heredia, *La Consagración del Ecuador al Corazón de Jesús [The Consecration of Ecuador to the Heart of Jesus]* p. 338; cf. Severo Gomezjurado, S.J., *Vida de Garcia Moreno* (Editorial Ecuatoriana, 1975), vol. 11, pp. 36-37.
[2] Gomezjurado, *Vida de Garcia Moreno*, vol. 11, p. 38.
[3] *Idem.* p. 339 ff.
[4] In the place called *Belen* (or "Bethlehem" in English) is the *Church of Belen*, the first one that Quito had, at the same site where the first Mass was celebrated, as a result of the conquest of Quito by the Spaniards. We cannot keep from reproducing this paragraph by the historian Federico Gonzalez Suarez, copied from *La Republica del Corazon de Jesus [The Republic of the Heart of Jesus]*, p. 92:
"Those very bold and obstinate conquerors, who nonetheless knelt and bowed their proud heads, were mixed with the Indians. There, conquered and conquerors, masters and slaves adored God, calling him Father, some in the silence of prayer, others with the first words of a strange tongue, but all in the language of the soul which God understands. For, religion reminded all, conquered and conquerors, masters and slaves, of the sublime dogma of Christian fraternity..." Cf. Gomezjurado, *Vida de Garcia Moreno*, vol. 11, p. 57.
[5] Gomezjurado, *Vida de Garcia Moreno*, vol. 11, pp. 40-41.
[6] *Messenger of the Heart of Jesus*
[7] *La Consagración del Ecuador [The Consecration of Ecuador]*, p. 344 ff.
[8] *Echo of Cordoba.*
[9] Cf. the famous indulgenced prayer written by Father Nicola Zucchi, S.J. (†1670): "My Queen! My Mother! I give thee all myself, and, to show my devotion to thee, I consecrate to thee my eyes, my ears, my mouth, my heart, my entire self. Wherefore, O loving Mother, as I am thine own, keep me, defend me, **as thy property and possession**. Amen."
These words would be later incorporated into the *Prayer of Total Consecration* by St. Maximilian Kolbe: "O Immaculata, Queen of Heaven and earth, refuge of sinners and our most loving Mother, God has willed to entrust the entire order of mercy to thee. I, N___, a repentant sinner, cast myself at thy feet humbly imploring thee to take me with all that I am and have, wholly to thyself **as thy possession and property**. Please make of me, of all my powers of soul and body, of my whole life, death and eternity, whatever most pleases thee. If it pleases thee, use all that I am and have without reserve, wholly to accomplish what was said of thee: 'She will crush your head,' and, 'Thou alone have destroyed all heresies in the whole world.'
"Let me be a fit instrument in thine Immaculate and merciful hands for introducing and increasing the maximum in all the many strayed and indifferent

souls, and thus help extend as far as possible the blessed Kingdom of the most Sacred Heart of Jesus. For wherever thou enters, one obtains the grace of conversion and growth in holiness, since it is through thy hands that all graces come to us from the most Sacred Heart of Jesus."
[10] Gomezjurado, *Vida de Garcia Moreno*, vol. 11, p. 42.
[11] *Ibid.* vol. 11, pp. 42-44.
[12] *La Republica del Corazon de Jesus* [*The Republic of the Heart of Jesus*], p. 53 ff.; cf. Gomezjurado, *Vida de Garcia Moreno*, vol. 11, p. 45.
[13] I.e. a volcanic peak near Quito.
[14] Gomezjurado, *Vida de Garcia Moreno*, vol. 11, p. 46.
[15] *Republic of the Heart of Jesus.*
[16] *La Consagracion del Ecuador* [*The Consecration of Ecuador*], p. 354 ff.
[17] This was the motto on the first flag of Ecuador.
[18] Gomezjurado, *Vida de Garcia Moreno*, vol. 11, p. 48.
[19] *Idem.* p. 358; Gomezjurado, *Vida de Garcia Moreno*, vol. 11, p. 65.
[20] Gomezjurado, *Vida de Garcia Moreno*, ibid.
[21] *Idem.* p. 362 ff.; Gomezjurado, *Vida de Garcia Moreno,* vol. 11, pp. 65-66.
[22] *Idem.* p. 368 ff.
[23] Gomezjurado, *Vida de Garcia Moreno*, vol. 11, p. 67.
[24] Father Berthe, *Vida de Garcia Moreno* [*Life of Garcia Moreno*], vol 2, p. 451 ff.; Gomezjurado, *Vida de Garcia Moreno*, vol. 11, pp. 67-68. The aged Ecuadorian photographer Ribadeneira has an authentic photo in which Caamano and his Ministers are carrying candles alongside the Most Holy Sacrament in the Corpus Christi Procession.
[25] In the author's *Vida de Garcia Moreno*, this passage interestingly continues as follows: "There is also this other resolution: 'Considering that Catholics cannot look without sorrow upon the iniquitous imprisonment of the Supreme Pontiff, who has sacrilegiously been dispossessed not only of his States but also of the liberty and independence that befits the Vicar of Our Lord Jesus Christ for governing of Holy Church, resolves: To renew and strengthen the protest which the Republic made through its President, Senor Doctor Don Gabriel Garcia Moreno, in the year 1871, against the unjust and violent usurpation of the Pontifical States.'" (Gomezjurado, *Vida de Garcia Moreno*, vol. 11, p. 68.)
[26] Belisario Pena's eulogy, *La Republica del Corazon de Jesus* [*The Republic of the Heart of Jesus*], p. 178 ff.; Gomezjurado, *Vida de Garcia Moreno*, vol. 11, pp. 69-70.
[27] Gomezjurado, *Vida de Garcia Moreno*, vol. 11, p. 70.
[28] *The Catholic Standard*
[29] Berthe, *Vida de Garcia Moreno* [*Life of Garcia Moreno*], vol. 2, p. 454 ff.
[30] *The Cross.*
[31] Gomezjurado, *Vida de Garcia Moreno*, vol. 11, p. 71.
[32] *The Republic of the Heart of Jesus.*
[33] "When Victor Emmanuel completed his series of sacrilegious robberies by the seizure of the Papal capital in 1870, Garcia Moreno was the sole potentate in Christendom who protested against the iniquity. Immediately after the news

of the crime had reached Quito, the president of Ecuador dictated to his foreign secretary the following protest, which was sent at once, according to constitutional formality, to the Italian Minister for Foreign Affairs: 'The undersigned, Minister for Foreign Affairs of the Republic of Ecuador, has the honor of addressing the following protest to His Excellency, the Minister of Foreign Affairs of King Victor Emmanuel, because of the melancholy events which occurred last September in the capital of the Catholic world. Since the very existence of Catholicism has been menaced in the person of its august head, the representative of Catholic unity, who has been despoiled of that temporal dominion which is the necessary guarantee of his independence in the exercise of his divine mission, Your Excellency will admit that every Catholic, and with much more reason every government which rules over a considerable number of Catholics, not only has the right, but is also bound to protest against this hideous and sacrilegious crime. However, before raising its voice, the Government of Ecuador waited for protests on the part of the more powerful states of Europe against the unjust and violent seizure of Rome; and it waited for what would have been much more gratifying—that His Majesty, King Victor Emmanuel, would voluntarily do homage to the sacred character of the noble Pontiff who governs the Church by restoring its stolen territories to the Holy See. But the Ecuadorian Government waited in vain; the monarchs of the old continent remain mute, and Rome continues to suffer under the oppression of Victor Emmanuel. For this reason the Government of Ecuador, in spite of its feebleness, and in spite of the enormous distance which separates it from the Old World, now fulfills its duty by protesting before God and before men, and especially in the name of the Catholic people of Ecuador, against the wicked invasion of Rome and the subjugation of the Roman Pontiff—deeds which have been perpetrated in violation of repeated promises, and which are now disguised by derisory guarantees of independence which do not hide the ignominious servitude of the Church. The Ecuadorian Government protests, finally, against the consequences which the Holy See and the Church will suffer because of this shameful abuse of power. While addressing this protest to you by formal order of His Excellency, the President of this Republic, the undersigned still trusts that King Victor Emmanuel will repair the injuries which he has inflicted in a moment of madness, before his throne is reduced to ashes by the avenging fire of the Revolution.' (*El Nacional of Quito*, January 18, 1871.)

"Not content with this personal protest, Garcia Moreno urged all the governments of South America to follow his example; but, as he afterwards said: 'I had little hope that our sister republics would respond to the invitation; I merely wished to fulfill my duty as a Catholic by giving the greatest possible publicity to our own protest. Columbia replied in moderate terms, but negatively; Costa Rica answered negatively, and in an insolent manner; Bolivia informed me very courteously that she would consider the matter carefully; Chile and Peru did not condescend to acknowledge the receipt of my communication. But, after all, what does it matter? God has no need for us in order to accomplish His designs, and He will accomplish them in spite of hell, and in spite of the emissaries of hell, the Freemasons, who are more or less masters in every land of South America, saving our own' (Berthe, *Garcia Moreno*, vol. 2., ch. 2.). The Brethren of the Three Points were not then masters in Ecuador, but their perennial efforts to obtain the supremacy were redoubled when Garcia Moreno so nobly stigmatized the chief masterpiece of their craft in the nineteenth century." (Rev. Reuben Parsons, D. D., *Studies in Church History* (Philadelphia, John Joseph McVey, 1900), vol. 6, pp. 67-68.)

[34] The Basilica of the National vow is a memorial of the national consecration to the Sacred Heart of Jesus, which it is designed to honor.

[35] See Appendix IV below for the full eulogy of Louis Veuillot.

[36] *La Republic del Corazon de Jesus* (Quito, August 26, 1886), p. 200 ff.; Gomezjurado, *Vida de Garcia Moreno*, vol. 11, pp. 71-74.

[37] Order of Pius, founded in 1847 by Pope Pius IX, is one of seven elite equestrian orders whose members are named directly by the pope.

[38] Gomezjurado, *Vida de Garcia Moreno*, vol. 11, p. 74.

[39] About the bloodstained message, see *La Republica del Corazon de Jesus* [*The Republic of the Heart of Jesus*], vol. 5, p. 505 ff.

[40] *The New World*, December 24, 1887 issue.

[41] Gomezjurado, *Vida de Garcia Moreno*, vol. 11, pp. 75-76.

[42] Gomezjurado, *Vida de Garcia Moreno*, vol. 11, p. 76.

[43] Gomezjurado, *Vida de Garcia Moreno*, vol. 11, p. 77.

[44] About the blood-stained message, see *Escritos y Discursos de Garcia Moreno*, [*Garcia Moreno's Writings and Discourses*], second edition, p. 485 ff., compiled with notes by Monsignor Manuel Maria Polit.

[45] Gomezjurado, *Vida de Garcia Moreno*, vol. 11, p. 78.

[46] Expressions by the Franciscan orator Aguirre in the book entitled *A la Memoria de Garcia Moreno* [*To the Memory of Garcia Moreno*]. There is a copy in the Aurelio Espinosa Library. Cf. Gomezjurado, *Vida de Garcia Moreno*, vol. 11, p. 85.

# Chapter 7
# January 1890, The Heart of Jesus from the Consecration goes to Chile

It has been well said, "There is a Heart that watches over your Nation." To prove it, a new religious institute was established in Quito, whose nature is "Of the Sacred Heart."[1] Its apostles toil hard to construct the commemorative church in the Capital of Ecuador. Here is the history of that event:

Father Julio Chevalier founded the Archconfraternity of Our Lady of the Sacred Heart in the French city of Issoudun.[2] He himself affiliated Garcia Moreno in that confraternity, and since then cherished the idea of sending some of his Missionaries to Ecuador. This idea became a firm resolution on the day that Father Chevalier received the news of the assassination of Garcia Moreno. "He is a victim of the Heart of Jesus," he exclaimed. "Our place is there where he fell."[3]

Nevertheless, eleven years went by without the fulfillment of those vows. Finally, when the Most Reverend José Ignacio Ordonez, Archbishop of Quito, was in Rome, he saw one of these Missionaries of the Sacred Heart from Issoudun and said, "My choice is made. It is you to whom I entrust the work of the National Vow in Quito." Issoudun was telegraphed immediately and Father Chevalier answered in turn by telegram: "I leave it to the decision of His Holiness." Then Ordonez told Pope Leo XIII, and from his august lips heard these words, "Tell Father Chevalier that I not only approve the project willingly, but I also desire that this Society will be in charge of this beautiful work for the Sacred Heart."

It was on May 10, 1887, when Fathers Marisseau, Caer, Derichemont and Barral, together with the Coadjutor Brothers Andre and Reichert, boarded ship at the port of Saint Nazaire. Their leader and companion for the voyage, Archbishop Ordonez, became their teacher, stimulus and model.

A month went by and the ship entered into the broad Bay of Guayaquil. A setback: an epidemic of yellow fever was spreading in that city. Consequently their bearing turned to the right, to the bay and fluvial port of Naranjal. The Missionaries rode horses for the first time and began to ascend the Andes Mountain Range. At the highest point, Father Caer dismounted and planted a cross from which hung a medal of Our Lady of the Sacred Heart.

The city of Cuenca impressed them favorably, as is evident from a letter written by Father Caer. "Today," he wrote, "on the feast of the

Heart of Jesus, I celebrated Holy Mass in the cathedral. We were witnesses of the people's enthusiasm for the Sacred Heart. The entire city celebrates the holiday; streets are carpeted; churches are packed with faithful; the confessionals are besieged. We have only to appear for an instant with the Sacred Heart on our chest to be the object of general attention and friendliness. All hats are removed; all heads are bowed; all stop to watch us go by. Ah! If we are up to our sublime vocation, how much good might we do in the church of Ecuador! In the afternoon the statue of the Sacred Heart is carried through the streets of the city."

On June thirtieth they arrived at Quito in the company of Archbishop Ordonez and in the midst of the people's general enthusiasm. Naturally the Missionaries from Issoudun established the Archconfraternity of Our Lady of the Sacred Heart with good auguries in the capital of Ecuador. As to the memorial church, they resolved to look for a more attractive site for its location. They were right.[4]

Meanwhile Divine Providence played in a strange way with the painting of the Heart of Jesus that had presided over the famous consecration made on March 25, 1874.

While in Cuenca, the author of these pages heard this plausible piece of information:

Agustin Serrano, native of that city, let himself become seduced by spiritualist practices during his early youth. Through Garcia Moreno's advice he entered the Catholic Protectorate[5] and then not only did he correct those errors, but he also left for Valparaiso, wearing the religious habit of the Sacred Hearts, a Picpus foundation near Paris.

In the month of June, 1889, Agustin Serrano, now a priest, returned to Ecuador to recruit vocations for priests as well as for nuns of the Sacred Hearts.

What were some of the stories that Serrano heard when passing through the city of Quito? Well, he heard that Garcia Moreno's image of the Heart of Jesus had been looked for by irreligious individuals. In which year? No answer has been obtained about this particular. The author of these pages supposes that it was around 1877, when Masonry made a show and demonstration of power by assassinating Monsignor Ignacio Checa.

The fearful dwellers of Garcia Moreno's house took the painting down from its place of honor and hid it. Inquiries by the persecutors were repeated and then the widow of the Head of State who had died before his time entrusted the sacred canvas to relatives living in another house. That house was also the object of unlawful entry and search on the part of the ominous escort. The painting went successively to the care of other families without remaining in the same house for more than three months whenever possible. The criminal gang even searched buildings where the famous oleograph had never been. The owner opted to deliver the venerable image to a Canon. Which one was it? Father Mateo Crawley and Monsignor Jose Felix Heredia have written the history of this matter and neither of them obtained the name of that prebendary. However, the author of these pages, in his little work entitled *Abanderado del Corazon de Jesus*,[6] specified the name Juan de Dios Campuzano. From whose lips was this name heard? It is not remembered with certainty. But he is almost sure of having heard it from the lips of the above-mentioned Monsignor Heredia, with whom he spoke about it more than once.[7]

That Garcia Moreno's image of the Heart of Jesus had been hidden for some years becomes more evident by the fact that it was excluded from the Eucharistic Congress of 1886, in spite of President Caamano's regime being very devoted to Garcia Moreno. Let us remember that it was a statue of the Heart of Jesus that presided over the functions in the Cathedral, including the act when the consecration was renewed. If this chronicled canvas were in no danger, it would have been the most appropriate one to use for the ceremony.

In the year 1889, Doctor Antonio Flores' presidency also showed deep affection for the President-martyr. However, the political situation could change. Did it not perchance change only one year after Garcia Moreno's death? If it truly were Canon Campuzano who kept the precious oleograph, it was clearly remembered that he had to change residence and live hidden during Veintimilla's regime and that his very house was searched by the henchmen.

In an interview with Father Agustin Serrano, the enthusiastic affection of the people of Chile for Garcia Moreno was discussed. Even among their anti-Catholics such a strong virulence did not exist against him as in Ecuador. Then, was it not convenient for the historical image to be removed to Chile, where it could receive the corresponding homage without danger?

However, the above-mentioned Canon, since he was not the owner of the picture, had to consult with Mariana del Alcazar, Garcia Moreno's widow. Now, this matron consigned her donation to the Congregation of the Sacred Hearts of Chile in writing which was witnessed by Father Serrano in the presence of some Ecuadorian nuns residing in Valparaiso. Among them was Sister Enriqueta Granda, who retransmitted it to the author of these pages in an interview that took place in Cuenca on September 25, 1949. To make the testimony more solemn, the author took Father Misael Vasquez with him [to be a witness].[8]

And so the sacred canvas passed into the hands of this priest of the Sacred Hearts from Cuenca. Was some kind of contract formulated about it having to be returned to Ecuador in the future? There was no such contract. This was affirmed by Father Mateo Crawley, the future distinguished propagandist of the above-mentioned image. From whom did the famous Crawley hear this? It was from his French Provincial, Father Romain. And from whom did the latter hear it? This was from one of Father Serrano's subjects.

In the above-mentioned September 1949 interview, another one of those questioned was Sister Agustina Cueva, who spoke in these very words:

> It was in the year 1889, the month of July, when I met the Reverend Father Agustin Serrano in Cuenca. I showed him an oleograph of his glorious Patron, Saint Augustine. Father Serrano in turn told me, "I also have a very beautiful and important oleograph of the Heart of Jesus," and he indicated the place with his arm where it was rolled up. It was the one that had presided over the National Consecration and later was enthroned in Garcia Moreno's house.[9]

Some bad news reached Father Serrano: the disease of cholera was spreading throughout Chile. Therefore he postponed his return to Valparaiso until further instructions. Only at the beginning of the new year of 1890 could he undertake the journey, riding on the back of a mule over the Cajas Mountains; later boarding a small sailboat on the Naranjal Creek, and crossing the Gulf until he reached Guayaquil; finally setting sail from this city in a deep draft ship bound for Chile.

A few days later a group of vocational students from Cuenca took the same route. Among the boys was Benito Velez, who became a priest of the Sacred Hearts. He was the son of the famous sculptor. Among the girls were the previously mentioned Sister Agustina Cueva and Sister Enriqueta Granda.

In the year 1890, Mateo Crawley was an adolescent of fifteen and he affirms that then he saw Father Agustin Serrano arrive at the port of Valparaiso. In another report he said that this Serrano was the bearer of the famous oleograph. Consequently, the assertion by Monsignor Jose

Felix Heredia, S. J., is demonstrated as false, according to which Father Romain, the Provincial of the Congregation of the Sacred Hearts, was the one who brought that painting from Quito to Valparaiso. It is seen that with the passing of the years the story is being expurgated and the store of documents is becoming enriched.[10]

Father Serrano, having arrived in Valparaiso, delivered the rolled oil painting to his Provincial, and narrated for him the genesis and celebrity of that painting. He said that its creator was Antonio Salguero Salas from Quito. This assertion by Serrano shook the belief that Rafael Salas, who was on a scholarship from Garcia Moreno in Rome, had painted the famous picture. From whom did Serrano hear this? Undoubtedly he heard it from the lips of the priest who entrusted the painting to him; and the priest was informed by Garcia Moreno's widow.

When the author was in the rural parish of Chambo in the month of May, 1970, Josefina Salas from Larrea made a visit. She was interrogated: "Who was the painter of the Heart of Jesus for the National Consecration?"

"It was my Uncle Rafael Salas. That is what my sister Gabina told me."

"What relationship did the painter Antonio Salguero Salas have to Rafael Salas?"

"He was Rafael's nephew."

"How many years younger was Antonio Salguero Salas than his Uncle Rafael?"

"He was some twenty-two years younger."

This last information reveals that Antonio Salguero Salas was only about twenty-five years old when the Heart of Jesus was painted for the Consecration. It is improbable that Garcia Moreno would have turned to an inexperienced painter, when he could turn to Luis Cadena and Juan Manosalvas, residents at that time in Quito. Greater research is needed in this regard.

What is certainly obvious is that the famous oleograph was deposited among some of the Provincial Father's objects of little interest. This superior, his head crammed with government matters, paid little attention to that religious treasure: games of Divine Providence, which, according to a German adage, has mills that grind slowly but grind well. While the venerated image continued to be hidden in Valparaiso, the construction of the National Basilica in Quito was steadily advancing.

Our story continues in the same year of 1890. In the month of February the site of Belen was abandoned and San Juan Hill was preferred.

There were more difficulties at the former site and therefore more expenses; at the latter site it was quite the opposite, which had a panoramic view besides. The Missionaries of the Heart of Jesus from Issoudun were the arbitrators of that change, and established their residence on that hill. They began by raising a provisional chapel; its blessing took place on March nineteenth with extraordinary solemnity.[11]

The streets leading to the site of the Basilica were adorned with flags and bouquets of flowers. Beautiful triumphal arches had been improvised at intervals. The entire residence of the Missionaries was also adorned with exquisite taste, especially one of the corridors, in the center of which an image of the Most Sacred Heart of Jesus was prominent.

In the middle of the main patio an enormous cross was raised between garlands and wreaths. It was a souvenir of the Missions preached by the Redemptorist Priests in April, 1874—the cross that President Garcia Moreno had carried on his shoulders, and at the foot of which he had expired on that ill-fated sixth of August, 1875. Two standards with two inscriptions were raised at its sides. The one on the right read: "Blessed Margaret Mary, protect Ecuador's National Vow to the Sacred Heart of Jesus." On the left was: "Blessed Mariana de Jesus, promote the prompt construction of the Basilica of the Sacred Heart of Jesus and the efforts of the people for whose salvation you gave your life."

The attendance was elite and numerous. Soul and body of the religious event, Fathers Jouet and Barral, had come from France. At the head of the nation was the Most Excellent President Doctor Antonio Flores with the Ministers of Worship and of the Interior, and the Governor of the province. The presence of the Most Illustrious Archbishop Ignacio Ordonez was missed, who for reasons of health had to leave for the countryside a few days earlier. However, on the eve of his departure he had given the sum of five hundred sucres to begin work on the Basilica. Substituting for the Metropolitan, the Vicar General of the Archdiocese, Doctor Juan de Dios Campuzano, occupied the place of honor, followed by several members of the Metropolitan Chapter and the superiors of some religious communities. Also in a preferential place were the members of the "Permanent Basilica Committee."

Monsignor Jose Macchi, Apostolic Delegate of the Roman Pontiff for the Republics of Ecuador, Peru and Bolivia, gave the opening address. Here are some paragraphs:[12]

Today the piety of the Supreme Government, the zeal of the illustrious clergy and the unblemished faith of the people have brought about this gathering here, to show the fulfillment of a vow that binds the whole Nation to God...

Ecuador has desired to be inspired by the magnanimous example of Catholic France, which in the height of the nineteenth century has raised a monument to the Heart of the God-Man, where the majesty of His glory marvelously shines here on earth. Nothing could be more just. In a century when an unworthy son of France had committed an outrage against the divinity of Our Lord Jesus Christ to destroy all the regenerative effectiveness of His love for men in a single blow, France herself, although she has made every effort to go astray, has also exceeded herself by the generosity of her atonements. She rendered worship and honors to the Divinity of Jesus Christ and more directly to His Heart, the center of the mysteries of the Redemption, by erecting the majestic and gigantic Church of Montmartre. In this way, while blasphemy passes away with the air that it splits, the glorification of Jesus is eternalized in the marble that overlooks the city of Paris.

It was also just, following the example of the Eldest Daughter [of the Church], that the voice and work of the most loving and predilect Daughter of the Church would correspond; I mean to say, the Ecuadorian Nation...

Quito, the highest of the most elevated cities on the globe, will also have her Montmartre. On her summit, dominating, so to speak, the whole world, will be erected the graceful temple glorifying Him who conquered the world. Yes, ladies and gentlemen, Quito will have her Montmartre if you want...

In the name of the Great Pontiff, I bless this holy undertaking. And during the unbloody Sacrifice that I hasten to celebrate, I will invoke Heaven's help and protection over Ecuador, especially over her Most Excellent Head of State, his most worthy Metropolitan, and over all who with their small contribution and work assist in her happy coronation. Nor will I forget on this day that Great Person who gave the best tribute to this pious idea that a believer can give: his own blood. Neither will I forget these meritorious Missionaries of the Sacred Heart, sons of France, for whose activity and zeal, always superior to any obstacle, Providence has reserved the realization of the National Vow of Ecuador. [13]

In turn the reporters of *La Republica del Corazon de Jesus*[14] manifested their euphoria in these terms:

> We have the satisfaction of having made known in other countries of Europe and America the religious movement that is the life and glory of this Republic, and attracted to her the affection of Catholics spread over all the earth by the millions. Therefore, we could well say that nowadays few people still do not know of the existence of the Republic of the Sacred Heart of Jesus, the Homeland of Garcia Moreno, the Martyr of Christian Justice.

Three months went by and fourteen members of the Legislative Chambers ascended San Juan Hill and renewed the consecration of Ecuador to the Heart of Jesus. It was June 22, 1890. The author has obtained the names of those Honorable members: Julio Matovelle, Leon Piedra, Camilo Ponce, Franciso Jose Moscoso, Benjamin Chiriboga, Modesto Jaramillo, Vicente Paz, Ramon Riofrio, Angel Polibio Chaves, Gabriel Ignacio Veintimilla, Jose Justiniano Estupinan, Remigio Crespo Toral, Manuel Maria Polit and Aurelio Espinosa.

The French architect, Emilio Tarlier, drew the definitive design for the Basilica.[15] It would be cruciform, in gothic style, four hundred and forty-three feet long by one hundred and twenty-one wide, and thirty-three feet wider at the towers. Its three towers would be in the facade of the church, the two side towers each having a height of three hundred and seventy-seven feet, and the central tower having a height of two hundred and sixty-two feet.[16]

The following year, 1891, the magnificent periodical entitled *La Republica del Corazon de Jesus* was discontinued because its main writer, the young Manuel Maria Polit, traveled to Rome to enter the South American College, and its Director, Father Julio Matovelle, had to spend almost all his time on the foundation of his "Oblates of the Heart of Jesus." This vacuum was being filled, only in part, through the Bulletin written by the Missionaries from Issoudun. They also had the credit of initiating the construction of the foundations that should support the heavy bulk of the Basilica on San Juan Hill.

Unfortunately it did not take long for an unexpected impasse to arise with the Ecclesiastical Government of the Archdiocese. Besides promoting the erection of the memorial church, the Missionaries administered the maintenance and worship of *El Sagrario* Church in the very center of Quito. Now, they wanted to continue their apostolic activities, but on the condition that no other entity would be able to have juridical interference in that church. On the contrary, the canons of the Chapter did not want to cede their rights of patronage conceded by a bull from the Roman Pontiff. The result was that the Missionaries from Issoudun decided to leave Ecuador and return to France. They gave the statue of Our Lady of the Sacred Heart of Jesus to Gabriel Garcia Alcazar[17] and left the capital of the Shyris[18] forever. It was the month of June, 1892.[19] What an incredible antinomy! For a trifle they turned back, who had said, "There is our place where Garcia Moreno fell." And for a mere nothing the Missionaries were left to go, whom Monsignor Ordonez had obtained with such hope and at the expense of such a great effort.

The valiant Archbishop, although deprived of those helpers, continued the work of the National Basilica. United with the other prelates of Ecuador, he set the following tenth of July as the date for the solemn placing of the first stone on San Juan Hill. It was the second stone placed with the nature of a first. Let us recall that the true cornerstone was placed in the area of Belen on October 5, 1883, that is, eight years, nine months and five days previously, with great solemnity and a discourse by Pentavirate member Luis Cordero. In a collective pastoral letter dated July ninth, the Ecuadorian episcopate said:

> The Basilica of the National Vow will be the palace from which the Supreme Monarch of the entire universe will reign in this nation. This church will be the throne of the divine mercies and the fount of graces for the whole Republic. Against the walls of this shrine the waves of revolution and of impiety will crash powerlessly. Against them the lances will break that Hell never ceases to hurl at the Ecuadorian Church: this small but chosen portion of the flock of the Eternal Shepherd. This temple will be the harbor of refuge for this nation in the storms through which the future threatens it. In its vestibule the little ship of the State will rest peacefully like the Holy Ark on Mount Ararat after the deluge of so many political upheavals and revolts. Just as the Hebrew nationality was consolidated forever with the Temple of Jerusalem, we too hope that Ecuador will fully enter the firm path of peace in the shade of the Basilica of the Sacred Heart of Jesus.[20]

Later the Most Illustrious Bishops said that since Ecuador was already consecrated to the Heart of Jesus, it was imperative to consecrate her also to the Most Pure Heart of Mary. Consequently they added:

> As the Pastors which we are of this Church, we solemnly and irrevocably consecrate the Republic of Ecuador to the Most Pure and Immaculate Heart of Mary; starting today we are obligated to recognize the Divine Mother of the Redeemer as the special Patroness, Protector and Advocate of our nation, and our effective Intercessor before the throne of mercy.

At the same time, each one of the dioceses of the Republic was ordered to ratify that consecration in a plebiscitary and spectacular manner, on the date that the respective prelates would designate. Lastly, it was resolved that, in accord with the monumental character of this consecration, a chapel would be built in honor of the Heart of Mary. That chapel would be located in the apse of the Basilica of the Heart of Jesus.

The next day, on San Juan Hill, the Most Excellent President of the Republic, Doctor Luis Cordero, met with his ministers and all the civil government officials. Monsignor Ignacio Ordonez, Archbishop of Quito, with the bishops from the rest of the dioceses, and all the clergy who could be present were there, together with educational groups, the people, the army, musical bands, etc. The first stone was blessed and the President of the Republic pronounced a discourse from which these paragraphs are selected:

> If there are some who look at this work with dislike, and who vex with insults those that work for its construction, I want no one to deprive me of the share of supposed ignominy that is mine as well. Ignominy in the eyes of a few unbelievers, not in the eyes of the men and nations who recognize the path of civilization, guided by the beacon of the faith..."[21]
>
> In religion, I am sincerely Catholic, and I submit without restriction to all that the holy Church of Christ teaches and commands, without having in such a grave matter any other constitution than the august one of the Gospel. In politics, I am sincerely republican. And I can say that my gospel is the Constitution of my native land, together with the laws that arise from that same Statute. In any case when a true conflict might be possible between sound politics and the true religion, I would opt for

the triumph of the latter, because the interests that it defends and safeguards are infinitely superior to the wretched and transitory ones of the world.

Never have I believed that Catholicism could clash with true freedom; never can there be the least antagonism between it and the Republic. All modern institutions that constitute what we properly call civilization spring from Christianity like a pure and plentiful fountain whose torrents, hidden at times, are the fruitful sap of civilized societies.

The system of government that we have adopted as the best is truly that, since it is found to be the most consistent with the sublime doctrine of Jesus, so favorable to human equality and reciprocal love. And notice that this form is not less worthy than others of fatherly fondness by our immortal Pontiff. As wise and prudent as he is, he has felt that the time has come to manifest to the world that Catholicism in religion and republicanism in politics can well cooperate simultaneously for the progress of a modern society.

And so we can be sincerely Catholic without the least diminishment of our character as republicans. On the contrary, the greater our submission is to the holy doctrine of the Gospel, the greater will be our diligence in observing the law, our exactness in fulfilling our duties and our consideration for the rights of others. It can be truly stated that there is the most exact synonymy between these two expressions: exemplary Christian, excellent citizen...[22]

Today when the venerable Princes of the Ecuadorian Church bless the cornerstone of our Basilica, emblem of the future greatness of Ecuador, which must be based on moral fundamentals, I raise my heart to the Almighty, to ask Him not to leave me alone to work for the good of the Republic. Only from Him can I receive the light, courage, and fortitude that are indispensible to me. May His sovereign munificence grant me these and the other gifts proper to a good ruler, not for my individual honor which means nothing, but for the prosperity and glory of my dear country.

Just twenty-seven days later and an intense light shone brightly on the four regions of Ecuador,[23] and the following decree thundered from the Legislative Chambers:

The Congress of Ecuador, considering:
1. That the Most Illustrious Prelates of the Ecclesiastical Province have consecrated the Republic to the Immaculate Heart of Mary, and
2. At all times this nation has obtained the most signal favors and graces from Heaven through the mediation of the Most Holy Virgin.
3.

Decrees:

Art. 1. The Legislature, for its part, also consecrates Ecuador to the Immaculate Heart of Mary and recognizes the august Mother of God as exalted Queen, most loving Mother and special Protectress of this Republic.

Art. 2. The Executive Power, in agreement with the Most Illustrious Prelates, will ask the Holy See for the Immaculate Heart of Mary to be declared, after the Divine Heart of Jesus, Principal Patroness of this Republic.

Art. 3. As a perpetual remembrance and testimony of this consecration, a bronze statue of the Most Holy Virgin will be erected with National funds in this capital on the top of Panecillo Hill with this inscription: "Ecuador, to the Immaculate Mother of God, August Queen, Most loving and Sovereign Protectress of this Republic. Legislative Decree of 1892."

Art. 4. For the expenditures of the statue's purchase in Europe and placement at the designated site, the sum of ten thousand sucres is voted which will be taken from the quantity assigned in the budget for religious expenditures.

Given in Quito, Capital of the Republic of Ecuador, on the fifth of August of 1892.

President of the Honorable Chamber of the Senate: Vicente Lucio Salazar

President of the Honorable Chamber of Representatives: Santiago Carrasco.[24]

Palace of the Government in Quito, on August 6, 1892. Let this be published and enforced. Luis Cordero.[25]

Without a doubt it was Divine Providence which disposed the approval of this decree on the seventeenth anniversary of Garcia

Moreno's death. This President-martyr spent the last minutes of his earthly life before the altar of Our Lady of Sorrows, and close to the cross that he had carried in procession on April 26, 1874. He was assassinated by the Masonic Sanhedrin, stabbed by an individual who had the thirty coins from the Lodges in his pockets, and who, before rushing at his victim, had addressed him with a respectful greeting. He was a victim who, before dying, forgave his assassins. Who cannot see the parallel to the Divine Model of the predestined on Calvary! Christ said, "Behold thy mother." How could Garcia Moreno, in turn, not say to Ecuador: "Behold thy mother," and to the Sorrowful Mother, "Behold thy son." Of course, not with the perceptible voice of his chest, but certainly with the voice of his blood that cries to heaven like Abel's blood.

The Decree of August 6, 1892, was the realization of Garcia Moreno's desires on August 6, 1875. The desires were from the brave Lion, and doing the work was from the meek Lamb.[26]

# Endnotes

[1] "Another one of the fundamental devotions of the Institute is that of the Sacred Heart of Jesus, since the Church teaches that the primary object of this devotion is the infinite charity of God towards men, primarily shown in Christ's Passion and in the institution of the Adorable Eucharist (the Servant of God, Father Julio Matovelle, Founder of the Oblates of the Sacred Hearts of Jesus and Mary (Original Constitution, n. 7)).

[2] "In 1864 [this] association of prayer was founded which has since been honored with the official title of Universal Archconfraternity of Our Lady of the Sacred Heart, and enriched with numerous indulgences." ("Missionaries of the Sacred Heart of Jesus," *Catholic Encyclopedia* (1912 ed.), vol. 13, p. 306.)

[3] *La Republica del Corazon de Jesus* [*The Republic of the Heart of Jesus*], vol. 4, p. 693 ff.; Cf. Gomezjurado, *Vida de Garcia Moreno*, vol. 11, p. 95.

[4] *Idem.* p. 698.

[5] The Catholic Protectorate was an educational institute of industrial arts for boys founded in 1871 and was run by the Brothers of the Christian Schools from New York in answer to the invitation by Garcia Moreno.

[6] *Standard-bearer of the Heart of Jesus*, 1945.

[7] The biographical data about Agustin Serrano was already published on page 59 of the pamphlet entitled *Abanderado del Corazon de Jesus* [*Standard-bearer of the Heart of Jesus*], 1945, first edition. It was the Marianite nun, Sister Lucia Carrasco, born in Cuenca, who told the author about the spiritualist practices and the intervention of Garcia Moreno. That information was transmitted in Riobamba in the year 1943.

Also see the author's little work entitled *¿Martir Garcia Moreno?* [*Is Garcia Moreno a Martyr?*], p. 155 ff., edited in Cuenca, 1952.

[8] That Juan de Dios Campuzano had suffered such vexations in the days of Veintimilla is clear from Severo Gomezjurado, S. J., *Vida de Garcia Moreno*, (Imprenta ARPI, Quito, 1979), vol. 10, p. 476.

[9] Gomezjurado, *Vida de Garcia Moreno*, vol. 11, p. 98.

[10] Father Mateo Crawley's assertion that there was no contract for the return of the painting is clear from the Chilean periodical *El Mensajero del Corazon de Jesus* [*Messenger of the Heart of Jesus*], August 1946, Santiago, 164th issue, and likewise from *¿Martir Garcia Moreno?* [*Is Garcia Moreno a Martyr?*] p. 155 ff. In Valparaiso during the informal meetings that Father Agustin Serrano held with the Ecuadorian expatriates, he told them all he knew regarding the important oleograph, and therefore about the persecution.

[11] *Mensajero del Corazon de Jesus*, [*Messenger of the Heart of Jesus*], Santiago, August, 1946. Also *La Republica del Corazon de Jesus* [*Republic of the Heart of Jesus*], vol. 6, p. 80.

[12] *Idem.*

[13] *Idem.* Continuation of Monsignor Macchi's discourse; Gomezjurado, *Vida de Garcia Moreno*, vol. 11, p. 101.

[14] *The Republic of the Heart of Jesus.*
[15] *Idem.* January, 1890, prologue. On p. 274 of Father Matovelle's biography, composed by Doctor Wilfrido Loor, it is mistakenly said that Francisco Tardieu was the French architect who designed the plan for the Basilica. Actually it was Mr. Emilio Tarlier, as the author of these pages was told by Reverend Father Correa, Superior General of the Oblates of the Sacred Hearts of Jesus and Mary and director of the work of the Basilica, around the year 1971.
[16] Gomezjurado, *Vida de Garcia Moreno*, vol. 11, p. 102.
[17] About the gift of the statue of Our Lady of the Sacred Heart, it is a most certain fact verified by Jose Maria Lazcano Orbe, who was one of Garcia Alcazar's favorite employees. The latter gave it in turn to the Church at Salcedo. [Editor's note: Gabriel Maria Garcia del Alcazar was the son of President Gabriel Garcia Moreno and his second wife, Mariana del Alcazar y Ascasubi. He died on August 22, 1931. (His father's first wife, Rosa de Ascasubi y Matheu, died in 1865.) In Spanish speaking countries, people generally bear two surnames. A person's first surname is the father's first surname, and the second one is the mother's first surname.]
[18] The Shyris were an ancient indigenous people who ruled the Andean region of Ecuador for 700 years before they were conquered by the Incas about the year 1500.
[19] Gomezjurado, *Vida de Garcia Moreno*, vol. 11, p. 104.
[20] *La Libertad Cristiana* [*Christian Liberty*], a biweekly Quito periodical, whose editor in chief was Juan de Dios Campuzano; page 39, No. 4, April 9, 1890. Likewise, p. 276 of the above-mentioned biography of Matovelle. According to the above-said pages of *La Libertad Cristiana,* it is clear that the departure of the Issoudun Priests took place in the month of June, 1892. And on p. 144 it is said that the priests from Issodoun had gathered much spiritual fruit on the feast of May 31, 1892, in *El Sagrario* Church.

See also, Father Jose Felix Heredia, S. J., *La Consagracion del Ecuador al Corazon de Jesus,* [*The Consecration of Ecuador to the Heart of Jesus*] which was written in 1935], p. 372 ff.
[21] *La Consagracion del Ecuador al Corazon de Jesus,* p. 374. See also, *La Libertad Cristiana,* p. 208 ff, July 16, 1892.
[22] *La Libertad Cristiana,* p. 267 ff.
[23] Ecuador can be divided into four geographic regions: the coast, the highlands, the east and the islands.
[24] *Idem.* Santiago Carrasco was the nephew of the sadly famous parish priest, Francisco Carrasco, who supported Urbino's revolution and who is mentioned in Severo Gomezjurado, S. J., *Vida de Garcia Moreno,* (Imprenta ARPI, Quito, 1979), vol. 9, p. 136. Around the year 1874, Santiago Carrasco, a youth of some twenty-two years of age, witness of the amazing material and spiritual progress promoted by Garcia Moreno, renounced his inherited hostility and declared himself Garcia Moreno's admirer and partisan through this statement: "I am taking off the tunic of Nessus," which according to Greek mythology was a talisman with powers for changing opinions and feelings. His daughter, Sister

Leticia Carrasco, a nun of the Congregation of the Sacred Hearts in Rumipamba, testified to all of this to the author in 1970.

[25] Gomezjurado, *Vida de Garcia Moreno*, vol. 11, pp. 106-107.

[26] A play on words since the President's last name, Cordero, means lamb. [translator's note]

## Chapter 8

# The Name "Garcia Moreno's Heart of Jesus" Conquers the Homes of the World

Mateo Crawley-Boevey,[1] born in Peru but of foreign parents[2] as is clearly seen from his last names, entered the Religious Congregation of the Sacred Hearts of Picpus. Being about eighteen years old around the year 1893, he heard these words from the Reverend Father Romain, Provincial of that Congregation in Valparaiso, "Please put all the many papers and notebooks in my room in order." The young religious went to work and found a rolled oleograph while looking through the objects locked in a trunk. He unrolled it and contemplated a picture of the Heart of Jesus that gave him pleasure and devotion. "Father Provincial! Does Your Reverence have any information about this painting?" Father Romain briefly told him what our readers already know.

Four years went by before Mateo Crawley dared ask Father Romain to entrust him with that picture, which greatly interested him. His request was granted, but on the condition that the picture would never leave the Community. A year later, that is, in 1898, Crawley was ordained a priest and celebrated his first Mass. A rich and also fervent Catholic lady revealed her desire of giving him a gift in remembrance of his first Mass.

"Give me an artistic frame for a picture of the Heart of Jesus that I value highly."

His desires were amply satisfied with a rich and beautiful frame. It is impossible not to mention the name of the donor: Sara Vives y Pomar from Chile. From then on, the Heart of Jesus from the Ecuadorian Consecration presided in a place of honor in the main hall where the members of the Literary Academy of the Corazonists in Valparaiso held their sessions. A few years later it was taken to the room where the University School of Law operated.[3]

Father Mateo's joy increased with the reading of the encyclical issued on May 25, 1899, by Pope Leo XIII, entitled by its first words: *Annum sacrum*.[4] Let us see the most impressive paragraph:

> When the Church, in the days immediately succeeding her institution, was oppressed beneath the yoke of the Caesars, a young Emperor saw in the heavens a cross, which became at once the happy omen and cause of the glorious victory that soon followed. And now, today, behold another blessed and heavenly token is offered to our sight—the most Sacred Heart of Jesus, with a

*Father Mateo Crawley-Boevey, founder of the Apostolate of the Home Enthronement of the Sacred Heart*

cross rising from it and shining forth with dazzling splendor amidst flames of love. In that Sacred Heart all our hopes should be placed, and from it the salvation of men is to be confidently besought.

It pleases us to note that there is an analogy between the words of Leo XIII and this announcement by Garcia Moreno, pronounced twenty-four years earlier: "After my death, the Revolution will again take possession of my land of birth, and will govern it tyrannically under the deceitful name of Liberalism. But the Heart of Jesus, to whom I have consecrated it, will wrest it from their claws, to make it live free and upright under the protection of the great Catholic principles."[5] Extend that farsightedness to all of mankind and the reason will be seen why the Catholics of Barcelona, during the evening literary gathering of February 12, 1914,[6] said that Garcia Moreno was the Constantine of modern times.

The above-mentioned encyclical, *Annum Sacrum,* was the announcement of another exceedingly important act to be carried out: the consecration of the entire world to the Heart of Jesus. That took place on the eleventh day of June of the same year in all the churches throughout the world. Here are some expressions from the formula sent by the Pope:

> Most sweet Jesus, Redeemer of the human race ..., we are Thine, and Thine we wish to be ... behold each one of us freely consecrates himself today to Thy Most Sacred Heart ... Many indeed have never known Thee; many too, despising Thy precepts, have rejected Thee. Have mercy on them all, most merciful Jesus, and draw them to Thy Sacred Heart. Be Thou King, O Lord, not only of the faithful who have never forsaken Thee ... make the earth resound from pole to pole with one cry: Praise to the Divine Heart that wrought our salvation ...[7]

On August 15, 1906, a violent earthquake shook the city of Valparaiso. It is unnecessary to consider the ruin and destruction, including that in the University of the Priests of the Sacred Hearts. And what happened to the historical picture of the Heart of Jesus? The episode bordered on a miracle. The main hall of the School of Law collapsed, but the canvas remained high on the wall where the precious painting had been hanging. The picture was unharmed.[8] A sign full of meaning from

Divine Providence! The Heart of Jesus from the Ecuadorian Consecration, symbol of firmness and anchor of salvation! And so it was worthy to receive the homage of peoples and nations. That is just what happened, as we shall now see.

Father Mateo Crawley was in Europe, enriching his soul with a greater abundance of virtue and science, and eager to transform this magnificent motto into a reality: "To conquer the whole world for the Heart of Jesus, through its Enthronement in every home, family after family, home after home." What picture should be adopted for this? His favorite painting, the one in Valparaiso, to which that religious had given a singular, acquired name: "Garcia Moreno's Heart of Jesus." By then it was the year 1907. Crawley left for Rome, obtained an audience with His Holiness, Pope Pius X, and asked him to kindly approve and bless his apostolate for the Enthronement. The Holy Father, assuming an air of mystery and authority answered him in these words; "Not only do I approve and bless this, your apostolate, but I also command you to travel the entire world for its propagation."

"Most Holy Father, please accept this photograph of the picture that I desire to adopt for Enthronement in homes."

Pius X received it kindly and smilingly, and had it put up in his private room until the last day of his life. The frame for the photo was golden.[9]

Father Mateo returned to Valparaiso and edited a pamphlet with the ceremonial and its explanation, approved by the Archbishop of Santiago on August 11, 1908. On October twenty-first of the same year he made the first solemn Enthronement in the home of Juana Rosa de Edwards in Valparaiso and on the sixth of February of the following year, the Enthronement in his mother's house in Arequipa. When he returned to Chile, there were two more Enthronements, in *El Chileno* and *La Union*[10] newspaper offices respectively. As is obvious, copies of Garcia Moreno's Heart of Jesus were the ones used, which were put in places of honor in the aforesaid homes and establishments. Here are Father Mateo Crawley's own words: "Although it is true that we never desired to impose this picture on families, for there is no accounting for tastes, and some tastes deserve a beating; nevertheless, it was always considered everywhere as the most appropriate and tacitly official picture of our beloved work."

Another of that apostle's successes consisted in arousing and obtaining a great number of priests and parishes to carry out the Enthronement in hundreds of families. Therefore they had to multiply the editions of the pamphlet as well as the aforesaid picture, not only in Chile, but also in France, Switzerland, Germany, Spain, Portugal, the United States and other nations.

In Santiago, the indefatigable priest of the Sacred Hearts had the pleasure of verifying the Enthronement in person in several drawing rooms of the children of Pedro Pablo Garcia Moreno, the brother of the martyred President. In testimony of their gratitude they gave him a photograph of their illustrious relative with this inscription: "Photograph taken in the sacristy of the Cathedral at Quito when our Uncle Gabriel Garcia Moreno had just expired on August 6, 1875, the First Friday of the month." Crawley said, "When preaching to the men of Catholic Action, I frequently show them and let them admire the photograph of the Martyr of the Sacred Heart."

He did not delay to set off and begin traveling throughout the whole world to undertake his Crusade, in obedience to the Pope's command, and stimulated by the fruit obtained everywhere. These are also his own words: "In 1915 at the height of the European war, I had the honor to personally offer this picture to her Majesty Queen Maria Cristina of Spain."

His stay in Canada produced very abundant fruit. For one thing, a young lady, whose name was not easy to ascertain, was persuaded that Garcia Moreno's intercession was more powerful than that of other saints to obtain divine favor. She wanted particularly to obtain special graces for her family. So, to that effect, she composed the following prayer.[11]

> Sacred Heart of Jesus, we beseech Thee, through the Immaculate Heart of Mary, deign to glorify Thy zealous servant Gabriel Garcia Moreno, who dedicated his efforts and his life for the establishment of Thy social reign in souls as well as in the State; and grant us the graces that we ask through his intercession.
>
> Most Sweet Heart of Jesus, victoriously extend Thy reign of love to all hearts. Jesus, King of Peace! Hasten the reign of Thy Loving Heart in our home, in our souls, and in all Christian homes. Sweet Heart of Mary! Prepare the reign of the Sacred Heart of Jesus in our souls!"[12]

Once the preceding prayer was composed, its author petitioned the Archbishop of Montreal to enrich it with indulgences. But his Illustrious Eminence refused, adducing that such a thing was the concern of the

Archbishop of Quito, under whose jurisdiction the President-martyr had died. Then the Canadian lady directed her letters and supplications to Sister Maria de San Jose, the superior of the Convent of the Good Shepherd in Quito, asking her to interpose her influence with the Archbishop of the Ecuadorian capital for the aforesaid effect. Sister Maria de San Jose did it, although not immediately, but after a notable time had lapsed from the reception of the letter from Canada. She did it on February 23, 1919; and she took advantage of that opportunity to also implore indulgences for another prayer that had been composed by the nuns of the Good Shepherd in Quito, and was recited in the Enthronement of the Heart of Jesus that had already taken place at that convent. Sister Maria de San Jose presented these reasons: "We desired then to take Garcia Moreno as our Protector, in order to obtain, also through his intercession, the grace of propagating the Enthronement in homes."

Monsignor Manuel Maria Polit, then the Archbishop of Quito, received and read the letter, the petition and both prayers; and what did he answer? And what procedures did he adopt? It is not clear from anything written or any oral tradition. It is certain that it might not have been convenient to officially approve a prayer that was recited in Quito, for Ecuadorian politics at that time were very hostile toward Garcia Moreno. But officially to approve the prayer composed for Canada seems not to have run up against any difficulty.[13]

The impression left by Father Mateo Crawley when passing through Scotland was none the less profound. It is proved by the thousands of holy cards of Garcia Moreno's Heart of Jesus that circulated there, in color and of fine quality, just like the original, with the rays of the Divine Heart over Ecuador. Whereas in the holy cards edited for France and for Spain, for example, the rays fall over French territory or on the Iberian Peninsula. The following paragraphs appear on the back of the Scottish copy:

> Picture adopted by the Christian Statesman Garcia Moreno for the consecration of Ecuador to the Sacred Heart of Jesus in the year 1873. Garcia Moreno was assassinated in 1875. Father Mateo Crawley, founder of the Enthronement of the Sacred Heart in homes, adopted this picture as the banner of his world-wide crusade for the social reign of that same Sacred Heart. He preached on that subject for fifty years.
>
> Prayer to Christ the King: Oh, Jesus Christ! I recognize Thee as Universal King. All that exists was created for Thee... I renew

my Baptismal promises, renouncing Satan and all his pomps and works, and I intend to live as a good Christian. I will try especially to obtain the triumph of the rights of God and the Church. Divine Heart of Jesus! I consecrate my humble apostolate to Thee, tending towards obtaining that all hearts accept Thy reign of peace to be established in the entire world. Amen. (Plenary indulgence upon completion of the usual conditions. Once daily. R. 273).

Even in recent years, a Scot named Hamish Fraser sent that picture to all English-speaking countries and he propagates the canonization of Garcia Moreno besides.[14] He is such an ardent devotee of the President-martyr that his home has this sign in Spanish: *Casa Garcia Moreno*, which even appears in his postal street address.[15] This is one of so many cases in which it is verified that Garcia Moreno's Heart of Jesus induces the faithful to venerate him who was the Standard-bearer and Martyr of His Social Reign.

Three years ago in Riobamba, Father Jose Bolanos, S. J., died with the reputation of sainthood. Now around the year 1943, the *Revista Catolica*[16] in El Paso, Ecuador, printed an article of his, containing this paragraph:

> In Garcia Moreno's picture, the Heart of Jesus seems to be saying: "I offer Thee, My Father, together with My sorrows and My Blood, the sorrows and blood of My servant Garcia Moreno, shed for Me and for this painting of Mine; for this reason I want it to be called "The Sacred Heart of Garcia Moreno."[17]

That same priest, as Director of the Apostolate of Prayer in Riobamba, also drafted the following paragraphs:

> We even suspect that in the plans of God, this oleograph could be adopted by rulers and nations as their picture when the horrendous war ends, a war without God and against God. They may then wish to consecrate their nations to the Sacred Heart, recognizing Him as their God and their King, as Garcia Moreno and Ecuador did, giving them the magnificent example of clearly constituting Christ as King with his Heart as the only unshakable basis of the New Order longed for by all. The picture's very name, "The Heart of Jesus of Garcia Moreno," induces us to suspect this. As if the Divine Heart wanted to reward His President-martyr,

making one of His sacred pictures bear Garcia Moreno as its **last name**. It is as though the picture, with this presidential last name, reminds and incites all rulers to accomplish the same thing in their nations that the Great Ecuadorian accomplished in his. It is as though it were meant to motivate them to choose for this purpose the portrait in which Christ is clearly shown as Monarch of all peoples, races, nations and continents under the celestial sphere held up by His Divine left hand, while His right hand holds the royal scepter.

Since not even the leaf of a tree moves without God's Providence, we believe that the Sacred Heart for some such reason wanted the very name of the Ruler, who was chosen by His Heart for the Republic of His Sacred Heart, to be added irrevocably, inseparably to His picture. So, no one can hear the name of that picture without hearing the name of Garcia Moreno, his faithful servant who shed his blood for Him on a First Friday after having received Him into his heart that morning and visiting Him, solemnly exposed in the cathedral, on the way to his martyrdom. No one can honor that picture without honoring him who ordered it to be painted and who honored it in public before the entire nation, and in private before his family. No one will be able to love the Sacred Heart represented in that picture without loving Garcia Moreno, whose heart loved God and his country so much. No one will be able to worship the Sacred Heart represented in that picture without also desiring to venerate his faithful servant, Garcia Moreno, who was not ashamed before his ministers and the city of Quito in an attitude of a penitent Head of State, to bear the cross on which His God and Lord died, the King of rulers and of those ruled. In conclusion, no one will be able to separate Garcia Moreno from the Sacred Heart, Who has united him to Himself forever on earth and in heaven with the bond of eternal love."[18]

The preceding paragraphs manifest that for Father Jose Bolanos and for all those who adhere to him, Garcia Moreno is already extra-officially canonized. Canonized by whom? By the Heart of Jesus![19] Such optimism increases when one considers that it was Father Mateo Crawley, a holy religious of the Sacred Hearts, who first added the name of **Garcia Moreno** to the famous picture.[20]

In the year 1931, the author was in Paray-le-Monial, the town justly considered as the capital of the world of the Heart of Jesus. There the author met Father Mateo, when he was preaching in the Chapel of the Apparitions. As is obvious, the center for selling holy cards of the Heart of Jesus is in the shops of Paray. I went to one of them and asked the lady who owned it, "Please be so kind as to show me the different holy cards of the Heart of Jesus."

"With the greatest pleasure!" and she began showing me several copies from a thick stack. When she came to one of them she said with the greatest naturalness, "The Heart of Jesus of Garcia Moreno."

"This name pleasantly impresses me," I told her, "because I am from Ecuador, from Garcia Moreno's homeland."

"Well, that is the way this holy card is called here," the kind saleslady replied.

Four years later, that is, in 1935, Father Mateo embarked upon an extended tour through the nations of the Far East. Thus, for example, he visited and expanded his Crusade in Hindustan, in Portuguese India, Indonesia, Ceylon, Java, the Philippines, Manchuria, China, Hong Kong, Indochina, and so on. Let us again hear words quoted from his lips:

> When traveling through the lands of the Far East for six years, I found it everywhere enthroned in homes, schools, hospitals, parish priests' rectories, palaces and huts, and bishops' residences. What else? When hearing these words, "The Heart of Jesus of Garcia Moreno," these people asked, "And who is Garcia Moreno?" Then the distinguished priest of the Sacred Hearts narrated the life and death of the President-martyr, together with the history of Ecuador to ignorant audiences, who were not at all concerned about Columbia, Peru, Chile, Venezuela, etc.[21]

Crawley himself concludes this chapter, letting us once again hear his own words:

> Not many years ago a Catholic from Brussels had the courage to undertake sculpting the statue of The Heart of Jesus of Garcia Moreno. And it truly was an artistic success. Full of surprise and joy I have found reproductions of that sculpture in all climates and latitudes, for example in the Cathedral of Saigon (French Indochina) and in a High School Academy in Chicago...
>
> Now making a mental effort of reconstruction, according to time and space, I imagine what follows:

Mixed up with other objects of more or less relative interest, the precious canvas was found in the bottom of a trunk, waiting for God's timing to begin to diffuse splendid light like a Sun of love and divine glory. I had the happiness, or better yet, the grace as enormous as unmerited to bring it out of the shadows and carry it on my shoulders like a flag of victory from one pole to the other. And I do not think that I sin by audacity if I suppose that Garcia Moreno, incomparable Martyr of the Heart of Jesus, was not unaware of this predestination of which I was the object with no merit of my own.[22]

Even more, I dare say that it was Garcia Moreno who, with his hands anointed with his glorious blood, put the precious Labarum[23] into my hands. Oh! And how happy I would consider myself to be if one day it were given to me to contribute in some way to his exaltation on the altars, in order to pay for the gift that he gave me, which gave a definitive direction to my vocation of social apostolate! If then, one day, the Church renders such glory to the President-martyr, the Congregation of the Sacred Hearts should attain that Rome would assign him to us as Patron of the Enthronement Crusade, since I made my debut in the shadow of his standard.

# Endnotes

[1] Remember, Boevey is his second last name, i.e. his mother's maiden name, of lesser importance than Crawley, which is often used alone. [Translator's note]
[2] Father Mateo's last names are English. In the *Mensajero del Corazon de Jesus* [*Messenger of the Heart of Jesus*] from Santiago, Chile, August 1946, what is in the text is narrated by Father Mateo himself.
[3] Gomezjurado, *Vida de Garcia Moreno*, vol. 11, pp. 121-122.
[4] "The Holy Year." The text and date of the consecration of the world are clear in the work by Father Arturo Vermeersch, S. J., entitled *Practica y Doctrina de la Devocion al Corazon de Jesus* [*Practice and Doctrine of the Devotion to the Heart of Jesus*], vol. 2, p. 300 ff.
[5] *Idem*. Around the year 1920, a Catholic from Canada wrote a letter to Ecuador asking whether Garcia Moreno had gotten ahead of Leo XIII or not regarding relations between Church and State. Let us see Leo XIII's doctrine consigned in his Encyclical *Arcanum* of February 10, 1880:

"It is befitting to the two authorities [the Church and State] and beneficial for all mankind that between these two reign union and concord; and that, in those matters which even though under different appearances, are, by right and by common sense, one, the authority which has in its charge human affairs, depends aptly and fittingly upon the authority to which has been confided heavenly matters." It is clear, therefore, that Garcia Moreno was ahead, as is verified in the Concordat. Cf. Gomezjurado, *Vida de Garcia Moreno*, vol. 3, p. 415 ff and also vol. 7, p. 415 ff. Thanks to his Concordat, Garcia Moreno was also ahead of the *Syllabus* that Pius IX promulgated in the year 1864. Many of the propositions condemned by the *Syllabus* can be found in *Vida de Garcia Moreno*, vol. 5, p. 236 ff.
[6] Barcelona's original program lies in a special glass case in the "Aurelio Espinosa" Library at Cotocollao. [Editor's note: The Cotocollao Parish is a parish in northwest Quito, Ecuador. It contains the "Aurelio Espinoza Pólit" library which is valuable for researchers since it has one of the most complete collections of old Ecuadorian books.] On the first page appears a bust of Garcia Moreno. Doctor Aurelio Espinosa Coronel, a resident at that time in France or in Belgium, transmitted the news to Quito and it is published in a clipping from the newspaper that lies in the aforesaid library. The program deals with a collection of clippings.
[7] Gomezjurado, *Vida de Garcia Moreno*, vol. 11, pp. 122-123.
[8] About the saving of the painting, see Monsignor Jose Felix Heredia, S. J., *La Consagracion del Ecuador* [*The Consecration of Ecuador*], p. 258. See also the above-mentioned *Mensajero* [*Messenger*] from Santiago, No. 4, 1960, where the whole life of Father Mateo is told and his holy death is related. Also the French magazine *Le Regne des Sacres Coeurs de Jesus et Marie*, [*Reign of the Sacred Hearts of Jesus and Mary*], pp. 19 and 36, by the Priests of the Sacred Hearts

of Picpus, a neighborhood near Paris, November 1946. Finally, again see the *Mensajero* from Santiago, Chile, August 1946.

[9] Gomezjurado, *Vida de Garcia Moreno*, vol. 11, p. 123.

[10] *The Chilean* and *The Union*.

[11] This prayer was first translated from French to Spanish, and now to English.

[12] Gomezjurado, *Vida de Garcia Moreno*, vol. 11, pp. 124-125.

[13] What is written about the letter from Canada is in the archives of the Archdiocese of Quito.

[14] The author of these pages has the holy card in lovely colors sent by Hamish Fraser and also letters from him where that gentleman makes known his activities for the canonization of Garcia Moreno. He also asked for several pictures of the President-martyr, to publish them with prayers, especially in Washington, thanks to Father Larkin, a Yankee priest of the Sacred Hearts, likewise devoted to that canonization. The result: in the magazine *Men of the Sacred Heart*, December 1970, edited in Chicago, it seems that Hamish Fraser had been a red Communist leader who promoted Communism in Spain and defended it with arms. Through the convert's efforts, not only a beautiful portrait of Garcia Moreno appears in that magazine but also the prayer to the Heart of Jesus, composed by the author of these pages in 1940, for the canonical glorification of the President-martyr.

Mr. Hamish Fraser's postal address is none other than this: "*Casa Garcia* ... Scotland." He finally got some fifty Scottish, Irish and British Catholic signatures addressed to Monsignor Pablo Munoz Vega, Cardinal Archbishop of Quito, asking him to promote the cause of canonization for Garcia Moreno, whose triumph would be the triumph of a regime apt to overthrow social injustices and wars.

[15] I.e. he named his house after Garcia Moreno.

[16] *Catholic Magazine*.

[17] Cf. Gomezjurado, *Vida de Garcia Moreno*, vol. 11, p. 126.

[18] Gomezjurado, *Vida de Garcia Moreno*, vol. 11, pp. 126-127.

[19] About Father Bolanos, see our pamphlet entitled *Abanderado del Corazon de Jesus* [*Standard-bearer of the Heart of Jesus*], edited in Riobamba, 1945, p. 76 ff.

[20] It is unthinkable that God could possibly have wanted to associate the last name "Garcia Moreno" with the Heart of Jesus, without that President being at least a man of notable holiness.

[21] Gomezjurado, *Vida de Garcia Moreno*, vol. 11, p. 128.

[22] *Mensajero del Corazon de Jesus* [*Messenger of the Heart of Jesus*] from Santiago, Chile, No. 4, 1960. Also the issue from August, 1946. And finally, *Le Regne des Sacres Coeurs* [*The Reign of the Sacred Hearts*], 1948, p. 72 ff.

[23] The labarum was a military standard that displayed the symbol ☧, formed from the first two Greek letters of the word "Christ." It was used by the Roman Emperor Constantine the Great.

# Chapter 9

# Heads of State Who Followed Garcia Moreno's Example

Mateo Crawley had initiated his Crusade in Chile. Let it be known that this nation had witnessed the awakening of its pious people's eager desires to invoke the Heart of Jesus through Garcia Moreno's intercession. Here is the quoted account of a miracle:[1]

In La Serena, Chile, Mrs. Juana Rodriguez reports that the glorious martyr Garcia Moreno, President of Ecuador, obtained an extraordinary favor for her from the Sacred Heart:

Being seriously ill in my left leg, especially my knee, and with very sharp pain and no improvement in a long time, it occurred to me to invoke the glorious martyr Garcia Moreno, so he would obtain improvement for me from the Sacred Heart, promising Him that I would place his portrait in a frame. It was twelve midnight. I fell asleep until two in the morning. I awoke completely healed. I thankfully make known the favor from my glorious intercessor and famous martyr of the Sacred Heart of Jesus.

In August of the following year the same magazine printed a poem in honor of Garcia Moreno composed by the Chilean Ramon Rojas Penafiel, the prize-winning poet at the Floral Games of 1926, who received the Flower of Gold in 1927. Let us see some stanzas:

There are men who are symbols; there are men
Who cross History like suns,
Shining with the brightness of their names
Like light trails of eternal glory.

Such a man was Garcia Moreno. That devotion to public welfare
Of this exemplary statesman and great Christian
Was a hymn to the truth and patriotism
Set on high before the gaze of the American World.

The sinews of his breast palpitated
With the rhythm of the Martyr on Calvary.
He was an apostle of law and justice
In his triumphal throne as Commander in Chief.

To the blow of the dagger he yielded his life,
As the oak before the lightning that wounds it;
And even then he palpitates the trembling phrase
Of his sublime credo: "God does not die!"

He was a star of blazing brilliance
Who in Quito had its immortal proscenium;
And his eminent children and grandchildren
Are today the heirs of his genius.

His virtues as leader and statesman
Arose in the temple of History.
For which reason the world, as long as God exists,
Will render eternal veneration to his memory.[2]

In Spain, also, the memory of Garcia Moreno continued to arouse feelings of affection, admiration and enthusiasm. Such can be seen, for example, in Cardinal Ignacio Moreno's biography, written by his brother, Manuel, in 1879. Let us listen to the following paragraph:

> What is worth more, incomparably more than this magnanimity of character and nobility, is that many of the persons who belonged to this lineage have shed luster upon it, through an exemplary life and heroic virtues, including among them a saint of the first magnitude, and a martyr, a very famous martyr. That saint was Saint Toribio Alfonso de Mogrobejo, Archbishop of Lima... The martyr is our first cousin, Gabriel Garcia Moreno, President of the Republic of Ecuador. His extraordinary deeds, known the world over, encircle that great man of the nineteenth century like a refulgent halo, making us confidently hope that the day will come when the Church bestows upon him the honor of the altars for having been, as on a solemn occasion the Holy Pontiff Pius IX said, a martyr for religion and country.[3]

Ten years later, another tribute emanated in Spain itself from that personage who justly bears the name of Prince of Literary Criticism, Marcelino Menendez Pelayo. Let us listen to him:

> It is right to close this section with a name that is as pleasant to believers, as it is hated by sectarians, the name of the champion and

## Heads of State Who Followed Garcia Moreno's Example 149

martyr of the Catholic cause in Ecuador, President Gabriel Garcia Moreno... The greatness of his administration, the integrity of his character and the glory of his death make him one of the noblest types of human dignity that could glorify our race in this century. The Republic that produced such a man may be poor, obscure and forgotten but with him it has enough to live honorably in history.[4]

In Germany the poet Leo Fischer extolled him with these verses:

1. The past Age recounts
That it had virtue and heroism;
But still they are not strangers,
Thankfully, to our Age.
Iron-willed characters
Are not of legend:
Upright, on his path today
Walks a hero indeed.

2. The wide granite base
Of the Andes shudders
When Garcia the Great
Appears as a king.
He is king from an unknown lineage,
There is no throne for his royalty,
The greatness of the nation
Is his heraldry and legitimacy.

3. In virgin forest and jungle,
Wherever he sets his foot,
There virtuous life
Blooms in peace.
With a tenacious hand
He banishes from his country
Hate from old barbarians,
Civil war from the new.

4. And when his athletic soul
Yielded to the cruel blow,
His lips could still utter
His last word.

> From his Olympian repose
> He made his nation his heir:
> Saying, "I succumb, yet,
> Know this: God does not die."
>
> 5. What a beautiful life of a hero,
> Of a fortunate noble martyr
> An offering, even in death,
> To God and to his duty!
> He fell like a shining star;
> And then like a condor
> He soared to the heights
> To drink in pure Light.[5]

From France, at the beginning of the year 1886, the poet E. Villedieu sent Ecuador a composition of his in which he deplored the decadence that the Land of Garcia Moreno underwent during Veintimilla's dictatorship, and jubilantly cheered the Catholic reaction in President Caamano's regime. But nevertheless, he discerned Ecuador's glorious destiny as the herald of the Social Reign of Christ in the whole world. It pleases us to recognize the likeness of inspiration and style shown between Villedieu and Paul Claudel. Let us now hear the former's verses:

<u>Angel or Devil! Which one are you?</u>

> Is life and light the magnificent ideal that your vision reveals to us, oh great Republic! Or is it mortal illusion...? During your years of silence and in your volte-faces without proper support, should our restless century accuse your cruel impotence, or rather the impotence of your own age?
>
> The past knew you as beneficent, in those times of confused rumors, in which the Faith, the torch of the Church, was the guide of reason. Herald of the God of liberty, like swift lightning that shatters the darkness; you showed men an unknown land where the truth was shining.
>
> Your name that bears the brilliance of Heaven, will it perhaps be the plaything of empty illusions? Will it be the flag of passions that trample upon justice and the altar? Will we see

under its folds the savage horde that devastates everything, to impose everywhere the terror of its abominable yoke...?[6]

What is the noble singing that suddenly and from afar resounds on our shores like the echo of a world of light, prayer of a prophet and voice that descends from the heavens? It is a hymn similar to the song of nature, when she is free of winter and with majestic rustling reclaims more beautiful horizons. It is a symphony that modulates notes from on high, to celebrate a new world. It is the canticle of peace in order. It crosses the Atlantic on the wings of the winds. It resounds from the cliffs of the snow-capped range,[7] in the vast pampas[8] and in the estuaries tinted with enchanting reflections...

<u>A great voice!</u>

You come to us like an immense gust, a rushing stream, an irresistible power that stirs up the oceans; like the forces of the ethereal heavens, which, uncontainable, drive the whirlwinds.

You come to us from that very fertile region where the roaring cyclone flies, the son of torrid Ecuador...

Your singing, like the voices of the ancient prophets, resounds in the nights, dominates in the storms with which an irritated sky deafens; and from on high bursts forth in strange harmony, telling us: "Triumphant love, eternal praise, vision of immortality."

It is your voice, Oh Republic! Serene in your joy and praying with head bowed before the altars. The tribute of love that you prepare for yourself takes you to immortality.

Oh generous Nation! Be proud of your children, whose gratitude rises up to God, like a melodious prelude to the hymn of triumphant heaven.

Probity, intelligence, the brilliance and honor of the State, the Authority, Magistrates of the Republic, Parliament that oversees its laws: all join their hearts and voices in the noble Catholic faith and patriotic ardor. The North, the South, the Coast, worthily represented, offer the image of the homeland, in the most impressive homage that our tormented age has seen.

There you invoke, oh valiant ones! that heart whose indomitable trust in God made the splendid day shine when faith like heaven's flower, finally opened, rests in love on the most luminous heights.

You are thinking of that strong athlete, Garcia Moreno, the pure martyr, whose mind conquered a nation that rises up to summits, ennobled by holy love. Cowardly sects plotted against him in their delirium, arming their band of hired assassins, ferocious minions of evil, they became drunk with his blood. Blasphemy, leaving a mark on the sides of the snow-capped Chimborazo, driven on by hell itself, immolated the Hero. And he, dying in the most beautiful combat, exclaimed the sublime words: 'I am leaving but God does not die.' Renowned Champion, he goes away, but does not die completely. This splendid day is his work. A nation that has God for an inheritance, these are his eternal laurels. On the sepulcher of the ardent initiator must be carved this inscription: 'A martyr, he succumbs; but what has fallen has risen again and extols God his Savior.' And his name has been lovingly remembered by a nation on this blessed day. It is a divine poem. It is a resplendent crown whose brilliance will never fade...[9]

A year and a half later, that is, in June of 1887, another illustrious son of France, Baron Leon de Maricourt, dispatched a proclamation, exhorting the whole world to follow the example of Ecuador, whose pact of October 18, 1873, must be considered as a forerunner and a herald that marks the course of a better world. Here are some of his expressions:

Turn your eyes toward the small Republic of Ecuador ...all Catholics who hear and understand the powerful voice of Christ, that demands the observance of the pact that all societies originally have formed with Him; and He claims the scepter of the world terrified by the crash of thrones that are overthrown, of nations that collapse, and of lightning bolts that pulverize civilization. The reason is that this country, pioneer of social salvation, is the first modern nation to indicate the way to be followed for the true solution to the problems that oppress contemporary society.

Therefore we do not cease talking about that glorious Republic of the Sacred Heart, which after two centuries of waiting, has finally managed to accomplish the desire that Christ manifested to Blessed Margaret Mary... If the world will be saved, it will be though the restoration of the Social Reign of Christ over nations.[10]

The effects resulting from the Eucharistic Congress of Quito were like the effusion of graces from the Holy Ghost in Gaul after Clovis' outcry in Tolbiac.[11] A powerful movement of restoration shook the whole country. In the enthusiastic discourses of the students and young men of letters, orators were inspired by Heaven, who filled the clergy and magistrates with admiration, obligating them to exclaim: "Without the Cross, it is impossible to govern this nation..."

History shows that each modern nation was born from a contract, from a pact between the founder of the nation and Jesus Christ... Let us cite some examples:

In the year 495, Clovis, King of the Franks, proclaimed the royalty of Christ and made an oath of alliance with the God of Clotilde on the battle field of Tolbiac, and France was founded.

In the year 737, Pelagius, King of Asturias, proclaimed the royalty of Christ and made an alliance at Covadonga, the only place in the country not invaded by the Arabs. He renewed this oath when he was consecrated in Lugo, and Spain was founded.

In the year 1167, the several States of Italy, invaded by the Germans, formed the Lombard League and proclaimed the royalty of Christ, taking the same oath in Milan, and long live Italy!

In the year 1307, Switzerland, oppressed by Austria, proclaimed the royalty of Christ, and renewed that same oath in Rutli, and their Nation was founded.

In the year 1337, the League of Belgian cities proclaimed the royalty of Christ in Ghent, and Belgium was founded...

In the year 1576, Venice, in danger of succumbing to sudden attacks from Protestantism, renewed the oath of vassalage to Christ that the Doge had sworn centuries before, and the most complete anarchy was succeeded by a social order whose magnificent development advanced from Tuscany to Rome and to the entire world...

The proclamation of the social kingship of Christ, put into effect, is implicitly or explicitly the basis of all the constitutions of modern nations. It is such an obvious fact that this author defies any freethinker to deny it, history in hand. All modern nationality has as its basis a solemn pact sworn to Christ...

The new and valiant little American Republic has renewed the pact of the likewise small and valiant French Nation. Ecuador, by renewing the contract of Tolbiac, Covadonga, Milan, and Rutli with Christ, has placed itself in the front of the line and at the vanguard of the modern world, a position occupied before by France.[12]

The New World began the same way as the Old World, placing Him as the foundation of sovereign authority, His through Whom and for Whom nations have been created. All the amazed Spanish-American republics attentively contemplated the deeds and exploits of their sister nation. Thus the small barbaric nations had contemplated France in the sixth century, which, thanks to the powerful influence of Christ, were to be transformed in turn into great nations. Soon the Latin republics will imitate Ecuador; and the virgin soil of the immense South America will give birth to powerful nations; and once again civilization will obey the mysterious law that guides and impels it in each one of its stages, from east to west...

That phrase, "Soon the Latin republics will imitate Ecuador" has proved to be a prediction by a good prophet. In 1898 the Republic of Colombia was consecrated to the Heart of Jesus conjointly by the ecclesiastical hierarchy and the supreme civil government. Furthermore, in 1952, the consecration was made by a decree of the Legislative Chambers.[13]

On May 30, 1919, Alfonso XIII, King of Spain, consecrated his Kingdom to the Heart of Jesus, solemnly and officially reading the act of consecration himself. That King was an admirer of Garcia Moreno. Here is a gesture that proves it:

In November, 1923, he officially visited the Pope. During his stay in Rome, one of the tributes of which he was the object consisted of the salutation that the students from the South American College addressed to him. On behalf of Ecuador the young Manuel Maria Polit Moreno made his intervention. When rendering his homage to the Queen of Spain, seated on a luxurious throne, she questioned him, "Do you Ecuadorians love Spain?"

The answer was, "Your Majesty, would you ask a Spaniard whether he loves Spain?"

"It is just that you were the first ones to demand independence," she replied.

"That is true, my Lady," the Ecuadorian answered, "but we were helped by the English."

These words could only cause a bit of uneasiness in the Queen, since she was English. Happily her husband, King Alfonso, intervened immediately with a frank laugh, and then with these expressions uttered now in a serious tone, "So you are from Quito, Ecuador, from the land of Garcia Moreno, the foremost man of America and the glory of his race?"

"My feeling of pride and satisfaction was indescribable," said Polit Moreno, "when I heard these words from the mouth of a king who in those days enjoyed so much popularity due to his works of charity during the European War."[14]

In the same above-mentioned year of 1919, the ecclesiastical hierarchy and their Majesties King Albert and the Queen of Belgium made the consecration of their kingdom to the Heart of Jesus.

In 1921, there was an identical act in the Republic of Costa Rica by the ecclesiastical authorities and the supreme civil government.

In 1922, the island of Malta was consecrated to the Heart of Jesus, through the decree of its legislative chambers.

In 1925, the same consecration was made by the ecclesiastical hierarchy and King Alexander of the Kingdom of Yugoslavia.

On August twelfth, of the same year of 1925, the President of the Republic of Bolivia publicly and officially read the act of consecration.

In 1934, in Argentina, the same was done by the ecclesiastical hierarchy and the president of the republic.

In 1940, the ecclesiastical hierarchy and the supreme civil government, having gathered together in the Basilica of Montmartre, consecrated France to the Heart of Jesus.

In 1959, in Honduras, the President of the Republic read the act of consecration.

In 1960, in Nicaragua, the consecration was made in the identical way as Honduras.

On May 30, 1969, the consecration was renewed in Spain, read by its Caudillo, Generalissimo Francisco Franco.[15]

## Endnotes

[1] *Mensajero del Corazon de Jesus ("Messenger of the Heart of Jesus")*, Santiago, Chile, September 1953.
[2] *Ibid.* August, 1954. Original poem:
Hay hombres que son símbolos; hay hombres / Que cruzan como soles por la Historia, / Irradiando el destello de sus nombres, / Como estelas de luz de eterna gloria. / Tal García Moreno. Su civismo / De ejemplar estadista y gran cristiano / Fue un himno a la verdad y al patriotismo, / Alzado frente al Mundo Americano. / Palpitaban las fibras de su pecho / Con el ritmo del Mártir del Calvario. / Fue apóstol de la ley y del derecho / En su solio triunfal de Mandatario. / Al golpe del puñal rindió su vida, / Como el roble ante el rayo que lo hiere; / Y aun palpita la frase estremecida / De su credo sublime: "¡Dios no muere!" / Fue un astro de fulgores esplendentes, / Que tuvo en Quito su inmortal proscenio; / Y sus hijos y nietos eminentes / Son hoy los herederos de su genio. / Sus virtudes de prócer y estadista / Figuran en el templo de la Historia. / Por eso el mundo, mientras Dios exista, / Rendirá culto eterno a su memoria.
[3] Manuel Ignacio Moreno, p. 5; Gomezjurado, *Vida de Garcia Moreno*, vol. 11, p. 135.
[4] Menendez Pelayo, *Historia de la Poesia Hispano-Americana* (*History of Spanish American Poetry*), pp. 60-61.
[5] Leo Fischer, *Gabriel Garcia Moreno. Sus pensamientos y Sentencias,* (His Thoughts and Sayings), the "Dios y Patria" (God and Country) Academy of San Felipe School in Riobamba. Edition by the Destellos Biblioteca, Quito, 1941, pp. 63-64. The first stanza has been added from Gomezjurado, *Vida de Garcia Moreno*, vol. 11, pp. 136-137.
Original poem:
1. Cuenta la Edad Pretérita / que hubo virtud y hazañas; / mas aun no son extrañas, / por dicha, a nuestra Edad. / Los caracteres férreos / non son de la leyenda: / erguido hoy va en su senda / un Héroe de verdad.
2. La ancha base granítica / se estremece del Ande, / cuando García el Grande / se ostenta como Rey. / Es rey de estirpe incógnita, / No hay trono a su realeza, / del pueblo la grandeza / es su blasón y ley.
3. En bosque y selva vírgenes, / doquier su planta posa, / allí vida virtuosa / florece con la paz. / Odio de antiguos bárbaros, / de nuevos civil guerra, / de su país destierra / él con mano tenaz.
4. Y cuando su alma atlética / rindióse al golpe rudo, / su labio aun lanzar pudo / la postrimera voz. / De su quietud olímpica / al pueblo hizo heredero: / "Sucumbo, dijo, empero, / sabed: no muere Dios."
5. ¡Que hermosa vida de héroe, / de mártir noble suerte / ofrenda, aun en la muerte, / a Dios y a su deber! / Cayó cual astro fulgido; / y cóndor, a la altura / cernióse luego, pura / la Luz para beber.

⁶ Villedieu, *La Republica del Corazon de Jesus,* p. 667 ff, April 1886. Translation from French to Spanish by Doctor Manuel Maria Polit Laso:
"¡Angel o Demonio! ¿Qué mismo eres? ¿Es vida y luz el magnífico ideal que nos revela tu visión, ¡oh gran República! o es ilusión mortal...? En tus años de mutismo y en tus virajes en falso, ¿deberá nuestro siglo inquieto acusar tu cruel impotencia, o más bien la impotencia de tu misma edad? / El pasado te conoció benéfica, en aquellos tiempos de confusos rumores en que la Fe, antorcha de la Iglesia, era el guía de la razón. Heraldo del Dios de Libertad, a guisa de veloz relámpago que rasga la oscuridad, mostraste a los hombres ignota tierra donde resplandecía la verdad. / Tu nombre que lleva el brillo del Cielo ¿será quizás el juguete de hueras ilusiones? ¿Será la bandera de pasiones que huellan el Derecho y el Altar? ¿Veremos bajo sus pliegues a una horda salvaje que todo lo devasta, imponer doquiera el terror de su execrado yugo...?
⁷ I.e. the Andes mountain range.
⁸ "The Pampas" (from Quechua *pampa*, meaning 'plain') are the fertile South American lowlands that include parts of Argentina, Uruguay, and Brazil.
⁹ *Idem.*

¿Cuál es el noble canto que de repente y desde luenga distancia resuena en nuestras riberas como el eco de un mundo de luz, oración de profeta y voz que baja de los cielos? Es un himno semejante al canto de la naturaleza, cuando ésta se libra del invierno, y con majestuoso murmullo reclama horizontes más hermosos. Es una sinfonía que modula notas de lo alto, para festejar un mundo nuevo. Es el concentro de la paz en el orden. Cruza en alas de los vientos el Atlántico. Resuena en los riscos de la nevada Cordillera, en las extensas pampas, y en los estuarios matizados con reflejos encantadores...

Grande voz. Tú nos vienes a manera de soplo inmenso, corriente impetuosa, potencia irresistible que solevanta los océanos; como fuerzas del éter que incontenibles empujan los torbellinos.

Tú vienes de aquella zona feracísima donde vuela el rugiente ciclón, hijo del tórrido Ecuador...

Tu canto, como las voces de los antiguos profetas, resuena en las noches, domina en las tempestades con que atruena un cielo irritado; y desde lo alto prorrumpe con extraña armonía, diciéndonos: "Amor triunfante, alabanza eterna, visión de inmortalidad".

Es tu voz, ¡oh República!, serena en tu regocijo, y orando, inclinada la cabeza en los altares. El homenaje de amor que se prepara te conduce a la inmortalidad.

¡Oh Pueblo generoso!, ten orgullo de tus hijos, cuya gratitud sube hasta Dios, cual preludio melodioso del himno de los cielos triunfantes.

La probidad, la inteligencia, el brillo y honor del Estado, el Poder, Magistrados de la Republica, Parlamento que vela por sus leyes: todos juntan su alma y su voz en la noble fe católica y en el ardor patriótico. El septentrión, el austro, la costa, dignamente representados, ofrecen la imagen de la Patria, en el homenaje más imponente que haya visto nuestra edad atormentada.

Allí evocáis, ¡oh valientes!, a ese corazón cuya indomable confianza en Dios hizo brillar esplendente día en que la Fe, como flor del cielo por fin abierta, descansa en el Amor sobre las cumbres más luminosas.
Pensáis en ese firme Atleta, en García Moreno, el mártir puro, cuya mente hizo la conquista de un pueblo que asciende hasta el cenit, ennoblecido por el santo Amor. Conjuradas contra él en su delirio las sectas cobardes, armando el brazo de sus sicarios, feroces satélites del mal, se embriagaron con su sangre. La blasfemia, dejando huella en las faldas del nevado Chimborazo, impulsada por el mismo Infierno, inmoló al Héroe. Y éste, muriendo en la más hermosa lid, exclamó sublime: "Yo me voy pero Dios no muere". Ínclito Campeón, él se va, pero no muere por completo. Este día espléndido es obra suya. Un pueblo que tiene a Dios por herencia, he ahí su laurel eterno. En el sepulcro del ardiente iniciador ha de ser esculpida esta inscripción: "Mártir, él sucumbe; pero ha vuelto a levantarse lo caído, y enaltece a Dios su Salvador". Y su nombre ha sido recordado amorosamente por un pueblo en este día bendito. Es un poema divino. Es una resplandeciente diadema cuyo brillo no se apagará jamás…"

[10] *Idem*. p. 606 ff., October 1887.

[11] In the distress of the battle of Tolbiac against the Alamanni barbarians in the year 496, King Clovis, the first king of France and still a pagan, loudly invoked the God of Clotilda and the Christians. St. Clotilda was his Christian wife. He promised that if God would help to win that battle, he would convert to the Catholic Faith. God helped him to win the battle and thus he converted and led France to embrace the faith as well.

[12] *Idem*.

[13]Note added by the editor: "In 1973, encouraged by the Vatican to conform with *Dignitatis Humanae*, Colombia amended its constitution to state merely that Catholicism is the religion of the great majority of Colombians. This astonishing development, in which the Church voluntarily surrendered her privileged status appropriate to the 'true religion and the one Church of Christ' was repeated in Spain, Italy and Argentina. In the years immediately following Vatican II, Catholic nations across the world amended their constitutions in order to conform with the Council's teaching on religious liberty, which absolves the state from its obligation towards the Church and her Divine Founder, an obligation which exists because the reign of Christ the King does not stop at the doors of parliaments and legislatures, whether they deny His kingship or not.

"Archbishop Lefebvre said in his sermon during the Ordinations of June 29, 1976, at Ecône, Switzerland: 'They thought that they would attract the world by accepting the ideas of modern man… who is a liberal, who is a modernist, who is a man who accepts the plurality of religions, who no longer accepts the social kingship of our Lord Jesus Christ. This I have heard twice from the envoys of the Holy See, who told me that the social kingship of our Lord Jesus Christ was no longer possible in our time; that we must accept definitely the pluralism of religions. That is what they told me; that the encyclical *Quas Primas* which is so beautiful, on the social kingship of our Lord Jesus Christ, which was written by Pope Pius XI, would never be written today. That is what the official envoys of the Holy See said to me.'" (*A Bishop Speaks*, Kansas City, Angelus Press, 2007, p. 247.)

[14] See the magazine from Quito, *La Sociedad* (The Society), March 9, 1941, p. 3.

[15] The chronological list of Nations that have been consecrated to the Heart of Jesus was elaborated by Father Aurelio Aulestia, S. J., a specialist in topics related to the Divine Heart.

# Chapter 10
# Division among Catholics Ruined the Catholic Regime

In the year 1894, the war between China and Japan broke out. Officially notified of that event, the government of Chile declared itself neutral. Therefore, it could not sell Japan its cruiser named the *Esmeralda*, no matter how much it was interested in doing so. However, the government of Ecuador, which had not received official notification from the belligerents, could do a great favor in this respect to the nation that had always been a friend and ally. Ecuador would buy that ship and then sell it to Japan. This was done. What crime did the Ecuadorian government commit against national dignity? No crime appears anywhere.[1]

In Valparaiso the transfer of the cruiser *Esmeralda* took place through a contract of sale in absolutely juridical forms and procedures. Consequently, the Ecuadorian tricolor flag was raised on the mast of the warship, the *Esmeralda*. Was there any offense in this act against national decorum? It is not seen even with a microscope. Nevertheless, the enemies of the government of Ecuador, whose head was President Luis Cordero, raised a cry against it, saying that the honor of the country had been disregarded through the act they called "the crime of the sale of the flag." Actually, not even a hint of the sale of any flag really appeared, but rather the sale of a vessel by Chile, its purchase by Ecuador, and the sale of the same ship by Ecuador to Japan, moreover with juridical documents and absolute forms of contracts of sale. Cash payment and receipts were in the following chronological order:

On November 23, 1894, the Japanese representative, Kurino, paid three hundred thousand pounds sterling, which was received by Mr. Modesto Solorzano, the representative of Ecuador in New York. Seven days later, on the thirtieth of that month and year, Luis Noguera, the Consul of Ecuador in Valparaiso, paid two hundred twenty thousand pounds sterling to the government of Chile. Who obtained the eighty thousand pounds difference? Nobody. This dealt with simulated prices to cover up the negotiation in the international aspect, since without this profit it was not explicable why Ecuador bought a boat from Chile to sell it to Japan for the same price. It was said that Kurino actually paid the eighty thousand pounds. There is no proof. If it were true, the money would have vanished in the hands of Solorzano and unscrupulous subordinate agents. Friends and adversaries of President Cordero's regime are in agreement that neither the head of state, nor any member of his cabinet, nor Mr. Jose Maria Placido Caamano, governor of Guayaquil at that time, received a single cent.

Analogous cases are not rare, even with less juridical apparatus, without having roused any consternation or scandal. So, in October of 1862, Chile borrowed Ecuador's flag. In the war of the Moors against Spain, around the year 1924, England lent its flag—arms—to the former;[2] and around 1936, it did the same to the Republicans that were fighting against Generalissimo Francisco Franco, so that those arms would not fall into the hands of the Italian Dictator Mussolini, Franco's ally. So, many other nations in our time, great or small, have transported or do transport war material under a flag that is not their own to prevent capture. The government of Luis Cordero rightly said that regarding the use of flags the only thing forbidden is for a State to use another's flag without permission.

One year later, the Supreme Court of Justice, composed of individuals who had protested angrily against the alleged sale of the flag, now the masters of the Supreme government, declared that there was no place for a penal case against Luis Cordero and his associates. They wanted to go down in history as impartial and upright judges.

On December 3, 1894, the Ecuadorian flag was raised on the *Esmeralda*, and it left bound for one of the Galapagos Islands, where it received forty-three tons of coal at the State of Ecuador's expense. Was this expenditure perhaps covered by a portion of the eighty thousand pounds, if that really was the case?

When the cruiser arrived at the port of Honolulu, the Ecuadorian flag was lowered, and the Japanese flag was raised. The name "Yolanda" was given it and it joined the Japanese fleet.

Doctor Luis Cordero, in his speeches, used to speak like a Garcia Moreno. We have demonstrated this in the preceding chapters. In his private life he was an exemplary Catholic. But in the government of the nation he imitated Borrero, using silk reins with revolutionaries and the enemies of Holy Church. Just like Borrero, he was also an enemy of the Conservative Party, which advocated Garcia Moreno's system of a firm hand against anarchists and antichristian propagandists. Those in Cordero's faction were called "Progressivists." In the elections he had defeated Doctor Camilo Ponce Ortiz, leader of the Conservative Party; hence the animosity of the Conservatives towards the Progressivists became more acute. Consequently, the Conservatives joined the Alfarist

## Division among Catholics Ruined the Catholic Regime

liberals and Masons, to exaggerate "the disgrace" of selling the flag and to demand the resignation of Luis Cordero and his administration.

From the beginning of December 1894, mob riots against the current government followed one another in Guayaquil. Caamano asked for the intervention of the armed forces to dissolve the bands of guerilla fighters. But his commanding officer, Reinaldo Flores, answered that the troops were not meant for hindering the just venting of democracy. The aforesaid military man was a Progressivist.

Such lenience increased and the contagion of the revolutionaries' spirit spread. In Quito, seven thousand signatures were obtained against the alleged "regime of the flag" headed by Luis Felipe Borja and Camilo Ponce Ortiz, leaders of the Liberal and the Conservative Parties respectively.

In Guayaquil, three died and seven were wounded in a clash with the police. In Portoviejo armed guerilla bands were organized in the countryside.

In January of 1895 the new archbishop, Monsignor Pedro Gonzalez Calixto, promoted special worship of the Sacred Heart of Jesus, imploring peace. In February the special worship was transferred to the Church of Our Lady of Quinche in the capital city. But, would God force the freedom of those who, fancying themselves as exemplary Catholics, were obstinate in provoking war? Truly the immense evils that oppressed the country more and more on a greater scale were not so much a punishment from God as a product and effect of the envy and hate of very many cruel children of the Church. They paid no attention to the pastoral letters of the prelates. Monsignor Arsenio Andrado, Bishop of Riobamba said:

> Daily the image of God, which is the soul, is stained and dishonored with great sins and crimes. Religion and the priesthood are publicly insulted. The sacred mysteries are blasphemed in the **free press;** and no one protests. No one looks after the rights of God and his Church, publicly outraged and reviled. Do the interests of our Heavenly Country matter less than the interests of our earthly country?

There was a bloody battle in Guaranda, crowned with the triumph of the revolutionaries. In Quito on April 10, 1895, the Wednesday of Holy Week, a battle broke out in which more than forty corpses were left on the streets. Rifle in hand, the Chief of State himself, Luis Cordero, fought like a lion. He triumphed but ten days later he resigned from the Presidency with these words:

> I have incurred no blame. I acted licitly with right intentions. But if the honor of my country requires you to be unjust to me and my cabinet, do so opportunely. I will be sufficiently resigned to bear it. The attitude of the army has been worthy; and with their support I could continue in command. But I do not desire that my country's soil continue to be covered with blood through my fault.

If Cordero would have adopted power and rigor at the very beginning of the crisis the shedding of blood would have been less. Now he resigned so that the country would not continue shedding blood. It is a characteristic means of Progressivism: condescendence to crime, silk reins. Within a short time civil war would continue and blood would flow in torrents.

The vice-president of the republic, Doctor Vicente Lucio Salazar, occupied the presidential chair. He was a conspicuous member of the Conservative Party. In the mountains, calm was reestablished. But along the coast, the bands of guerrilla fighters continued with massacres and outbreaks of robbery. What a way to wash the stains from the flag! Manuel J. Calle, in spite of his liberal creed, wrote: "The flag that gave immense popularity to the revolution was an excellent pretext for committing numerous crimes." And we might add: the poor people let themselves be deceived by the ideas of honor and country which they understood one way and the liberal leaders in another, quite different way.

Especially along the coast, many liberals and Masons supported the candidacy of General Eloy Alfaro for chief of state, but not with elections; for such a legal expedient was synonymous with failure and defeat; but rather through arms and war. In the mountains the people were deceived, being told that Alfaro would not be a persecutor of the Church, since such conduct was absurd in Garcia Moreno's land. Nevertheless, a few anti-Alfarist liberals were not lacking, like Juan Benigno Vela from Ambato, who said: "The Indian Alfaro will not rise to power through my vote." Luis Felipe Borja sustained his own candidacy, whimsically stating, "Alfaro is worse than I am. He is the son of the Indian woman, Presentacion Delagado, who, in our midst, served as

## Division among Catholics Ruined the Catholic Regime 165

an Indian servant to a vice-consul from Spain, a certain Manuel Alfaro, who was Eloy's father."[3]

Since Vicente Lucio Salazar's government was weak and incapable of repressing outrages, a Committee of Notables was created in Guayaquil, made up of the top liberal leaders from Puerto and of two conservatives, with the object of safeguarding order and sponsoring the candidacy of Dario Morla for the Presidency. But another Dario—Dario Fiallos—had the ability to tell direct lies.[4] He seized the Alausi telegraph office. He transmitted these dispatches to Guayaquil: "The Interior is in the hands of the revolution. Colonel Antonio Bega is asking to be granted personal guarantees to lay down arms. The same should be done in Guayaquil, since fighting is now useless." This was all a lie. Nevertheless the hoax worked. The Governor of Guayaquil, Rafael Polit, member of the Conservative Party, and also the commander of arms of Guayaquil, Reinaldo Flores, fancying they were being respectful to public opinion, renounced their posts before the Committee of Notables.

The next day, June 5, 1895, the soldiers from the artillery barracks were indignant and protested against the puerile, cowardly resignation. Left deprived of their high-ranking officials, they abandoned the barracks and the city and took the road to the mountains to swell the ranks of the defenders of the legitimate government. The same procedure was adopted by the rest of the army units.

Then the reddest liberals penetrated the barracks, seized all the armaments and summoned the mob for the appointment of the chief of state of the republic, no longer in the person of the wishy-washy liberal Dario Morla, but in the person of a radical liberal Mason like Eloy Alfaro. In all, fifteen thousand seven hundred and eighty-four signatures in support of him were obtained, even those of numerous deceived Conservatives.

A cablegram notified Eloy Alfaro, who at the time was living in Managua, Central America. In the meantime, Mr. Ignacio Robles took charge of the civil and military headquarters for the province of Guayas. In Quito the news produced rejoicing in the liberals and some deluded Catholics. Monsignor Gonzalez Calixto wrote a pastoral letter on June fourteenth:

> The enemy knocks at the doors of the Republic of the Sacred Heart of Jesus. Scour the nations where Liberalism has penetrated, and you will find churches destroyed; priests persecuted, exiled and martyred; Sacraments profaned; marriages dissolved;

property seized; tyrannical governments given over to all the fury of anarchy; godless people; hapless generations; unrestrained passions; unprecedented vices; nameless scandals; the horror of death. Liberalism and Radicalism are the denial of the truth and the precocious affirmation of lies and error. Liberalism comes to break our Catholic unity...

In turn, Monsignor Pedro Schumacher, Bishop of Portoviejo, addressed the voice of alarm:

> Radicalism, thinking it has triumphed, knocks on the doors of Manabi. To the shout of "Long live Alfaro!" launched with deafening applause, the announcement is now greeted for a new order of things. The shout so often launched by town criers of current disturbances: **"Down with priests; death to Jesus Christ!"** seems like it will be accomplished. And not to leave you with the possibility of a doubt about what is to come, two agents have been sent to you which are the genuine expression of the radical program: dismal Masonry represented by an excommunicated individual,[5] and the profanation of the sanctuary, symbolized by an apostate priest[6]... Felicisimo Lopez and Manuel Ontaneda come to propose an alternative to you: Christ or the devil...

Let us listen to the expressions of the Most Illustrious Arsenio Andrade, Bishop of Riobamba:

> The present revolution is radical, the destroyer not only of political order, but also of social and religious order. This revolution is the same as that which triumphed in Colombia in 1863 through Cipriano Mosquera, the same that persecuted the Church of Colombia with tyrannical laws and persecuted and expelled bishops and clergy... Some virtuous Christian families are at present in the same state and disposition as many Catholic families of Colombia were when Mosquera rebelled in the radical revolution...

He agreed with the criteria of Wilfrido Loor, who said the following:

Since this nation had a profound religious spirit, Alfaro's small amount of piety frightened it. The nation was not, therefore, Alfarist, but had the desire for social change and to do away with certain decadent men then in power which enervated the defense of the nation. And perhaps unwittingly, it unconsciously desired that Alfaro would be the winner... Progressivism had formed managers of public finances to direct the Nation in a prosperous era, but not men who knew how to sacrifice themselves in adversity for the good of the nation. The Conservatives had not operated during recent years and they lacked men to direct a campaign successfully...[7]

The situation was similar in the year 1869 when General Urbina wanted to usurp the Supreme Command, availing of a revolution. The Constitutional President, Javier Espinosa, was incapable of hindering the revolution due to his lack of political vision and weakness of character. And then Garcia Moreno deposed that inept president and flung the detestable Urbina far away. But now there was no strong, sagacious leader.

On June 18, 1895, General Eloy Alfaro reached port at Guayaquil. A large multitude shouted, "Long live Liberalism! Long live the Old Fighter! Down with the Big Ring!"[8] In the midst of popular enthusiasm, the Caudillo went to the Governor's Palace. He was fifty-three years old. He had rugged features; was short of stature; had wide shoulders; bronzed skin; close-cut short hair, already prematurely white; lively and penetrating eyes; a wide and clear forehead; wide nose; thick lips especially the lower one; gray mustache and goatee; wore a frock coat, white vest, and sported a gold-handled cane and a Panama hat. The multitude clamored, "Let Alfaro speak!" He came out onto the balcony. Applause. He wanted to speak but could not. He stuttered and kept quiet definitively. Liberals of the pen were disillusioned. In his place some of his followers give speeches. A printed proclamation also circulated on the night of that same day. Without a shadow of a doubt with the help of some man of letters, for Alfaro's literary culture was null. Let us hear these expressions:

> The country is exhausted from the Theocratic regime. I come without hate or vengeance to give a fraternal embrace to all my fellow countrymen. I vouch for victory with my head...

The following day wreaths of flowers began to arrive at the dwelling of the Old Fighter. With political finesse he had them taken and placed at the foot of the statue of the Sacred Heart of Jesus in the Church of San Francisco. It was the eve of the feast day of the Republic's Celestial Patron. In the Corpus Christi procession the troops rendered honors to the Most Blessed Sacrament, in accordance with Garcia Moreno's laws. The newspaper entitled *El Monitor Popular*[9] dedicated its editorial columns to the Reign of the Heart of Jesus in Ecuador, and ended with the well-known hymn, *Corazón Santo, tú reinarás; tú nuestro encanto siempre serás.*[10]

In Quito, since his softening of the brain was getting worse, President Lucio Salazar had resigned the Supreme Command to dedicate himself to dying well. Mr. Carlos Mateus Pacheco replaced him in all legality, for he had been president of the senate.

Meanwhile the situation of the Catholics in Manabi was becoming desperate due to the increase of Alfarist guerrilla bands, the prolonged lack of communication with the capital of the Republic, the scarcity of supplies and ammunition for the troops, and finally the lack of money for their food and wages. After much pondering, one of the top commanders, Ricardo Cornejo, approached Monsignor Schumacher, Bishop of Portoviejo, and told him:

> If you stay, they will assassinate you. Plans for this crime have been made in Jipijapa, in Chone and in Manta on board the Cotopaxi. They do not leave the slightest doubt in this respect. You will be a martyr, and we would not like to deprive you of this happiness. But, as a prelate, you are obliged to avoid such a horrendous sacrilege, for which your diocesan priests will be falsely accused. God commands us to be simple like doves, but with the prudence of serpents. In the Roman persecution the Christians who went and provoked the pagans in their temples and were put to death were deprived of the glory of martyrdom. Maybe it would not be virtue for you to expose yourself to their killing you by remaining in Manabi.

The plan of the military leaders was for Monsignor and all the clergy to leave Manabi for Quito through the woods. The troops would march with them and guard them. The bishop and some priests abandoned Portoviejo on horseback the morning of June twentieth. The inhabitants contemplated the exodus with truly incredible indifference,

## Division among Catholics Ruined the Catholic Regime 169

given the enormous amount of benefits that His Excellency had rendered to the immense diocese for ten years: primary and secondary schools, seminaries, printing presses, newspapers, the introduction of missionaries and religious for teaching, the construction of churches, roads and bridges, the influx of enormous monetary alms from Germany and other foreign countries.

A few hours later the troops also left. Two days later, that is, June twenty-second, was the Feast of the Sacred Heart of Jesus. Monsignor was in the neighborhood of Junin in the company of the battalion. Further on, in the village of Calceta the priests also left Manabi. One of the guerilla bands entered the latter town and started to insult the clergy and the religious who ran a school. They shot at, and hit the doors of the convent with machetes. They uttered blasphemies: "Death to Christ; long live Ramos Iduarte!"

Ramos Iduarte, a Mexican, had been made the leader of the guerilla bands of Manabi. In a skirmish against government forces two months previously he launched his favorite blasphemy, "Death to Christ!" And at that instant he received a bullet in his heart and was dead.

Government troops went to Calceta with the determination of occupying it by blood and firearms. Bishop Schumacher was in their company. The combat began. The victory delayed in being decided.

Meanwhile, twenty-five outlaws assaulted the spacious convent of Calceta. Sister Genoveva raised the North American flag, for they were all of that nationality. A useless resort! The outlaws broke the doors and invaded the cells and chapel shouting, "Long live Liberalism! Long live Alfaro! Long live Ramos Iduarte! Death to Christ! Death to the Curuchupas!" [11] They rushed forward inside the chapel, swinging machetes or rifles against the priests who were praying there. The nuns intervened, raising their arms and standing in the way. Nevertheless, the seminarian Eduardo Dickert was wounded in the head and fell unconscious to the floor. A machete blow was aimed at Father Herbrand's throat, but was deflected by Mother Genoveva's arm, who shouted, "For Jesus Christ's sake, do not kill this priest." The fanatic answered, "Death to Christ!"

They dragged Fathers Herbrand and Haecker by the feet, hitting their heads on the stairs. Father Haecker continued being dragged through the streets and received blows from rifle butts and was shoved. The victim questioned, "O child of God, you do not know me nor do I know you. Then, why do you mistreat me?" The reply was, "Because you are a priest." Father Avinonet was another of those dragged and ended up hung upside down from a beam, receiving sharp blows on his head. In any case the nuns had persisted in intervening, and therefore they suffered slaps on the face and their habits were torn. Locked finally in jail, they were the victims of other abuses and the last gunshots. Father Avinonet was bleeding profusely.

The bandits returned to the chapel, destroyed the corpus of the crucifix, and stole everything they thought would be useful; always to the shouts of "Long live Alfaro! Long live Ramos Iduarte! Long live liberty! Death to Christ!" The persecutors of the Church are God's instruments for the martyrdom of good Christians. But afterwards they have to suffer their punishment from Heaven. Such was Mr. Medardo Alfaro, one of the Coryphaei [12] of the sacrilegious outrage. Within seventeen years he was to be the victim of a shooting, dragged through the streets of Quito, together with his companions in crime, stripped of his clothing and burnt to ashes.

The diabolic drama of Calceta was upset presently with shouts of "Long live Religion!" launched by the loyal troops who conquered in battle and brought Monsignor with them. Of the liberal combatants twenty died, of the Catholics not even one died, although they had attacked unarmed. This prodigy is attributed to the Heart of Jesus on whose feast day they had engaged in battle.

The next day, at four in the morning, a voracious fire took place in the town. Was it an intentional work of the revolutionaries? So it is conjectured. Did they perhaps suppose that the Government troops, to put out the fire, would neglect their weapons, which could be taken to aid the rebels? Commander Alvarez, the first officer in command of the battalion, was aware of the probable ruse, and did everything possible to extinguish the calamity, but without disregarding the armament in the least. Because of the abundant timber and thatched roofs, thirty houses were reduced to ashes.

At five in the morning the military, the bishop and the rest of the priests began the march, initially along traversable paths, later through fields and crossing virgin jungle, headed for Santo Domingo de los Colorados.[13] The route was the same one that Garcia Moreno had wanted to make into a very good road, to be finished in a little more than six months of work. But he was hindered from doing this work by the machete of Masonry.[14]

After twenty-eight days of clearing the way for themselves amidst immense hardships, they finally reached the outskirts of Quito. It was

## Division among Catholics Ruined the Catholic Regime 171

July twentieth. The Archbishop came to meet them, the representative of the executive branch, the president of the municipal council, the governor, clergy, auxiliary civil servants, soldiers and a mass of people. There were arches of triumph at intervals with the Papal, Ecuadorian and German flags. Bells pealed. "Hurrahs," acclamations of *Viva*,[15] and all kinds of ovations! A crown was placed on the forehead of each soldier. The leaders were decorated with gold medals; the officers, with silver; and all the soldiers, with bronze.

On the sixth of August it had been twenty years since the death of Garcia Moreno. Many buildings in Quito awoke with black flags, or the tricolor national flag at half-mast and with black ribbons attached to it.[16] The Archbishop once again exhorted all to pray insistently for the triumph of the good cause.

Prelates and clergy continued preaching that the war was unleashed against the Catholic religion. It was demonstrated by the revolutionaries' cries, "Let Christ die." Nevertheless, hate between Progressive and Conservative Catholics continued to rise. Before, there were Conservatives who said, "As a last resort let Alfaro assume power, so that the Sly Fox,[17] Luis Cordero, will fall." Now the Progressivists retorted, "Rather the liberals; rather Alfaro than Camilo Ponce."[18]

On that same day, the sixth of August, gunfire broke out in the town of San Miguel de Chimbo. The legitimate government triumphed. In fact, Colonel Julio del Hierro, a Conservative, continued controlling that town. Besides, the adversary leader himself, Colonel Vernaza, recognized that his battalion, Babahoyo, had been destroyed, the Vinces was in ruins, the Medardo Suarez and the Guaranda were decimated. Well then, the next day, Colonel Julio del Hierro and his valiant men abandoned San Miguel and retreated. Who ordered that unjustifiable retreat? It was ordered by General Jose Maria Sarasti, Director of War for the legitimate Government but a bitter enemy of the Conservatives, who would have strengthened their political predominance if the Alfarists had been defeated. In fact, the current president of the republic was Carlos Mateus Pacheco of the Conservative Party. Then, why was Sarasti appointed? A governmental error! On the other hand, the Conservatives lacked good generals. The result was that General Veranza entered San Miguel de Chimbo as if it were his own house, and sent a report of his triumph to Guayaquil.[19]

# Endnotes

[1] Gomezjurado, *Vida de Garcia Moreno*, vol. 11, p. 181 ff.
[2] The Rif War, also called the Second Moroccan War (1920 – 1926).
[3] Biographical data about Alfaro's previous years appear in our volume 3, p. 456; in our volume 4, p. 328; in our volume 7, p. 36; and in our volume 9, pp. 338 and 391.
[4] In the Spanish, it is said that he had the ability to lie *a plomo*, ("with a plumb line") which is a Masonic expression that indicates that something is very much in place, especially that a Mason has fulfilled his current obligations to his Lodge. So there may be an inference here to say that he can lie like a good Mason! [Editor's note]
[5] I. e. Felicisimo Lopez, who had been accused of atheism and was excommunicated by Bishop Schumacher for publishing an article in which he referred to Catholicism as a sect (suggesting that it was one among many religions). (A Kim Clark, *The redemptive work: railway and nation in Ecuador : 1895-1930* (Latin American silhouettes Series: Studies in History and Culture, Wilmington, SR Books, 2001), p. 59.)
[6] I. e. Manuel Ontaneda, who joined the revolution and served as chaplain for Alfaro's army. (Alfredo Pareja Diezcanseco, *La Hoguera Bárbara II: Vida de Eloy Alfaro*, (Ariel, 1970), p. 265.)
[7] *Vida de General Eloy Alfaro* (*Life of General Eloy Alfaro*), p. 362.
[8] See endnote 18 below.
[9] *The Popular Monitor*.
[10] "Holy Heart, Thou shalt reign; Thou shalt ever be our delight."
[11] An indigenous term referring to members of the Conservative Party of Ecuador or those deemed to be "ultra-conservatives." The word is a mixture of Spanish and Quechua (the native language of the central Andes of South America), and means "a person who lives according to the letter as dictated by the priest of his village." It is derived from the Spanish words, *rabo de cura*, meaning "the priest's tail."
[12] Or "leaders." "Coryphaei" is derived from the Greek word, *koruphaios*, meaning "leader."
[13] I. e. the fourth largest city in Ecuador.
[14] Loor, p. 313 ff. *Historia del Ecuador, en Tiempo de la Republica* [*History of Ecuador in the Time of the Republic*] by Father Jose Legohuir, S. J., vol. 3, p. 458 ff. About the road through the jungle, see my vol. 8, p. 324.
[15] "Long live..."
[16] In Spanish they are called *crespónes negros*, which refers to the black ribbons usually attached to flags or clothing when mourning some tragic event. Since 1913, I have spoken with Jesuits, advanced in age, in Quito and heard them say that for twenty years that capital decked their houses with black flags on the anniversary of Garcia Moreno's assassination. But in 1896 that custom

# Division among Catholics Ruined the Catholic Regime 173

began to wane because of threats of fines against whoever raised such flags of mourning.

[17] *El Morlaco.*

[18] Throughout the pages by Wilfridod Loor the hatred of the Conservatives against Cordero, the Progressivist, is felt. The phrase, "Even though Alfaro comes to power, just so that the Sly Fox falls," was quoted to me by Mrs. Amelia Salazar de Salazar, daughter of Doctor Vicente Lucio Salazar. She quoted it to me in Sangolqui, about the year 1940. In the presidential elections Camilo Ponce Ortiz was defeated by Luis Cordero. It explains the dislike of the former for the latter. President Antonio Flores, founder of Progressivism, had a moral influence in Cordero's triumph. This Flores-Cordero support and machinery is what was called "Argolla" [the Big Ring] in a hateful and derogatory manner.

[19] Loor, p. 388 ff. On page 359, Rafael Polit appears as an Alfarist, not so much for love of Alfaro as for his hatred for Progressivism.

# Chapter 11
# October 21, 1900: De-consecration

At the beginning of the year 1895, a Masonic Congress took place in the Honduran town of Amapala, made up of Cipriano Castro, who at the time was the President of the Republic of Venezuela; Santos Zelaya, President of Nicaragua; Eloy Alfaro; Uribe y Uribe; Vargas Santos; Herrera; and other Central American individuals of lesser importance. The fruit of the reports and discussions was what is called the "Pact of Amapala." Its content was:

To promise under oath to lend reciprocal aid with the object of forming a common political cause, and to revolutionize the nations by all means they had at hand until they obtained success in Ecuador, in Colombia and in Costa Rica, Republics in which the supreme power of Masonry did not rule.[1]

Eloy Alfaro was the one who took advantage of the first fruits of the Pact of Amapala by obtaining better quality Krupp[2] cannons and modern rifles, thanks to the support promised under oath by General Santos Zelaya, President of Nicaragua. For spending on the campaign, he obtained a public loan from the banks for two hundred thousand sucres, equivalent to two hundred thousand dollars in those times.[3]

Since he was a man with the gifts of a *caudillo*, or warlord, he went ahead and placed his army in the middle of the mountains, in the town of Guamote, at near nine thousand eight hundred and fifty feet (three thousand meters) above sea level. In order not to frighten the Catholics, he had the cannons blessed by the parish priest of that community. And on the tenth of August, the anniversary of the first proclamation of independence, his battalions attended the Mass of thanksgiving.[4]

In Quito, Doctor Vicente Lucio Salazar, having slightly recovered from his illness, returned to take the reins of the Supreme Government and appointed for the Ministry of the Interior, the expert jurist, Aparicio Ribadeneira, a conservative and adversary of the Progressivists. Some young men, staunch Catholics, had enlisted in the army voluntarily. And what about Garcia Moreno's son, Gabriel Garcia Alcazar, a youth of twenty-five years of age...? His father had cherished the idea of making him a worthy successor, a Catholic leader. And to that end he gave him a solid education, yet compatible with the early years of his childhood.[5] Fatherless before he was six years old, Garcia Alcazar completed his primary education in the school of the De la Salle Brothers. At eight years of age he made his First Communion and was given the gift of a book in French which was a complement to the *History of the Church* written by Father Rohrbacher. The concordat inaugurated by the President-martyr in 1862 appeared on page two hundred forty-two. On the first page was a dedication by Father Dominico Jacinto La Camera written in his own hand in Quito, June 9, 1878:

"To the boy, Gabriel Garcia Moreno. In eternal memory of his First Communion." Then in Latin was verse twenty-five of chapter forty-nine of Genesis. It is translated in these terms:

"The God of thy father shall be thy helper, and the Almighty shall bless thee with the blessings of heaven above, with the blessings of the deep that lieth beneath." They were the words with which the Patriarch Jacob blessed his most beloved son, Joseph.

Around the year 1881 Garcia Alcazar began his secondary education at the Jesuit College of Saint Gabriel, named in honor of the distinguished President who founded it.[6] There the young man was outstanding among the best students and on at least two occasions obtained the first prize. In the University he was also among the best students. In his handwritten class papers, he signed himself Gabriel Garcia Moreno, and even in the flourish of his signature, he imitated his father exactly. He did not take the final exam to receive the title of Doctor of Jurisprudence, which does him no credit. Strictly speaking, he did not need it because caring for and administrating his mother's estates kept him honorably busy.[7]

He did not enlist among the combatants for God and Country, which does him no credit either.[8] The author attributes this to his mother, since he was her only son and support. Whoever knew him extolled the respect and submission that gentleman had to her for this reason.

The loyal army camped at Riobamba where discord and arguments between Conservatives and Progressivists continued stridently in spite of the teachings and pleadings of the bishops who urged concord for the sake of the Catholic religion and the nation. On August fourteenth it left the city and headed for the battle ground. In the neighborhood of Lican, the Garcia Moreno column advanced to explore the area and encountered the "Vencedores"[9] battalion, the vanguard of the enemy army. It was two-thirty in the afternoon. The battle began. The "Quito" and "Patria"[10] battalions came in defense of the government. The "Chimborazo"[11] and the "Daule"[12] came to fortify the "Vencedores." Later, two

*Gabriel Garcia Alcazar,
son of the President-martyr*

other units intervened: the "Sucre"[13] and the "Vengadores,"[14] the first in favor of the government and the second against it.[15]

The fighting was bitter. Eloy Alfaro in person went through the different groups of soldiers and attended to reinforcing the weakest or most decimated. "Take care of yourself, my General," his men told him when he entered the places most peppered with bullets by the enemy. But he answered, "My boys, the bullets don't touch me." His courage, serenity and presence of mind are undisputable, but victory did not smile on him. And after nearly four hours of fighting, the liberal troops had to abandon the trenches which the government troops occupied. The latter ceased to pursue the enemy, not so much because night had come as because General Sarasti, the leader of the government troops, had not indicated anything beyond a general plan.

The Alfarist side recognized its difficult situation. General Ulpiano Paez from the "Vencedores" said that the liberal troops retreated because munitions ran out. Commander Campi from the "Daule" battalion confessed that after three and a half hours of shooting, he had to abandon the field to Sarasti's soldiers. They were in agreement that the troops from Quito took possession of the trenches, in spite of the heroism of the "Vengadores" who had to fight hand to hand.

The following facts are against General Sarasti:

> Only some eight hundred and fifty men from the government forces had fought. Nevertheless, they took over the enemy trenches. Why didn't Sarasti support these valiant men with at least part of the two thousand soldiers in the rearguard?
> 
> The result of the battle was more advantageous to the government troops than to the Alfarists. Maintaining those advantages and keeping the trenches would have been sensible so that the next morning they could resume the battle with greater optimism. However, Sarasti ordered those brave men to abandon the trenches and retreat from that scene of the war. They protested and refused to obey. A second command came through General Miguel Paez: "Obey and observe discipline. Sarasti is the chief and he knows how to direct operations." They obeyed but launched shouts of rage, spite and accusations against the Commander in Chief.[16]
> 
> The retreated men interrogated the chief, "Why did you order us to retreat?"

"So that you would go fight against General Vernaza's battalion in Chuquipocyo."

They left for that place and found no enemy to fight.

The next day, August fifteenth, early in the morning, six cannon balls shot by Alfaro incited the battle to be resumed. The government troops wanted to return to the field of honor, but there were only a handful of soldiers. And the bulk of the army? It had marched to Riobamba. Angry voices exploded, "Treason, treason!" The shouts disseminated throughout all the units. They looked for Sarasti to quarter or shoot him, but could not find him. He had gone into hiding. This is the sad outcome of the battle which had taken place in a region called "Gatazo" and was thus named the "Battle of Gatazo."

Monsignor Pedro Schumacher, Bishop of Portoviejo, wrote, "The defeat at Gatazo was not the fault of the government troops from Quito, but rather Sarasti's infamous treason." Gonzalez Suarez had this same criterion, according to the writer Pedro Monsalve's assertion. Wilfrido Loor shared this opinion which he based on the following: "A victory in Gatazo would have strengthened the Conservative Party, to which the current President, Lucio Salazar, belonged. General Sarasti was of the Progressivist Party and did not want to give the victory to the former."

Alfaro was puzzled. He feared an ambush. He knew that the Conservative troop from Quito would at least resist in Riobamba. That was quite obvious, for a battalion of reinforcements had just arrived from the north, the same one that had left Manabi accompanying Bishop Schumacher. But, alas! Its commanding officer, Jose Alvarez, was not with them. He had been shot by some liberals who were hiding in ambush when he was passing through Ambato. Now Sarasti did not hinder the troops from returning to Quito. In fact it would have been useless or disastrous to continue fighting under the command of a completely discredited and loathed leader.[17]

When the disaster was discovered in the capital of the republic, the valetudinarian, Lucio Salazar, resigned irrevocably, and following legal procedures, Doctor Aparicio Ribadeneira, who, as was said above, belonged to the Conservative Party, assumed the presidency.

On the advice of accredited ecclesiastics, Bishop Schumacher left Quito for the north and sought refuge in Colombia. He settled for a long time in the town called Samaniego where he constructed buildings for the apostolate, which have both religious as well as cultural importance. Faced with the fury of the liberals in Manabi, the Franciscan nuns who ran a school in Chone also fled to Colombia. The Benedictine nuns of Rocafuerte, Calceta and Jipijapa returned to the United States. The priests of the Sacred Heart returned to France. The parish priests from Portoviejo and Pajan embarked for Europe. All priests had to flee. The parish priest from Rocafuerte, whose last name was Rieger, on the verge of being assassinated, was eventually able to flee. Father Avinonet, after having recovered from his wounds, also went to exercise his apostolate in Colombia. Ten years of the episcopate and sacrifices disappeared in a moment. Manabi, which was advancing with giant steps under the protection of Catholicism and the leadership of a genius like Bishop Schumacher, regressed under Alfaro almost to the extent of savagery. It remained without schools, without priests. And churches like the cathedral of Portoviejo were converted into horse stables.[18]

With keen instinct, Canon Jose Maria Terrazas was sure that liberal Masonry would also persecute Garcia Moreno's memory. Consequently he arranged for the removal of the President-martyr's remains from their hiding place in the Cathedral to conceal them in a more discreet and secret place.[19] In what ingenious way did he carry out the transfer? The details are unknown for sure. During the 1940's, Father Antonio Benitez, well known for his pronounced limp and ever present cane, and very likeable for his virtues and good manners, said to the author:[20]

> Garcia Moreno's remains were wrapped in an enormous, thick rug and the voluminous roll was transported by Indian porters through the public streets in midday.

Mr. Jose Maria Lazcano Orbe enjoyed the trust and particular esteem of Gabriel Garcia Moreno Alcazar,[21] whom he called his *"patron"* or "employer." Now this Mr. Lazcano told the author in more than one interview, "My *patron* was upset that the transfer of his father's remains should have taken place without his being informed. He knew that Rafael Varela was one of those who had helped Canon Terrazas in that venture, and for that reason he showed him greater affection and esteem than ever."[22]

On his part, President Aparicio Ribadeneira judged armed resistance in Quito to be impossible. Therefore, on the morning of August twenty-fifth he left the capital in the company of a party of soldiers and sixty mules loaded with ammunition. After a nine day march they arrived at Tulcan where he cherished vain hopes. Since Quito was without a government, the liberals proclaimed General Alfaro the supreme chief there; and as he was still in Riobamba, they named Doctor Alban Mestanza as civil and military chief of the province of Pichincha. Mestanza declared freedom for all political prisoners, even Roberto Andrade, Garcia Moreno's assassin.

The vanguard of the victorious army did not take long to arrive in Quito. And a few directed their steps to the statue of Major General Sucre, supposing it to be that of Garcia Moreno. They showered insults upon it and began to break off the marble plates with their honorific inscriptions. Soon the liberals of Quito made them realize their mistake and told them that the small pyramid with Garcia Moreno's image was thirty-three yards away, close to Saint Dominic's Arch. The destroyers ran there and repeating the preceding curses, broke off the honorific marble and the medallion from the bust of Garcia Moreno. Thus the obelisk looked ugly, with cavities or incredible holes.

In the main hall of the University the enormous painting of Garcia Moreno was removed from its place of honor.[23]

Eloy Alfaro entered Quito on September fourth, with no solemnity or multitudes to acclaim him. There were three or four speeches by his partisans. But the liberal press of Guayaquil lied, saying that the allocutions totaled the number of thirty-seven. Alfaro did not answer them, for he did not have enough ability. His troops occupied the monasteries of the Dominican, Augustinian, Mercedarian and Franciscan friars, converting them into barracks.[24]

The Usurper ordered Gabriel Garcia Alcazar to be put into prison. What was he accused of? Of nothing! Undoubtedly it was presumed that such a gentleman, by being the son of the greatest of all Ecuadorians, could be a dangerous element for the prevailing regime. The ground floor of his house was now occupied by the *Garroteros*.[25] The persecuted man managed to get a message to his cousin, Neptali Bonifaz Ascasubi, who went into the street covered with a waterproof cape, for a heavy downpour was then falling. He boldly opened a way among the soldiers and went upstairs where Gabriel was. It was the first time the *Garroteros*, and even the people of Quito, had ever seen a waterproof cape like this, brought from France by Mr. Bonifaz. So the military men identified this especially with Bonifaz.

Gabriel Garcia covered himself with his cousin's waterproof cape, and with the greatest naturalness walked through the throng of soldiers, went out into the street and made his way to his cousin's house. Note that the two cousins were tall young men with little difference in age.

When the squad forced entry to the upper floor, they found Neptali Bonifaz. Brother Alfaro, the Mason, furiously threatened to confiscate the Bonifaz-Ascasubi fortune. But the mother of young Neptali, Mrs. Josefina Ascasubi de Bonifaz, sent him the warning that this fortune was under the protection of the Government of Peru, since her husband was of Peruvian nationality. Then Brother Alfaro, recalling that Peru's Masonry was above Ecuador's, abstained from continuing his threats. At that time it was more advantageous to be Peruvian.

The pursued Gabriel Garcia Alcazar fled to Quinche where he spent the night hiding in the side chapel of the miraculous statue of the Blessed Virgin, thanks to the exquisite carefulness of the priest. From there he left for Guachala, accompanied by his cousin Neptali. He spent a whole month at that farm. His favorite pastime was hunting, in which he displayed his ability to handle arms and his good aim, which would soon be useful to him for the guerrilla campaign.[26]

From Guachala, bordering the eastern mountain range, he arrived at his "Cumbujin" hacienda in the province of Cotopaxi. There he could easily be safe from government persecution.

On September thirteenth, Alfaro visited the Panopticon[27] and freed more than seventy prisoners confined there for misdemeanors. Naturally they went out into the streets shouting, "Long live Alfaro!" The most thankful one wrote on the door of the jail, "Long live our Caudillo!"

Twelve days later the first edition of the newspaper entitled *La Ley*[28] appeared, in which its editor, Victor Vivar, making use of freedom of the press, expression, thought and conscience, so much vaunted by the liberal regime, said that the liberals had conquered on the battlefield but not in regard to reason and justice. The people did their utmost to buy that newspaper. The Dictator, inflamed with rage, made prisoners of its writers, Pablo Borja and Leon Vivar. The next day the second edition came out with these expressions:

> The will of the supreme chief overruled the principles of science, the dictates of justice, the calculations of expediency, and opened the doors of the house intended for the punishment and reformation of delinquents. The ability to forgive should exist in every civilized country, and it exists in ours. But the foundation of this ability is none other than justice. If justice is broken, the exercise of that faculty is an act of tyranny... The freedom conceded to Roberto Andrade should have its corollary...

The Usurper ordered a squad of people armed with clubs to the clergy's printing house, led by a layman, Francisco Ribadeneira. And the printing house was turned into a pile of debris by force of the volley of blows it received. Immediately afterwards the *Garroteros* invaded the adjacent bishop's palace and set the extremely valuable archive on fire. They seized Monsignor Gonzalez Calixto, made him kneel and obliged him to shout, "Long live Alfaro!" The innocent victim said, "May he live until he dies," and the tormentors were satisfied with that. Let us listen to His Excellency the Archbishop in his own words:

> I should have died on the memorable night of Thursday the twenty-fifth (of September), because innumerable daggers and machetes, in the hands of men drunk with liquor and satanic fury, fell on my head and all around me to tear me to pieces... But the Sacred Host was exposed in the main chapel and the faithful were praying for me. Those prayers certainly prevented my death. They did not kill me because the palm of martyrdom is not bestowed by Our Lord God upon everyone. In the midst of the danger the thought was consoling me that I was going to die for the Church...

In January of 1896, the President of the Municipal Council of Quito asked the students of the De La Salle Brothers to sing the glories of Alfaro when this Caudillo returned from Guayaquil to the capital. Those distinguished educators refused. Then Manuel Franco, a kind of leader of the Alfarist Gestapo, ordered the *Garroteros* to invade the Brothers' school grounds and mistreat them through actions. Note that those *Garroteros* were nothing other than soldiers disguised as civilians, and they passed themselves off as the people: the people of Quito, the people of Riobamba, the people of Cuenca.

Those religious took refuge in time: from the French in the embassy of their country, from Ecuadorians in the convents of the Mercedarians, of Saint Francis, and of Don Bosco. One thousand five hundred students were left in the street. The persecution spread to all of Ecuador and of the thirteen schools run by the Brothers, only the ones in Latacunga, Cuenca and Azogues remained in operation.

Here it is appropriate to cite the following data taken from the "1926-1927 Masonic Annual," printed in Guayaquil, pages 104 and 105:

> It is only since the Liberal Party returned to power, embodied in the great figure of the Old Fighter, Brother Caballero Cadosh, thir-

tieth degree Mason, General Eloy Alfaro, that some Masons have formed an association and on January 31, 1897, established the "Luz del Guayas,[29] No. 10" under the jurisdiction of the Very Respectable Grand Lodge of Peru, which granted a charter to it on April 2, 1897.

Chile's Masonic magazine, entitled *La Cadena de la Union*,[30] sang congratulations in these terms:[31]

> Masonic Lodge of Ecuador. This great National Masonic Lodge does not exist and Masonry is forbidden and punished with very severe penalties. Fortunately the triumph of our dear Brother Alfaro will bring prosperous and happy days to the Order. Nevertheless, the persecution of the clergy is working in Guayaquil. And now we can proclaim loudly, "The *Luz del Guayas* Masonic Lodge under the dependency of the Grand Masonic Lodge of Peru." The former lodge did not have a fixed residence. Its archives are in Peru hidden from Jesuit espionage. The venerable master invited them to a specified place, taking the charter, and there the Workshop operated. Oh, how different it will be now, thanks to the triumph of liberty personified in the unbeaten Brother Alfaro!

Did Brother Alfaro perhaps imagine that the Christian Brothers were Brothers from some Masonic Lodge?

Father Juan Bautista Menten had been Dean of the Polytechnic founded by Garcia Moreno, and moreover, the builder and Director of the Astronomical Observatory of Quito. He was in Guayaquil in February of the same year, 1896. To avoid being abused by Brother Alfaro's *Garroteros*, he left Ecuador and sought refuge in Colombia.

Roberto Andrade, Garcia Moreno's assassin, was rewarded with the post of director of the School of Art in Portoviejo, where, making use of the printing press left behind by Bishop Schumacher, he edited his book entitled *El Seis de Agosto*,[32] full of innumerable errors and calumnies.[33]

Abelardo Moncayo, also an assassin of the President-martyr, after twenty years of life in dens and hiding places, was now the governor of the province of Imbabura. In agreement with Brother Alfaro, he ordered the Capuchins to leave Ibarra in six hours. It was March 16, 1896. Of what were they accused? Of causing the guerrilla warfare.[34] The terrorist Manuel Franco threatened, "I will have half the city shot, if the fanatics try to oppose the expulsion." At eleven o'clock at night and in the midst of a downpour, the religious emerged from their convent.

Placed in the center of an escort of seventy drunken men armed to the teeth, they marched on foot heading for Colombia. When they arrived at Tulcan, the Capuchins from this city joined them and they crossed the border.

To mitigate the fury of the Catholic people, Alfaro assisted at the Holy Week religious ceremonies, the feast day of Blessed Mariana de Jesus and that of the Sacred Heart, patron of Ecuador.[35]

On February 18, 1896, Doctor Pablo Herrera, Garcia Moreno's famous friend and collaborator, died. The next day Father Manuel Proano pronounced the funeral prayer. Victor Leon Vivar, Vicente Enriquez and Telmo Viteri spoke in El Tejar cemetery and were accused of being anti-liberals. The Dictator ordered them to be put in prison. Leon Vivar fled in time. Enriquez and Viteri were taken prisoner. In jail they were subjected to a torture invented by the liberals: ice water baths at eight o'clock at night as well as at five o'clock in the morning.

Flyers were published in Mr. Manuel Flor's print shops that were not to Alfaro's liking. He ordered his *Garroteros* to destroy that printing press, and that gentleman to be put into prison. That outrage took place on February twenty-first.[36]

The liberals stole furniture, foodstuffs and agricultural machinery from the Cumbijin hacienda, whose owner was Mariana Alcazar, Garcia Moreno's widow. The Governor of Latacunga, an individual named Narvaez, took her cattle, had them butchered in Saquisili, and the meat was sold for the benefit of that official.[37]

On the fifteenth, sixteenth, seventeenth and eighteenth of May, 1896, popular elections took place for the representatives of the Constituent Congress. In a great number of towns the urns were transported to the military barracks. And everywhere the only electors were the soldiers and the *Garroteros*. This electoral farce lasted for the period of forty-five years. This ignominy was recognized by the liberals themselves, who used to say, "We must not lose through ballots what we won with bayonets." As was obvious, only liberals were elected.

In the month of June, Canons Juan de Dios Campusano and Jose Maria Terrazas were sent into exile, as well as the priests, Father Jose Joaquin Borja and Father Ulpiano Perez Quinonez, and the gentlemen Jose Modesto Espinosa and Carlos Ordonez Munoz, together with their two brothers, Alejandro and Gabriel.[38]

In the province of Azuay, at Carlos Ordonez Lazo's hacienda, the "Machangara," the soldiery did not leave even a single piece of furniture or a single plant in good condition. From Benigno Jara's farm, they took seventy head of cattle, thirty beasts of burden, and all the pigs, goats, turkeys, hens, furniture, books and documents. And, as a bonus, they destroyed the alfalfa fields and sugar cane plantation by putting animals there for nine days. They also ransacked the "Ushupud," "Giron," and "Yunguilla" haciendas as well as the house of Doctor Juan de Dios Corral. The number of horses and mules that the conquerors took is calculated at three thousand, with no other right than that they were liberals and the owners, *curuchupas*.[39] The pillage lasted for three months and when the invaders returned to the coast they took with them whatever livestock there was on the ranches and farms along the way. One author, after referring to these deeds, adds, "If the houses and haciendas had been transportable, from 1895 on, the geography of Azuay would have changed."[40]

The Republic turned into a firestorm of guerrillas. Under the influence of Aparicio Ribadeneira, the Catholics fought at Caranqui on September 22, 1895, and at Chapues on December second. They did not win, but they were not disheartened.[41]

On June 2, 1896, Antonio Vega was in Azogues with a handful of ardent Catholics. He was acclaimed General and received a flag with this inscription: *Dios no muere*.[42] He headed north, at the head of a battalion that kept growing more and more on the way. Having arrived at the province of Chimborazo, he joined combat against Alfaro's forces on the highlands of Pangor. And since he was supported by another conservative unit from Tungurahua under the orders of Colonel Folleco, the victory for the good cause was resounding.

On June eighteenth the conservative troops from Azuay joined those from Chimborazo. The latter were under the command of Colonel Pedro Lizarzaburo. They joined in combat against the liberals who were again defeated. The next day in the hamlet of Tanquis, a third defeat for the liberals. On the farm called "Florida" close to Riobamba, a fourth defeat for the liberals.

The union of the conservatives had made their strength overwhelming. "Let's march united against Quito, take it and throw out the Usurper. Who will be the commander in chief?" Those from Azuay said, "Antonio Vega." Those from Chimborazo replied, "Pedro Lizarzaburo." The former complained that those from Riobamba took the victories as their own, and the latter acclaimed: "The *morlacos*[43] think they are the arbiters of the war." Besides, the latter wanted to return to Azuay to throw the Alfarists, who tyrannized Cuenca, out of that city. The division was fatal. Whose fault was it? The conservatives themselves.

With one hundred and twenty men Antonio Vega opened fire against Cuenca to the cry of "God and Country. Long live the Catholic religion!" It was July 5, 1896. The Alfarists rose to the number of six hundred well-armed men. It was the war of the Machabees against the armies of a greater number of pagans. Cuenca's fifth column, or internal front, was a tremendous factor against the liberals, attacked from without and from within. Two women, the famous Rosario Crespo and the shoemaker Bahamonde, attacked the garrison with knives and distributed cartridges to the conservatives. The children diverted the water from a canal towards the place where the Alfarists had taken refuge. They fled and were captured. Those inside even fought with bottles and threw boiling water, ashes and chili powder at the eyes of the liberals. The victory of the Catholics was overwhelming.[44]

Due to the dreadful experience of the internal front at Cuenca, the government was devoted to weakening it in Quito, putting Catholic leaders in prison including women such as Alegria de Mata and Juana Torres Barba, who even had to suffer ice water baths.[45]

In the artillery barracks a picture of the Lord of Justice still hung on the wall: Jesus Christ seated on a bench, holding in His right hand the reed given Him by the Roman soldiers to mock His Divine royalty. The Apostle Saint Peter was kneeling at one side, begging pardon for his denial. The Blessed Virgin was at the other side, also kneeling, to accompany her Son in sorrow. On top of a column was the cock, which by its crowing reminded Saint Peter of the Lord's prophecy: "Before the cock crow twice, thou shalt deny me thrice." As was obvious, the soldiery from the coast did not take long to let blasphemies fly at that picture and even threatened to destroy it. Sergeant Muela, from Quito, reprimanded them, exposing himself to be knocked down in the act. To remedy it all, the Catholic artilleryman removed the picture from the wall and took it to his house. Years passed and Sergeant Muela was sick and dying. He had a Dominican priest come. He confessed and entrusted the picture to him. It was placed in the Church of *Santo Domingo*,[46] to the right of the sacristy door and is the object of special devotion by the faithful.

In the diocese of Riobamba Father Raimundo Torres was captured and weighed down with shackles. In Quito the Dominican priests, Father La Camara and Father Duranti, were condemned to exile. The Seminary was constrained to pay a fine of sixteen thousand sucres, and its Rector, Father Juan Stappers, was sent to jail.

Victor Leon Vivar had made his names come true[47] in the battles of Pangor, Tanquis, Columbe and Guaranda. He took advantage of a short break in the war to enter Quito incognito and visit his family. But a few days later the house was razed to the ground and the brave warrior of pen and sword was taken prisoner. It was three o'clock in the morning on August 6, 1896, the twenty-first anniversary of the assassination of Garcia Moreno. Vivar was made to emerge from the prison and to direct his steps amidst a squad of soldiers to *San Diego*[48] cemetery. Once he was inside the graveyard, he received three, four, five rifle bullets. Immediately he was favored with a last sacramental absolution given by Father Eudoro Maldonado, a holy priest who was in the cemetery praying. Who cannot marvel at the paternal Providence of God towards the victims of liberal fury? In spite of such an unforeseen time of day, a chaplain was not lacking.

Victor Leon Vivar, extremely similar to Garcia Moreno in the field of Catholic journalism and in battle, had also been an admirer of Garcia Moreno's writings. In this respect he had written a literary review entitled *Carta – Prologo*.[49] Here, as an example, is a short quotation: "About his translation of the *Ave, Maris Stella*, the fearsome Conqueror in the naval battle of Jambeli[50] succeeded in translating it better than my teacher, the Illustrious Mr. Federico Gonzalez Suarez, who enjoys a well-deserved reputation as an admirable translator of Latin."[51]

Already during Alfaro's regime, he had made a contract with the printing house of the Salesian Fathers for a new edition of Garcia Moreno's famous satire against General Urbina. When the printing began, those religious noticed that the abuses of authority perpetrated by Alfaro were depicted in those by Urbina and they suspended the work, due to the well-founded fear of the *Garroteros*' reprisals. In truth Urbina was a precursor of Alfaro. The former expelled the Jesuits; the latter expelled the Capuchins, Bishop Schumacher and many priests and religious. The former had the soldiery named *Los Tauras*[52] as his instrument; the latter, the soldiery named the *Garroteros*, or Ecuadorian Gestapo. The former and the latter misused the word "people" to give their crimes a "certificate of citizenship." The former could not continue oppressing the Republic because he came up against Garcia Moreno, who destroyed and crushed him.[53] Alfaro, on the other hand, would continue tyrannizing because he only ran up against a Cordero, a Vicente Lucio, a Mateus and a Ribadeneira, a Sarasti, etc., who let themselves be destroyed and crushed. Through this brief list of atrocities committed by Alfaro and those noted below, Alfaro is on a par with the most dreadful and pernicious man that has existed in the nation.

Six days after the assassination of Vivar, the priest who attended him in the cemetery, Father Eudoro Maldonado, while sleeping in his bed during the small hours of the night became the victim of a formidable knife gash in the back of his neck. Undoubtedly the *Garroteros* wanted to be free of a witness.

Eleven days went by and the Salesian priests from Quito were exiled and a little later, those from Cuenca. Everything was done at night, for fear of the true "people."

Two days later, on the night of August twenty-fifth, a battalion entered the monastery of the Franciscans, demanding that they leave the city and Ecuador. But, as that community is in the center of Quito, an immense crowd rose up in their defense. The troops fired. Many Quitonians died. Faced with the Catholics' persistence, Masonry's *Garroteros* had to desist.

The following month, a ukase by the usurper government ordered the Jesuit missionaries of the eastern region of Ecuador to be exiled and leave, en route to the Maranon River or Brazil. Here is a crime detested by the liberals themselves, who had a bit of patriotism. Those religious had founded and civilized fifteen towns, endowed with their respective schools, and maintained Ecuador's ownership up to the village named "Destacamento," at the confluence of the Napo with the Amazon River.[54] A short time earlier the Sisters of the Good Shepherd, who ran schools for children, had left there because of the outrages whereby the liberals made their stay impossible. Now, on September 22, 1896, the Jesuits, whose superior was the holy priest Father Maurillo Detroux, left those towns and those Ecuadorian rivers, respected by Peru because of the presence of the missionaries, who wore the crucifix and carried the Ecuadorian flag. Once the Salesian school in Gualaquiza was destroyed and that of the Franciscans in Zamora, the entire, immense eastern province was at the mercy of Peruvian invaders. These were the effects of Peruvian Masonry that had Brother Alfaro, Cadosh of the thirtieth degree, under its obedience and submission.

The assassination of Leon Vivar incited the guerrilla fighters and brought the young Gabriel Garcia Alcazar out of hiding and inaction. He named Don Rafael Varela as his main adjutant, the same man who had cooperated in the transfer of Garcia Moreno's remains to a more secret place. As was obvious, almost all the employees and farmhands were converted into guerrilla fighters from the "Bella Vista" and "Cumbijin" haciendas that belonged to Mariana Alcazar, Garcia Moreno's widow. Some young men from Quito joined. And the resulting column adopted the name of "Vengadores de Vivar".[55] Note that another column already existed, also of guerrilla fighters, with the name of "Garcia Moreno."

Garcia Alcazar invited the men from the "Chimborazo" column to a conference in "Bellavista" which took place on August 9, 1896. After a brotherly agape paid for by the host, they decided they would all march to take Latacunga.[56]

Gunfire broke out on the eleventh. The conservatives attacked the city on three sides: Donoso and Melchor Costales of Riobamba, from the south and the east; Garcia Alcazar, from the north. The Alfarists, who took refuge in the tower of the Matriz church and the Christian Brothers' school, launched a shower of bullets, first against those from the north and east, then against those from the south. Melchor Costales made an assault with his company, shooting with such success that he seized the enemy barricades located close to the impregnable tower. But Costales fell to the ground, wounded in one leg, and as his adjutant, Zapata, was lying dead, the rest began to flee, but were stopped in time and joined the forces of Garcia Alcazar and of Donoso Herboso. The former went up the tower of Santo Domingo accompanied by a handful of courageous men, and with steady shots cleared the plaza of the principal church. They came down from the tower, charged the enemy barracks, and by Garcia Alcazar's express initiative and command, one of the walls was drilled open and through the hole they got inside where they finished off the resistance.

As for the role of Donoso Herboso, being stationed at the foot of the tower that constituted the Alfarists' main stronghold, and taking advantage of their discouragement, he had his bugler play ceasefire, imitating the enemy's key. They fell into the ruse and stopped shooting. Donoso entered the barracks and embraced Garcia Alcazar.

All agree that the sharpshooting from the tower of Santo Domingo and the open breach in the barracks constituted the main factors of the victory for the good cause and for the taking of Latacunga. They captured seventy prisoners. Twenty of the dictator's soldiers had died. About ten of the Conservatives had perished. Melchor Costales was promoted to General; Garcia Alcazar and Donoso Herboso to Colonels.

Leaving aside the tale of the other battles in which Garcia Alcazar intervened, during this time this gentleman received a letter written by the director of the construction of the Basilica of the Heart of Jesus on Montmartre, Paris. What did it say? It dealt with one of the stained-glass windows of that church, which would represent President Garcia Moreno consecrating his nation to the Divine Heart of Jesus, and that this window could be paid for by the son of that great man. Without a doubt, the addressee answered. But he did not contribute the quantity that they asked of him. This does not honor him. It is true that his fortune was quite broken due to the Alfarists' pillages and his help to the Conservatives. Nevertheless it seems that a sacrifice was imperative so that the President-martyr would have his place of honor in such a symbolic and important church as Montmartre.[57]

Without the shadow of a doubt, the Usurper wanted to implant liberal errors and Masonic predominance in all of Ecuador. Here are those words of Alfaro's: "The country is oppressed due to the theocratic regime that has filled it with ignominy." There in the very Catholic province of Azuay was heard the cry of "Long live the devil!" in answer to "Long live Christ!"[58] Even in Quito there was the foundation of the Lodge called "Light of Pichincha," whose first meeting took place on May 3, 1897, with around one hundred individuals. Let us listen to the Peruvian Masons' announcement:

> The liberal science of General Alfaro, Supreme Head of Ecuador, exercising the eminent gifts with which Providence endowed him, has powerfully driven away the terrorists of the doctrines of Christ crucified to the nation in the north.
>
> In the trimestral session held by the very respectable Grand Lodge of Peru, on Sunday the thirteenth of the present month, it was seen fit to expedite the charter for the establishment of a Lodge in Quito dependent on our jurisdiction, under the historical name of "Light of Pichincha" Number 31. Here is the circular that was transcribed by the Grand Secretary for that purpose:
>
> Lima, June 15, 1897. To Q. (three dots), H. (three dots), Vn. (three dots), M. (three dots) of the R. (three dots).
>
> With enthusiasm and pleasure I notify you that the Masonic New Year, even at its dawn, now counts on another workshop. Our very beloved and decided Grand Master Mason commands me to communicate this plausible event to your Resp.[59] (three dots) L.[60] (three dots), so that you can enter into fraternal and official relations with that workshop. For, it has been constituted legally and properly

under the auspices of the Very Resp. (three dots) Grand Lodge of Peru.

The Workshop has the name "Light of Pichincha," its own number, 31, and the place of its operation is Quito.

That capital, nest of the abominable ravens who sustain fanaticism and Jesuitism, has therefore a light and a group of workers who will begin to demolish the foundations of obscurantism there.[61]

The Very Resp. (three dots) Grand Master believes that you will receive this birth with jubilation; and when entering into relations with "Light of Pichincha," you will try to support and encourage it.

Your H. (three dots) Jose B. Ugarte, Grand Secretary, sends you fraternal greetings.

Regarding the guerrilla fighters at Riobamba, the heroism of a woman named Rosario Betancourt should be noted. She had studied at the School of the religious of the Sacred Hearts in Cuenca, thanks to a scholarship conceded by President Garcia Moreno. Due to her intrepid character, she was particularly esteemed by that great man.[62]

She married a gentleman from Riobamba whose last name was Leon. They had children, of whom two perished on the battlefield for God and country. On different dates, but close together, the corpses of both youths were brought into their mother's house for the wake. She saw them enter and did not shed a tear. "I would like to have more sons," she exclaimed, "to combat and die for the Catholic religion and country." The people called her "Spartan woman." They would have better said, "Rival of the Mother of the Machabee martyrs."[63]

It was May 4, 1897. In the early morning hours, Melchor Costales and his brave men took their stand in the tower and the interior of the Saint Philip's chapel, hoping that the majority of soldiers from the nearby barracks, *Pichincha,* would surrender in favor of the good cause, as they had promised. Costales appeared at the door of the above-mentioned barracks and shouted, "Long live the Catholic Religion!"[64] He was answered by silence and shortly afterward with the bustle for fighting in favor of the Usurper. Costales ran to join his men and had to be resigned to fight in the proportion of one to fifty. Why such recklessness? Because Donoso Herboso had a good number of guerrilla fighters on the outskirts of Riobamba with the plan to attack the government troops caught in the crossfire. But this fighting was to happen starting at six o'clock in the morning. It was five fifteen and the struggle was already in an uproar. Besides, part of the government troops made a front against the possible intervention of Donoso Herboso. After an hour of combat, Costales and his survivors fled. A few went inside the adjoining Jesuit school.

The Alfarists broke the chapel door with axes and rifle butts. They found no guerrilla fighters inside the sacred place. With gunfire and blows they opened the little door of the Tabernacle, took out the pyxes, uncovered them, strewed the consecrated hosts over the floor, ate them, and stepped on them. They poured liquor into the chalice and drank it. They dressed in the ornaments for Holy Mass and went out on the streets.

Another contingent of Liberals invaded the cells of the community. They fired two mortal shots at the rector, Father Emilio Moscoso. On his corpse they put a cartridge belt of cases on a slant across his chest and a rifle over his shoulder, so they could invent the story that this religious had been fighting. They hit Father Buendia on the forehead. They pushed Father Guzman flat on his face; they punched Father Valdecasas in the face; they rolled Father Gabela down the stairs; they kicked Father Bond onto the street; they broke Father Santocildes' head because he refused to shout "Long live Alfaro." Then they tied them all by the neck and hands and drove the prisoners to the barracks. One of those who tied Father Lopez told him, "Now let God come and free you." It must be pointed out that especially those who profaned the Eucharist were punished by God with a tragic and impenitent end.

Aristocratic ladies entered the barracks that was used as a jail for the Jesuits and served them food on their knees.[65] Students of the Jesuits continued to swell the numbers of the guerrilla groups and their heroism wrested these verses from a poet from Cuenca:

> Waving sacred banners
> For religion and country
> The sons of Chimborazo
> Go out to a noble crusade
> They are delicate youths,
> Sons of an illustrious family
> Who leave the bosoms
> Of tender mothers and sisters.
> Good-bye, they say, let us
> Leave for a noble campaign
> Let us, because it is glorious
> To die for God and Country.

They forget classes and books.
They need heavy arms,
And on their spirited steeds
Rush to the field of honor.[66]

The Bishop of Riobamba, Monsignor Arsenio Andrade, and the priests, Father Felix Proano, Father Alfonso Auderreguen, and Father N. Izurieta, had to go into exile. Others had to live in hiding. The same fate was shared by many other priests in the rest of the Republic. Before long Monsignor Massia, Bishop of Loja, found himself exiled in Peru. The printing presses that defended Catholicism continued being scattered in pieces or thrown into ravines. The famous Father Matovelle extended his "Act of Reparation for the Crimes of Ecuador" with those of May fourth: "For the crimes of August sixth, March thirtieth and May fourth, forgive us, O Lord, forgive us!" In some churches the painter drew a bramble bush with tremendous thorns whose trunk contained this date: August sixth; one of its branches: March thirtieth; and another: May fourth. But before long, Father Matovelle, the ardent apostle of the Heart of Jesus, also had to take the road to exile.

The farce of Father Moscoso's corpse with the cartridge belt of shells across his chest and the rifle was circulated by liberals to the four winds. The self-styled National Congress gathered in Quito utilized this farce to decree the expulsion of the Jesuits from all Ecuador. But, as soon as the people from the capital learned of it, they made an uprising against that ukase. Thousands of signatures, proceeding from high ecclesiastical authorities as well as from the most humble Catholics, overwhelmed the Congressmen who had no other recourse than to withdraw the decree. It was May 7, 1897. Garcia Moreno's prediction was fulfilled which is found in chapter four: "The Reds will dare not expel them."[67]

Pope Leo XIII ordered all the members of the Apostolate of Prayer to pray to God for Ecuador. This order was obeyed by the general director of that Apostolate, who, in turn, made it known to the thirty-nine superior directors, and they transmitted it to the 41,558 local directors. The result was that sixteen million associates from every tribe and tongue began to pray for Ecuador starting on July 1, 1908. Also the thirty magazines entitled *El Mensajero del Corazon de Jesus*,[68] written in fourteen different languages, published an article under the heading of "Catholics in Ecuador." Here is a sample, the translation of which appeared in the *Petit Messager* from Toulouse, France:

## October 21, 1900: De-consecration

A few months ago the papers reported the news that in one of the cities of Ecuador, called Riobamba, Saint Philip's School was invaded by the soldiery, the superior of the Jesuits assassinated, the other priests harassed and reviled, the church devastated and the Sacred Species sacrilegiously profaned. These facts, having been verified and proven, constitute an extremely sad reality. And even though it has not been generalized throughout Ecuador with identical savagery; and although the revolutionaries, once they obtained command, may have seen the need for moderation: it cannot be denied that we are quite far from the time when Garcia Moreno the Great consecrated his nation to the Heart of Jesus and when the People gloried in calling themselves "The Republic of the Sacred Heart."

The Masonic Lodges, not content with having assassinated the Hero, persist in undoing the ideal of the Christian State achieved by that man helped by his genius and by his faith. Once this new Judas Machabeus perished, the sects launched a war without respite against the institutions that he founded or reestablished. In the end they have just obtained victory; but in the people educated by Garcia Moreno they find elements of resistance that do not let them do all the evil they would like.

Let us pray for that bold nation which formerly gave such beautiful examples of Christian faith and valor. Let us ask the Heart of Jesus, Patron of Ecuador, to shorten the length of the trial and to manifest the truth of the dying martyr's last words: "God does not die."

Daily prayer for this month:

O Divine Heart of Jesus, I offer Thee, through the Immaculate Heart of Mary, all the prayers, works and sufferings of this day, for the intentions for which Thou dost immolate Thyself upon the altar. I especially offer them so that Ecuador will again be, as it was under Garcia Moreno, "the People of the Heart of Jesus."[69]

Alfaro was not in Quito on January 28, 1899. His vice-president, Benigno Cueva, sent this order to the rector of the Jesuits in the capital:

By the special power entrusted to me and with the consent of the president of the Republic, I decree that all the Jesuits in Quito vacate it in the space of six hours, and set out for the north with all possible care that their departure may not be noticed; because if a disturbance should be provoked in the people, the latter will suffer the consequences. For you are the causes of all the evils in the Republic and of the guerrillas.

Naturally the priests had to make the day students and the boarding students leave under some ingenuous pretext. They were bewildered. They had noticed that the priests seemed to be preparing a trip. Had not other communities already been expelled? The voice of alarm spread like fire in gunpowder. Some messengers of theirs showed to the public the notices and petitions relating to the banishment of the Jesuits from Quito. Thousands of men, women and children advanced to the house of those religious, already surrounded by troops armed with rifles and cannons. The shouts of protests and threats against the usurper Government were tremendous. They did not take long to reach the people in the neighborhood of San Blas, brandishing stones they had extracted from their streets. The example spread. The battalions were oppressed by a huge crowd. Women of all kinds took complete control of the cannons. Those from the neighborhood of San Roque surrounded the Panoptico to break the doors and release numerous Conservatives from there, whose contribution must have been considerable.

One of the commanders ordered: "Shoot at the people." But the soldiers answered, "For every shot we fire, they answer us with twenty stones." It is expected that the firearms would have won, although it would have been at the price of a slaughter. But the moral influence of the masses and the fear produced in the troops defeated the vice-president, who hurried to give a countermand, once and again and a hundred times, in writing and by word.

It was already seven o'clock in the evening and the multitude did not withdraw from the religious house and roared with threats. The government men, Jose Peralta and Abelardo Moncayo, managed to enter where the Jesuits were and begged them to appease the people. Two priests, the most popular ones in Quito, Manuel Proano and Enrique Faura, went out into the streets and with gestures and words did everything possible to persuade the people: "The order of ostracism against the Jesuits has been shelved forever."[70]

For greater security there were groups who spent the night next to the Jesuit School and at the crossroads of the exit ways from Quito going to the north and to the south.

## October 21, 1900: De-consecration

Let us pass over an innumerable number of other acts of violent robbery, killing, blasphemy and sacrilege perpetrated by Alfarism, and let us end this chapter with the following ukase by the National Congress on October 21, 1900:

> The legislative decrees of April 22, 1861; October 18, 1873; and August 4, 1892, are repealed: the first declares the Virgin Mary under her name of Our Lady of Ransom as the Patroness of the Republic; the second consecrates it to the Most Holy Heart of Jesus; and the third resolves the erection of a statue of the Blessed Virgin on Quito's Panecillo Hill.

Let us recall that it was Garcia Moreno who approved with his signature the consecration of Ecuador to Our Lady of Ransom.

Alfaro abstained from subscribing *Ejecutese*[71] to this blasphemous act of his Congress. Was it a remainder of a holy fear of God? According to the legislatures, the decree of the Chambers, lacking the sanction of the executive branch, is approved by the Ministry of Law. So the blasphemers from the Masonic Sanhedrin stopped worrying.

It is clear that this decree of October 21, 1900, is null:

> Because without authority there can be no decree at all. Who confers authority? God; and God does not confer it against Himself.
>
> A decree, to be worthy of the name, has to have the common good as its end. This decree of October 21, 1900, did not have that purpose. Therefore it is null.
>
> Those congressmen were the makings of Alfaro and were not elected by the people. They said, like the Jews in other times, "We will not have Jesus reign over us."[72] Nevertheless, the vast majority of Ecuadorians protested against that contrivance of Masonry.

The Catholic press was in ruins because of the *Garroteros*. Even so, a flyer immediately appeared in Quito with these words:

> The outpouring of sectarian fury, unable to change the religious faith of a people born and raised in the warmth of Christianity... We, as Ecuadorian Catholics, declare before the face of all nations, that the legislative decree that repeals those decrees, by which the

Republic was consecrated to the Sacred Heart of Jesus and to the Immaculate Mother of God and our Mother Mary Most Holy, is not the expression of the will of Ecuadorians. They place their welfare and honor in the immutability of their Catholic beliefs. And therefore, they profess and will always profess the most consoling and honorable dogma for man, regarding the social sovereignty of Jesus Christ, a dogma that, exalting the freedom of man, dignifies him and makes him happy.[73]

The preceding confession of their faith by the inhabitants of Quito was reproduced, commented upon and approved in all Ecuador. In Lima, the exiled Father Julio Matovelle promoted the publication of the protests signed by the Illustrious Bishops Massia and Andrade, and by Ecuadorian priests and laymen who underwent exile there. Besides, he published a pamphlet with this title: *La Causa del Sagrado Corazon en el Ecuador*.[74] Let us listen to a paragraph by the above-mentioned bishops:

> Among all the perverse laws that have been published in this Republic by impious Radicalism, this is the most wicked and monstrous because it goes directly against the adorable Person of the Redeemer and His Most Holy Mother. Through it was the desire to wound the most delicate and sensitive heartstrings of that pious nation with no consideration for the holy beliefs and the august religion which that extremely Christian and unfortunate nation professes... We ask the Heart of Jesus, through the intercession of His Immaculate Mother, not to impute the tremendous responsibility to the Ecuadorian People that weighs upon all who have contributed to the enactment of that law; and to forgive, in the excesses of His infinite mercy, the blindness and deviancy of those who have perpetrated such a scandal. Let us confide in that extremely infinite mercy, so that, in spite of all the efforts of Hell, Ecuador will always continue under the protection of the Most High, and will never stop being the Republic of the Sacred Heart and beloved portion of the inheritance of the Most Holy Mother of God.
> Lima, November 15, 1900, Fray Jose Maria, Bishop of Loja. Arsenio, Bishop of Riobamba.[75]

The impious press, on the contrary, approved and applauded the sacrilegious decree of October twenty-first; and even the devil, in person, became an Alfarist, or better yet, more Alfarist than ever.

Father Maurillo Detroux himself who, as was previously said, was thrown out of the East by Alfaro, told us young Jesuits the following in 1917:

> In Guayaquil I was asked to exorcise a man possessed by the devil. I went to him with holy water and the ritual with the exorcisms. Above all I ordered the possessed man to say, "Long live the Heart of Jesus." The answer of that unfortunate man was "Long live Alfaro!" At that, the author dared ask the priest, "What was the possessed man's voice like?" The holy missionary answered, "Loud, coarse and ugly."

Since 1913 the author began to hear this interesting case from the Jesuits with whom he began his priestly studies:

> In Spain another possessed man shouted in the presence of several individuals, "Long live Alfaro!" Everyone wondered, "Why such an acclamation and what is it about? And who could that Alfaro be?" The exorcist interrogated him, "Why do you shout 'long live Alfaro'?" The possessed man's answer was, "Because through him I reign in Ecuador." Shortly thereafter the exorcist or some other witness wrote to the Archbishop of Quito, telling of that fact so full of meaning. This letter, they say, must be in the archives of the Metropolitan Curia in Quito. The author went to the Reverend priest, Father Alfredo Ponce, in charge of the above-mentioned archives; but he answered, "I am revising and ordering what relates to the colony; I still have not come to the republic."
>
> The devil is the father of lies. Consequently we are not obliged to believe that he controls all of Ecuador absolutely, although he certainly reigns over Masons, apostates and unbelievers.[76]

In fact, forty-one days after the infernal decree, the immense majority of Ecuadorians renewed their consecration solemnly and in a plebiscitary manner, inspired by the initiative of Pope Leo XIII to consecrate the entire world to the Heart of Jesus on the eve of the new century, the Twentieth Century.

It was December 31, 1900, when the consecration of Ecuador was renewed and the consecration of the whole world was recited in all the churches and chapels of Ecuador. The next day, January 1, 1901, pictures of the Heart of Jesus were displayed on the fronts of their houses and even altars with His image. In Cuenca, they even inaugurated a new church on that date, the *Templo del Santo Cenáculo*,[77] principally devoted to honoring the Most Holy Sacrament, and to satisfying for the horrendous sacrilege perpetrated by the Alfarists in Saint Philip's Church in Riobamba on May 4, 1897.

It is clear that the Ecuadorians also ignored the abominable decree pertaining to the consecrations to Our Lady of Ransom and the Most Pure Heart of Mary. But the splendid, plebiscitary manner of renewing the filial dedication took effect four years later, on December 8, 1904, on the occasion of the fiftieth anniversary of the dogmatic definition of the Immaculate Conception of the Blessed Virgin. The entire Ecuadorian nation rendered fervent tribute to the Mother of God and of men; but in Quito the homage took greater meaning and unction, because the chapel dedicated to the Heart of Mary was inaugurated then.[78]

# Endnotes

[1] Doctor Wilfrido Loor, *Vida del Padre Julio Matovelle* (*Life of Father Julio Matovelle*) (first edition), p. 331. Cf. Gomezjurado, *Vida de Garcia Moreno*, vol. 11, p. 193 ff.
[2] The long-renown Krupp steel company, based in Germany, is one of the world's largest and best steel manufacturers of ammunition and armaments. It produced superior quality weapons which played an important role in the Franco-Prussian war, as well as in both World Wars.
[3] $200,000 in 1895 would be equivalent to $5,360,000.00 in 2010.
[4] Wilfrido Loor, *Vida del General Eloy Alfaro* (*Life of General Eloy Alfaro*), vol. 2, p. 371 ff.
[5] For more details in this regard, see the author's vol. 5, p. 334 ff.
[6] I. e. his father, President Gabriel Garcia Moreno.
[7] *Idem*, p. 392 ff. The good grades that Garcia Alcazar earned at the *College* of *Saint Gabriel* are recorded in printed booklets from that high school on the occasion of the final exams and distribution of prizes. They are in the "Aurelio Espinosa" library in Cotocollao. In the archives of that same place there are handwritten papers in philosophy by the above-mentioned young Garcia Alcazar. Mr. Jose Maria Lazcano Orbe was Garcia Alcazar's loyal and devoted servant from childhood. He told me that the university professors, among others Doctor Jose Maria Penaherrera, extolled Garcia Alcazar's successful progress and that he was extremely submissive and affectionate toward his mother.
[8] We want to correct an error [in our book, *The Consecration*] that Garcia Alcazar did not fight at Gatazo. We have found his contribution in the battle against General Alfaro in the book by Miguel Angel Gonzalez Paez entitled *Genesis of Ecuadorian Liberalism: Its Triumph and its Works*, in the chapter concerning the battle of Gatazo. Moreover, Garcia Alcazar contributed financially to the completion of the Church of the Heart of Mary.
[9] "The Conquerors."
[10] "The Homeland."
[11] "Chimborazo" is the name of a volcano located 93 miles (150 km) south of the capital, Quito.
[12] "Daule" is a city of Ecuador, 30 miles (46 km) north of Guayaquil.
[13] General Antonio Jose de Sucre assisted Simon Bolivar's campaign of separating the South American colonies from Spain, and led the first attempt to "liberate" Quito from Spain in 1821.
[14] "The Avengers."
[15] Father Jose Legohuir, S. J., *Historia de la Republica del Ecuador* (*History of the Republic of Ecuador*), vol. 3, p. 512 ff.
[16] Wilfrido Loor, *Vida de General Eloy Alfaro*, p. 394 ff.
[17] *Idem*, p. 396 ff.
[18] Gomezjurado, *Vida de Garcia Moreno*, vol. 11, p. 197 ff.

[19] "In what place in the Cathedral was Garcia Moreno's corpse laid from August 9, 1875, until March 27, 1883? The author thinks no one currently knows. Therefore it was providential that it was transferred to the convent of the Sisters of Saint Catherine who, through a community tradition, have kept the more or less precise and exact place in its memory. Some twenty years ago the priest, Father Antonio Benitez, a little lame and of refined manners, told me that the cadaver was buried in front of Saint Joseph's altar in the Cathedral. But his testimony is the only one." (*Ibid.*, pp. LXII-LXIII.)

[20] Wilfrido Loor, *Vida de General Eloy Alfaro*, p. 406 ff. Also on p. 386, vol. 1. Jose Maria Lazcano Orbe told the author that it was the Canon Jose Maria Terrazas, born in Gonzanama, Loja, who had promoted the transfer.

[21] He is the son of Mariana del Alcazar, the second wife of the widower Garcia Moreno. Hence, according to Spanish custom, his name incorporates the surnames of both his father and mother. Here Gabriel is designated with both of his father's last names: Garcia and Moreno, which is unusual, but is used to emphasize their relationship.

[22] From his youth, Rafael Varela from Latacunga was favored by the President-martyr, as is recorded in the author's vol. 9, p. 478 ff.

[23] This matter was recorded in the author's vol. 8, p. 122 ff.

[24] Loor, *Vida de General Eloy Alfaro*, p. 408 ff. Luis Robalino Davila told the author in person that the victorious soldiers in Gatazo, whether by treason or not, who were the first to enter Quito, were the ones who mistakenly reviled Sucre's statue. Then they went on to revile Garcia Moreno's obelisk. Wilfrido Loor records the profanation of the little monument to Garcia Moreno on p. 435 and states that this act took place on October 11, 1895.
On the other hand, a Spanish Jesuit, passing in front of the above-mentioned statue of Sucre, made a respectful bow or salute, believing it to be Garcia Moreno. He himself told this to the priest Doctor Eudoro Ribadeneira Bermeo, who transmitted it to the author of these pages in Quito at the beginning of the year 1972. But that priest did not recall the Spaniard's name.

[25] The *Garroteros* were Alfaro's henchmen, or gang of "thugs."

[26] Neptali Bonifaz Ascazubi himself recounted this to his son, Cristobal Bonifaz Jijon, who told the author in Quito in February 1972. About being hid in Our Lady of Quinche's side chapel, Jose Maria Lazcano Orbe transmitted this to the author in Quito at the beginning of the year 1971.

[27] The "Panopticon" is a prison in Quito, still in use, whose construction was ordered by Garcia Moreno in 1869. A panopticon is a building so constructed that it is possible to observe the whole interior from a single point. The design consists of a circular structure with an "inspection house" at its center, from which the managers, or staff of the institution, are able to watch the inmates, who are stationed around the perimeter.

[28] "The Law."

[29] "Light of Guayas" [Guayas is a coastal province of Ecuador wherein Guayaquil is located].

[30] "Chain of the Union."

[31] *Idem*, p. 448 ff. Also Father Matovelle's biography by the above-mentioned author, p. 332, note. Again, the above-mentioned biography on Alfaro, p. 417.
[32] "The sixth of August."
[33] The above-quoted biography on Alfaro, pp. 457 and 455. In the Aurelio Espinosa Library there is a copy of the work *El Seis de Agosto* with a great many notes written in the margins by Doctor Aurelio Espinosa, a Colonel, refuting Roberto Andrade's assertions.
[34] This occurred in Caranqui on September twenty-second and in Chapues on December second.
[35] Gomezjurado, *Vida de Garcia Moreno*, vol. 11, p. 203.
[36] Gomezjurado, *Vida de Garcia Moreno*, vol. 11, p. 201.
[37] *Idem*, p. 458 ff. Besides, p. 468 ff. Lastly, p. 473.
[38] Gomezjurado, vol. 11, p. 202.
[39] "Curuchupas" is a local derogatory epithet for an "ultraconservative" as mentioned above in endnote eleven of chapter ten.
[40] Gomezjurado, vol. 11, p. 203.
[41] *Idem*, p. 475 ff. Besides, p. 482. Also, the above-mentioned biography on Matovelle, p. 336 of the first edition.
[42] "God does not die."
[43] I. e. those from Azuay. The *Morlacos* are Ecuadorians who speak the local Spanish dialect of *Morlaco*, spoken in the Ecuadorian city of Cuenca and the surrounding provinces of Azuay and Canar.
[44] Loor, *Vida de General Eloy Alfaro*, p. 489 ff.
[45] Gomezjurado, vol. 11, p. 205.
[46] "Saint Dominic."
[47] *Victor* in Spanish means "conqueror" and *Leon* means "lion."
[48] "Saint James."
[49] "Letter – Prologue."
[50] Garcia Moreno personally commanded at the naval battle at Jambeli (June 27, 1865), in which the forces of his old adversary, General Jose Maria Urbina, were completely defeated.
[51] *Escritos y Discursos de Garcia Moreno* (*Garcia Moreno's Writings and Speeches*), vol. 1, second edition, p 473, compilation and notes by the Illustrious Archbishop of Quito, Monsignor Manuel Maria Polit.
[52] The *Tauras* were Urbina's "thugs." See endnote one in chapter one.
[53] Those who would like to know more about Urbina can read the first chapters of volume 2 of the author's work, *Vida de Garcia Moreno*.
[54] The Jesuit, Father Caceres, traveled throughout the East in 1891 and wrote, "From Mazan there is a dirt road to Iquitos, taking approximately seven hours. Six hours down from Mazan is the "Destacamento," acknowledged as being under Ecuadorian jurisdiction until recently. The Governor of Napo has from time immemorial appointed the local administrator (*teniente politico*), and it was the place where Ecuadorian escorts stopped whenever they brought out an exile that way." (Ricardo Caceres, S. J., *La Provincia Oriental de la Republica del Ecuador. Apuntes de Viaje.* (*The Eastern Province of the Republic of*

*Ecuador. Travel Notes*), Quito Imprenta de la Universidad ("Quito University Press"), 1892, p. 34.)
[55] "Vivar's Avengers."
[56] Garcia Alcazar, vol. 3 of the magazine *Dios y Patria (God and Country)*, p. 304 ff. Account made by the campaign eyewitness, Doctor Javier Bustos H. In vol. 5 of the same magazine, p. 177, Mr. Arcesio A. Vela Flores appears as a very Garcia-like guerrilla fighter, whom the author mentioned in his vol. 5 of *Garcia Moreno*, p. 266.
[57] Again, the magazine *Dios y Patria,* vol. 5, p. 178 ff. The author heard about Montmartre from the lips of Jesuits, but did not read it written anywhere.
[58] Shouts of "Long live the devil!" in the province of Azuay are recorded. (Wilfrido Loor, *Vida de General Eloy Alfaro*, p. 501.)
[59] "Respectable."
[60] "Lodge."
[61] The capture of Cuenca by Alfaro took place on August 22, 1896. (Wilfrido Loor, *Vida de General Eloy Alfaro*, p. 459 ff.)
[62] Some details are given in the author's work, *Vida de Garcia Moreno*, vol. 5, p. 85 ff.
[63] Her surviving children, both in Riobamba and in Quito, narrated this about Rosario Betancourt to the author. Besides it is common knowledge in the former city.
[64] Wilfrido Loor, *Vida de General Eloy Alfaro*, p. 561 ff. The shout of "Long live Religion!" pronounced by Costales facing government troops is known from the testimony of the Jesuit Father Guillermo Schlimn who lived for many long years in Riobamba immediately after the sacrilegious events. That Jesuit was the author's professor in Cotocollao around the year 1922 and narrated it to them.
[65] That there were ladies who served the Jesuit prisoners on their knees is clear from the testimony of the Jesuit temporal coadjutor brother, Abel Coronado, who was also in the prison. Years later that brother relayed it to the author in Riobamba around the year 1932. A temporal coadjutor is an official assistant to a religious order who does not officially join that order or take the vows to do the spiritual work associated or directed by that order. "Temporal" refers to their situation in a secular, worldly setting.
[66] The verses by the poet from Cuenca to the boy heroes of Chimborazo are recorded in *Alfaro* by Loor, p. 498. Original verses in Spanish:
Batiendo sacros pendones / por la Religión y Patria / los hijos del Chimborazo / salen a noble cruzada. / Son delicados garzones / hijos de familia hidalga / que abandonan el regazo / de tiernas madres y hermanas. / Adiós les dicen, dejadnos / salir a noble campana / dejadnos porque es glorioso / morir por Dios y la Patria. / Clases y libros olvidan. / Requieren pesadas armas. / Y en sus briosos corceles / al campo de honor se lanzan.
[67] For the context of the prediction, see Gomezjurado, *Vida de Garcia Moreno*, vol. 9, p. 164.
[68] *The Messenger of the Sacred Heart.*

[69] Wilfrido Loor, *Vida del Padre Julio Matovelle* (first edition), p. 365.
[70] *Historia de la Compania de Jesus en el Ecuador* (*History of the Company of Jesus in Ecuador*), vol. 3, still unpublished, p. 465 ff, by Father Jose Jouanen, S. J., a Frenchman who lived many years in Ecuador as a professor, rector, provincial, missionary and historian. The Spanish priest, Father Manuel Puertas, told the author in Quito about the women taking control of the cannons. Among the Jesuits of those times the words, "Shoot the people," are common knowledge, as well as the soldiers' answer, "What about the shower of rocks?" See also the newspaper from Riobamba, *El Templo* (*The Church*), July 16, 1898.
[71] *Publiquese et ejecutese* in Spanish is a general legal closing statement used to enact a law, and it means, "Let it be published and enforced."
[72] Luke 19, 14.
[73] *Idem*, p. 467 ff. See also the book entitled *La Consagracion del Ecuador al Corazon de Jesus* (*The Consecration of Ecuador to the Heart of Jesus*) by Monsignor Jose Felix Heredia, S. J., p. 403 ff. Father Matovelle wrote the following: To prepare minds, the impious press of Guayaquil for many months outdid itself with blasphemies, clamoring that the law should be repealed as soon as possible which consecrated Ecuador to the Heart of Jesus.
[74] "The Cause of the Sacred Heart in Ecuador."
[75] Again, *La Consagracion del Ecuador,* p.405 ff. The protests by Bishops Massia and Andrade were taken from the newspaper *El Observador* (*The Observer*), June 27, 1919.
[76] Other Jesuits told us that, to exorcise the possessed man, Father Detroux was chosen because of his sanctity, well-known to those from Guayaquil.
[77] "Church of the Holy Cenacle."
[78] The chapel of the Immaculate Heart of Mary, which was constructed from 1892 until 1909, is the Lady Chapel found behind the main altar of the Basilica of the National Vow in Quito. Again, See *La Consagración del Ecuador*, p. 406 ff.

# Chapter 12
# The Mason, Alfaro, and Six of his Minions Are Lynched

In October of 1896, Monsignor Schumacher published a pamphlet printed in Pasto, Columbia. Its content referred to Ecuador. The title was *Theocracy or Demonocracy? Christ or Lucifer? Who will conquer? Who is like God!* Let us select a few sentences from its pages:

> "I come to put an end to Theocracy in Ecuador." This was the program of Eloy Alfaro, the man sent by Masonry.
> Those who had the joy of knowing Garcia Moreno intimately, especially in the latter years of his life, saw him perfecting and transforming himself with the acquisition of properly heroic virtues...
> Garcia Moreno was a Martyr of the Catholic Religion. How did he reach this triumph, and why did the satanic sect of Masonry immolate him? Ah! Everything that I have said about Garcia Moreno's private and public virtues pales before the titles that merited him Masonry's hate and the death sentence pronounced there in the nocturnal sessions of the synagogue of Satan...
> Only in eternity will Garcia Moreno's merit before God be understood, for having procured a holy priesthood for his nation's Church, a priesthood that would honor Jesus on the altar and would sanctify the people by its preaching and example...
> He crowned his work by consecrating his country to the Word made flesh: he surrendered it to His Divine Heart, which is the only and constant source of all good and of all happiness...
> Either Garcia Moreno, as the personification of Christian politics, justice, peace and prosperity, that is, Theocracy, the reign of God; or a Masonic *jefe*, with fierce and blood-stained liberty, arbitrariness, injustices and revolution without end, that is, Demonocracy, the reign of Lucifer... Such is the alternative which is now presented to Ecuadorians. The middle course would be to return to the treacherous Liberalism that opened the doors to the Masonic hordes...[1]

Fulfilling what was arranged in the Masonic Congress of Amapala, Brother Alfaro dispatched a regular contingent of his liberal troops to combat the Conservative Government of Colombia. Reciprocally, Ecuadorian Conservatives departed for Ipiales to swell the Catholic army of the neighboring nation. They joined battle. "Long live Alfaro! Death to Christ!" was the cry of the Alfarists, who suffered such a phenomenal defeat that, abandoning arms and munitions, they retreated blindly to the Chota River.

With the booty of such war provisions, the Catholic Ecuadorians decided to attack and take the city of Tulcan. Not a few Colombians joined this unit. Shooting broke out and the Conservatives had to flee. This support by Catholics from the neighboring nation was considered by Monsignor Gonzalez Suarez, Bishop of Ibarra, as a scandalous and intolerable Colombian invasion. And on May 31, 1900, he had these opinions published:

> Our priests must stay high above all political parties, whatever they may be called. To cooperate in one way or another with the Colombian invasion would be an act of treachery to our country. We priests must not sacrifice the nation to save religion... Our priests must work for peace; and as prelate I impose on them the duty of working in such a way that public tranquility will not be disturbed... In my dioceses I am as much a bishop as any other Catholic bishop is in his; and it is not my faithful who should direct me, but rather I who have to counsel and direct them... I demand obedience and submission of my priests to the direction of their prelate...

These directives were received with joy by the Alfarists, who propagated them abundantly in the Masonic newspapers and fliers throughout the Republic and beyond its borders, as proof that the Conservatives were fighting against the bishop, and that the bishop was in favor of the liberals.

Garcia Moreno's assassin, Abelardo Moncayo, wrote:

> The sacred character and self-assurance of the Bishop of Ibarra were an overwhelming phalanx for the Liberal Party. Was not his cooperation most effective for the pacification of the country, for the illumination of the conscience of the multitudes and the ensuing calm, amidst the splendor of the truth? And given the character with which he is invested and the rage it must have produced in those with long hair, does not that stentorian cry, "Country before Religion," border on the sublime, a cry that terrified those who irresponsibly lent their hand to our invaders?[2]

For Catholics, this doctrine constituted a scandal, which was condemned by the Bishop of Pasto, Monsignor Ezequiel Moreno, and by the victims of Alfarism: Schumacher, Andrade and Massia. Let us attend the dispute:

> "One cannot take up arms against Alfaro because he is the government," said Gonzalez Suarez.
> "Yes, they can," replied Schumacher, "because the legitimate government is in the Conservative Party, stripped of power by the misuse of force in the battlefields of Gatazo. Alfaro is a usurper and a tyrant."
> Gonzalez Suarez said, "A bishop should maintain neutrality between the Conservative and the Liberal Parties because that is the teaching of the Roman Pontiffs."
> Schumacher answered, "You have very poorly understood that doctrine. The Pope commands maintaining neutrality when the political parties are Catholic and disagree on points that have nothing to do with religion, such as the royalist and republican parties in France. But he has never commanded neutrality between truth and error; between the Conservative Party, the only one in the Republic of the Sacred Heart that works for Christian politics, and the Liberal Party that, by its very nature, its history and its actions, strives to implant anti-Catholic teachings many times condemned by the Supreme Pontiffs."

In agreement with Schumacher was Julio Matovelle, who called the Catholics martyrs who had fallen in the battles of Cuenca, and who in Gonzalez Suarez's mind were revolutionaries who had died in the grave sin of rebellion.

A Catholic layman in turn opposed the bishop of Ibarra in these terms:

> It is clear that what Your Illustrious Lordship calls Colombian invasion is the reaction of the Ecuadorian Conservative Party that has opened operations against Alfaro on the northern border of the Republic. You could have then said more frankly, "The Conservative restoration of Ecuador will not contribute to the good of the Catholic religion; and even if it did contribute, it would not be licit to cooperate with it, because the fall of Alfaro would be a very grave evil…" But is there no kind of peace that is disgraceful and

no war that is glorious? It does not matter. "In exchange for the benefit that our friend Alfaro will reign, let us love disgrace, let us strive for disgrace to reign..." Monsignor Gonzalez Suarez sheds tears of tenderness, if Alfaro calls him his friend, if Moncayo attends his discussion groups."[3]

Saint Thomas Aquinas, to whom, because of the reliability and sublimity of his doctrine, is given the name of "Angelic Doctor," states that in spiritual matters greater obedience is due to the spiritual power than to the temporal. Vice versa, in what pertains to the purely civil good, greater obedience is due to the temporal power than to the spiritual, in accordance with the words of Jesus Christ, "Render unto God, the things that are God's; and unto Caesar the things that are Caesar's."

Schumacher, by leaving Conservatives their freedom of action so that they could duly evaluate the events and judge the legitimacy of the armed movement, followed the Angelic Doctor and marvelously fulfilled Gonzalez Suarez's principle, "Our priests must remain high above any political party, whatever it may be called." On the contrary, the bishop of Ibarra, instead of putting his own doctrine into practice, plunged into party politics by condemning the Conservative guerrillas; and he covered himself with ignominy and opprobrium by favoring, by that condemnation, a usurper, Masonic, assassin and sacrilegious political party.

In chapters two and three we saw that Monsignor Esteves Toral, Bishop of Cuenca, slipped into an analogous error, but of much less transcendence. He ran up against Garcia Moreno, who appealed to the Pope, and the latter imposed the obligation on that prelate to retract and amend his ways. But now there was no Garcia Moreno. The result was described by an Alfarist in these words, "Thanks to the sagacious intervention of Gonzalez Suarez, Alfaro ended his period of government by seeing the emergence of peace."

After the electoral pantomime in the barracks, General Leonidas Plaza had the majority of votes, and was proclaimed president of the Republic. It was August 31, 1901. There was an amnesty by virtue of which nearly all exiled persons returned.[4]

Continuing the religious persecution initiated by Alfaro, President Plaza, or the Congress of his handiwork, on October 3, 1902, promulgated the Law of Civil Matrimony and Divorce. The bishops launched protests for this assault on the Catholic conscience of the nation, but the

## The Mason, Alfaro, and Six of his Minions Are Lynched

government closed its ears. However, his Holiness Pope Leo XIII addressed these words of encouragement to Their Excellencies:

> Do not lose heart, Venerable Brothers, that in spite of your protests those laws, so opposed to the progress of civil order and the rights of the Catholic religion, have been approved and sanctioned, ... Beseech the Heart of Jesus assiduously, to whom your country was the first of all nations to be solemnly consecrated, that, through the abundance of His mercy, He would deign to grant better times to the Ecuadorian church.

The same year, on October 18, 1902, the twenty-ninth anniversary took place of Garcia Moreno's executive approval of the legislative decree for the consecration of Ecuador to the Heart of Jesus. Touched by that memory, Father Julio Matovelle took up residence next to the work on the Basilica of the National Vow, promising to bring the construction to a happy end. He had three religious Oblates of his recently founded congregation as helpers.

November 22, 1903, was the golden anniversary of the beatification of Mariana de Jesus. It is unnecessary to ponder the splendor with which such an anniversary was celebrated, especially in the Church of the Society of Jesus,[5] where the remains of the Lily of Quito[6] repose. Among the literary pieces in that regard, we are pleased to present some stanzas of the poetry composed by the Peruvian poet Jose Panizo, S. J.[7]

1. [O Mariana de Jesus Paredes...]
   Did your Ecuador do no more?[8] Heaven be praised!
   It gave an example to the New World.
   The soaring eagle sees the ground,
   It descends not, but flies farther on!
2. Ecuador followed the sad fate of the Church
   For your country is the nation of the faith.
   And Ecuador lovingly united itself to the Divine Heart;
   Since it, too, was the nation of Love.
3. Ah! Your lips perhaps on that day
   Were what whispered the beautiful idea
   Into the ear of the man who ruled
   Your country, when it was seen as great.
4. And when the light of one morning dawned
   I saw your streets in Quito decked,

> And in unison with the sound of the bell,
> I heard the soldier's cannon thunder.
> 5. And the noble youth and the pure virgin
> To the holy temple eagerly flew;
> And to that temple too, from the heights,
> Jesus descended amidst his angels.
> 6. See Him, Mariana: His chest exposed,
> His wounded Heart He shows.
> See that ring I notice in His hand,
> Your beloved nation to receive it goes.
> 7. The veiled face, modest and lovely,
> Advances now toward Christ's throne.
> Oh! How beautiful and how loving is she!
> Oh! How loving and how beautiful is He!
> 8. Finally she bows in adoration and with a burning sigh,
> She said and cried, "Thine, I must be called";
> He put the ring upon her, and on her forehead
> He impressed a wedding kiss;
> 9. And she, inspired by holy affection
> Also kissed the wounded Heart;
> And meanwhile the angels kept silence,
> Gazing at the lovely scene with envy.
> 10. Ecuador, Ecuador, beloved name,
> As though I hear "My Homeland!"
> Indeed, I love you. And why not? Man has never
> In this world loved only his mother.[9]

On August 15, 1904, the Oblate Priests founded the fortnightly magazine entitled *El Voto Nacional*[10] whose purpose was to promote the continuation of work on the great Basilica.

On October thirteenth of the same year, President Plaza gave his executive approval to the "Law of Worship," through which religious communities were deprived of their economic possessions. Those possessions became the property of the State, and their administration was placed in the hands of its employees. This robbery was also given the name of "The law of the Dead Hands." What was pillaged passed into living hands.

During those days, Quito was shocked by the news that the Peruvian invaders had killed twenty Ecuadorian soldiers in the eastern settlement of Solano. The former had fought with modern rifles while the defenders, with rifles from the time of the Independence called "Kropacher," which could serve more as clubs than firearms. President Plaza, with criminal cynicism exclaimed, "We should not fight for a piece of land that we are unable to colonize." Then why did they expel the Jesuits, who certainly were able to colonize it? The Usurper and his ministers did not take long to visit the Peruvian Legation in Quito, where they drank champagne and danced. Here is another revealing case of the subjection of Ecuadorian politics to Peruvian Masonry.

On May 5, 1904, the Ecuadorian Plenipotentiary, Carlos Tobar, and the Brazilian Plenipotentiary, Baron de Rio Branco, signed a protocol and alliance, to militarily oppose the Peruvians who were occupying territories that did not belong to them. However, that very beneficial treaty was not ratified by the Congress of Quito or by President Plaza. Who does not see the black hand of the Great Peruvian Lodge holding superior authority?

On July 2, 1905, the Redemptorists from Riobamba were expelled from that city and from Ecuador. Needless to say, this outrage was perpetrated in the dead of night.[11]

Towards the end of the year 1905, over in Belgium near Namur, a small village with the name of Beez gave the asylum of a guest to Doctor Aurelio Espinosa Coronel, a Quitonian, who, persecuted in Ecuador, had left for the Old World with his whole family. He enrolled his children in the best schools. During vacation time he resided in the aforesaid village, where he conversed during long hours with the parish priest, who did not delay in uttering these complaints to heaven:

> "Oh, Jesus and my God! How canst Thou allow the Land of Garcia Moreno, so glorious at a time not very long ago, which bore witness to a splendid faith; how canst Thou now allow it to be oppressed by Thine enemies, and in peril of continuing to cede more and more Catholic ground?"
>
> "It is because Ecuadorians do not ask Me; they do not plead or pray to Me," was Our Lord's answer. Such a response may or may not have been of a strictly miraculous character.[12]

Then the inspired priest wrote a prayer expressly destined to be prayed for Ecuador, which, having been translated into Spanish from the French by Doctor Espinosa Coronel, reads as follows:

Arise and defend us, Lord God of Hosts! Raise men powerful in deeds and words that they may gain victory against Thy enemies. Dispel, Lord, as smoke, those impure legions that blaspheme Thy Holy Name. Unfurl, O Jesus, the standard of Thy Holy Cross and do Thou Thyself defend Thy precious inheritance. Who is like Jesus, the Son of the living God? Most loving Hearts of Jesus and Mary, have mercy on us!

These prayers, having been sent to his country by the distinguished Quitonian exile, were prayed by Catholics in Ecuador and without a shadow of a doubt, have influenced the events that followed.[13]

Close to the end of his presidential term of four years, Leonidas Plaza decreed another electoral farce, by making his friend Lizardo Garcia receive the majority of votes, who assumed the Supreme Leadership on August 31, 1905.[14]

Unable to contain his yearning to rule, General Eloy Alfaro launched a revolution. He had in his favor an enormous sum of money placed at his command by Mr. Harman, an entrepreneur of the railway under construction. Some battalions allowed themselves to take bribes. There were war meetings of an oppositional fate. Liberals against liberals; Masons against Masons. The decisive battle took place on the highland plateau of Chasqui, near Cotopaxi, on January 15, 1906. The Alfarists won and their caudillo entered Quito and was proclaimed Supreme Head.[15]

On April twentieth of the same year a miracle took place at the College of Saint Gabriel.[16] This name or title had been given by Monsignor Ignacio Checa thirty-four years earlier, since its new building had been constructed by President Gabriel Garcia Moreno. The wonder was seen in an oil painting of Our Lady of Sorrows. Her exposed heart, pierced by seven swords, appears on her chest. The picture was hanging on a wall in the boarding students' dining hall. At seven forty-five at night, while they were engaged in after-dinner conversation, some three or four boys noticed that the Blessed Virgin closed her eyes slowly and then slowly opened them likewise. To be more certain, they rose from their seats and went close in front of the picture. Without any doubt they saw the Virgin continue closing and opening her eyes. They shouted out excitedly. Faced with the novelty, all the other boarders came close, thirty-five in all. Two Jesuits approached, Brother Luis Alverdi, the temporal coadjutor,[17] and a priest, Father Andres Roesch, the first of whom exclaimed, "This is a miracle." The latter, making an

## The Mason, Alfaro, and Six of his Minions Are Lynched 215

effort not to give credence, nailed his eyes to the image and clearly noticed that the Blessed Virgin closed and opened her eyes. A glacial coldness came upon his whole body. The students unanimously shouted, "Now she's closing her eyes; now she's opening them." And they trembled before a wonder that surpassed all natural laws. A quarter of an hour passed and the image continued working the miracle. Bewildered, Father Roesch clapped his hands to leave the dining hall and go to chapel.

Five days later a Canonical Process was established. Theologians and medical doctors examined the witnesses and their declarations. The result was that the metropolitan ecclesiastical authority said the prodigy was historically certain and authorized public veneration of the holy image.[18]

Undoubtedly it was an omen of the misfortunes that would still befall the country. Therefore, the Virgin chose an image with the expression of her sorrows and her sad eyes shedding tears. It was also a sign of her motherly solicitude, especially for the childhood and youth of Ecuador. Truly the miraculous image, called the *Dolorosa del Colegio,* contributed to sustaining the faith of the Ecuadorian people, in spite of the persecutions. How many unbelievers were converted! How many lukewarm Catholics became fervent! Our Heavenly Mother was troubled and shed tears because she foresaw Alfaro's September 24, 1906, decree abolishing the teaching of the catechism in municipal as well as national schools; a decree that became a law of the Constitutional Charter, sanctioned by Alfaro himself on December twenty-third of the same year.

Many Ecuadorians had already apostatized from their faith, seduced by money and jobs given by the Usurper. Now they wanted to destroy the root of Catholicism in Ecuador by stopping children from learning the faith. Fortunately there were numerous, energetic protests. The Archbishop of Quito at this time was His Grace Gonzalez Suarez, appointed by the Roman Pontiff, Pope Pius X. Faced with laicized education, the brand-new Metropolitan now applied a cautery of indelible ignominy by means of his discourses; and upon the promoters and executers of godless education he imposed the name of "the Nation's Gravediggers."[19]

The miracle of April twentieth put fear into the legislators of that year, who again wanted to decree the expulsion of the Jesuits. They recalled that their identical resolution had failed nine years earlier when confronting the terrible Quitonian crowd armed with rocks. Now that the College of San Gabriel had been converted into the Sanctuary of the Virgin of Sorrows, resistance would be much more vehement. Primitivo Yela, representative of Los Rios province, publicly declared that the new attempt to expel the Jesuits was annulled by the miracle of April twentieth.[20]

Here a Providential connection can be noted:

Garcia Moreno, bathed in blood, died at the foot of Our Lady of Sorrows. On the seventeenth anniversary of his death, the Republic was consecrated by President Luis Cordero to the Most Pure Heart of Mary. Fourteen years later, the miracle of April twentieth occurred in an image that united the Virgin of Sorrows to the Heart of Mary. Moreover, this prodigy not only saved the existence of the college founded by Garcia Moreno, but also increased its renown, since the miraculous image began to be called "Our Lady of Sorrows of the College of Saint Gabriel."[21]

Let us return to the year 1906. In Guayaquil there were newspapers such as *El Ecuatoriano, El Grito del Pueblo, El Telegrafo,* and *La Dictadura*[22] that dared oppose Alfaro's Government. Now, on September seventeenth, at night, the *Garroteros*, to the cry of "Long live Alfaro!" attacked the print shops and destroyed the machinery, scattered the type and broke the furniture.

The next day, the same damage was done in Cuenca against the editorial press, the *Eco del Azuay.*[23]

As to the guerrilla fighters, only the now famous Antonio Vega resumed his armed attacks. On December 9, 1906, gunfire broke out in the place called "Ayancay," in the province of Canar. He was defeated, taken prisoner and assassinated with two bullet holes in his head. In the state of agony he was transported to Cuenca where he received the holy oils and absolution by the Redemptorist Esteban Maret. Half an hour later this Catholic soldier worthy of being compared to Judas Machabeus expired. The Alfarists disseminated that Antonio Vega had committed suicide. No impartial person believed such nonsense.

On January 15, 1907, Vicente Nieto, Director of his newspaper entitled *Fray Gerundio,*[24] wrote and published a few litanies "to be prayed by Father Abelardo Moncayo," Garcia Moreno's ex-Jesuit assassin and now a famous Alfarist. Here as a sample are four of the invocations:

> Alfaro, thief of the bonds issued from Lima with your signature: be ye accursed.

Alfaro, thief of all fiscal Treasuries: be ye accursed.

Alfaro, thief of the cattle from Chisinche, Buena Vista, El Salto, Machangara, Nino Jesus, Santa Rosa, Ucubamba, Galte and Changala: be ye accursed.

Alfaro, Assassin of Tello, Vivar, Bowen, Guillen, Francisco Vasconez Maldonado, Moscoso, Santana, Bustamante, Spons, Rosillo, Sanchez, Briones, Canto's wife, Coronel, Vega, etc: be ye accursed.[25]

The following day the *Garroteros* appeared and beat poor Nieto, took him prisoner and destroyed his printing press. That was in Quito. We pass over the repeated assaults, outrages and slaughtering by Alfarists against Placistas,[26] Conservatives and young people who had asked for electoral freedom.[27]

It was November 1, 1907, when Monsignor Manuel Maria Polit was in Rome and received episcopal consecration. In an audience with His Holiness Pope Pius X, he heard these words from his lips:

"You ought to introduce Garcia Moreno's cause of beatification. Take advantage of my Pontificate. You Ecuadorians will never find a Pope like me, so desirous of placing your Hero on the altars, nor a College of Cardinals like the present one, so eager to contribute to the glorification of such an exalted person."

"Oh, Holy Father," the newly-consecrated bishop answered, "the situation in Ecuador, as Your Holiness well knows, is horrifying. The government would never permit the least step in this regard. Unfortunately, in our country antichristian political circumstances prevail to such a degree that it would be a dangerous temerity to initiate this so praiseworthy cause. For now, it only remains for us to wait in patience and to trust in God for a favorable, or a perhaps less adverse, future time for our immortal hero."

His Holiness listened to these words with sorrow, and went on to treat other matters. Monsignor Polit was correct. Any step by the Ecuadorian Church supporting the pope would have been violently attacked by the Alfarist *Garroteros*. This was for sure. The *Garroteros* would have intervened.[28]

By this time Masonry had duplicated its tentacles. In Guayaquil a Masonic Temple already existed. There were two more lodges: one was called "Fraternal Chain and Temple of Friendship," and the other, "Natural Law." Finally, there was "The Society to Protect Childhood," whose purpose was to stop the teaching of the catechism to children.

The following document has particular significance, published in the "Masonic Annual of the Great Lodge of Ecuador from 1926 to 1927,"[29] printed in Guayaquil:

> The Masonic life of the Illustrious Brother Gaspar Alamiro Plaza, thirty-third degree. Due to his important performance as a Rosicrucian, the Peruvian Supreme Council wanted to raise him to the rank of Knight Kadosh; and since Guayaquil then lacked an Areopagus, for that purpose it expressly commissioned General Eloy Alfaro, who possessed that high degree and, at that period of time, was invested with the constitutional presidency of the Republic of Ecuador. The act of investing Brother Plaza was carried out on February 13, 1909.[30]

The following year began with Alfaro's frequent visits to Guayaquil. It was rumored that these visits were due to the delicate health of the Dictator, who needed to be in a tropical climate. Soon afterwards the Old Fighter himself roused the Ecuadorians' patriotism, in favor of a war in defense of the Amazon borders. The events that followed engendered a well-founded belief in the country that such stays by Alfaro in Guayaquil had the object of putting him more in contact with the Peruvian President Leguia, to prepare the subterfuge of an international war, advantageous to Peru and to Alfaro's interests.

The Political Leader of Rimac[31] also provoked desires for war in his people. In Lima the people attacked the Ecuadorian Embassy, tore off the shield, dragging and stepping on it. In Quito the people did the same with the Peruvian shield. Archbishop Gonzalez Suarez stated publicly that Alfaro's conduct was patriotic and sincere, worthy of all support; and electrified the multitudes with this highly rhetoric paragraph: "If Ecuador must disappear, let it disappear; but not tangled in the threads of diplomacy, but rather in the open air and carrying arms."

On the other hand, a good number of Ecuadorians said that Alfaro had sold himself to Peru, since he had to obey the Peruvian Lodges like a vassal. Here are some facts and sayings to prove it:

> 11. Promotions in military rank in the Ecuadorian army were made from Lima.

12. Since 1900 there was a newspaper in Guayaquil by the name of *La Razon*,³² written by Peruvians, for intervening in Ecuador's internal policies.
13. On March 20, 1909, the newspaper Fray Gerundio published these concepts: "It is not difficult for the Supreme Council of Peru to order Brother Eloy Alfaro to sacrifice the army to the Peruvian hordes in an upcoming conflict; or to call upon him to deliver the Ecuadorian territory to our neighbors to the South. Is not the Peruvian invasion of the East and Alfaro's silence a Masonic plan?"
14. In June of 1909, the Peruvians did in fact peacefully invade Zarumilla, without meeting any effective attempt by Alfaro to resist. *Fray Gerundio* in its issue number one hundred ninety-four raised this question, "Did not the Supreme Federated Council of Peru involve itself in the intrigues by obliging these known Brothers in apron and compass to take the step that they did?"
15. On May 6, 1910, the daily Quitonian newspaper, *El Comercio*,³³ stated that the disorder and the rabble-rousing speeches in Ecuador had their origin in Peru, and that from there the order came to carry them out.³⁴
16. Luis Carbo, of a liberal creed, wrote, "The war between Ecuador and Peru will be a great crime and an unforgiveable error."
17. Alfaro's Ecuadorian army was in a very inferior situation to Peru's. The Alfarist, Roberto Andrade, himself confessed the truth in these terms:

> Peru mobilized over thirty thousand men and began to send them to the border. It put abundant war material and many troops in Tumbes and the surrounding area. Its army was relatively respectable, due to its better organization and discipline. It had better war equipment at its disposal than we had, especially maritime equipment.

18. The journalist, J. Calle, of a liberal creed, wrote these lines:

> We have in the Republic Alfarist Generals and Colonels incapable of killing a hen; who never smelled gunpowder or entered a barracks except to drink beer and

eat meat on anniversaries and the name days of their patron saints; they would faint in the case of danger, and are only good for giving beatings with clubs to defenseless people and receiving salaries...

The governmental program is carried out by calling Peruvians *Bertoldos*, cowards and queers; without war provisions, without effective resources, without naval units...

19. Once again, on March 13, 1910, the newspaper *Fray Gerundio*, written in large part by Vicente Nieto, stated the following:

> Does Alfaro perhaps think he will defend Ecuador with the mob of *Garroteros* and the rabble of illiterates that surround him? Perchance the lots deciding the fate of our country will be cast upon the green table cloth of the Masonic Lodges![35]

20. The Guayaquil newspaper *El Guante*[36] ratified the above with the following words:

> Today soldiers' individual bravery and the troop's collective courage is a secondary factor for victory in armies that fight and destroy at great distances. But, how can it be thought that Alfaro takes the conflict seriously, when Ecuador did not have an army and did not improvise one; when the immense majority of the reserve corps did not have target practice; when, if they did practice, it was with Kropacher and not with Mannlicher rifles, which were the rifles that they should have used...?
>
> How can the war be believed in when, notwithstanding extraordinary taxes, not even one lousy canon was bought for the defense...?
>
> How can victory be dreamed about when the sights on the majority of the rifles were skewed, and you could not kill an iguana with them, as the soldiers from *El Oro* substantiated?
>
> ...not even the first division could be formed from veterans and necessary recourse was to mix soldiers from

## The Mason, Alfaro, and Six of his Minions Are Lynched 221

the battle line with reserve soldiers, the latter without the most indispensible strategic notions of modern war...

Ecuador's wretched military situation was no secret even outside the nation, for the London *Times* pointed it out in these terms:

> Peru has five million inhabitants, obligatory military service and five warships. The population of Ecuador is one million and a half inhabitants, of which some two hundred thousand are whites. It lacks a navy, and could not sustain war, for, in all probability, it is the most backward nation in South America.

In November *El Guante* published a caricature in the form of a monument in which Alfaro, with a whip in his right hand, was mounted astride the shoulders of a woman in rags, her hands in chains and her eyes blindfolded. On her skirt were these words: "The Nation." Under her feet lay a sheep with the name of "Laws." Underneath sat a naked man, chained by the ankles: he is the Ecuadorian people. Finally, on the bottom or pedestal was this inscription: Eloy Alfaro, in his youth he was a pirate. The people acclaimed him as President. He was a Dictator. He took possession of power by force and was a tyrant.[37]

In another issue of the same newspaper Alfaro appears hanged, dangling from a tree. Underneath is this inscription: "The death of Judas."

The political atmosphere in 1910 was such that in the month of June, an express mail reached Quito, sent by the President of Peru, Mr. Leguia. It was [carried by] a young Ecuadorian whose last name was Duran, who, unable to obtain an audience with Alfaro immediately, mounted a horse and went to the town of El Quinche, saying to himself, "I am going to visit my mama and will return to Quito tomorrow." It was June 8, 1910. Halfway there, at the Puru-anta hacienda, the traveler drank a few glasses of sugar cane liquor and some glasses of brandy. He became so sick that he had to be carried in the arms of another horseback rider. When he arrived at El Quinche, the region of his birth, he entered into agony, received the holy oils from the parish priest, Father Felix Granja, and died at seven o'clock in the evening, as is recorded in the civil register of deaths in that neighborhood. He was thirty-two years and three months old. His full name was Justo Arsenio Duran Jimenez.

The next morning his mother, Mercedes Jimenez, found an envelope with President Alfaro's written address in her ill-fated son's briefcase. She went to the above-mentioned priest and put it into his hands.

Mr. Gregorio Salcedo, a friend of the Duran family, was then thirty- some years old. Well, years later that man in turn said to his son, Eli Jacinto Salcedo: "The ill-fated young Duran came from Peru. At Puru-anta he felt the effects of a violent colic. He died on reaching Quinche. Among the objects that he had brought, there were documents written by the Peruvian President Leguia and addressed to President Alfaro."[38]

The parish priest, Father Felix Granja, was surprised to see that the Peruvian correspondence was sealed, not with gum but with sealing wax, and showed Masonic symbols such as triangles and three dots. "Beware! I smell a rat!" he exclaimed to himself. "A Masonic communiqué, and from Lima and in these times when we are feverishly preparing for war against Peru...? Alfaro does not concretely know of the arrival of such a document. The bearer has just died unexpectedly. Perhaps here is the key to the international conflict and the finger of God." He hurriedly tore open the envelope and read the contents, which were told by that priest to a few persons. But since it was important, it has been published in many pamphlets and even printed books, for example in the weekly *La Bomba*, in the magazine *El Voto Nacional*, and in the newspaper *Frente a Frente*.[39] The priest, Father Manuel Maria Betancourt, was the chief editor of the latter newspaper. The author went to him on Monday, April 17, 1972, looking for reliable testimony. That priest, now a canon in the Metropolitan Cathedral, satisfied those desires in the following terms:

> In Quinche I heard the dreadful story twice from the lips of the parish priest himself, Doctor Felix Granja. At the beginning of the year 1934, that priest came to the Eugenio Espejo Hospital in Quito to be attended by the doctors. Then the Jesuit priest, Father Felix Heredia and I presented ourselves at that health center and begged Doctor Granja to repeat the breathtaking account to us. Father Heredia made the sign of the cross upon himself when I asked him to write down the priest's report. Here is, in substance, what Father Granja called "The Protocol between Augusto Leguia, President of Peru, and Eloy Alfaro, President of Ecuador":

## The Mason, Alfaro, and Six of his Minions Are Lynched   223

Article 1. There will be a fake war between Peru and Ecuador.

Article 2. So that the reasons to justify that war would be more impressive, the respective governments will promote violent rallies, attacking the Ecuadorian Legation in Peru and the Peruvian Legation in Ecuador. Those acts had in fact already been carried out.

Article 3. Ecuador will mobilize its army at the southern border, in the province of Loja as well as in that of El Oro. Its officers must be in Alfaro's absolute confidence.

Article 4. Combat will be enjoined, and the Ecuadorian army, always defeated, will retreat until it reaches Quito.

Article 5. The Peruvian army will enter and take over the Ecuadorian capital.

Article 6. Peru, by way of indemnification for war expenditures will demand the occupation and property of the whole Eastern Region of Ecuador, whose limit will be the mountain range.

Article 7. An ad hoc convention will meet which will approve the transfer of all those immense territories to the Peruvian nation.

Article 8. In exchange, the government of Peru will deposit the quantity of twenty-five million soles[40] in the Bank of London, payable to Alfaro's Government.[41]

It should be made known, dear reader, that Father Granja was the parish priest in the town of San Felipe, close to Latacunga, around the years of 1930. And so, he also told about the Protocol there. One of his listeners, the Jesuit priest, Father Jose Bolanos, who was there as a missionary, did not cease telling what he had heard, and the author of this book was one of his listeners. Now then, the author can assure that what Father Bolanos transmitted does not differ in anything substantial from what was transmitted by the most Reverend Father Betancourt. Only one detail was added by Father Bolanos, that is, that this document was inside a metal tube, a detail that seems very likely considering the great importance of the document.

Returning to the month of June, 1910, and to Quinche, Father Granja, carrying the sensational protocol in his pocket, mounted a horse and went to Quito, where he showed those pages to the Archbishop,

Gonzalez Suarez, who, angered and amazed, exclaimed, "Alfaro has deceived me. The Virgin of Quinche has saved Ecuador!"

He did not take long to address a few lines to the Dictator, letting him know the atrocious discovery and entreating him to liquidate that farce of a war with its dreadful consequences. If he did not do so, the Archbishop would inform the public about that infamy.

It is a fact that Alfaro hurried to suspend all war rallies, which produced enormous surprise in the Ecuadorian people. Humbly he deferred to the United States Ambassador, settler of the conflict through peaceful means.[42]

Four days before the death of Justo Duran in Quinche, Alfaro decreed that the armed forces should continue in the state of combat. Twenty days after that death, the Ecuadorian Chancellor Peralta said that the Ecuadorian troops had already retreated from the border; but that those from Peru did not retreat. President Leguia was still not informed of the failure of his courier, Duran. Besides, for the very superior Peruvian army, the retreat must have been very disgraceful. The following paragraph by Wilfrido Loor fits well here: "When the people of Quito realized that the conflict had been a farce, they hunted down Roberto Andrade as a traitor, who was a perpetual guest of the Peruvian Legation in July 1910. What was he doing there?" The author's answer is obvious: the commissioned Alfarist needed to inform the Peruvian Ambassador about the setback that had occurred, exhort him to have patience and make the Peruvian forces retreat, lest Gonzalez Suarez publish the fateful document.[43]

The citation of this sentence, very common at that time in Quito, also fits well here: "Alfaro fears Gonzalez Suarez's pen more than an army." The knowledge that His Grace had the document brought by Duran instilled dread in all the Masons. To what did they resort against an archbishop who had supported Alfaro's government in the war against Peru, and who had previously defended it against Catholic guerrilla fighters? The following paragraph serves as an answer, written by His Grace in his own handwriting, signed on February 2, 1912:

> Every day I receive reports, notices and warnings about the plans that unjustified enemies have prepared against my life. I consider them unjustified, because not even in thought have I done them any evil, nor do I now desire them any evil. It is publicly affirmed that the Masons are the ones who have decreed my death. I confess that I have always been convinced that secret soci-

eties are the worst enemies that the Catholic Church has; and that the nations in which those societies manage to take control of the government are miserable and hasten to their ruin. May God forgive my assassins as I forgive them."[44]

By virtue of such antecedents, the author judges as historically certain the farce of the war and the existence of the protocol whose carrier was Justo Arsenio Duran Jimenez. This last attestation by Felix Granja can serve to support the author's judgment, "Duran said to one of his friends or companions: 'With my own hands I have to place this document in Alfaro's. I have only twenty-four hours to remain in Quito, at the end of which I must return to Lima.'"[45] The author is in agreement with the assertion of a liberal writer quoted by Wilfrido Loor: "If some day raising a statue to General Eloy Alfaro is attempted, it should be erected in the eastern territories ceded to Peru."

According to the French erudite LaSallian, Remigio German, His Grace Gonzalez Suarez gave the authentic protocol to the priest, Father Luis Escalante, so that he would put it in the archives. This priest made allusion to that crime of Alfaro's in the newspaper entitled *La Hermandad Ferroviaria.*[46] The author looked for that newspaper, but could not find it.

The magazine *Boletin Eclesiastico*[47] added the following recollection to the necrology of Father Felix Granja, who died in Quito on September 17, 1939:

> The Reverend Father Granja related that during our conflict with Peru in the year 1910, when he put a document with Masonic seals into the hands of the Most Excellent Archbishop Gonzalez Suarez, the sale of our Ecuadorian East to Peru by high magistrates of our nation was made evident. The Reverend Father Granja related this event on several occasions to distinguished persons. The weekly magazine from Guayaquil, *La Bomba,* also dealt with this crime of high treason against the nation, and no one, to our knowledge, contradicted that publication presented in two issues. Undoubtedly the surviving traitors feared that the original document would be published.

Towards the year 1955, the priest, Father Efrain Santeli, saw that protocol on a desk in the Curia and exclaimed, "But how can they have this in sight and in public!" Now, a few hours later this document was then hidden. But Canon Betancourt is of the opinion that what Santeli saw was not the Peruvian original, but rather one of the five copies that the aforesaid Prebendary wrote as a result of the interview with Doctor Granja in 1934.

The year 1911 arrived, and they proceeded to the familiar electoral fiction conducted especially in the barracks. Alfaro's friend, Emilio Estrada, received the majority of votes and was acclaimed President of the Republic. But after a few days Alfaro suspected that his elected man was capable of betraying the Liberal Party. Consequently he fought to hinder his ascension. How? Through a dictatorship of Alfaro himself.

On August eleventh of the same year, Quito was the theater of battle between Alfarists and Estradists. The latter sang victory. The people and the army insulted, reviled and vilified the Old Fighter, and did everything possible to kill him. With great difficulty a few Alfarists managed to bring their Caudillo into the Chilean Embassy.

On August thirty-first, Estrada began his Presidency. Alfaro and his family, protected by a powerful escort so as not to be lynched, abandoned the capital, went down to Guayaquil, boarded a ship and went to Panama.[48]

Emilio Estrada did not betray the Liberal Party, but he remained in power for only four months, being the victim of a heart attack which brought him to eternity on December twenty-first. According to the law, he was replaced by Carlos Freile Zaldumbide, whose duty it was to convoke new presidential elections. But in Guayaquil an Alfarist leader, General Pedro Montero, sent messages to Eloy Alfaro who was in Panama, and conjured him to return to Ecuador, to save the unity and harmony of the Liberal Party. Intoxicated by reckless ambition, Alfaro left Panama and disembarked in Guayaquil. It was January 4, 1912.

In Quito and in the other towns in the mountain region, anti-Alfarist fury was at its height. The army and the people threw themselves onto the field of honor. On the eleventh of that same January, both armies engaged in combat at the place called Huigra, with the defeat of the Alfarists. The conquerors advanced toward the coast, and in the neighborhood of Naranjito, the Alfarists were defeated for the second time. It was the fourteenth of the same month. The Alfarists suffered a third disaster in Yaguachi, a torrid and swampy land. It was the seventeenth of that same January.

In Guayaquil, after a skirmish, the defeat of the Alfarists was definitive; the sun of the twenty-second of that same January was shining. Eloy Alfaro, his nephew Flavio Alfaro, his brother Medardo Alfaro,

## The Mason, Alfaro, and Six of his Minions Are Lynched 227

along with Pedro Montero, Ulpiano Paez and Manuel Serrano were taken prisoners. The people from Guayaquil as well as those from Quito shouted, demanding that the prisoners be shot; but the Quitonians, moreover, asked for the penalty and punishment to be inflicted in the capital city.

The twenty-fifth of January: the prisoners' trial. Pedro Montero appeared in court, and tried to justify himself before the judges by dint of lies. Civilians and soldiers invaded the courtroom and killed the defendant with bullets, stabbing him with a dagger and beating him with a small chair. They threw the corpse into the street where they tied it with a rope and dragged it to the Rocafuerte Plaza. Here they cut off his head and testicles. They opened his chest and tore out his heart. Everything was thrown into a bonfire.

If the trial of the other defendants would have continued, they would have suffered the same tragic fate. Therefore they were transferred immediately to Quito. At two o'clock in the morning, on the twenty-sixth, the Alfaros and the rest of the defendants left the Governor's palace and were taken to the Duran railway station.[49]

The twenty-eighth of January, 1912, was a very famous tragic day in the highest degree. The defendants got off the train almost a mile before the station in Quito so they would not be lynched by the people who waited for them there. It was eleven o'clock in the morning. They got into an automobile that drove on roads and less populated streets. Nevertheless, a multitude of civilians threw rocks at the vehicle. Finally, opening a way through the dense crowd, the car reached the curb of the Panoptico, the enormous and beautiful stone jail built by Garcia Moreno.

Meanwhile fliers circulated on the city streets from hand to hand with the following in print:

> I beg and implore all the inhabitants of this Catholic city to abstain from making any hostile demonstration against the prisoners. Conduct yourselves toward them with sentiments of Christian charity. I beg and implore it in the name of our Lord Jesus Christ. Federico, Archbishop of Quito.

Here is the official reciprocation of the Catholic Church in favor of those who for sixteen years had persecuted and reviled it. Some individuals tore up those fliers, others wanted to have a rally against the Archbishop, labeled as an Alfarist.

The first one to leave the automobile was Eloy Alfaro, then the rest: that is, his brother Medardo, his nephew Flavio, Ulpiano Paez, Manuel Serrano and Luciano Corral: six in all. A soldier from the multitude dashed forward and kicked the ex-dictator. The bodyguard made efforts to stop the prisoners from being lynched by the immense multitude of people that crowded together. Finally each one was inside their respective little cells, well locked with crossbars and bolts.[50]

The crowd began to withdraw in despair and disappointment. But within the Panoptico itself there were bitter enemies of Alfarism: soldiers in charge of guarding them and a few prisoners for common offences. While the latter removed the adobe bricks that blocked the entry to the people, who were going away, the soldiers, with rifle shots, broke the bolts, crossbars and bars that secured the main door; and then, with shouts, arm motions and waving handkerchiefs, invited the people to return and take over the prison. Civilians and soldiers hugged each other with emotion. Rifles and sabers were distributed. "Let us avenge the blood shed by those bandits in criminal campaigns!" they shouted, and penetrated the jail. They began by entering the ex-Dictator's cell, whom they interrogated, "Where are the millions, old shameless man, which you have robbed?" And they immediately dealt a blow with a club and killed him off with bullets. Then they went to Paez's, Torres', Medardo's, Serrano's, Coral's and Flavio's rooms and exterminated them.

Partly to take possession of the money that might be in their pockets and partly to vent their revenge the more, they stripped the corpses and immediately threw them from on high to the patio and from there to the street. There were shouts of rejoicing in the immense crowd. Even the women, although lying, boasted of having contributed to killing the evildoers. An old corpulent woman, nicknamed "Cimborazo," dressed festively in a pink suit, raised the bloody saber and exclaimed, "I come from killing the Old Bandit." Meanwhile, a woman, dressed in black, who was mourning the death of a loved one, a victim in the latest combats, stabbed the ex-Dictator's corpse, shouting insults at him, "Old bandit, thief, you still wanted to rule!" A third woman with a club was hitting his head, exclaiming, "You paid me back, Indian executioner." A religious Mercedarian reprimanded her, "Do not do that." She replied to him, "You did not lose a husband and a son in the war; I did." The soldiers fired shots into the air, after the manner of salvos of triumph and joy.

## The Mason, Alfaro, and Six of his Minions Are Lynched

They tied the corpses' feet with ropes and began to drag and parade them through the streets, three miles in the direction of *Ejido Norte* Park. Flowers were thrown from some balconies at the dragged bodies, and they applauded frenetically. The children went behind the corpses and kept plucking their beards and hair. There were voices that shouted, "Now we will have peace, because this criminal has died who never tired of waging war." The crowd was calculated at twenty thousand persons, an extraordinary number in a city of only ninety thousand inhabitants. Almost all were armed, even the little girls, at least with a knife, to kill the criminals in a kind of communal work party. The Army musical band was requested to play jubilant songs. But there was no one to grant permission, since Mr. Carlos Freile Zaldumbide, the appointed commander in chief, was sick.[51]

The multitude arrived at the *Plaza de la Independencia*.[52] A group invaded the Archbishop's Palace to ask the Illustrious Archbishop to ring the bells in celebration of the triumph; but permission was denied. On the corner where Garcia Moreno's assassin, Faustino Rayo, had been lynched, they wanted to incinerate Eloy Alfaro. During preparations for making the bonfire, the majority prevailed by shouting, "To the park, to the park."

In front of the Archbishop's Palace they clamored, "Long live the Catholic Religion! Down with Masonry!" Some also shouted, "Down with the Archbishop," perhaps because of the support that Gonzalez Suarez gave Alfaro's government in 1910. "That shout did not find its echo in the people," wrote that Prelate and he added, "I tried to do something to prevent the profanation of the corpses, but the people that accompanied me made me desist from that endeavor. My presence, on the other hand, would have been not only useless but also dangerous for sacred dignity."

During one of the stagnations of the human avalanche, the ex-Dictator's testicles were ripped out, drenched with fuel oil, put on fire and used as a game for the children who kicked them or threw them up high.

The multitude was now at the park at two in the afternoon. Three pyres were made and the incineration began. The majority of the crowd dispersed. There were groups who planned to invade the Panoptico again to kill the eighty-seven political prisoners, Alfaro's partisans. In order to stop it, the Governor, Carlos Alberto Arteta, had recourse to the Archbishop. The latter came out in the company of Monsignor Riera and Father Aguirre, highly esteemed by the Quitonians. They went around, pacifying the people. There were shouts against Gonzalez Suarez, who disappeared into the monastery of *Santo Domingo*. The presence of Riera and Aguirre prevented the continuance of the massacres.[53]

It is a fact that not a few writers and philosophers have recognized a parallel and antithesis between Eloy Alfaro and Garcia Moreno. As proof, here are some words by Bishop Schumacher, a victim of Alfarism:

> Garcia Moreno, as the personification of Christian politics, that is to say, theocracy and the reign of God; or a Masonic *jefe*, that is to say, demonocracy, or the reign of Lucifer—this is the alternative that is now presented to Ecuadorians.

On the other hand, Pio Jaramillo Alvarado, a thinker of the liberal creed has written:

> Once General Alfaro triumphed, the two antagonistic political parties were clearly defined: Garcia's clericalism and doctrinaire liberalism.

Here are the positive beneficial works carried out by Alfaro during his eleven years of administration:

In Quito, the Santa Clara Market; for its construction the executive-in-chief helped with fifty thousand sucres to the Municipal Council. Also constructed was a vast, beautiful building where an international exposition took place to celebrate the centenary of the "First Shout of Independence."[54] It is located in the *Plaza de la Recoleta*. In the *Plaza de la Independencia*, was raised the truly artistic monument to Liberty. The Conservatory of Music and Fine Arts, on a mediocre level, was established. In Ambato was raised the statue of Juan Montalvo.[55]

Garcia Moreno's principle works during his twelve years of administration were:

In Quito: the Panoptico; the Protectorate, for the technical teaching of arts and trades and which was shut down by Alfaro, and the School of Obstetrics. The Astronomic Conservatory, equipped with an internationally famous telescope and under the direction of the German Jesuit, Father Menten, the best astronomer that has walked the lands of America, who was expelled by Alfaro twenty-one years later. Also, the College of San Gabriel building and the Conservatory of Music, and the Academy of Painting and Sculpture with professors such as Antonio Neumane, who composed the national anthem, Juan Manosalvas, Luis

Cadena, Rafael Salas, and a Spaniard, Jose Gonzalez, professor of sculpture. The Polytechnic was established, rival of the best in the world, because of its machinery and museums of the highest quality, and universally famous professors such as Sodiro, Kolberg, Wolf, Dressel, etc. The enormous *Tunel de la Paz*,[56] the *Gallinazos* Bridge; introduction of the mulberry tree for silk raising; introduction of the eucalyptus tree whose benefit is incalculable, etc.

In Guayaquil: the construction of an artillery barracks called *El Modelo*.[57] Public gas street lights; the pier; the first artificial ice; the first dredges and buoys; the multiplication of lighthouses, etc.

In Imbabura, which was destroyed by the earthquake, the new Ibarra is the work of Garcia Moreno with government buildings, seminary, the Church of Our Lady of Ransom, hospital, bridge over the Tahuando River, etc. Also accomplished was the reconstruction of Otavalo; the Hatunyacu Bridge; the streets of Cotacachi, drawn by the engineer MacClellan; as well as new schools in all of Imbabura.

Babahoyo in its new, better site was Garcia Moreno's work, with its new church, Government buildings, military barracks, San Gabriel bridge, etc.

In Cuenca: its first hospital and leper hospital; the government building, designed by the Scottish architect, Thomas Reed; the Chicti, Yanuncay and Rumiurco bridges; the parish house and the Chahuarurco and the Naranjal jail, etc.

In Latacunga: the house of correction, hospital and barracks.

Garcia Moreno left in service the first railroad using the nation's money. Laying of track was continued during the Borrero, Veintimilla, Caamano and Flores administrations. In all, sixty miles of track was laid in the tropical and marshy area along the coast.[58]

Eloy Alfaro made a contract with the Yankee engineer, Archer Harman, to prolong rail laying to Quito, more or less one hundred and seventy-six miles in ten years of work, using non-Ecuadorian capital but rather money from the United States. Consequently the profits or returns from the railroad had to serve for the amortization of the debt contracted. Instead of taking advantage of the paths and bridges already constructed by Garcia Moreno, Alfaro committed the blunder of going down the deep valley of the Chanchan River, whose flooding has knocked down the bridges and destroyed the railway countless times with the consequent suspension of the service. The expense for repairs amounted to millions of dollars, paid for not by the Harman Company but by the nation of Ecuador. Hence the legislative chambers, even though most of its members were Alfaro's henchmen, asked him to show them the original contract. The dictator commanded his secretary, Alejandro Moran, to eliminate the pages in which the loss to Ecuador was the most blatant; and forwarded the document thus truncated to the national congress.[59] Here we have Alfaro's most important work.

Garcia Moreno built one hundred and eighty-six miles of highways and two hundred and forty-nine miles of bridle paths. Alfaro did absolutely nothing in this department.

Garcia Moreno kept the eastern area intact, ceded criminally to Peru by General Guillermo Franco, Alfaro's precursor. Moreover, he placed self-sacrificing Jesuit missionaries there who insured sovereignty better than soldiers. Alfaro removed the Jesuits and let the invaders from Cuzco advance freely. The farce of the war of 1910, with an increase of taxes to the poor nation and the contract of sale of the East for twenty-five million soles in Alfaro's benefit, are crimes that sink the Old Fighter to the depths of moral disgrace.[60]

Garcia Moreno founded and constructed schools such as the Bolivar in Ambato and the girls' school in Guayaquil, in addition to hundreds of primary education centers in the whole Republic; while Alfaro founded only the Mejia School in Quito, a building stolen from the Christian Brothers. One of the principals named by Alfaro was Abelardo Moncayo, Garcia Moreno's assassin.

Garcia Moreno promoted the erection of the bishoprics of Ibarra, Loja, Riobamba, and Portoviejo. Instead, Alfaro expelled the bishops from Loja, Riobamba and Portoviejo.

Garcia Moreno introduced in Ecuador the religious communities of the Jesuits, Lazarists, Redemptorists, Capuchins, De La Salle Brothers, Carmelite nuns, Augustinian nuns, Sisters of Charity, of Providence, of the Sacred Hearts and of the Good Shepherd. Alfaro expelled the De La Salle Brothers, Capuchins, Salesians, Religious of the Sacred Heart, and the Benedictine and Franciscan nuns.[61]

Garcia Moreno, in spite of the large amount of works of public utility that he accomplished, decreased taxes year after year. Alfaro increased them year after year. With Garcia Moreno the purchasing power of Ecuadorian money was great. Under Alfaro it depreciated on a large scale. Let us listen to the comparison written by Doctor Aparicio Ortega, a witness of Garcia's period and of the Alfarist period:

> During Garcia Moreno's tyranny, these were the prices here (in Quito) for food articles:

Top quality meat, five *centavos*[62] for a whole Spanish pound; eggs, twelve for one *real*;[63] pure milk, three quarts for five *centavos*. For a loaf of bread that is worth one *real* today, it cost half a *real* or simply five *centavos*. Potatoes, barley, etc., one-fourth of today's value... Then a craftsman could eat meat, eggs, milk and bread in abundance for four *reals* a day. Today, earning one *sucre*,[64] if he has anything to eat, he hardly has barley flour and broth with the shadow of meat.

Garcia Moreno founded the Normal School for whites and for natives. Alfaro re-established it only for whites.

Garcia Moreno established the Cadets' School, with professors even from the Polytechnic, such as the wise Dressel for military chemistry, and Mullendorf and Brugier for mathematics applied to war science. The Lazarist priest, Father Claverie, delivered the classes on religion and French. Let us listen to the following view expressed by Colonel Adolfo Zambrano:

> Very soon its results made known the excellence of the scientific military education in the barracks. Within the eight years of its existence, it gave the army fifty-seven officers in the three branches, which began by banishing from the practices observed in the army corps, all the corrupt practices kept and followed through habit. With the death of that great man, his great works also had to die. The Military School ceased.[65]

Alfaro re-established it. Its poor quality was described by the biographer Wilfrido Loor in these terms:

> The studies were too superficial and completely theoretical, which led to nothing practical. No one but inept persons came out of there; and Calle, in justice, was able to write: "We have Alfarist Generals and Colonels in the Republic incapable of killing a hen, who never smelled gunpowder or entered a barracks except to drink beer and eat meat on anniversaries and the name days of their patron saints: they would faint in the case of danger, and are only good for giving beatings with clubs to defenseless people and receiving salaries."

In Garcia Moreno's regime approximately seventy men guilty of great crimes were shot. Not even the enemies of that ruler have been able to accuse him of having shot delinquents of little account and even less, innocent persons. Alfaro, in the campaign against Veintimilla, had twenty-one shot, almost all deserters because of diseases and the tyrannical government; almost all the individuals were of no importance and even included some unknown persons. Maria Reyes Prieto, the sister of one of the victims, wrote, "The greatness of Garcia Moreno disturbed Eloy Alfaro; but take into account that the former shot generals and not corporals."

Alfaro made an armed revolution against Caamano's government, a government that was legal, democratic, and moreover beneficial. In naval combat, he ordered his troops to inspect a transshipment and attack a government ship, *Huacho,* whose crew and soldiers, when seeing themselves attacked by surprise, surrendered themselves as prisoners. But the liberal Caudillo led the massacre of the defenseless and innocent. Over three hundred persons, including some women and two children, perished by machetes and lances.[66]

Alfaro attacked the commander in chief by the force of arms, and during his regime the following were assassinated: Victor Leon Vivar, Father Eudoro Maldonado, the Jesuit Father Emilio Moscoso, General Antonio Vega, Juan Tello, Boven, Guillen, Francisco Vasconez, Maldonado, Santana, Bustamante, Spons, Rosillo, Sanchez, Briones, etc.

During Garcia Moreno's regime, the number of newspapers doubled, as was done during the regime of his predecessor, President Robles. Only two journalists, Valverde and Proano, were exiled for being subversives. During Alfaro's regime, sixteen printing presses were smashed to pieces; the journalist Julian de San Martin was put in jail, beaten by the *Garroteros*, and bathed in ice water early in the morning. The same torment was suffered by the columnists Rafael Polit Narvaez, Luis Felipe Lara, Javier Espinosa Coronel, etc. He had some soldiers publicly flogged as a reprisal for protesting against so much cruelty toward the innocent. The writers of the newspaper *La Palabra Libre*[67] were taken prisoner and tortured. Some were confined in Guayaquil where they died of yellow fever.

Garcia Moreno, on April 2, 1861, when assuming his first constitutional presidency, said to the members of the Convention:

> To re-establish the rule of morality, without which order is merely a truce or weariness, outside of which freedom is a decep-

tion and a chimera. To moralize a country where bloody fighting between good and evil has lasted for a space of half a century; and to moralize it through the energetic and effective repression of crime, and through the solidly religious education of the new generations. To respect and protect the holy religion of our elders, and seek from its beneficial influence the reform that laws and governments cannot obtain by themselves... These are the difficult duties that I have just imposed on myself, duties that I would not hope to fulfill, if I did not trust in the kind protection of Divine Providence.

On August 19, 1862, he responded to Monsignor Tavani's discourse with these words:

> Mr. Apostolic Delegate, seeing you among us on the memorable day of such jubilation and hope for the people and government of Ecuador, I am animated with the deepest gratitude towards Him who is the Eternal Source of all good, toward our Holy Father who has given us so many proofs of his fatherly tenderness, and toward you, His worthy representative, who, as the Messenger of the Good News, comes in his name and in the name of the Lord. The mission is as great as it is honorable with which you have been invested of putting the Concordat into execution which, tightening the bonds ever more that unite us to the center of Catholic unity, will be the cornerstone of the Republic's happiness.

On May 16, 1869, he said to the new Convention members:

> Modern civilization, created by Catholicism, degenerates and becomes debased in the measure that it departs from Catholic principles... A wall of defense must be raised between the people kneeling at the foot of the altar of the true God and the enemies of the Catholic religion that we profess.

Consequently, the Convention approved as law this subparagraph recommended by Garcia Moreno: "to be a citizen it is necessary to be Catholic."[68]

In his spiritual retreat of 1871 he wrote these resolutions, "All for the greater glory of God exclusively. Mass, daily rosary and Kempis,[69] and preserve the presence of God."

On January 18, 1871, Garcia Moreno's government protested officially against the usurpation of the Pontifical States. His was the only government in the world to show this loyalty to the Vicar of Christ.

In 1873 he also officially consecrated Ecuador to the Heart of Jesus.

In his Message of 1875, Garcia Moreno launched these brilliant expressions, "Never lose sight, Legislators, that all our little advances would be ephemeral and unfruitful if we had not founded the social order of our Republic upon the ever combated and ever triumphant rock, the Catholic Church. Her divine teaching, which neither men nor nations renounce without perishing, is the norm of our institutions and the law of our laws." This Message was sealed with the blood of its author, who carried it in his hands when he was assassinated. Having then received fourteen machete wounds and six gunshots, he exclaimed, "God does not die!"

All that was expressed on the pages of this Message constitutes the national reign of Christ in Ecuador, which the liberals refer to as "Garcian Theocracy." It lasted for twenty years, recognized by the above-mentioned Pio Jaramillo Alvarado with these words, "Garcia Moreno's shadow cast its morbid influence directly until 1895, and subterraneanly until our days, in 1923, when Liberalism takes on a nationalist modality."

Eloy Alfaro, Garcia Moreno's antipode, said on the first day of his political rule in Guayaquil, "I come to destroy Theocracy." He did everything possible for that, as has been proven in this chapter and the previous one: violent persecution of the clergy and of Catholic newspapers; trampling upon the Garcian decree of Consecration; suppression of the catechism in national and municipal schools, etc.[70]

Here is a comparison of both policies in regard to benefits. Miguel Valverde, although a liberal who had been exiled by Garcia Moreno to the Amazons, said that the Republic progressed under Garcia Moreno more than under all the other administrations from the foundation of the Republic in 1830 up to that of Antonio Flores in 1890. Under Alfaro's regime, we saw that there were more curses than blessings.[71] Aparicio Ortega, a liberal, who died without the last rites of the Catholic religion, said that Alfaro's era had been the most disgusting that the Republic had undergone.[72]

## The Mason, Alfaro, and Six of his Minions Are Lynched

The assassination of Garcia Moreno was decreed by the Masonic Lodges of Germany and Peru, and executed by four perverted individuals, of whom the principal one was, moreover, salaried. The assassination of Alfaro was decreed by the people of Ecuador and executed by the same. The death of Garcia Moreno has been the one most mourned by the Ecuadorians; there was collective weeping, even by soldiers. The death of Alfaro was celebrated with pleasure and euphoria of the masses, like that of a national triumph, with cries of jubilation. A woman of the common people, seeing Alfaro's corpse next to her house, threw a sizable stone upon his head, saying at the same time, "*Now you can blaspheme!*" That is, "Now, destroy the Theocracy!"[73]

# Endnotes

¹ Booklet entitled *Theocracy or Demonocracy?* p. 62 ff. second edition, by Monsignor Schumacher, in 1907, Herder editorial, Freiburg, Germany. Cf. Gomezjurado, *Vida de Garcia Moreno*, vol. 11, p. 218 ff.
² Doctor Wilfrido Loor, *Vida de Eloy Alfaro,* vol. 2, p. 617 ff.
³ *Idem*, p. 685 ff.
⁴ *Idem*, p. 688 ff. Also vol. 2, p. 199 ff.
⁵ The Church of the Society of Jesus is known colloquially as *La Compañía*.
⁶ Saint Mariana of Jesus de Paredes (+1645) is the first canonized saint of Ecuador. During the earthquakes and subsequent epidemics in Quito in 1645, she publicly offered herself as a victim for the city and died shortly thereafter. It is also reported that, on the day she died, her sanctity was revealed in a wonderful manner: immediately after her death, a pure white lily sprang up from her blood, blossomed and bloomed, a prodigy which has given her the title of "The Lily of Quito."
⁷ *Idem*, vol. 3, p. 729 ff. See also Wilfrido Loor, *La Vida del Padre Julio Matovelle* (*The Life of Father Julio Matovelle*), p. 405. Father Panizo wrote this poem while he was studying theology in the town of Pifo, near Quito. (Cf. Gomezjurado, *Vida de Garcia Moreno*, vol. 11, p. 222.)
⁸ There are eight stanzas that precede this one but are omitted here. (Gomezjurado, *ibid.* pp. 222-223.)
⁹ The pamphlet *Bodas de Oro de la Azucena de Quito* (*Golden Anniversary of the Lily of Quito*), p. 56.
Original verses:
1. ¿No hizo más tu Ecuador? ¡Alaba al Cielo! / A dar al mundo nuevo ejemplo va. / El águila remóntase, ve el suelo, / Y no baja, ¡se aleja más allá!
2. El siguió de la Iglesia el triste sino, / Que tu Pueblo es el Pueblo de la Fe. / Y unióse amante al corazón Divino; / Que el Pueblo del Amor también él fue.
3. ¡Ah! Tu labio quizás en ese día, / Fue quien la hermosa idea susurró / Al oído del Hombre que regía Tu Patria, / cuando grande se miró
4. Y al apuntar la luz de una mañana, / Vi sus calles a Quito engalanar, / Y acorde con el son de la campana, / Del soldado el cañón oí tronar.

5. Y el noble joven y la virgen pura / Al templo santo con afán voló; / Y a ese templo también, desde la altura, / Jesús entre sus ángeles bajó.
6. Vélo, Mariana: el pecho descubierto, / Su herido Corazón mostrando está. / Mira ese anillo que en su mano advierto, / Tu amada Patria a recibirlo va.
7. La faz velada, pudibunda y bella, / Avanza ya de Cristo hacia el dosel. / ¡Ah, cuán hermosa y cuán amante ella! / ¡Ah, cuán amante y cuán hermoso El!
8. Se postra al fin, y entre un suspiro ardiente, / "Tuya me he de llamar" dijo y lloró; / Y El le puso el anillo, y en la frente / Un ósculo de alianza la imprimió;
9. Y ella, inspirada por afecto santo, / Besó el herido Corazón también; / Y los ángeles callan entre tanto, / Y el bello cuadro con envidia ven.
10. ¡Ecuador, Ecuador, amado nombre / Que al par que de mi Patria escucho yo! / Sí, te amo, ¿y por qué no? Jamás el hombre / Sólo a su madre en este mundo amó.

[10] *The National Vow.*
[11] Again see *Vida del Padre Julio Matovelle*, p. 409 and also *Vida de Eloy Alfaro* by Wilfrido Loor, vol. 3, p. 730 ff.
[12] Cf. Gomezjurado, *Vida de Garcia Moreno*, vol. 11, p. 264 ff.
[13] The history of the prayer "Rise up and defend us, Lord God of Hosts" was described in the Riobamba newspaper entitled *El Templo del Corazon de Jesus* (*Temple of the Heart of Jesus*), just as Father Jose Bolanos, S. J., told me. But unfortunately the issues of that newspaper are not complete in the Aurelio Espinosa Library at Cotocollao, and this account is not recorded in the issues that are there. Happily, Father Bolanos and Father Manuel Espinosa Polit, S. J., son of Doctor Aurelio Espinosa Coronel, told me enough about it.
[14] Gomezjurado, vol. 11, p. 225.
[15] Wifrido Loor, *Vida de Eloy Alfaro*, vol. 3, p. 742 ff.
[16] St. Gabriel College is a secondary school. In Spanish countries, "college" often refers to a secondary school.
[17] Temporal coadjutors among the Jesuits are brothers who assist the professed priests by undertaking the more "worldly" jobs.
[18] Again see Wifrido Loor, *Vida de Eloy Alfaro*, p. 768 ff. See Gomezjurado, *Vida de Garcia Moreno*, vol. 3, p. 443 ff., on the founding of the College of San Gabriel. See also the pamphlet entitled *El Milagro de la Dolorosa del Colegio. Estudio Critico* (*The Miracle of Our Lady of Sor-*

*rows of the College. Critical Study.*), p. 13 ff., anonymous author who in reality is the very talented French Jesuit, Father Jose Jouanen, Professor of Theology and author of the *Historia de la Companía de Jesus en el Ecuador* (*History of the Society of Jesus in Ecuador*) in three volumes.

[19] Gonzalez Suarez's pastoral letters against the secular school can be read in the *Boletin Eclesiastico* (*Ecclesiastical Bulletin*), Quito, November 1 and December 15, 1906. The sentence "They endeavor to quickly dig the grave into which the Ecuadorian people must be thrown" was parodied by the people themselves into "the Nation's Gravediggers."

[20] Primitivo Yela was a student the College of San Gabriel. Because of a mistake, not at all impossible to human fragility, he was unjustly punished by one of his professors, the German Father Eduardo Kaesen. In the Congress of December, 1906, he did everything possible to take revenge through a legislative decree for the closure of the College of San Gabriel and the expulsion of the Jesuits. Yela himself narrated that his intention and that of many legislators failed because of the miracle of April twentieth. This was common knowledge in the Jesuit community of Quito, and Father Kaesen declared that he was willing to ask forgiveness on his knees from his former student, Yela.

[21] I. e. *La Dolorosa del Colegio San Gabriel.*

[22] *The Ecuadorian, The Cry of the People, The Telegraph* and *The Dictatorship.*

[23] *The Echo of Azuay.*

[24] *Brother Gerund.*

[25] Wifrido Loor, *Vida de Eloy Alfaro*, vol. 3, p. 776 ff.

[26] The *Placistas* were the supporters of President Plaza.

[27] *Idem.* p. 798 ff.

[28] This fuller account of this important discussion and subsequent comment from Fr. Gomezjurado's *Vida de Garcia Moreno*, vol. 11, p. 268, replaces the summary version given in the text here.

[29] *Anuario Masónico de la Gran Logia del Ecuador, de 1926 a 1927.*

[30] Gomezjurado, vol. 10, pp. 21 and 26. Alfaro's commissioning to invest Alamiro Plaza as Kadosh is in Father Matovelle's biography, p. 322, note, written by Wilfrido Loor.

[31] One of the districts of the province of Lima, Peru.

[32] *Reason*

[33] *Commerce*

[34] Again, Matovelle's biography, p. 462. Also Alfaro's biography, vol. 3, p. 872 ff.

[35] Alfaro's biography, p.875 ff.

[36] *The Glove.*
[37] *Idem*, p. 880 ff.
[38] *Idem*, p. 884 ff. The author of this work went to Quinche on Monday, May 8, 1972, and recorded the ecclesiastical as well as civil death certificates, vol. 7, p. 153; and vol. 2, p. 132, respectively; and found what is described in the text. In 1910 only three deaths appeared with the last name of Duran: a child, a woman, Julia Duran, and Justo Arsenio Duran, of thirty-two years and three months of age. There are conjectures that some Mason gave Duran a poisonous potion that made him die on the night of June 8, 1910, therefore after the document was to be delivered to Alfaro.

In the above-mentioned year of 1910, Miguel Del Hierro was in his hacienda "San Miguel de Car," adjacent to the Colombian border. A man approached him, barefoot and dripping wet, for it was raining heavily. "I am a Mason," he said, "and Alfaro's government wants to kill me. As a Catholic with a good heart and rich, give me a three-piece suit and help me cross the border." The petition was fully satisfied by Miguel, who inquired into the fate of that Mason once in Colombian territory. The report he received was: "After a few days of residing in Colombia, he was assassinated."

The next day, on Tuesday morning, May ninth, the author went to the tailor Eli Jacinto Salcedo in Quinche itself and asked him for some information that would confirm what was told by the parish priest, Father Felix Granja. The answer was: "My father, Gregorio Salcedo was a friend of the Durans, and therefore he managed to find out that the above-said traveler had come from Peru, was attacked by colic in Puruanta, and died on the night of the same day that he arrived at Quinche. Papers sent by President Leguia to President Alfaro were found among the objects in his briefcase."

[39] *La Bomba* (*The Bomb*), May 24, 1934, Guayaquil; *El Voto Nacional* (*The National Vow*), August 1941, Quito; and *Frente a Frente* (*Face to Face*), April 25, 1942, Quito.
[40] The *sol* was the currency of Peru at this time. It has since been replaced by the *nueva sol* in 1985.
[41] With little difference the articles of the Protocol are also reproduced in Matovelle's above-mentioned biography, p. 462 ff., where Wilfrido Loor clarifies Alfaro's continuous trips to Guayaquil during the first months of 1910. The priest, Father Segundo Moncayo Benavides, conversed with Gonzalez Suarez, who hit his forehead with his palm and said, "Alfaro, what a rogue! He deceived me."

[42] The author formulated this objection to Betancourt and some Jesuits, "Could not all this have been a hoax invented by Father Granja?" Surprised at such a question, they answered, "This is not invented. Father Granja could never have invented such a story." The docile deference to the United States American mediator's request was noted likewise in *La Bomba,* on the above-mentioned date.
[43] Gomezjurado, vol. 11, pp. 273-274.
[44] See *Registro Oficial (Official Record),* year 1910, No. 1265, June eighth, and No. 2384, July first, about the army on campaign and the unexpected cessation of hostilities.

See Alfaro's biography, vol. 3, p. 878 ff., about Roberto Andrade, continual guest in the Peruvian Embassy, and the *Boletin Eclesiastico (Ecclesiastical Bulletin),* March 1, 1918, last page, photocopied, about the Archbishop pursued unto death.
[45] About "with my own hands,...." Was referred by Father Bolanos who heard it in San Felipe.
[46] *The Railroad Brotherhood.*
[47] *The Ecclesiastical Bulletin.*
[48] Again, Alfaro's biography, p. 884 ff.
[49] Alfaro's biography, vol. 3, p. 907 ff.
[50] *Idem,* p. 989 ff.
[51] *Idem,* p. 995 ff.
[52] "Independence Square."
[53] *Idem,* p. 1003 ff. Also *Boletin Eclesiastico (Ecclesiastical Bulletin),* Quito, year 1913.
[54] On August 10, 1809, Ecuador declared its independence from Spain and hence this day is called the "First Shout of Independence," for independence was not actually obtained until May 24, 1822.
[55] *Teocracia o Demonocracia? (Theocracy or Demonocracy?)* by Monsignor Schumacher, p. 78 of the second edition. Also the work entitled *Anoranzas (Nostalgia)* by Abelardo Moncayo, prefaced by Pio Jaramillo Alvarado, p. XLVIII. *Vida de Eloy Alfaro,* vol. 2, p. 433, by Wilfrido Loor. Alfaro's biography by Roberto Andrade, p. 414 and the pictures at the end of the book.
[56] "Tunnel of Peace."
[57] "The Model."
[58] The author's vol. 7 of Garcia Moreno's biography, chapter 4; vol. 8, chapters 2, 4, 11, and 12; vol. 9, chap. 3; vol. 8, p. 341 ff.
[59] The previous two sentences were taken from the author's *Vida de Garcia Moreno,* vol. 11, p. 283.

## The Mason, Alfaro, and Six of his Minions Are Lynched

[60] "I am in agreement with the assertion of the liberal writer cited by Wilfrido Loor, "If some day raising a statue to General Eloy Alfaro is discussed, it would need to be erected in the eastern territory ceded to Peru." (Gomezjurado, *ibid*.)

[61] *Ibid*. vol. 8, p. 397 ff., p. 236 ff; vol. 8, chapters 6, 7, and 8; vol. 3, chapters 3 and 7; vol. 6, chapters 3 and 8; vol. 4, chapters 2 and 4, p. 156 ff. Regarding the Christian Brothers see vol. 9, chapter 5.

[62] "Cents."

[63] I. e., a ten *centavo* coin.

[64] One *sucre* was one hundred *centavos*.

[65] Gomezjurado, *Vida de Garcia Moreno*, vol. 8, chap. 19. Also the magazine *El Foro (The Forum)* by Aparicio Ortega... Gomezjurado, *Vida de Garcia Moreno*, vol. 6, chap. 9 and vol. 7, chap. 1.

[66] Alfaro's biography by Wilfrido Loor, p. 879 ff. Gomezjurado, *Vida de Garcia Moreno*, vol. 9, p. 375 ff. Alfaro's biography by Wilfrido Loor, p. 120 ff.; p. 267 ff.

[67] *The Free Word*.

[68] Alfaro's biography by Wilfrido Loor, p. 890. Gomezjurado, vol. 8, p. 485 ff; vol. 3, p. 348; vol. 4, p. 70; and vol. 6, pp. 59 and 89.

[69] I. e. a reading from *The Imitation of Christ*.

[70] Gomezjurado, *Vida de Garcia Moreno*, vol. 7, pp. 258 and 333; vol. 9, p. 128.

[71] Father Jose Legohuir, S. J., *Un Gran Americano (A Great American)*, second edition, p. 401.

[72] *El Foro,* by Aparicio Ortega.

[73] "*Now you can blaspheme*," was heard by the priest Doctor Eudoro Ribadeneira in Quito from the lips of Julia Ribadeneira, his relative, a visual and auricular witness.

# Chapter 13
# Fiftieth Anniversary of the Consecration

After having been terrified by contemplating Alfaro's and his principal cohorts' bad end, it is fitting to put on the lips of the country these words of Judith, who beheaded Holofernes: "Woe be to the nation that riseth up against my people: for the Lord almighty will take revenge on them, in the day of judgment he will visit them. For he will give fire, and worms into their flesh, that they may burn, and may feel forever."[1]

Pedro Aviles: here is a priest who is Garcia Moreno's admirer and devotee. When hearing the name of the President-martyr, he doffed his biretta. Suffering the illness called fistula[2] in one foot, he had recourse to a certain powder applied very many times without the least benefit. He spent the night from the fifth to the sixth of August in prayer, asking for health through Garcia Moreno's intercession, martyred one August sixth. The result was the beginning of evident improvement, which soon reached complete healing. He was euphorically and proudly in the habit of saying, "Garcia Moreno healed me."[3] He composed some stanzas that could be sung to the music of the national anthem. Here they are:

> Hail, O homeland consecrated to Jesus!
> Glory to you; your heart now overflows
> With rejoicing and peace, your forehead radiant
> More than the shining sun we contemplate.
>
> Loving Heart of Jesus,
> Today we humbly ask Thee to take possession
> Of this people and teach it patiently
> To be faithful and live like Christians.
>
> O, Jesus, do not let this country
> Die that was the happy mother
> Of Mariana, the Lily of Quito,
> Of Moreno, Thy blessed athlete.[4]

Pedro Aviles died in the odor of sanctity on February 3, 1913.[5]

The Ecuadorian church celebrated the fortieth anniversary of the Consecration with special solemnity.[6] The iconography was enriched with the following symbolic painting:

The nation is characterized by a very modest, majestic lady with one knee on the ground. She holds the tricolor flag in her left hand and raises her right hand in the direction of Christ suspended on high from whose Heart flows two streams of light, the first towards her and the second towards the future Votive Church. Four angels surround Christ and display these two inscriptions: "Consecration of Ecuador to the Sacred Heart, 1873," and "National Basilica of the Sacred Heart, 1913."

The State took no part in this anniversary. General Leonidas Plaza was the president for the second time, imposed by the electoral farce typical of Masonry. Religious persecution continued, no longer violently but rather quietly and surreptitiously, impeding public worship and the establishment of new educational centers run by the clergy. The punishment inflicted on the memorable January 28, 1912, produced salutary effects. Here is a typical case:

After Plaza, Doctor Alfredo Baquerizo Moreno ascended to the presidency, who took to heart making the Conceptas Nuns leave their enormous and very old convent in the center of Quito to go to another building constructed on the outskirts. The reasons provided were just: the ancient central convent should be transformed into beautiful, modern buildings worthy of the capital, and the religious would enjoy greater comfort in the suburbs. But a crowd presented itself in front of the Presidential Palace with shouts of protest. Baquerizo Moreno came out onto the balcony and addressed the multitude in measured discourse. Then a robust voice launched this shout: "To the park! To the park!"[7] The President, full of fear, interrupted his allocution, turned around and entered his palace. The nuns remained at their original site.[8]

On June 10, 1915, the Jesuits from Riobamba inaugurated their own Votive church to the Heart of Jesus. It was an extensive, lovely, circular building, baptized by the people with the name of "The Rotunda." There were delegations from all Catholic Ecuador. Father Manuel Proano preached, narrating the genesis of the official consecration, since he himself, as Director of the Apostolate of Prayer in Riobamba, had written to Garcia Moreno and the bishops, exhorting them to consecrate the Republic to the Sacred Heart. A literary poetry contest was sponsored; the gold medal was awarded to the Quitonian canon, Father Luis Escalante. Let us hear a couple of stanzas:

> From the hand of God a glowing fingerprint,
> A jewel of art detached from heaven,
> The great Rotunda, majestic and lovely,
> Between the Andes hurls

Its daring pinnacle into space...
Eternal monument on which
Astonished centuries will read
A date indelibly consecrated
Through faith, science and sword.
Its gigantic dome
Rival of the lofty Chimborazo
Like a herald of peace and concord
Invites with sovereign tone
The people of Ecuador
To unite their hearts in a fraternal bond
And before the Divine King of nations
To humble and render their hearts.[9]

Around this same time the Bishop of Riobamba, Monsignor Andres Machado, made his visit *ad limina*, that is, to Rome. He stopped in Buenos Aires where the Jesuits entertained him with a small literary act in which Garcia Moreno's heroic religious deeds were celebrated. The proscenium displayed the portrait of the eminent Ecuadorian surrounded by flowers. At the end of the act, the Monsignor felt very deeply moved and turning to his secretary, Father Javier Bayas, he said, "The day will come when Garcia Moreno will be exalted on the altars."[10]

In 1921, there was enthusiasm and jubilation because of the celebration of the centenary of the birth of the President-martyr. The Lazarist priests, Father Carlos Villavicencio from Ecuador and Father Julio Candau from France, contributed with a very beautiful religious hymn that put the heroic deeds of that great man into relief. Villavicencio composed the words and Candau applied them to the melody of a French hymn to Joan of Arc. Well then, soon we shall see that the French bishops wrote a beautiful comparison between Joan of Arc and Garcia Moreno. Here are two stanzas of Villavicencio's words:[11]

Stand up, People of Ecuador!
Stand up, valiant youths.
You should fight in Christian combat
To give the victory to virtue.
Jesus the King shows you His heart
Full of love and compassion;
If a tempest threatens disaster,
Look to Him for salvation.

Oh, Jesus, with wasted efforts
Has Lucifer tried to fill us with terror;
Since by the Christian Hero's law
Ecuador with tender love
Proclaims Thee its Sovereign.

Ecuador, put on the armor
Of the champion of King Jesus.
To triumph is the glory of the race
That was born at the foot of the exalted Cross.
If the Tempter offers you peace,
Perfidious, sly, Satan,
"Who is like God?"
Is the cry that makes him tremble.
Tell him, "Get behind me! That, I will never do."
Oh, Jesus with wasted efforts, etc.[12]

The bishops addressed pastoral letters to their diocesans. Here are some words of the Metropolitan, Monsignor Manuel Maria Polit:

> Garcia Moreno's homeland is the title by which we are known everywhere... The glorious and most faithful son of Holy Church, the support and comfort of Christ's Vicar, Confessor of the Faith, and no matter how much it is claimed to the contrary, martyr of the Catholic idea and sentiment...

Cardinal Gasparri, Secretary of State to His Holiness Pope Benedict XV, said:

> A man of solid piety, Garcia Moreno has the merit of being the first to consecrate officially the nation which he governed to the Sacred Heart of Jesus, thus giving it glorious primacy. A most devoted son of the Catholic Church, he stood up as a fearless upholder of her sacred rights, thereby drawing the wrath of sects upon his head...[13]

These verses are presented from the Jesuit, Father Luis Velasco:

Hero! I greet you.
Martyr! I venerate you.

A more enviable destiny
I could not allot you
For your great deed
Than immortal life
From that death.[14]

The Ecuadorian episcopate unanimously wrote Pope Benedict XV, rendering him thanks for his tribute to Garcia Moreno. A few lines are extracted here. "A word from Your Holiness in memory and honor of the Hero-martyr of Catholicism among us and even in America and in the entire Catholic world, corroborating those that Pope Pius IX and Pope Leo XIII dedicated to him, renews and enhances his glory."[15] It was signed by Manuel Maria Polit, Archbishop of Quito; Andres Machado, Bishop of Guayaquil; Carlos Maria de la Torre, Bishop of Riobamba; Alberto Maria Ordonez, Bishop of Ibarra; Daniel Hermida, Bishop of Cuenca; Guillermo Jose Harris, Bishop of Loja; Virgilio Maldonado, Apostolic Administrator of Portoviejo; Domingo Comin, Apostolic Vicar of Mendez and Gualaquiza.[16]

Here is another declaration by Monsignor Manuel Maria Polit:

> The Archdiocese of Quito, together with the other dioceses of the Ecclesiastical Province of Ecuador, its prelates, clergy and faithful with the highest admiration and affectionate gratitude commemorate the first centenary of the birth of Garcia Moreno, proclaiming him once again the eminent President of the Republic, distinguished benefactor of his people, hero and martyr of Catholic civilization...
>
> He took his Republic, pacified, instructed and morally revitalized by him, adorned now with the precious jewels of genuine culture, and he raised it in his powerful arms and consecrated it to the most loving Heart of the God-man, who until then for two centuries had asked and waited in vain for this homage from kings and emperors. Oh great, beautiful and incontestable primacy of Ecuador, which a short time ago the Holy See recognized again, and of which no one can deprive you! Since then we are and will be, thanks to God and to Garcia Moreno, even though hell may rage, the Republic of the Heart of Jesus.[17]

The words of His Excellency Carlos Maria de la Torre, Bishop of Riobamba: "The moral greatness of Garcia Moreno had soared to such a height that without the glorious martyrdom that was its worthy conclusion, God's work would have been unfinished and imperfect..."[18]

The above-said Prelate sent his Pastoral letter to his old professor, Cardinal Luis Billot, who answered him with these expressions:

> Your allocution about the great man and renowned martyr, who was Garcia Moreno, has awakened in my soul such a lively joy that I cannot find words to express it. I have read it from beginning to end. Oh, what a beautiful figure, truly worthy of being placed on the altars; worthy of being proposed as an example to our modern Catholics who, unfortunately, let themselves be more and more corrupted every day by the deadly principles of Liberalism! I fervently pray that the political conditions of Ecuador will finally permit his cause to be initiated in the Sacred Congregation of Rites. How happy I would judge myself to be if I were the Postulator![19]

Let us hear these paragraphs from the speech pronounced by the Very Reverend Tomas Vergara, Pro-vicar of the Archbishopric:

> A century ago, in the year 1821, there among the waves of the immensity of the ocean, in the solitude of an island, a catafalque was raised and a regal sepulcher was dug. Here, in that same year, in our then practically unknown Republic, an illustrious cradle rocked in which a beautiful child was caressed in the Pearl of the Pacific by the soft breezes with which the gentle Guayas greeted him, when giving him its welcome to the world.
>
> There on the island of Saint Helena, with military and religious pomp, amidst the sound of cannon fire and prayers by the Church, always generous and prompt to forgive, funeral rites were held for the eternal repose of the great Napoleon. Here, at the same time, in our country, the dreams of baby Gabriel, later Garcia Moreno the Great, were interrupted by the din of cannons and rifles that then, in the final and bitter battles, decided the bloody victory with which the national heroes of our Independence crowned their great deeds.[20]
>
> Napoleon eternally closed his eyes to life; that powerful breath was coming to an end. His glorious sword fell from his stiff hand; the crucifix received the last palpitations of his chest; he was heard to say, "I believe in God, and I profess the religion of my

fathers. Can you cease to believe in God when everyone proclaims His existence, and when the most gifted men have believed in Him? I die in the Catholic, Apostolic, Roman Religion, in whose bosom I was born more than fifty years ago." Thus the genius of war sank into the sunset of life, when in our country, allow me the expression, the genius of Nineteenth Century Christianity arose. This child will wipe away the tears of the Vicar of Jesus Christ in the person of Pope Pius IX which Napoleon, momentarily dazzled by the brightness of glory, was wrenching from Pope Pius VII. He will be the favorite son of the Church, the comfort of her elderly and loving Father. He, being indignant, will make the voice of justice be heard; and his cry and challenge against the chains riveted on the benevolent hands of the representative of Christ, will heap impiety with shame, and Garcia Moreno and his Country with glory. The sword that this child will take up later will never be placed at the service of injustice, of impiety, of tyranny, but rather for the sake of honor, of freedom, always on the side of the people and of their faith...

It was August 6, 1875, a Friday, consecrated to the Heart of Jesus, the Feast of the Transfiguration of Our Lord Jesus Christ on Mount Tabor. On that day and during that feast day, Garcia Moreno was to climb the Tabor of eternal glory. The angels adorned a magnificent throne in heaven; they weaved a most beautiful wreath with the ornaments of glory and enthusiastically prepared a hymn of triumph to the awaited Champion of the Immaculate Lamb. On earth firearms were loaded and the homicidal machete was sharpened. "My Father, here is the fire and the wood," said Isaac to Abraham, "where is the victim for the holocaust?" Garcia Moreno had exclaimed in the secrecy of his prayer on the day of his death, "My Lord Jesus Christ, grant me love and humility and let me know what I ought to do today in Thy Service!" Here is the victim. God will show him what he should do on his last day on earth. God will show him His will: martyrdom and glory...

About five years ago a foreigner visited our capital. He was a venerable old man, a Catholic priest of North American nationality... He spoke with a few of us priests and with great enthusiasm told us, "The (Protestant) American Consul in Guayaquil recommended that I place a flower on the monument to Garcia Moreno. And his Catholic wife has asked me for a prayer at his tomb. Where is his monument? Where is his tomb?" You can imagine our shame and speechlessness. His tomb is not accessible; his monument does not exist...

In Guayaquil, where Garcia Moreno was born on the night between the twenty-fourth and the twenty-fifth of December of 1821, the main speech was made by the Jesuit, Father Miguel Martinez de la Vega. The expression that seemed the most accurate was: "Garcia Moreno, ladies and gentlemen, is not only a genius. He is many geniuses in a single giant."[21]

In Cuenca, Doctor Remigio Crespo Toral made a literary study that received the gold medal. Here are some of his concepts:

> To measure his stature with God's measurement, may the Immortal, the Strong one, the Saint of saints grant us a glimmer from the sun of His justice...[22]
>
> In him burns the flame of seers, the fire of the apostles and the constancy of heroes. These words by the immense and most holy Savonarola could easily have been his: "I wanted to rest and found no place for it; I wanted to remain silent and not to speak, but it is impossible for me, for the word of God burns in me like fire and consumes me if I do not express myself freely..."[23] All the vehemence of the passion that agitated this noble human model, Garcia Moreno, is translated in an explosion of ingenuity that proclaims the vocation of that soul for the fight, for the apostolate and for martyrdom: a man of God, a missionary, a knight of the cross; the Hero, the Madman... the Genius...[24]

In the poetry contest a priest from Cuenca, Father Manuel Palacios Bravo, was also honored with a gold medal. Here are some stanzas:

That man was the honor of humanity.
Beautiful Homeland of mine,
Forgotten delight of the mountains,
He, loving you with the greatest concern,
Aggrandized your name in history,
He embroidered the fine scarlet cloth of your robe with gold
And imprisoned light in your diadem.
He, while gazing on you, beautiful and noble, to Christ
Who showed His sweet Heart in Gaul,

As an instruction to great nations,
Presented you as a holy offering,
To serve as the royal silk of His sandal,
Like a flower of the Andes...

Alone, he awaits the martyr's wreath.
Let the impious mob fall upon him,
And from humanity at the front of the stage,
Stained by waves of his blood, let him pass away.
Enveloped in red light the star eclipses,
Stained with red clouds the day dies.
Sons of the crime, immolate the Genius;
Shed his blood, savage human beasts!
Martyrdom crowns his greatness:
Lofty Christian domes are crowned with the cross.[25]

Many other literary tributes are passed over to put into relief the enthusiasm which was not lacking for the erection of a bronze statue of Garcia Moreno. Regarding its cost, Mr. Carlos Fernandez Madrid covered it by himself. "I am paying a debt of gratitude," he exclaimed, "for my fortune is due to the bus service the length of the southern highway. Who made that highway? Gabriel did!"[26] In turn it can be asked, "Who was the main motor of the national movement for Garcia Moreno's glory, in spite of the Masonic regime and government, the persecutors of the Church and of the President-martyr's memory? It was Monsignor Manuel Maria Polit Laso, the Archbishop of Quito, who nevertheless did not manage to succeed in reference to the statue. President Luis Tamayo and the ruling municipality forbade that monument to be raised."

The culminating tribute took place in the Metropolitan Cathedral on December twenty-fifth, with a Pontifical Mass in thanksgiving and an allocution by the above-said Prelate. Here are a few of the most interesting lines:

> He was born exactly one hundred years ago; and by a singular coincidence, on the same night from the twenty-fourth to the twenty-fifth of December, as Jesus, whom he would serve as a docile and powerful instrument, bearing the name of Gabriel worthily, which means "strength of God"...[27]

There were also tributes in foreign counties. Let us keep to Spain, where the Jesuit, Father Constantino Bayle, published a much applauded pamphlet. We extract these paragraphs:

> Far from his intention was the idea of the Theocratic Republic or slave of Rome, as his rivals calumniated him and raging liberals or half-baked Catholics calumniate him. However, he believed that out of propriety the State should restore what did not belong to it; and out of justice should leave the Church all the freedom and all the privileges that her Divine Founder granted her for the good of the world; and by helping her and offering her the support of the secular arm, he did nothing other than to place that protection and that arm at the service of the Catholic sentiments of his people, benefits to be prized, even in this world, as much as any other terrestrial good.
>
> He put forward this reason, on a solemn occasion, when the miniscule Republic of Ecuador appeared before the world one hundred cubits above the colossuses of cannons and of banks. When Pope Pius IX was dispossessed and taken prisoner by the sacrilegious Piedmont troops; when European governments, either traitors or cowards, looked at the robbery and shrugged their shoulders; Garcia Moreno was the only head of state who raised his noble, valiant, Christian voice in protest. He did not have armies nor did he have battleships to stop the usurpation, but weakness that recognizes it is weak and still dares to protest against the injustices of the strong, takes on something of the majesty of the Baptist and of the words that made the petty king tremble: "It is not lawful for thee to have thy brother's wife."[28]

In Rome the poet Blas Vergehtti sang Garcia Moreno's heroic deeds in his Latin hexameters. Now, this writer was in charge of composing poetry in verse suitable to be incorporated in sacred liturgy. Here is the translation of some of his hexameters:

> Great jubilation, when, on your knees,
> Your hands raised to heaven,
> You surrendered your Kingdom
> To the Divine Heart of Jesus,
> Who approved you from on high,
> Constituted the anchor, harbor, salvation,

Life and Shepherd of your people.
The threats and dangers of a bloody death
Did not daunt you...[29]

In Paris, there was a religious service in Saint-Sulpice Church[30] where Garcia Moreno used to attend Mass and recite the rosary sixty-five years previously.[31] Before a numerous and select audience, Monsignor Baudrillart, Member of the French Academy and Rector of the Catholic University of Paris, gave a long discourse, from which this maxim is taken: "Bountiful fruit of the Spanish genius in the New World, Garcia Moreno was a martyr of Christian civilization."[32]

Catholic France, represented by its most conspicuous bishops sent Monsignor Manuel Maria Polit a message of admiration for Garcia Moreno.[33] Here are some paragraphs:

> Garcia Moreno, during the final days of his second presidential period, had the right to sign this declaration: "The Republic has enjoyed six years of peace, and has marched resolutely along the path of true progress, under the visible protection of Providence."
>
> He did not have time to read the message, from which this declaration was taken, to the Congress. Stained with blood it was picked up off his chest, wounded by the dagger of the enemies of order and of the Faith. Garcia Moreno had foreseen this tragic end without fearing it. Let us say even more: he had longed for it. Forewarned of the danger, he thanked heaven for granting him "the happiness of shedding his blood for Him who, being God, wanted to shed His blood for us upon the Cross."
>
> His life, on the other hand, had prepared him for such a death and we even dare say: it had merited it. Does not such a death assure the victim of a twofold immortality: happiness in heaven and glory on earth? God reserves this kind of death for his greatest servants. He permitted the bonfire that burned a Joan of Arc, and the machete that wounded a Garcia Moreno. Joan of Arc and Garcia Moreno! Your Grace, it is not without an express purpose that these two names are joined by our pen. Between our Holy Liberator and your Heroic President, despite the profound differences of situation, age, times and nations, we not only find a simple analogy of supreme destiny, but also a true and admirable identity of principles and ideals.

The shepherdess from Domremy was called by a miraculous vocation to free her country from the exterior enemy, in order to restore it to itself and to its destiny, that is, to restore it to Jesus Christ, whose soldier she was. The student from Guayaquil was clearly prepared by providential circumstances to free his country from interior self-seeking factions, so that Ecuador, by its awareness of the duty and security of order, could become a model Catholic nation.

For Joan of Arc, the King of France was Christ's *vice-regent*. Did not Garcia Moreno, to the extent of his power and ability, perhaps merit this same title and fulfill this role?

Finally, just as the martyr of Rouen, condemned to the flames, appealed to God's representative, so also the Victim of Quito, while expiring under the assassin's steel, had recourse to God Himself: "God does not die."

No, God does not die. We repeat it with you, Your Grace, in these commemorative celebrations. And those who die for Him and in Him, like the Hero of Ecuador, survive forever.

May the Sacred Heart, to whom Garcia Moreno, the first among heads of state, consecrated his country, maintain and fructify this continued remembrance of the great Christian who was "in the government of the people a man of Jesus Christ." This is the prayer that we in the name of the archbishops and bishops of France and of the whole of Catholic France make today, not only for the moral and material good of the Republic of Ecuador, but also for the progress of civilization in the world.

Luis Jose Cardinal Lusson, Archbishop of Rheims.
Francois Cardinal de Cabrieres, Bishop of Montpellier.
Paulino Cardinal Andrieu, Archbishop of Bordeaux.
Luis Cardinal Dubois, Archbishop of Paris.
Luis Jose Cardinal Maurim, Archbishop of Lyon.[34]

The above letter was answered by Monsignor Polit on January 22, 1922. Let us listen to some of his words:

Garcia Moreno, in a small land but located at the center of the New World, continued the work of your greatest kings, Charlemagne and Saint Louis... Fulfilling the desires of the Divine Redeemer manifested to His servant Saint Margaret Mary Alacoque, he did what he ought to do and that which perhaps your great king, Louis XIV, did not know: the official consecration of his nation to the Divine Heart of Jesus Christ... Victim of his love for the Church and his country, as Pius IX exclaimed; martyr for his Catholic religion and patriotism; to the like of your incomparable Joan of Arc, to whom Your Eminences nevertheless have deigned compare him with such authority, tracing an eloquent parallel that will remain forever... He too had freed his country from the enemies that invaded it; had oppressed rebellious and internal discord; had enthroned legitimate and national authority.

Like Joan, he wanted Christ's Church to anoint this authority, no longer monarchic according to the usages of the Middle Ages, but rather popular and democratic, according to modern trends. He accomplished what your holy heroine so eagerly desired: intimate union between the Catholic religion and the nation, between Church and State.[35]

Just as she inscribed the sweetest names of Jesus and Mary on her banner, so he gloried in stamping them reverently on his most solemn official messages, where they sounded like a battle cry, whether in triumph or before falling bathed in his own blood... He attained what he desired: he was insulted, calumniated and persecuted, the same as Joan of Arc, no longer only by the enemies of his nation, but also by those of Christ and His Church... The Plaza Mayor of Quito and the Old Market of Rouen appear together in the same perspective of the panorama of history... There from the iniquitous blaze, the immaculate Lark of Gaul flew to heaven, fixing her eyes on a rough cross and repeating in anguished chirps, **Jesus, Jesus!** And here, he went about mightily as the Lion of the Andes, crying out with a roar that filled the world, **"God does not die"**; while with his mangled hand he pressed against his chest the *Lignum Crucis*[36] of Christ, the rosary of Mary, and the First Vatican Council medal of Pope Pius IX: a triple and blood-stained relic that I possess as a treasure and always venerate with ineffable emotion.

The Ecuadorian Hero whom I firmly hope will rise one day to the altars as a martyr of Jesus Christ; and the French Heroine who has already been placed upon them as the saint of patriotism: both symbolize the union that has existed and will always exist between Catholic France and Catholic Ecuador. Both pray to the God of mercies so that the one Republic and the other, the great one and the small one, will faithfully fulfill their mission; and the

Deified Heart of Jesus reigning in them, from them His social reign will be spread throughout the old and the new continents.[37]

In Mexico, in the city of Zamora, the Centenary was celebrated with the martyrdom of some of the President-martyr's admirers. The best celebration: Divine Providence's generous contribution. They were young men belonging to the "Garcia Moreno Center," of such fiery piety that they soon merited the name of "Lunatics for Christ."

The top leader of the "Garcia Moreno Center" was twenty-three year old Joaquin Silva. Soon they admitted his younger brother Ignacio to the group. Manuel Melgarejo also stood out for his ardent Catholicism. These three and a few more from that entity started to edit flyers and distribute them among the thousands of workers in danger of abandoning the Catholic faith and yielding to Communist materialism. It was in the years of the bloody persecution headed by the Mexican dictator, Plutarco Calle. They were put in prison. Soon they were freed under the threat of being imprisoned again if they repeated that propaganda against Communism. They resumed the campaign no more and no less than before and were again punished with prison.

The most capable and heroic apostles, Joaquin Silva and Manuel Melgarejo, exhausted the regime's patience and were condemned to capital punishment. They went through the public streets praying the rosary out loud and showing off the string of blessed beads. Their escort intimidated them, "Throw away that rosary." "As long as I have life," Joaquin responded, "no one will succeed in separating me from my rosary. Kill me; do as you like with me. I only ask you to free Manuel who is only seventeen years old." But Manuel, full of fright, exclaimed, "No, Joaquin, I want to die with you."

When they reached the cemetery, Joaquin stood facing the squad of riflemen and shouted, "Long live Christ the King! Long live the Virgin of Guadalupe!" He had not finished pronouncing the last syllables when he fell to the ground with his head destroyed by the bullets; minutes later, the same scene with Manuel. It was the month of December of 1921.[38]

In October of 1922 the announcement appeared in print of the upcoming Fiftieth Anniversary of the Consecration of Ecuador to the Heart of Jesus. Let us hear the most significant paragraph:

> Garcia Moreno subjected the law of the Nation to the law of God, without appeasement or subterfuge to weaken his deep con-

viction in the least; and he longed for his governed to be true Catholics in their private life the same as in public. If not, recall how, on the memorable March 25, 1874, with the majesty proper to the head of a nation, he repeated after the Metropolitan Prelate, in a loud voice, so the people congregated in the Cathedral could follow him, the act of consecration of the republic to the Most Holy Heart of Jesus, the God-man, Our Savior, "in whom we were created and for whom God created all things."[39]

On December 14, 1922, in a Pastoral Letter, His Excellency Carlos Maria de la Torre, Bishop of Riobamba, said:

> To use the comparison of the Psalmist, Ecuador in 1873 was the chosen vine planted by God whose branches gave shade even to the mountaintops, whose trunk climbed vigorously among secular trees, whose green foliage was bathed in the waters of the sea, and whose vines offered rich, tasty, abundant fruit everywhere. It is because Garcia Moreno, Garcia the Great, the extraordinary and extremely upright head of state in whose brain the light of the faith burned with the fire of genius, in whose chest glowed an iron will purified and beautified in the forge of charity, had been predestined by the Lord to be the wonder-working Moses who, breaking the chains forged by the Revolution, would return the freedom of God's children of the New Israel; valiant Josue who introduced them into the promised land that flows everywhere with the streams of the milk and the honey of temporal happiness; and the most wise Solomon who would bathe his intelligence in the radiance of wisdom and would delight his heart with the sweetness of peace...

On his part, the Illustrious Bishop of Guayaquil, Andres Machado, in his Pastoral Letter of January 25, 1923, narrated the most glorious heroic deed of the Nation in these words:[40]

> It is March 25, 1874... The venerable pontiff, the future martyr, stands up and with his rich priestly vestments, gravely and majestically approaches the feet of the Savior. He kneels down on the ground; and holding a sacred script in his hands, trembling with emotion, he starts reading from it while loving tears fall from his cheeks. What is it that his lips pronounce? The immense,

devoted congregation listens to him breathlessly and without turning their eyes away for even an instant from the Savior. The pontiff is silent and retires to his throne.

Immediately the exceptional man of this nation stands up, the model leader of leaders, he who encloses in his chest an entire volcano of faith and of Catholicism; and his gallant erect figure, with his flashing eyes, his brow raised to heaven, and his majestic countenance, advances gravely and measuredly toward the same place where the pontiff had knelt; and before the image of Christ, Garcia the Great, reins in his genteel greatness and adores his God. Then his vibrant, melodious voice resounds, a mixture of love, tenderness and majesty; and with an air of immense resolution, he reads the same words that the pontiff had said:

> Adorable Heart of Jesus, King of kings and Lord of lords, by Whom and for Whom all the peoples and nations of the earth have been created. In deference to Thy most lovable and infinite sovereignty, kneeling in Thy divine presence, we, the public powers of Church and State, all offer and consecrate, henceforth and forever, the Republic of Ecuador to Thee as Thy exclusive possession and property. Deign to take this nation as Thy inheritance; reign perpetually in her. Receive her under Thy sovereign protection. Free her from all her enemies. Show all nations that Ecuador is Thine. Prove to the world that the nation which chooses Thee as Lord and God is blessed; and make the glory of Thy Most Holy Name shine forever in our Republic.[41]

Profound silence... emotion... tears... The President is silent, but the angels, above the clouds, jubilantly intone, "Glory to God in the highest; and on earth peace to men of good will." The crowd leaves for their homes singing, "We are Thine, we swear it, O Heart of the Savior. We are Thine, we beseech Thee, save, save Ecuador."

This is how the greatest act of the religious history of our country took place... "A sublime act," it was said in Europe, "whereby Garcia Moreno, crowning all his feats as a Catholic ruler, made the Republic of Ecuador the Republic of the Sacred Heart. A grandiose act that of itself is enough to immortalize his memory and place him beside Charlemagne and Saint Louis, Isabella the Catholic and Saint Ferdinand III..."[42]

Regarding a partial celebration of the Golden Anniversary, here is the account that appeared in the Ecclesiastical Bulletin of the capital in the month of June, 1923:

> By a very special grace obtained not without difficulty by our most worthy Metropolitan, the Sacred Congregation of Rites, in view of the fact that our country had the merit of being the first nation in the world that was officially consecrated to the Divine Heart of Jesus, has permitted it to celebrate a special feast with a proper Mass and Office every year on the octave day, which is the Friday following the feast of that same Sacred Heart, to commemorate the aforesaid Consecration, against which the impious blaspheme, because they understand that because of it their satanic efforts are like "beating the air,"[43] according to the expression in the Scriptures...
>
> In Quito, on the days of the eighth to the ninth and the fifteenth of June, 1923, the program formulated by piety was observed. In the artistically illuminated Cathedral, the sweet, attractive and compassionate image of the Sacred Heart was raised upon an altar embellished with red, a symbol of love. At its feet, on each one of those days, the Most Illustrious Archbishop celebrated the Pontifical Mass. Speakers of merited reputation, such as Canons Pozo, Escalante and Vergara displayed all their eloquence. The multitude, with raised voices, ratified the consecration. The Presidential chair remained empty, which Garcia Moreno had occupied half a century before; but not that of the Most Illustrious Archbishop Checa, now occupied by his worthy successor, the Most Illustrious Polit, who renewed the act of Consecration, seconded by the "Garcia Moreno Worker's Association," that was founded some two years previously to keep alive the memory of the most Christian President.[44]
>
> All strata of society: clergy, religious congregations, confraternities, colleges, schools, artisans' guilds, private associations, members of the press, businesses and banks, had their representatives at the act of consecration, which was repeated in successive hours during the entire day on the fifteenth, before the real presence of Christ in the Blessed Sacrament, exposed above the altar.[45]

On March twenty-fifth of the following year, 1924, acts of worship took place similar to those just mentioned; again the religious iconography was enriched with the following symbol:

The Ecuadorian coat of arms, made of gold and precious stones, was in the arms of the glorious Patriarch Saint Joseph, who is symbolized by an enormous golden lily. This inscription was above and in the form of an arch: "Who is like God!" Two hearts were incrusted in this apothegm: that of Jesus and that of Mary. At the pinnacle was a dove, symbol of the Holy Ghost.

In a second image, the golden lily served as a pedestal for a cross; in its center glistens a holy host encircled with this caption: "Ecuador to the Sacred Heart, on the fiftieth anniversary of its Consecration." Underneath appear the initials of these names: Jose Ignacio Checa, Manuel Jose Proano and Gabriel Garcia Moreno.[46]

Ten years later the author of this book began his crusade for the canonical glorification of the President-martyr, adding the name of "Garcia Moreno" to the Eucharistic Crusade founded in Riobamba.[47] Its members did not take long at all to revive enthusiasm for the figure of the great man. The following year, that is, in 1935, there was this noteworthy document: a photograph in which the portrait of Garcia Moreno stood out with the initials of his apothegm, "God does not die." Underneath were the components of the military staff with their standards. The two children aroused particular attention because of the metal armor on their arms and legs, imitating the bronze trappings of the Medieval Crusades.[48]

One of the associates, Mr. Alberto Muyrragui, came to me one day with one of his writings. "Father Gomezjurado, please correct this."

"Your poetry again!" was the author's slightly harsh reply.

"They are not verses, Father, but this," and he put in my hands a composition in prose. I read it; I corrected its grammar, and euphorically said to the interlocutor, "Now you have really composed something of great merit. Have the Vicar General approve this prayer, and then disseminate it on holy cards. I will help you distribute them and you will not have any financial loss." Here is the result:

### Prayer to ask God for the glorification of the Martyr of the Faith, Gabriel Garcia Moreno:

O Lord! God of goodness, who makes the virtues of Thy servants to shine forth before the face of the world, grant us, we

*Father Gomezjurado. To his right, the boy Alberto Pipa. To his left, the boy N. Anda Escobar. Behind him in the center, Mr. Neptali Cisneros, President. To his right, Mr. Pacifico Merino. To his left, Mr. Alberto Muyrragui, author of the prayer.*

humbly beseech Thee, that by the virtues practiced during the mortal life of Thy faithful servant and martyr of the faith, Gabriel Garcia Moreno, to have the unspeakable joy of seeing him exalted to the honor of the altars, so that he may be held up and imitated in the world as the perfect model of those who govern, for Thy greater glory, the spiritual good and benefit of our souls. Amen.

A.M.D.G.[49] A Franciscan tertiary. Riobamba.
Diocesan Ecclesiastical Government. Riobamba. September 29, 1938. Imprimatur. The Vicar General
Note: We call Garcia Moreno a martyr with merely human criterion, without intending to anticipate the decision of the Church.[50]

Therefore, the first prayer approved officially by the Church to implore the canonical glorification of Garcia Moreno had its beginning on the feast of Saint Michael the Archangel. "Who is like God," the latter had said. "Strength of God"[51] was the name of the former, who had said, "God does not die."[52]

Four days later two thousand holy cards began to circulate in Riobamba with the picture of the bust of Garcia Moreno on the front and the above prayer on the back. The next day the author gave a conference on the subject at the College of the Sisters of St. Mariana of Jesus, having obtained beforehand the permission of his rector, Father Luis Mancero; and they made the aforementioned holy cards available to the public at a low price, so that Mr. Muyrragui would not suffer economic loss, being poor of fortune. Immediately the author's rector was besieged by individuals who branded this propaganda as a spark that would provoke a Masonic arson attack against the Jesuits. They said, "It is rashness. It is a challenge to the ruling Masonic government, which will retaliate and persecute the Jesuits violently." The matter was communicated to Quito and there the Jesuits also answered, even those most devoted to Garcia Moreno, "The time and season has not yet come to promote such great glorification of the man who did honor to humanity. His enemies still have a fierce hatred for him and they are powerful. God will indicate when such an apostolate can be undertaken."[53] The Head of State then was Doctor Manuel Maria Borrero, one of the arms of the Masonic pincers.

Consequently, the boxes of holy cards had to be put "on ice" and hidden, even though their owner was a layman, who bore it with patience, convinced that alone he would not be able to make use of these holy cards, and was strengthened by the author's words, "This opposition shows that the work is from God, and has to culminate in triumph." Bishop Alberto Ordonez did not take long to return to Riobamba. He gave an audience to the Jesuit priest, Father Alfonso Escobar, Director of the Apostolate of Prayer, who had contributed money to editing the cards and had with him the original approved by the Very Reverend Vicar Camacho. He showed it to His Excellency saying, "See what your Vicar approved in the absence of Your Excellency." Monsignor read the prayers, reflected for a few minutes, took up a pen and also inscribed his approval on them next to that of the Very Reverend Vicar Camacho. These were sent by mail to Quito, to Father Ricardo Vasquez, also a Jesuit, who presented them to the Archbishop, Monsignor Carlos Maria de la Torre. The latter in turn read them, reflected for a few moments, brandished his quill, approved them, and added the following note: "Distribution is to be made in the religious associations and Catholic schools." Father Vasquez made a new edition in the capital and fear disappeared. The liberal daily, *El Día*,[54] took that propaganda in jest, and rather promoted it, by publishing the prayer and the picture of Garcia Moreno in its columns.[55]

The author of this book then hastened to compose another prayer, in which the heroic religious achievements of the President-martyr would shine in a concrete way. Not only the bishops of Ecuador approved it but also the Bishop of Pasto in Columbia, Monsignor Giraldo; Cardinal Archbishop Jose Maria Caro of Santiago, Chile; a bishop in Scotland, through the efforts of Mr. Hamish Fraser; and finally the Archbishop of Sao Paulo in Brazil, through steps taken by Mr. Hermes Di Ciero. So then, that prayer has been translated into English and Portuguese. Let us listen to it:

> O Most Sacred Heart of Jesus! Remember the consecration that President Gabriel Garcia Moreno made to Thee of his Republic; of the enthronement of Thy sacred image in his presidential home; and of his blood, shed to seal his unshakeable adherence to Thee and to Thy vicar, the pope, and grant us the canonical glorification of such an exemplary ruler, that men powerful in deeds and words may rise up for the cause of religion and of country, and finally the particular grace which we ask Thee, in accord with Thy good pleasure. Amen.[56]

There have always been extraordinary favors granted by God, thanks to Garcia Moreno's intercession. They have been published in the author's works, especially in *Is Garcia Moreno a Martyr?* Here is another one as yet unpublished:

While the author was in the city of Milagro in the province of Guayas, a woman of humble condition came to him and said, "The doctor prescribed a shot. Lacking resources, I invoked Garcia Moreno: 'Give me the money to buy it.' I was walking along a very deserted street. I tripped on a pile of dirt and at the top was incrusted upright a little roll of papers. I approached and took it. It was ninety *sucres* in bills, more than enough to buy the injection. Now I am well and healthy." This was around the year 1969. The author took down the name of that woman, but has much difficulty in reporting it because his writings are made up of an immense sea in lovely disorder.

The author has also composed a prayer to the Blessed Virgin that has been approved by the Church and widely circulated. Here it is:

> Remember, O most Pure Virgin Mary, that your servant Gabriel Garcia Moreno swore to defend the privilege of your Immaculate Conception. He was a member of your Congregation, and assiduously recited the holy rosary. He expired at the feet of your sacred altar, and according to the testimony of Pope Pius IX, who defined your exemption from original sin, "died as a victim for the faith and because of his Christian charity for his country." Obtain for us the canonical glorification of such an exemplary ruler, that men powerful in deeds and words may rise up for the cause of the same faith and their country, and finally grant us the particular grace which we implore through your intercession and for his glory, if it be for the good of our souls. Amen. [57]

It is fitting to reproduce here the prodigy already published in the author's pamphlet entitled, *The Virgin's Knight*.[58]

Around the year 1968, while the author was in the church at Jiron, a neighborhood near Cuenca, a lady approached him and said, "Garcia Moreno performed a miracle for me. I was the victim of a diabolic temptation of despair. I invoked the Most Blessed Virgin, 'My Mother! I do not ask you for wealth, neither for honors nor for a house. I want to be a good Christian, fulfilling the Commandments of God's Law and of the Church. But deliver me from this despair that makes my life unbearable and horrible.' Our Lady answered me interiorly, 'Invoke Garcia Moreno.'

I objected: 'Perchance, Mother of mine, are you not infinitely more powerful than Garcia Moreno and do you not love me like a daughter? I have heard that Garcia Moreno does miracles, but I have no devotion to him or confidence.' I continued suffering this distress of soul with greater anguish and distress. The next Saturday, bathed in tears, I knelt before the altar of the Virgin and repeated the prayer to her more vehemently. She responded to me as before, 'Invoke Garcia Moreno.' Then I obeyed her. I raised my eyes to heaven and said, 'Oh Garcia Moreno, since the Blessed Virgin wants me to invoke you, I do so. I do not ask for wealth or employment or a house. I want to be a good Christian. But deliver me from this despair that makes my life an insupportable torment.' Father, no sooner had I concluded this prayer than the temptation disappeared as if by magic, as though a strong arm had lifted off my shoulders a crushing burden that was torturing me, and it did not return again. From that moment I invoke Garcia Moreno in my difficulties and I feel his protection."[59]

The author also undertook to gather signatures to send to the Illustrious Archbishop Carlos Maria de la Torre, asking him to establish the cause of beatification of Garcia Moreno. Undoubtedly these documents are in the Curia archives of Quito, proceeding from the Artisans' Confraternity, the Minor Seminary, etc. He exhorted the members of the Third Franciscan Order to do the same and they corresponded with even greater enthusiasm. A delegation left for Quito which included the above-mentioned Mr. Alberto Muyrragui. They were introduced to the Most Excellent Apostolic Nuncio, Efren Forni, in whose hands they deposited the petition for this matter. Among the considerations it was included that Garcia Moreno was a model Franciscan Tertiary. Archbishop de la Torre's replies were very promising.[60]

In November of 1939 a reunion of all the bishops of Ecuador took place. There Archbishop Forni read the petition out loud and then laid it on the table near Archbishop de la Torre's chair, who took it up with an energetic gesture saying, "This matter is my concern, because Garcia Moreno died in Quito."[61] As a fruit of the petitions and the Metropolitan's drive and talent, the following decree was published in the Ecclesiastical Bulletin of January, 1940:

> Serious and prudent men, well-versed in Sacred Theology, who have studied with special care and diligence, inside and outside of the Republic, the death of Lord Doctor Gabriel Garcia Moreno and the cause that motivated it, believe they have discov-

ered in these the essential marks and characteristics of true martyrdom.

It seems to them that the deaths of Saint Canute, Saint Wenceslaus, Saint Thomas of Canterbury, and of the English Catholics sacrificed during the fateful days of Henry VIII and Elizabeth I, maintain perfect consonance and analogy to the death of the Ecuadorian President; and that, if the infallible decision of the Church has decorated them with the aureola[62] of martyrdom, she could well encircle the brow of this man with it also.

Such an assessment is far from negligible indeed, as is the interest that not only simple and devout faithful but even conspicuous members of the College of Cardinals have shown so that, within the canonical framework, everything possible would be done for the extremely upright President to be placed upon the altars, who, notwithstanding the incredulity and apostasy of his century, gloried in his Faith and his unwavering adherence to the Church and to the Vicar of Christ, in his innermost conviction, expressed by constant and superhuman efforts, that only the nation which recognizes Christ's sovereignty in its customs, its laws and its constitution will be happy. They have moved us to take the first steps toward the clarification of such an important point.

How much glory we would give to God, with what new splendor the Church would be clothed, and what unfading honor would redound to our country, if with his infallible lips the Roman Pontiff would declare that Garcia Moreno was and should be called a "martyr of Christ!"

No one is unaware of the protracted and delicate proceedings that have to be performed before the Church can, after having proved with unmistakable certitude the heroism of virtues or the reality of martyrdom, place one of her sons upon the altars. Moreover, the desired goal will not be reached if God Himself, by means of wondrous deeds, above all natural powers and wrought through the intercession of the Servant of God, does not put, so to say, His signature and His seal upon the Process to show that it is His will for a hero to be honored and glorified as a saint or martyr of the faith.

The first inquiry about heroism of the virtues or the reality of martyrdom pertains to the Ordinary in whose territory the Servant of God ended life's journey.

So that the Sacred Congregation of Rites, to which the process has to be presented, does not brand it as null, it must adhere strictly to everything that the canons have treated about so delicate a matter.

The whole second part of the fourth book of the Code of Canon Law is put together to give these rules and regulations and what regards historical Causes, that is to say, those in which so much time has passed since the death of the Servant of God, that it is not possible to receive statements from eyewitnesses. Pius XI, of holy memory, in his *Motu Proprio* of February 6, 1930,[63] marked out the lines that the Sacred Congregation of Rites ought to follow in processing these causes.

Recently the same Sacred Congregation of Rites, on January 4, 1939, published the "Norms to be Observed in the Formation of the Ordinary Processes concerning Historical Causes."[64] In number one of these Norms, it prescribes that the Ordinary, before beginning the Process, and having previously listened to the view of the Promoter of the Faith or the Fiscal Promoter,[65] will constitute a commission formed of three members, whose expertise concerning historical methods and concerning the investigation of the archives is fully attested, who are bound *in solidum*[66] "to gather all the historical sources about the life, virtues or martyrdom, the ancient fame of sanctity or of martyrdom, or the ancient veneration of the Servant of God."

Therefore, after invoking the light of the Holy Ghost, having heard the views of our Fiscal Promoter; we are fearful of incurring Divine indignation, if perchance we were to put forward some resistance to the designs which perhaps God may have upon the privileged soul of whom Pius IX said that "he had fallen victim of his faith and of his Christian charity," and Leo XIII that "he surrendered his life for the Church at the hands of the wicked": and the Congress of 1875, that "he shed his blood for the holy cause of religion, morality and order, peace and progress." In compliance with what has been ordained by the Sacred Congregation of Rites in the document cited above: we deem it beneficial to constitute the Historical Commission which will have for its end to gather all the historical documents relating to the death and the cause that motivated it or the long standing fame of martyrdom of Doctor Gabriel Garcia Moreno, who died riddled with gun wounds in the Plaza of Independence of Quito, on the First Friday, August 6,

1875. This commission will be composed of the Very Reverend Juan de Dios Navas, Magisterial Canon of our Metropolitan church and archivist of our Ecclesiastical Curia; of Reverend Father Joel Monroy, Provincial of the Order of Ransom: and of Reverend Father Jose Legohuir of the Company of Jesus.

Given in Quito on the twentieth of December of 1939. Carlos Maria, Archbishop of Quito. Angel Humberto Jacome, Secretary.[67]

Father Legohuir, a very competent man, as he had been the author of thick volumes about Garcia Moreno, such as *Un Gran Americano* and the second volume of *Historia de la Republica del Ecuador*, was writing his thesis about the Garcian Martyr, when he was surprised by death, just seven months after his appointment as a member of the Historical Commission. Unfortunately, it has not been possible to ascertain the whereabouts of that manuscript.

Archbishop de la Torre filled the vacancy left by Father Legohuir with another Jesuit, Father Jose Jouanen, who wrote his thesis in Latin as well as in Castilian Spanish, presenting Garcia Moreno as a victim or martyr of liberal errors. It has some force of logic, but its discrepancies in the religious-political order undermine it.[68]

Removed by the decree of the Fates, the above-said commissioners were replaced, with Archbishop de la Torre's prior designation, by Doctor Julio Tobar Donoso, Doctor Wilfrido Loor, and the author. Doctor Wilfrido Loor has published his book, *Garcia Moreno and His Assassins*. The author published a book entitled *Is Garcia Moreno a Martyr?*; thirteen volumes of the life of that great man; and this present book. Everyone who has read these books has declared them historically accurate about the intervention of German and Peruvian Masonry in the assassination of Garcia Moreno. Therefore with time more light is increasingly shed on a magnificent Cause of world-wide proportions. As for the recognition of his martyrdom, it is more or less universally acknowledged among Catholics and has its origin in testimonies by popes, cardinals, bishops and those most outstanding personages in Catholicism. This observation must be added: the majority of the declarations enjoy a beautiful literary form, enthusiastic and full of unction. This material can be found in the author's eleventh volume.

# Endnotes

[1] Judith 16, 20-21. Cf. Gomezjurado, *Vida de Garcia Moreno*, vol. 11, p. 289.
[2] An ulcer of a chronic type is commonly called a "fistula."
[3] "The malady worsened to the point that the doctors judged it necessary to amputate his diseased foot... During the course of the night the foot seemed to be so much better that, in the morning, the surgeons determined that the amputation was unnecessary." (Gomezjurado, *Vida de Garcia Moreno*, vol. 13, p. 406.)
[4] Original verses:
¡Salve, oh Patria a Jesús consagrada! / Gloria a ti; ya tu pecho rebosa / gozo y paz, y tu frente radiosa / más que el sol contemplamos lucir. / Corazón de Jesús amoroso, / hoy humilde rogamos te adueñes / de esta Patria, y paciente la enseñes / a ser fiel, y cristiana vivir. A esta Patria que fue feliz madre / de Mariana, Azucena de Quito, / de Moreno tu atleta bendito, / oh, Jesús no la dejes morir.
[5] Testimony by Sister Mariana Aviles, a Franciscan nun from San Diego, by Pedro's brother, and by the priest, Father Felix Aviles, who was a student in the Minor Seminary directed by the above-mentioned Pedro Aviles, who, to dispel sleepiness, also put his feet in cold water, imitating Garcia Moreno.
[6] Cf. Gomezjurado, *Vida de Garcia Moreno*, vol. 11, p. 289 ff.
[7] "These were the same words which reminded him how the Quitonian people burned Eloy Alfaro and his cohorts in the park." (*Ibid.* p. 309.)
[8] "He commanded that the crowd be told that the nuns would not leave their old convent." (*Ibid.*)
[9] The newspaper entitled *El Templo* (*The Church*), June 20, 1915, in Riobamba. Also the book entitled *Notas Bio-bibliograficas del Padre Manuel Proano* (*Bio-bibliographic notes on Father Manuel Proano*), p. 159, by Monsignor Jose Felix Heredia, S. J.
Original verses: De la mano de Dios fúlgida huella / joya de arte del cielo desprendida / la gran Rotonda majestuosa y bella / entre los Andes lanza / al espacio su cúspide atrevida... / Eterno monumento / en que los siglos leerán pasmados /una fecha imborrable consagrada / por la fe, por la ciencia y por la espada. / Su cúpula gigante / émula del excelso Chimborazo / cual heraldo de paz y de concordia / invita con acento soberano / al pueblo Ecuatoriano / a unir los pechos con fraterno lazo / y ante el Divino Rey de la naciones / a humillar y rendir los corazones. Cf. Gomezjurado, vol. 11, p. 308.
[10] The author heard this when he was in Riobamba in the year 1926.
[11] Common knowledge among the Lazarist Priests in the year 1944, confirmed by Father Garces, Provincial of the Lazarists, in April of 1972, in a conversation with the author in Quito. This hymn is usually sung on occasions of patriotic events. Cf. Gomezjurado, vol. 11, p. 328 ff.
[12] Original verses: ¡De pie, Nación Ecuatoriana! / de pie, valiente juventud. / Luchar debéis en lid cristiana / por dar el triunfo a la virtud. / El Rey Jesús el Corazón os muestra /lleno de amor y compasión; / si tempestad amenaza sinies-

tra, / en El buscad la salvación. / Oh Jesús, con empeño vano / tentó Luzbel infundirnos terror; / pues por la ley del Héroe Cristiano / el Ecuador, con tierno amor / te proclama su Soberano. / Ecuador, vestid la coraza / del Adalid del Rey Jesús. / Triunfar es gloria de la raza / nacida al pie de excelsa cruz. / Si tentador las paces os ofrece / pérfido, astuto Satanás / "¡Quién como Dios?", clamor que le estremece / "¡Atrás! decidle, eso jamás." / ¡Oh, Jesús, con empeño vano," etc.

[13] Cf. Gomezjurado, vol. 11, p. 333.

[14] Original verses: ¡Héroe! Yo te saludo. / ¡Mártir! Yo te venero. / A ti caberte / por tu hazaña no pudo / más envidiable suerte / que la vida inmortal de aquella muerte. *Ibid.* p. 354.

[15] *Ibid.* p. 335.

[16] *Boletín Eclesiástico de Quito* (1921), vol. 28, pp. 194, 484, & 487.

[17] December 12, 1921. *Boletin Eclesiastico de la Arquidiócesis de Quito* (1921), p. 487 ff. Cf. Gomezjurado, vol. 11, pp. 377-378.

[18] *Ibid.* p. 385.

[19] *Boletin Eclesiastico de la Arquidiócesis de Quito* (1921), p. 508. See also our book *¿Mártir García Moreno?* (*Is Garcia a Martyr?*), p. 151.

[20] *Idem.* p. 529. The speech by Father Martinez de la Vega is in a separate pamphlet. Cf. Gomezjurado, vol. 11, pp. 393-394.

[21] Martinez de la Vega's speech is in the Aurelio Espinosa Library in a separate pamphlet. Cf. Gomezjurado, vol. 11, p. 410.

[22] Gomezjurado, vol. 11, p. 429.

[23] Cf. Jeremias 20, 9.

[24] The study by Remigio Crespo Toral is in a separate book with all the tributes from Cuenca. Cf. Gomezjurado, vol. 12, p. 12.

[25] Ecclesiastical Bulletin of Quito, p. 550 ff. Cf. Gomezjurado, vol. 12, pp. 66-68. Original verses: 1. Fue ese Hombre honor del hombre. Hermosa Patria mía, de las montañas olvidado encanto, él, al amarte en ansiedad suprema, ante la Historia engrandeció tu nombre, bordó de oro la grana de tu manto, y aprisionó la luz a tu diadema. Él, al mirarte hermosa y noble, a Cristo que el dulce Corazón mostró en la Galia, para enseñanza de los pueblos grandes, cabe el regio tisú de su sandalia, te rindió en santa ofrenda, como flor de los Andes. 2. La guirnalda del mártir sólo espera. Caiga sobre él la multitud impía; y de la humanidad ante el proscenio, teñido en ondas de su sangre muera. Envuelto en roja luz se eclipsa el astro, teñido en arreboles muere el día. ¡Hijos del Crimen, inmolad al Genio; su sangre derramad, fieras humanas! El martirio corone su grandeza: con la cruz se coronan arrogantes las cúpulas cristianas.

[26] Cf. Gomezjurado, vol. 11, pp. 421-422.

[27] Carlos Fernandez 's enthusiasm was a topic of conversation in that year of 1921. The author's professor, Julio Vacacela, S. J., composed in turn an epic song and edited it in a separate pamphlet, together with clarifying notes and comments that the author has quoted at times in his other volumes. Polit's speech on December twenty-fifth is in the Bulletin, p. 490 ff., with the Pontifical Mass and *Te Deum*. Cf. Gomezjurado, vol. 11, p. 418.

[28] Mark 6, 18. Cf. Gomezjurado, vol. 11, p. 342.

[29] "Grande júbilo, cuando, hincadas las rodillas, y elevadas las manos al cielo, entregaste tu Reino al Divino Corazón de Jesús, el cual te aplaudió desde lo alto, constituido áncora, puerto, salud, vida y Pastor de tu pueblo. Las amenazas y peligros de una muerte sangrienta no te arredran..."
[30] December 22, 1921.
[31] I.e. during the years 1855 to 1856.
[32] Cf. Gomezjurado, vol. 12, pp. 90-94.
[33] What concerns Baudrillart and the correspondence between the French episcopate and Monsignor Polit are in separate pamphlets.
[34] *Idem.* Cf. Gomezjurado, vol. 11, pp. 371-372.
[35] *Idem.*
[36] I. e. "the wood of the Cross."
[37] *Idem.* Cf. Gomerjurado, vol. 11, pp. 374-376.
[38] Concerning the Mexican martyrs from the "Garcia Moreno Center," it is copied from a voluminous book relating to the religious persecution provoked by the Dictator Plutarco Calle which the author read around the year 1944. He retains his manuscript regarding it.
[39] This announcement was made by Canon Luis Felipe Sarrade. Cf. Gomezjurado, vol. 12, pp. 113-114.
[40] Again, the above-mentioned Bulletin, Vol. 29, corresponding to the year 1922, p. 227 ff. Likewise in Vol. 30, corresponding to the year 1923, p. 35 ff. Also, p. 147. Gomezjurado, vol. 12, p. 126.
[41] *Idem.* pp. 149 and 150. Monsignor Machado was an eye-witness. Therefore it seems to be without a doubt that the formula that is recorded in the text, quoted by Machado, was recited first by Checa and subsequently by Garcia Moreno. The prayer that begins with these words: *"Lord, this is Thy nation..."* was recited later as a corollary.
[42] Cf. Gomezjurado, vol. 11, pp. L-LIII and vol. 12, pp. 125-127.
[43] I Cor. 9, 26.
[44] *Idem.* p. 332 ff.
[45] "*Boletín de Quito*, May, 1923, p. 533 ff.
[46] Cf. Gomezjurado, vol. 12, pp. 128-129.
[47] I. e. "The Eucharistic Crusade of Garcia Moreno."
[48] The pictures from the Fiftieth Anniversary are in the pamphlet entitled "Souvenir from the Jubilee Year of the Consecration" and at the end of the collection entitled "To the Memory of Garcia Moreno," No. 1, final pages. All of this is in the Aurelio Espinosa Library at Cotocollao.
[49] *Ad majorem Dei gloriam* ("For the greater glory of God"); motto of the Jesuits.
[50] Cf. Gomezjurado, vol. 12, p. 226 ff.
[51] This is the meaning of the name "Gabriel" in Hebrew.
[52] The author has a few copies of the first edition of those prayers. On the back is the portrait of Garcia Moreno's bust with his insignias as President and as Army General. Later other editions were printed with the approval of other bishops.

⁵³ The Young Alberto Muyrragui, responsible for and owner of these prayers, could have propagated them with his own bank account, but the result would have been nugatory. During the first few days of October of 1938, Father Ricardo Vasquez addressed a letter to the author in which he sympathized with him on his failure, and ratified that it was not yet time, in spite of his being very devoted to Garcia Moreno and of having received singular favors through his intercession.

⁵⁴ *The Day*

⁵⁵ Fr. Gomezjurado gives more details in *Vida de Garcia Moreno* (vol. 12. p. 229): "Here is its article which appeared at the end of October. Unfortunately the collections which the author is reviewing are incomplete; but he remembers the substance well which is as follows:

> After the holy card of García Moreno and the prayer have been reproduced, it is said that General Elroy Alfaro also deserves to be raised to the altars, since he does not lag behind Garcia Moreno in that he had been barbarously assassinated. Still more, Elroy Alfaro has performed a portentous miracle, and it is the following:
>
>> A certain devotee of his, suffering from complete deafness, prayed before the portrait of Alfaro, and with a lit candle in his hand, was asking him to perform the miracle of taking away this ailment. Before he had finished the prayer, what an astounding miracle! The Alfarist devotee began to hear wonderfully with both ears in perfect condition. Even more, he began to perceive sounds with excessive intensity, like claps of thunder, even the buzzing of flies and the sputtering of the candle.

This was the whole Masonic arson attack against Father Gomezjurado and all the Jesuits.

See Gomezjurado, vol. 13, p. 408, for the account of the favor attributed to Garcia Moreno being mocked here.

⁵⁶ "His Excellency Alberto Ordonez, an ardent devotee of the President-martyr, and knowledgeable of his anecdotal features and even his unpublished feats, advised me." (Gomezjurado, vol. 12, p. 232.)

⁵⁷ The first prayer that the author composed to the Blessed Virgin was in Cuneca in the year 1954 on the occasion of celebrating the centenary of the dogmatic definition of the Immaculate Conception. Instead of the words "he was a member of thy confraternity" these appeared: "he belonged to thy sweet Archconfraternity." A little folded paper of four pages: on the first and the fourth were the image of the Virgin of Lourdes and the bust of Garcia Moreno respectively, with ecclesiastical approval. "The preceding prayer was also approved by other venerable bishops, and was even enriched with an indulgence of three hundred days by His Eminence María de la Torre, Archbishop of Quito." (Gomezjurado, vol. 12, p. 240.)

⁵⁸ Third edition, p. 34.

⁵⁹ Cf. Gomezjurado, vol. 13, pp. 409-410.

[60] The Tertiaries who went to Quito were Arturo Salazar, Aurelio del Pozo, Alberto Muyrragui and Javier Bustos. It was a mistake to have addressed the written application to the Apostolic Nuncio instead of to the Archbishop. What has been stated is found in the Franciscan Bulletin, Riobamba, June 13, 1940.
[61] It was Monsignor Alberto Ordonez Crespo, an eyewitness, who told me about the energetic gesture and words of the Metropolitan, who always prided himself in valiantly promoting the beatification of Garcia Moreno without paying the least attention to the Masons.
[62] I. e. "little golden crown."
[63] Apostolic Letter *Già da qualche tempo*" (AAS 22 (1930), pp. 87-88).
[64] *Normae servandae in construendis processibus ordinariis super causis historicis* (AAS 31 (1939), pp. 174-175).
[65] "The fiscal promoter (*fiscus*, public treasury) — though perhaps, if we attend to the most important part of his office, a better title would be "promoter of justice" — is a person who, constituted by the ecclesiastical authority, exercises in the ecclesiastical courts and in his own name the office of a public prosecutor, especially in criminal cases (*Instr. S. C. Episc. et Reg.*, January 11, 1880, art. 13). If we wish to include in the definition all that is comprehended in his office, he might be defined as a public person legitimately appointed to defend the rights of his church, especially in court. Peries, in his article *"Le procureur fiscal ou promoteur"* (*Revue des sciences ecclésiastiques*, April, 1897), rightly says that the whole office of the fiscal promoter may be summed up in three points: solicitude for the observance of discipline, particularly among the clergy; attendance at the processes of beatification and canonization in episcopal courts; and defense of the validity of marriage and of religious profession. All these functions, it is true, are not always carried out by one and the same person; they are all, however, included in the full idea of the *promoter fiscalis*, for it is this official's duty to defend the rights of the Church, the decency of Divine service, the dignity of the clergy, the holiness of matrimony, and perseverance in the perfect state of life" ("Ecclesiastical Courts" (*The Catholic Encyclopedia* (1908 ed.), vol. 4, p. 450).
[66] "His competit 'in solidum' officium colligendi omnes fontes scriptos circa vitam, virtutes vel martyrium, antiquam famam sanctitatis vel martyrii, aut antiquum cultum Servi Dei. His competit 'in solidum' officium colligendi omnes fontes scriptos circa vitam, virtutes vel martyrium, antiquam famam sanctitatis vel martyrii, aut antiquum cultum Servi Dei."
[67] This extract is taken from the archbishop's act establishing the cause of beatification of Garcia Moreno in the *Bulletin* of January, 1940. Cf. Gomezjurado, vol. 12, pp. 233-236.
[68] Regarding the thesis composed by Father Jouanen, a copy remains in the Aurelio Espinosa Library at Cotocollao and another one was given to the Metropolitan Curia.

# Chapter 14
# The Return of the Heart of Jesus of Garcia Moreno, January 29, 1942

Mr. Robert Parker, a noted physician, admired Garcia Moreno's head for its great size and configuration, and for having housed a great talent. Once he confided, "They say that Garcia Moreno was condemned to death by Masonry. Well now, I am a Mason. I would not have agreed with such a sentence." Mr. Parker was charitable to the poor and deferential to the members of religious communities. He cultivated friendship with Sister Carolina Escobar from the School of the Immaculate and he helped its apostolate with frequent alms. He was born in the United States and even so was the Grand Master of Ecuadorian Masonry, whose main headquarters was in Guayaquil. On a certain occasion he said to Sister Carolina, "Ecuadorians easily betray their convictions in exchange for money and jobs. In the last Masonic meeting it was determined that the president of the Republic would be Doctor Carlos Arroyo del Rio and this must come to pass." In fact, the elections were a brazen fraud, and Arroyo del Rio ascended to the Presidency.

Such was the Ecuadorian regime when a battalion of Peruvian soldiers began an invasion of the province of El Oro. The Ecuadorian patrol arrived at the violated spot, but was received with gunfire. As was obvious, a slight battle ensued. It was July 5, 1941. During the following days, Peruvian planes bombed the Ecuadorian towns of Chacras and Huaquillas. There were skirmishes in which Ecuadorian soldiers, inferior in number and lacking an air force, fought with heroic valor. Twenty-one days later, on July twenty-sixth, the Peruvian government was content with having seized the province of El Oro, and accepted a cease fire.[1]

There is a book written by an eyewitness, Major Leonardo Chiriboga Ordonez, with the epigraph, "It Happened at the Border,"[2] from which a few paragraphs are extracted:

> During all that nightmarish era, which we would like to erase from the annals of our country, an epic handful of Ecuadorian soldiers obscurely and heroically fulfilled their duty. They were poorly equipped, clearly abandoned, victims of a disoriented central command and political leadership reaching beyond the limits of incompetence. It makes us think something unspeakable and murky—that today's and tomorrow's men have a terrible duty to explain...

Those episodes will initiate an era, the age that the new youth eagerly desires, of a revision of values and realities, of a readjustment of positions, of awakening from the tragedy. An age that, with Wagnerian severity, with latent sorrow, with lacerated flesh, but with an indomitable spirit for rehabilitation and reconstruction, will know how to stamp on the foreheads of the holders of authority the ineffaceable stigma of their crime of high treason, whether it be with the whip of sanction or with the satire of history...

All the officers have requested the government to send us tools, at least to dig some trenches, but they do not want to send even that. We barely have a few old machetes and four useless pickaxes. And so, cholito,[3] if I begin to tell all the miseries of this poor border, perhaps I might start to cry and run away. But wait just a little while. Someday something serious has to happen, and then each of the ones on top will have to wash his hands like Pilate did, and in the end no one will know whom to blame.[4]

When the armistice was accepted, the foreign minister, Doctor Julio Tobar Donoso, had recourse to every diplomatic support so that the conquerors would not exact too much. The opportunity came when the Foreign Ministers of the American Continent met in Rio de Janeiro, the Brazilian capital.

At the same time there was an influx of bishops from that continent to Santiago, Chile, for the celebration of a Eucharistic Congress. It was the month of November, 1941. Our Metropolitan, Archbishop Carlos Maria de la Torre, left for the Chilean capital, and contributed with his words and example to the splendor of the Eucharistic event. However, with greater enthusiasm he also took the opportunity to make an excursion to Valparaiso, and deployed all his powerful influence there for the return of "The Heart of Jesus of Garcia Moreno" to his Ecuador, which had been defeated, invaded and was in the process of being greatly mutilated. "Lord, if Thou hadst been with us, such a disgrace would not have happened. Thy image hast already been enthroned in the homes of the entire world; it is now time for Thee to return to the chosen people, who nonetheless have been punished for their crimes."[5]

In chapter seven we saw that the precious oleograph was put into the hands of Father Agustin Serrano, as a donation to the Priests of the Sacred Hearts of Jesus and Mary in Valparaiso. And so it is understandable that those religious answered with an emphatic "No" to Archbishop de la Torre's request, who, on the contrary, argued in these terms:

> "When this painting was in danger of being profaned, it was sent secretly to Chile, on the basis of being returned. The time has come for it to be returned to Ecuador." The part about "on the basis of being returned" could not be demonstrated apodictically by the Ecuadorian prelate, who also had recourse to arguments of suitability given the sad internal and external situation of Ecuador. The author attributes the success of the negotiation to the charm produced by the eminent virtue, profound science and oratorical eloquence of the Quitonian Archbishop. The latter returned to his country with hopes of triumph and with the charism of a precursor. Upon leaving, he conferred with Reverend Mother Cornelia Rogier, who inevitably had to return to Quito, and told her, "Do not step on Ecuadorian soil unless you are bringing the painting with you."

The aforesaid religious continued the campaign. She believed in the existence of some writing where "to be returned" was recorded. But since such a document did not appear, the Superior of the Catholic University of Valparaiso maintained a negative answer. One morning when the Reverend Mother Cornelia was kneeling in her oratory, the chaplain passed next to her, put his hand on her shoulder and told her, "You will take the painting to Quito."

Having taken down the venerable image which presided over the stately reception hall, the persistent little nun received it in her arms, who, being the bearer of the magnificent trophy, and accompanied by a few other religious, left Chile in the middle of December, 1941.

She stopped in Lima for the space of three long weeks. On the terrestrial globe held in the left hand of the Heart of Jesus of Garcia Moreno, the nation of Ecuador was painted having the Amazon River as its border. Any Peruvian who fixed their glance on that detail must have been upset.

At the port of Callao, the travelers boarded the ship and began the voyage heading for Ecuador. It was January 24, 1942. The ship was named *The Imperial*. What an admirable disposition of Providence, since on that occasion sailed the Emperor of Heaven and Earth. Besides, *the Imperial* was escorted in procession by three Peruvian warships. From a human viewpoint, this accompaniment was necessary, because of the danger of Japanese submarines. Those were the years of the World War.⁶

It was two o'clock in the afternoon on January twenty-ninth when *The Imperial* entered Ecuadorian waters. And at the same hour in Rio de Janeiro the Protocol was signed that stripped Ecuador of her Amazon rights, depriving her of two thousand square kilometers in the Eastern Region, and transferring them to the ownership of Peru. This nation, having accomplished its criminal objective, retreated from the invaded province of El Oro, which it had taken as a hostage until then. A completely mysterious coincidence! The Heart of Jesus returns to His people at the time of tragedy. The Almighty, the Just One: a hope for the nation.

*The Imperial* anchored in the Bay of Salinas in the middle of the night of the thirtieth to the thirty-first of January of 1942. A group of religious of the Sacred Hearts was waiting there, who welcomed the Divine King as well as their sisters who came from Chile. A small procession took place from the dock to the community's residence. The painting was placed in the chapel and received its first homage from the land of Ecuador.⁷

On the ninth day of February it left Guayaquil on a train bound for Quito. In the Sibambe station Mother Cornelia Rogier had to tear herself away from the painting and from her sisters to change direction, since she had to go to the community of the Sacred Hearts in Cuenca, whose governance holy obedience had entrusted to her. Mother Mary de San Jose Velez took her place as the one responsible for the traveling image. At eight-thirty at night, near Ambato, the train had a violent crash. The three religious suffered frightful bruises and were injured, although not seriously. But the painting of the Heart of Jesus suffered no damage, despite the fact that it was not rolled up, but extended on the flat bottom of its case. None of the other passengers were injured.

It was February tenth and three o'clock in the afternoon, when the Heart of Jesus of Garcia Moreno arrived at Quito, and a quarter of an hour later at the School of the Sacred Hearts in Rumipamba, where it was transported to the chapel while the Community sang the jubilant *Magnificat*. On that night, two prayers were recited amidst tears: the act of reparation for the public crimes of Ecuador and the act of consecration made sixty-eight years earlier by Archbishop Checa and President Garcia Moreno.⁸

The next day, the feast of Our Lady of Lourdes, the eleventh of February, and at twelve noon, the incomparable little nuns of the Sacred

Hearts, having arrived at the Archbishop's Palace, put the very famous oil painting into the arms of Archbishop de la Torre. It remained in an atmosphere of silence and concealment for over three months, until May twenty-second when the following proclamation resounded in the ears of the Ecuadorians:

> *Evangelizo vobis gaudium magnum.* "I bring you good tidings of great joy."[9] The precious image of the Most Holy Heart of Jesus, before which our fathers knelt and made a thousand declarations of Faith, shed bitter tears of compunction and choosing Him as their Sovereign, offered humble vassalage and fervent love to the God-man. The artistic image before which the Ecuadorian Nation was officially and irrevocably consecrated to the most loving Heart of Jesus worthily represented by its authorities, magistrates and people, and especially by the martyr, His Grace Archbishop Checa, and by the President of the Republic, the honor of Ecuador and the glory of America, already purified from the dross of culpability and having reached a high degree of moral perfection, Garcia Moreno. This precious and artistic image, absent for many years from our native soil, is now in our midst...
> 
> Who is able to plumb the inscrutable secrets of Divine Providence?
> 
> The portentous image arrives at the saddest, most distressing, critical time of our national existence.
> 
> It plows through Ecuadorian waters during the precise moments when there in Rio de Janeiro, our country, obligated, constrained, forced by inexorable circumstances, tolerates them to rend her insides, tearing away from her, against all justice and rights, a notable portion of her territory, acquired with the gold from her coffers, with the valor of her sons, the sweat of her missionaries, and even with the blood of her martyrs.[10]
> 
> It comes in the precise moments when the sky of this most beloved country is enveloped in the shadows of gloomy night, and is covered with thick, black clouds, sinister forerunners of furious storms that, without the almighty and fatherly protection of the Heart of Jesus, King and Lord of Ecuador, would end her religious unity, and perhaps even the very existence of the nation.
> 
> What does this irrefutable witness of our National Consecration to the Deified Heart of Jesus come to do?

Does it perhaps come to fling in our faces our ingratitude for His love, our unfaithfulness to promises so solemnly made, our national apostasy?

Does it come perhaps in the midst of the sadness and agony that tortures our souls, to challenge us, as He did with the ungrateful Hebrew people, to look for salvation from the false gods that we have forged for ourselves?

Maybe those terrible, formidable words are going to strike our ears that struck those of Israel when the Lord, irritated, said to them, "Where are the gods that have supplanted Me? Let them arise and deliver thee in the time of thy affliction."[11]

Yes, He will undoubtedly reproach us, because we deserve it. But these same reproaches will be reproaches of love, reproaches that will invite us to put all our trust in Him, and to hope for everything from His infinite mercy.

When we offer ourselves to Him, He will let us hear those same most sweet words that once reformed the ungrateful Jewish people: "I have not been able to forget your former love and the tenderness with which you consecrated yourself to Me."

Thus we hold this as certain, when we reflect on the unfathomable abysms of love and mercy that are enclosed in that most sweet Heart, thus we are persuaded by the consideration of the moment chosen by Him for His image to return to Ecuador, that it actually reached our native soil when that uninterrupted Holy Hour was still being celebrated in which, amidst sighs and tears, we begged Him by His weariness, by His sadness, by His cruel agony and by His copious sweat of blood, to pity us and grant us true peace founded on justice...[12]

To correspond to these expressions of love, we ought to embark upon a moral and religious regeneration... The most loving Heart of Jesus expects this of us... Let us not forget that there is no vengeance more frightful than that of scorned love. Let us remember that, although for punishing individual sins there always remains eternal justice, the punishment of social crimes must necessarily be temporal, because in eternity there are no longer peoples or nations, rather only the immense multitude of the predestined or the damned.

If, then, we want the whip to be lifted that cruelly rends the back of our nation, let us make our country return contritely and humbly to Jesus.

Quito and the entire nation were touched. In the capital a novena took place in the form of a mission, beginning on June nineteenth, with the attendance of various strata of society and areas of the city each day. The crowning point of the novena culminated on Sunday, June twenty-eighth, with an open-air Mass on the esplanade called *Polo-Club*. There were sixty thousand faithful attending, and thirty-five thousand Communions.

In the afternoon, the number of those gathered was the same. The holy picture arrived and was enthroned on a majestic altar. "Long live the Heart of Jesus! Long live Christ the King! Long live the Sovereign of the Nation!" These shouts, like the roar of the sea heard from a great distance, were resounding unto those who were near; faint but mysterious and more surreal to those who heard them from afar. The numerous standards and flags swayed by the wind brought to a pinnacle the wonder of all. Archbishop de la Torre spoke into the microphone:

> Ecuador! Open wide your doors! Clear the way for the King of glory. It is He! He is the same One before whom our fathers knelt and swore fidelity and love. It is He. He does not come amidst the resplendence of glory and majesty to demand from us an account of the breaking of our word or to punish our crimes. He comes full of meekness and mercy to dry our tears and offer us pardon...[13]
>
> People of Ecuador! He is your King by a threefold title, each one more incontestable: King by natural right, King by the title of conquest, King by your own voluntary, free and loving choice. People of Ecuador! He is the Son of God; and if the Father, as David sings, erected for Him a throne on the holy mountain of Sion, one is also raised for Him at the base of Mount Pichincha. People of Ecuador! Long live Christ the King!

An ocean of voices answered, "Long live Christ the King!"

> Garcia Moreno, the ideal and model of a Catholic head of state, the man who honored mankind, and whose glory, as Menendez Pelayo said, is sufficient for Ecuador to take a seat with all fittingness in the concert of nations. Garcia Moreno, by publicly, officially and inviolably consecrating the Republic to the Most Holy Heart of Jesus, did not oppose, but rather most faithfully interpreted, the will and sentiments of the Ecuadorian nation...

Cast your gaze upon the artistic and historical painting that is before you. In a very lifelike manner, it reproduces one of the apparitions of the Deific Heart of Jesus to His most faithful servant Saint Margaret Mary. Look at it: the uncovered and visible Heart is surrounded by burning flames, encompassed by a ring of thorns, overwhelmed by the weight of a cross, slashed by a wound. Do not ask me for an explanation of this mysterious emblem. Our Savior Himself gave it when He said, "Behold this Heart which has so loved men that it has spared nothing, even to exhausting and consuming itself in order to testify to its love. In return I receive from the greater part [of mankind] only ingratitude, irreverence, sacrilege, and coldness and contempt."

But the crime that has grieved this most noble Heart the most is without a doubt the disregard for His social sovereignty. Ecuador appears as an atheistic nation before the face of the world. Jesus Christ has been disdainfully cast out of all manifestations of public life. Jesus Christ is Ecuador's great exile. He has been exiled from many families, schools, colleges and universities; banned from the Constitution and laws. He has been exiled from governmental assemblies and courts. He has been exiled from the army and even from cemeteries. This monstrous crime has provoked Divine wrath...[14]

"Jesus, Jesus! Who has wounded Thy Heart?" "Those have wounded My Heart who call themselves My friends." That is to say, we His chosen people, we His predilect people, we, the first nation consecrated to His Divine Heart, which now disowns His sovereignty and which is ashamed of appearing as a faithful, submissive and loving vassal.

Heart of Jesus, Thou didst not abandon the little lost lamb but went after it and did not stop looking for it until Thou returned it to the sheepfold! Have compassion and mercy on our country. Heart of Jesus, Thou didst receive the prodigal son with open arms and showered him with kisses and caresses, and restored to him all the tenderness of Thy love: mercy and compassion for our nation!

With a quivering voice and tearful eyes the multitude chanted this prayer in unison: "Mercy and compassion on our country!" The hearts of the multitude thus enflamed, His Grace proceeded to renew the Consecration, the formula of which was repeated aloud, word for word, by the immense crowd. Here are some of the words:

> Adorable Heart of Jesus! King of kings and Lord of lords... we offer and consecrate the Republic of Ecuador to Thee from this day and forever ... Show all nations that Ecuador is Thine... Prove to the world that blessed is the nation which chooses Thee as its Lord and God ...

It was six o'clock in the evening. The sun was setting over Pichincha. Faint light shone over the city. The high horizons were bathed in the last rays. The copious human river flowed to San Juan Hill, to the National Basilica, singing their popular hymn: "*Corazon Santo—Tu reinaras—Rey de mi Patria—Siempre seras.*"[15] The venerated picture, enthroned on a lavish bier that everyone strove to carry upon their shoulders, advanced slowly, surrounded by the pontiffs and clergy. As night fell, the wonder-working painting arrived at the Basilica, took possession of its palace; and, in the midst of frenetic cheers and acclamations, received clouds of incense and flowers upon the sumptuous altar.[16]

A long month passes by, and on August first the venerable image is transported by plane to Guayaquil, where it is received with triumphal pomp. Immediately a mission commences, which works extraordinary conversions of sinners. The Prelate, Bishop Heredia, takes advantage of the occasion to vindicate Garcia Moreno's eminent practice of Catholicism, for he has this thesis firmly fixed in his mind: "God demands two things for the rehabilitation of Ecuador: the greatest possible glorification of Garcia Moreno, and the completion of the construction of the Basilica of the National Vow." For the first, he recalled through flyers that Garcia Moreno was the one who gave the design to the renowned image, whose owner he was; at its feet he consecrated Ecuador to the Heart of Jesus; and in the whole world it is identified by these terms, "The Heart of Jesus of Garcia Moreno." However, there were not lacking women who crumpled up those papers and threw them into the waste paper basket right before the eyes of the bishop. Such was the bitter fruit of the Masonic campaign of pamphlets against the Great Man; and prejudices from families whose ancestors perhaps had to suffer some punishment from the just Head of State.

The same year, on October 17, 1942, the aforesaid icon was brought by automobile to Riobamba. The civil authorities asked that its passage through the city be made through the least populated streets, for fear that the multitude would cry out against the hated government of Arroyo del Rio. The answer was in the affirmative.

I would like to speak about myself, since I was an eyewitness and even an actor in the scenes. In the company of a group of Young Christian Workers, I set out to intercept the painting. At the edge of town I came upon steadily increasing groups of people from Riobamba. I also found some forty men who had come from the neighboring village of Calpi, led by their parish priest, Father Victor Ruiz, and with a band of musicians. Delegations from other rural parishes were not lacking.

From the corner of a less populated street they shouted and made signs: "The picture is coming this way; everyone run over here." In mass and as fast as possible, even running, we went there. I heard a furious craftsman exclaim: "Those bandits are trying to make sure that the image goes where there are no people."[17] The automobile stopped at the human barrier and was obliged to turn to the right to continue the procession down the main avenue. The painting was taken out, received and carried in the arms of matrons of rank, who did not cease praying and singing, by the initiative of the Jesuit Father Jose Bolanos, the Director of the Apostolate of Prayer. The river of people marched towards the Basilica of the Heart of Jesus.[18] A spirit of joy and unexpected bravery imbued us all. The acclamations resounded in unison of "Long live the Heart of Jesus of Garcia Moreno, long live the Savior of our country, long live the King of Ecuador!" This idea became firmly entrenched in my mind: "That God has given this image the charism of effectively promoting Catholic fervor among Ecuadorians, and of giving rise to a new Pentecost of which the prelates must take advantage."

Likewise, a schoolboy, in spite of being a student in a lay high school, said to me, "Father, lead a cheer for Garcia Moreno and we will join you all together." I hastened to do so, and it was a complete success. I have become more and more convinced that this picture has returned to Ecuador, in part, to take up the defense of Garcia Moreno's honor and his glorification, given the history of that picture and its name of "The Heart of Jesus of Garcia Moreno."

After nineteen days of homage in "The Sultana of Chimborazo,"[19] the Garcian painting returned to Quito. It was November fifth. Around midday the regal car reached the outskirts of Ambato and encountered a most gratifying surprise: children and youths from the Catholic schools, besides large groups of adults, had come to meet it, letting out cries of acclamation to the Divine Monarch and imploring for it to stop at Ambato for a novena. In an analogous way, twenty centuries before, the Divine Master, walking alone through Samaria, was obliged by its pious inhabitants to remain there a few days. In the present case, recourse was made to the most rapid means of communication, asking the Archbishop of Quito for his reply. Meanwhile the venerable image was the object of the most spontaneous and ardent homage. The magazine *Cristo Rey*,[20] of the Congregation of the Sacred Hearts of Jesus and Mary in Quito, was right when formulating the commentary that the author permits himself to touch up as follows:

> The bones of Juan Leon Mera would jump for joy, who not only approved the legislative degree of the Consecration, but also, as a renowned writer, gave it the final form in pure and elegant Spanish. On the contrary, the mummy of Juan Montalvo, if it truly is Montalvo's mummy, would tremble, who mocked that decree with these words: "The New World has still not stopped laughing from seeing that ingenious Caius, by a solemn act, dedicate the Republic to the Sacred Heart of Jesus."

In the endnote we present the arguments and testimonies which give rise to the suspicion that it is not the body of Juan Montalvo which reposes in the funeral chapel of Ambato.[21]

The response of the Illustrious Archbishop of Quito expressed that the detention of the painting was not appropriate, and that first committees should be organized which were to officially request its presence in the city of flowers, with preparations worthy of the majesty of the wonder-working image.

That is how it was done; and thirty-seven days later, that is, on December twelfth, the residents of Ambato went out to meet the King of the country with unsurpassable pomp. Desirous of reproducing the spectacle of Palm Sunday, some two hundred inhabitants of Ambato went out to meet it with palms in their hands, waving and fluttering them.

The culminating day was on Sunday, December twentieth, with the arrival of the Metropolitan Prelate, Archbishop Carlos Maria de La Torre, whose sermon gave express and enthusiastic mention of Garcia Moreno, to whom was due the fact that Ecuador was the firstborn among the nations officially consecrated to the Heart of Jesus. Just as in Quito, Guayaquil and Riobamba, so likewise in Ambato there was a resurgence of faith and Christian ardor, and even true conversions. The gesture of the distinguished gentleman, Alfredo Coloma, a victim of human respect in times past, was much enjoyed and disseminated. Now, he stood up with the greatest aplomb, when the loudspeaker had barely broadcasted these words: "All who are going to Communion, please stand." His friends around him, told him, "What a pity that you did not inform us in time; otherwise we would have accompanied you."[22]

Let us pass on to the village called *Tambo*, on the memorable day of March 17, 1943, at eight-thirty at night. At last the stentorian whistles of the railway car were heard, bearer of the miraculous canvas. The crowd, as though affected by an electric bath, rushed forward to meet the Divine King. Volleys of fireworks thundered in the sky. There was a triumphal entrance into the church with hurrahs and acclamations. Hymns and prayers continued in the church until midnight, the hour in which all the administrators from the town of Canar brusquely pounced upon the painting to take it to their village, putting it into the arms of the President. They interwove the painting with ribbons which the town councilors took in their hands with pride and joy. This altar composed of men ascended an adorned carriage and began a night procession of almost four miles. Having arrived at Canar, the picture was taken into the Municipal Palace, where its representatives, while kneeling, exclaimed, "Enter, O Lord!" The venerable image having been put in a place of honor on high, the following agreement was read:

The Municipal Council of Canar Canton, considering:
1. That, named through the people's free election, the Town Council is their genuine representative.
2. That, on solemn occasions such as the present one, it is an obligation of loyalty for the principal representatives to act for them.
3. That on the seventeenth day of the current month the sacred image of the Divine Heart of Jesus our King arrives from the capital of the Republic, before which the Ecuadorian Nation officially and publicly was consecrated during the Presidency of the renowned Gabriel Garcia Moreno:

Agrees:
1. To receive the historical oleograph officially in the House of the People in order to recognize in this way the divine sovereignty of Jesus Christ, universal Monarch of all nations.

2. To make a public manifestation of faith during this act, renewing, in the name of the people of Canar, the oath of fidelity to the Most Sacred Heart of Jesus.

>Given in the Blue Room of the Municipal House, on the seventeenth day of the month of March of one thousand, nine hundred and forty-three.
>
>President of the Council: Alfonso Munoz Andrade.
>Vice-President: Ezequiel Cardenas Espinoza.
>Council Members: Luis Antonio Crespo, Alfonso Maria Ortiz, Antonio Andino, Manuel Crespo Avila.
>Municipal Procurator: Antonio Santacruz.
>Treasurer: Jose Gabriel Andrade.
>Secretary: Alfonso Arce.

The people crowded together with the goal of contemplating the image up close. They noticed that at their feet lay the map of Ecuador with a black ribbon[23] on the region seized by Peru. They raised their eyes and noted that the Ecuadorian Nation held up by the Divine King was not mutilated but rather that it had the Amazon as its boundary: here was hope.[24]

It was like Christmas Eve, a night of no sleep.[25] In the Eastern horizon the first glimmers of dawn were breaking, when the painting was transferred to the principal church crammed with faithful who began the prayers and hymns of the Holy Hour. The day of March eighteenth having begun, the Illustrious Bishop of Cuenca appeared, His Excellency Daniel Hermida, who celebrated Holy Mass and distributed Communion to a large number of attendees.

The Heart of Jesus of Garcia Moreno resumed its triumphal march in the direction of the villa of Biblian where it arrived around midday and presided over an open-air Mass before crowds of people.

The Catholics of Azogues, the capital of the province of Canar, came in person to Biblian very early, to escort the Divine King in procession to their hearths. As vassals of the Church, they fearlessly endured the downpour that had broken out, without retreating from being next to His Majesty. In the principal church of Azogues, the painting was placed upon a sumptuous throne, to the concentric sounds of hymns, cheers and applause.

The following day, March 19, 1943, the holy image, the true Paladin of the Nation, made its entry into the very faithful and populous city of Cuenca. Along the way, the multitude cried out shouts of "Long live the Heart of Jesus of Garcia Moreno! God does not die!" Meanwhile two airplanes joined the procession, flying over the crowds of people and joining the chorus with the din of their motors. In addition, the verses that appeared in the newspaper from Cuenca, *El Mercurio*,[26] palpitated and seemed to resound in the hearts of each one of the attendees. Here they are: they are touching and beautiful:

> Welcome, Lord, to our hearths, to this sweet corner of the Andean rainforest. Thou hast returned, at last, from so long an exile, to the joy of Thy poor children.
> Extremely impenetrable are Thy mysteries, and I cannot understand, O Lord, why Thou didst leave, when a martyr and wise Head of State of the nascent Ecuadorian Republic, with ardent faith and desire, proclaimed Thee Sovereign and King of Ecuador... Thou didst leave us orphans and alone for such a long time. What days of mourning, tears and tragedy have been occurring year after year, during Thy long absence, to the extent that today Thou findest Thy nation mutilated!
> But Thou hast returned, O Lord, blessed art Thou! Place Thy feet with determination and firmness on the soil of Azuay.[27]
> Yet, do not arrive like a humble pilgrim, with quivering soles and tattered robes. Do not come with a traveler's staff, in search of hospitality, like a foreigner. Let Thy brow bleed no longer, be not a beggar for love with Thy sad gaze... Do not bring those scarlet wounds that hurt so much in Thy open side... I would not like to see Thee thus. Turn Thy thorns into a prince's crown, and Thy staff into a monarch's scepter. Come as King to govern us, like a Father to bless us. Come as a Friend to console us, for we all await Thee here, with the tenderness of serenaders in the countryside, with the endearment of love in our chests; and children, plucking petals from the best flowers, will give Thee their innocent souls.
> Thou hast done well in coming, O Lord! For, poets have now tuned their mystical lutes, to rhyme their poems with wonderful finesse.
> Thou hast done well in coming, O Lord! And those of us who have nothing to offer Thee hurriedly make iridescent prisms from tears to decorate the edge of Thy cloak.

> Thou hast done well in coming, O Lord! And as Master and Sovereign of souls and all things, establish Thy kingship in Thy loving city.
>
> Never ever leave anymore, because all of us shall know how to worship Thee. Do not leave us alone, Lord! We need Thee so much, in order to be good.
>
> Thou who dost imprison the disheveled furies of hell, and chain the storms of sea and clouds: fold once and for all their black wings from wickedness, and cover them with the blessed labarum of Thy mantle. Thou hast done well in coming, Lord, and leave us not![28]

Here are some lines also extracted from another column of the same *Mercurio*:

> Ecuador is still alive. But what a life is that of our nation! A mediocre, mutilated, moribund life! How the patriotic heart longs for other times, times brimming with national life that is lost in the resplendent and transparent distance. Then was Ecuador great, as also was the figure of its gigantic and brilliant leader ...
>
> The canvas of the Heart of Jesus has made immense propaganda for Ecuador in the world. Just as when the good patriot speaks of his homeland in exile, he does it honor, and suffers the nostalgia of separation, so the painting of the Heart of Jesus has spoken eloquently of Ecuador; and its echo, whose strong vibration from a powerful diffuser, has made itself heard to the ends of the world...
>
> May Ecuador readjust its life and institutions, and may this movement of national reconstruction be born of Ecuadorian Catholicism...
>
> Cuenca is today the Biblical Jerusalem.[29]

Omitting the account of the acts of intense Christian fervor that took place in Cuenca during the first twelve days, it is necessary to put into relief the stay of the sacrosanct image at the School of the Sacred Hearts, on April third, fourth, fifth and sixth, at the request of Reverend Mother Cornelia Rogier, the same sister who had an influence on the return of the miraculous painting to Ecuador. Again the multitude was elated and overwhelmed. The shouts were repeated of: "Long live the

Heart of Jesus of Garcia Moreno! God does not die! Long live Garcia Moreno!" In the portress' office, the little sisters formed a guard of honor, dressed in their splendid robes, veils and brocades, just as when they make their perpetual adoration. A new hymn was heard, expressly composed for the entrance of the famous oleograph in Cuenca. The words were written by the distinguished writer, Luis Cordero; the melody by the Salesian priest, Father Carlos Crespi. Let us listen to some stanzas:

1. Come, Jesus, to your people who one day
   Acclaimed Thee as their monarch and Lord;
   Come and reign in the nation that craves
   To be Thy perpetual throne of love.
2. Inebriated with deep joy
   Our beloved Nation was offered,
   The first among all in the world,
   As an altar for Thy royal Heart.
3. Always faithful to the happy oath,
   Through Thy name it kept up the fight
   And on Thy altar was the bloodstained martyr
   Its greatest and most noble Champion.[30]

In addition, the poem entitled *Canto a la Consagracion del Ecuador y a Garcia Moreno* was recited, whose author was Doctor Remigio Tamariz Crespo.[31]

The discourses and sermons always alluded to Garcia Moreno, especially to his heroic effort for the Catholic education of young children and older youths; and they applied the cautery of fire to the modern day governments that degrade their schools, without catechism and without God, a true gangrene of the nation.

Pilgrimages from the neighboring towns continued, headed by their parish priests and sometimes with their musical band.

The incomparable icon was in Cuenca for three long months, and would have remained there forever if the Quitonian Metropolitan had not urged its return insistently. This took place on June twenty-third by plane. The towns of Azuay mitigated their sorrow by lavishing silver and gold, with the object of fashioning a frame worthy of their ardent faith and of the venerable image. When its execution was completed, it was taken to Quito by a delegation headed by the bishop of Cuenca, His Excellency Daniel Hermida, on the sixteenth of November of the above-said year of 1943, and delivered into the hands of Archbishop de la Torre. Let us read a descriptive summary.

> It is entirely made of silver with incrustations of gold. The four sides consist of smooth polished moldings, made with eight bundles of rays or beams. At the middle of the upper side the shield of Ecuador is engraved, which is surrounded by a crown of pure gold, the same one with which the poet Luis Cordero had been crowned years before…, the accomplishments of this Catholic President have been stated in earlier chapters. The descendants of that personage were the ones who offered to the Heart of Jesus of Garcia Moreno this honorific memento and family treasure. On the right as well as on the left side, six polished medals jut out, consisting of the portraits of Garcia Moreno, Archbishop Ignacio Checa, Archbishop Carlos Maria de la Torre, Father Manuel Proano and the respective shields of Bishop Hermida and of the Religious Congregation of the Sacred Hearts. Lastly, on the lower side are mounted the shields of the city of Cuenca and of the city of Azogues.[32]

Just ten days went by, and the Divine Monarch of Ecuador took flight by airplane to the city of Loja. Here is some information about the reception:

The day before, Saturday November twenty-seventh, at twelve noon, there was a general ringing of bells; and at seven in the evening, there was an illumination of the entire city. On Sunday, November twenty-eighth, at seven o'clock in the morning, the procession went in automobiles to the Catamayo Valley and aviation field.

As soon as the airplane could be seen, the image would be greeted with the salvos customary for the arrival of kings and emperors, twenty-one cannon shots, in the absence of which, twenty reports or shots of powerful fireworks, under the direction of the Chuquiribamba Highway Administration Committee.

In the blue sky in the distance, the crowd finally sighted a gray dot which grew and grew, like hope in the Christian heart: "It is the airplane," said the news report: "It is the angel of the genius that advances, to strengthen the nation's unity, along the paths of hurricanes and lightning, and to announce the coming of the Messias…" Emotion shook their hearts. Some are touched by a divine impulse; they rush to the encounter and offer an uncontainable tear.

The plane thrice circles above the city, whose bells ring gloriously for a long time. At the moment of landing, the multitude breaks into thunderous shouts of "*viva*," applause and throwing flowers. The festive thunder of firecrackers is in the air. Musical bands play hymns of triumph.

When the Emperor of heaven and earth is at the city gates, the twenty-one salvos established by protocol are begun, each one at five minute intervals. The Palladium advances majestically on the shoulders of gentlemen. From the balconies the ladies give it a royal welcome not only with clouds of petals but also by spraying aromas and perfumes that make breathing a delight. Firecrackers, exploding on high, let fall a shower of little papers on which are written greetings and congratulations to the Sovereign. Let us hear the reporter again:[33]

> We cannot omit an exceptional case: the spontaneity in religious acts; the practical respect of those who do not agree with our religion; the absence of extravagant, pretentious individuals who disturb the majesty of the church. The Sacred Heart in its historic painting has penetrated hearts. The psychology of the people on these days was hardly a natural phenomenon in its multiple manifestations. Such a brusque change of sentiments to pious affection, to general veneration and respect, cannot be explained normally. The church was full of people all day long; and at the hours of special festivity the naves were overflowing. It can be said, without being mistaken, that there was a feeling of satisfaction in the soul of Loja. The spirit was satisfied: a phenomenon that only produces the feeling of happiness... There are times when language expresses with difficulty the psychological state of the crowd...

The glorious memory of Garcia Moreno was asserted strongly and gently thanks to a circular by Bishop Aguirre of Loja. The secular speaker, Enrique Paredes Larrea, expounded the following topic: "Garcia Moreno's Christian virtues and their influence on his work as President." These stanzas are found in the poetry composed by the Vicar General, Ernesto Castro:

> Sacred and beloved canvas
> On which the artist's brush
> Made the ideal conceived

> By the enlightened Man
> Radiate into our view:
> Kneeling, in you I adore
> The royalty of that King
> Who gave decorum to the nation
> When she codified in her law
> The treasure of greatness.[34]

One morning Brother Diego Navarrete, a Franciscan, said this prayer: "O Garcia Moreno, you who consecrated Ecuador to the Heart of Jesus before this picture, work a miracle; make me recover the use of my ears. I want to be a missionary in the East. But, being deaf, how can I teach the catechism to the little Jivaros[35] or listen to their answers?" Immediately afterward he opened his missal and began to participate at holy Mass. A few moments passed and he realized that he was now hearing the prayers of the faithful clearly and effortlessly, which he did not hear before in the least. His superiors no longer had any difficulty in sending him to the missions in Zamora.[36]

Around the year 1950,[37] Brother Diego Navarrete spoke with the author in Gualaceo. He related to the author the foregoing account and added these very words: "Father, the doctors in Quito declared that they were unable to help me and advised me to go to Guayaquil, in case the warm climate would make me better. The change was useless. I was treated by the doctors in Guayaquil. All in vain! Then I was transferred by my superiors to Loja where the doctors also attended me, but without any success; and without hope, when they had heard of the failure of the doctors in Quito and Guayaquil. Of course, treatment by the doctors of Loja was another disappointment. Father, my deafness lasted six months, until Garcia Moreno performed a miracle for me. I can swear that I was declared incurable in Quito, Guayaquil and Loja. For their part, the doctors in these cities can swear that they declared me incurable."

Around the year 1967 the author found Brother Diego in the city of Milagro, near Guayaquil, with the illness that brought him to his death. They told the author that his age was some eighty-seven years. The author was surprised that his ears were functioning perfectly, even though his other senses were failing, due to old age.

The remaining cities of Ecuador: Ibarra, Tulcan, Latacunga, Salcedo, etc., also got a view of the Heart of Jesus of Garcia Moreno, and they celebrated with analogous solemnity, spiritual joy and resurgence of our holy faith. Morally it visited Ecuador in its entirety.[38]

Let us place ourselves in thought and imagination in the city of Buenos Aires when, on October 14, 1944, millions of Catholics from the whole world celebrated an International Eucharistic Congress. When the Jesuit Father Benigno Chiriboga was obliged by the Directors to say a few words in the name of Ecuador in order not to disappoint the immense crowd, he could do nothing but recur to the topic of this book. Here are two paragraphs:[39]

> The participation could not be missing of the Republic of Ecuador, small in territory but great in the faith and love with which it comes into your presence, Argentinian brothers! To tell you with all my soul: well done and bravo for the admirable nation that is giving us such examples of religious fervor during these days! For the noble army that has surrendered its arms to the King of kings and Lord of lords. For the authorities who have such a clear concept of its nation's soul and of what we all owe to God; and who so courageously follow the intentions of their hearts and their consciences. Because they well know what has been said is true: never is man greater than when down on his knees. That is how a great statesman from my country understood it, the man who without any doubt is its greatest honor. He who one solemn day in 1874, with a vibrant and sonorous voice dedicated his nation to the Most Sacred Heart of Jesus, officially consecrating it, the first one in the world: Garcia Moreno. Garcia Moreno made the Republic of Ecuador, the Republic of the Sacred Heart. (Here there was prolonged applause by the immense crowd.) Well then, gentlemen, the Republic of Ecuador, Garcia Moreno's homeland, comes before the great nation of Argentina on the day of its consecration to Jesus in the Blessed Sacrament, to say that we applaud and congratulate you.

At once the commentator burst out with cheers for Ecuador, which were warmly answered by the enormous audience. The bishops approached to congratulate the Ecuadorian religious; and one of them, a Brazilian, said to him: "Garcia Moreno is worth more than the whole world." Some students from Buenos Aires made small Ecuadorian tricolor flags and exhibiting them on high, intervened in the great parade or procession, shouting "Long live Garcia Moreno! Long live Ecuador!"[40]

Returning to our country, let us place ourselves in Quito on June 19, 1949, in the presence of Christ in the Blessed Sacrament, since the Second National Eucharistic Congress was taking place; and in front of the wonder-working picture of the Heart of Jesus, which soon after was crowned by the authority and in the name of the reigning Supreme Pontiff, Pope Pius XII. Let us listen to two paragraphs from his radio message transmitted to Quito that morning:[41]

> A double sacred debt weighed over you: to commemorate the first centenary of that historic Archdiocese of Quito, and to remember the seventy-five years since the date that made your nation famous in the whole world: that March 25, 1874, when the robust voice of one of its most illustrious sons consecrated it to the adorable Heart of our Redeemer.
> The debt has been paid. It is witnessed by your impressive numbers, ardent fervor and unrestrained enthusiasm. Truly it was fitting to give thanks for that consecration, to which is undoubtedly due the safety of your faith amidst so many obstacles and attacks. It was opportune to dedicate a remembrance to that loyal son of the Church, the illustrious ruler, irreproachable gentleman and upright Christian, who with the same daring descended to the crater of a volcano, who fought like a Titan for the implanting of that ideal Christian Republic, for which he yearned, without retreating even before his own bloody sacrifice, generously foreseen...[42]

Once the Pontifical Mass was finished, Archbishop Efren Forni, as Delegate and representative of the Roman Pontiff Pius XII, took in his hands the gold crown set with diamonds and fastened it upon the divine forehead, while the crowd fixed their gaze on the sublime scene, holding their breath. But, when the delegated pontiff lowered his arms, once the coronation was finished, then an immense sea of jubilant shouts began to rise into the air: "Long live the Crowned King, long live the Monarch of Ecuador, long live the Savior of the Nation, long live the Heart of Jesus of Garcia Moreno!" Those shouts, heard close up, reverberated like thunder; heard from afar, they acquired a mysterious and dreamlike character, and just as the robust voices of the men drew tears, so likewise did the soprano voices of the women and children. The applause and the joyful waving of thousands of white handkerchiefs crowned the grandiose event.

Here is a new character and charism imprinted on the Garcian painting, besides those already displayed in previous years and events: a new character and charism of an unmovable Rock, acquired by the approbation and association with Pius XII, the ever-opposed and always triumphant Rock of Saint Peter. The gates of Hell shall not prevail against this painting either.

Father Mateo Crawley, who at the time was in Canada, had plenty of reason to exult with joy and to transmit the following cablegram to Quito: "May the Sacred Heart of Garcia Moreno triumph, rule and reign in Ecuador."[43]

When the crowd's ovations subsided, a delegation from Guayaquil approached, presided by their bishop, His Excellency Jose Heredia, and mounted the shield of Guayaquil, decorated with gold and precious stones, on the painting's frame. The same was done by the capitals of the provinces of Azuay, Cotopaxi, Canar, Imbabura and Carchi. Portoviejo gave the offering of a very artistic silver card.

In the afternoon the people again congregated on the esplanade or Eucharistic Field and renewed the Consecration. Here are some of their declarations:

> We wish to consecrate ourselves forever to the most lovable Heart of Jesus. We want this consecration to be absolute, total and perpetual. We do not want any other king besides Jesus. We want the light of His Gospel to enlighten all intelligences; may the easy yoke of His most holy law bend all wills; may His most sweet love consume and inflame all hearts.
>
> We will work without tiring and without ever ceasing so that this most loving Sovereign will reign without rival in the impenetrable sanctuary of the individual conscience, within the sacred walls of the domestic family, in schools, universities and colleges, in the courts, workshops and in the entire nation..."

There was a sad absence from these proceedings: that of the President of the Republic, Mr. Galo Plaza. The official presidency of the State was shamefully submissive and obedient to the absurd laws and a constitution that are without God and against God.

Thanks to Providence this vacuum began to be filled three years later. In fact, when celebrating the diamond jubilee of the official consecration of Ecuador to the Most Pure Heart of Mary, the new President of the Republic, Doctor Jose Maria Velasco Ibarra, unable to personally

*Alfredo Chiriboga Ch.,*
*Vice-president of the Republic.*

*José Maria Velasco Ibarra,
President of the Republic.*

attend since he was away from Quito, named two high officials as his representatives. Moreover, the most excellent Alfredo Chiriboga, Vice-president of the Republic, presided over the great solemnity from his place of honor, and turning toward the immense crowd on the esplanade, he pronounced an extraordinary discourse. Before he had finished, the people loaded him with applause, touched to witness an official religious intervention for the first time after fifty-seven years of persecution of the Church and apostasy of the State. Let us listen to a few of its paragraphs:

> As in the days of Garcia Moreno, the anguished nation sought its protection in God... The road which Ecuador has traveled has been rough... By turning its back on the Catholic religion, it suffered an agony, and it lacked the heroism necessary to defend its national patrimony... The treasure of freedom still remains to us; faith in Christ the King remains to us... His doctrine is the light of all lights; it is the strength and bond of charity among men... Ecuador returns to God through the maternal love of Mary, the Advocate of mankind. Ecuadorian Catholicism owes to Mary its vitality and vigor. Mary has defended the bastion of Catholicism, and from this bulwark she will save Ecuador... The greatness of nations, of our Spanish American people, is measured in proportion to their spiritual values and historical essence. Ecuador surpasses the level of other nations in this aspect, because always, ever since its political genesis, it has nourished its existence in the limpid fountains of the Catholic faith...
>
> I am proud to confess my Catholic faith, and I do so as an official of the Executive Branch of the Republic. I understand that in this way I am more in conformity with the unanimous view of my people, by whose will and mandate I am holding the vice-presidency of the nation. I humbly ask God's forgiveness for my sins and for those of my fellow citizens; and with the intention of offering something pleasing to the Heart of Christ, and in the name of the Ecuadorian nation, I am going to pronounce the renovation of the Consecration of the Republic to the Immaculate Heart of Mary...

A burst of applause and cheers erupted. Thousands of hands waved their handkerchiefs. Hearts were beating impelled by a mystical emotion.

Kneeling down and with the voice of profound conviction, the Representative of the Republic spoke in these terms:

> O most sweet and most lovable Heart of Mary, we ask and implore you to obtain from the Most Sacred Heart of Jesus that He deign to illuminate, defend, sustain and conserve under His sovereign protection the Episcopate, the Clergy, the Governing Administration and all the people of the Republic of Ecuador, consecrated to this Deific Heart, etc.

It was the glorious day of October 27, 1952.[44]

How did this happy political development come about? According to what we suggested shortly above, the Heart of Jesus having returned from Chile and having been received with fervent love in the Garcian land, worked the miracle. As a secondary cause, thanks to his prolific oratory and brilliant performance, Doctor Jose Maria Velasco Ibarra gathered the immense majority around himself which contributed to his victory in the electoral urns. In order not to seem ridiculous and enforce the farce to a monstrous degree, the Masonic clique had to leave the people their freedom and respect Velasco's triumph. This President broke the chains that had enslaved the Church regarding public worship, processions, open-air Masses, etc. He allowed free entry to foreign priests and religious. He broke the tyrannical yoke which had bound Catholic schools to the hostility and ill will of state and lay schools. Then he restored freedom of education. In his speeches and writings he showed himself a frank admirer of Garcia Moreno. During his presidential term of office, which we are currently chronicling, the Legislative Chambers and the City Council of Guayaquil decreed the erection of a first class monument to the most sublime man of Ecuador. Let us listen to two paragraphs by Velasco:

> I wholeheartedly endorse the homage that you, the members of the Popular Committee for the Monument to Garcia Moreno, are rendering to the greatest politician that Ecuador has had, as the eminent Archbishop Gonzalez Suarez told me one day. A brilliant vision of the future of the nation and its needs; the objective spirit for fulfilling them or to lay the foundations for their fulfillment; faith in the moral order and in the fact that only morals give nations patriotism; coherence and boldness; total and absolute dis-

interest and complete devotion of individuals to public service: such were the main characteristics of Garcia Moreno ...

You are doing a work of justice to him who, like Rocafuerte, knew how to understand the nation and serve it with genius and heroism. Nowadays it is in fashion to adulterate history and praise everyone, either due to party spirit or personal commitments. It is not known where good and evil lie. Austerity has been lost. Youths are being corrupted through the adulteration of history. To honor Garcia Moreno is to honor virtue, to honor heroism, and to teach youths the norms for serving humanity and for redeeming Ecuador. Your labor is not only for the good of a great man, but also for the good of the Republic...[45]

Nearly two years later, on June 27, 1954, the aforesaid Vice-president, Mr. Alfredo Chiriboga, renewed, in an official manner, the Consecration of Ecuador to the Most Sacred Heart of Jesus, in memory of the eightieth anniversary of the original Garcian feat. Chiriboga made this magnificent act in the Basilica of the National Vow, before Christ exposed in the Blessed Sacrament and a large crowd that cheered and applauded. The formula used was the historic one, whose first words are, "This, O Lord, is Thy people..."[46]

Two years later, on April 22, 1956, the canonical coronation took place of the miraculous image by the name of *Our Lady of Sorrows of the College.*[47] During the culminating ceremony, his Excellency, President Doctor Jose Maria Velasco Ibarra, was the one who, in the name of the State, put into the hands of the Cardinal Archbishop, His Grace Carlos Maria de la Torre, the crown that would shortly afterwards encircle the Virgin's forehead. The multitude applauded that gesture of harmony between the Church and the State.

Another two years passed and another National Eucharistic Congress was convoked, which now had Guayaquil as its seat. His Excellency the President, Doctor Camilo Ponce Enriquez, assisted in an official manner and received Holy Communion. It was September 28, 1958. His speech was broadcast over the radio stations of the Supreme Pontiff, Pope Pius XII. One of his expressions was in the following tenor:

> The Republic of Ecuador boasts of holding the primacy in the Eucharistic annals of America, for hosting the first Congress celebrated in the New World, and for having borne the name of "Land of the Blessed Sacrament," whose Confraternity was the first reli-

gious matter settled when its cities were founded. O Guayaquil! You are as noble as you are beautiful. Is it not true that you moreover have the privilege of the Permanent Jubilee obtained already in 1776, by having been the cradle of the Great Garcia Moreno, or by possessing the distinguished name that the industriousness and ingenuity of your illustrious sons have given you...?[48]

December 24, 1962. The Ambassador of his Ecuadorian homeland in Paris, Mr. Cristobal Bonifaz Jijon, visited the village of Paray le Monial and its sanctuary of the apparitions of the Sacred Heart of Jesus. He noticed that many countries were represented there by their national flags and that Ecuador's was missing. He stirred up the zeal of the Ecuadorian bishops gathered in Rome on the occasion of the Second Vatican Council and obtained the making of an Ecuadorian tricolor flag displaying the exceptionally deluxe national shield. That flag was blessed personally by his Holiness Pope Paul VI and transported by the above-said prelates, and put in the most honorary place among the other emblems.

October 27, 1963, came, which was the Feast of Christ the King, and moreover the ninetieth anniversary of the official consecration of Ecuador to the Heart of Jesus by the episcopate, the Legislative Chambers and President Garcia Moreno. The Ecuadorian flag was raised in a preferential place in the Chapel of the Apparitions. Bishop Benigno Chiriboga of Latacunga celebrated Mass, in representation of his Eminence, Cardinal Archbishop of Quito, Carlos Maria de la Torre, who because of his old age and ailments had been unable to go to Europe. After the Gospel, Father Albisser, a Corazonist priest who had been in Quito some years previously, mounted the holy pulpit. Here are his first words translated from the French:

> There is a country among those of South America, particularly privileged by the blue of its sky and the opulence of its rays of sunshine, beautiful in its scenery and the good character of its inhabitants. It is a country of God's predilections, and destined to give a great example to the world. It is Ecuador, the Ecuador of the President-martyr Garcia Moreno, of little Saint Mariana de Jesus Paredes, the Republic of the Heart of Jesus...

When Mass ended, and in the midst of a profound silence, the archbishop of Guayaquil, His Grace Antonio Mosquera humbly raised

*Bishop Echeverria of Ambato with the Ecuadorian Pavilion blessed by the Pope, on their way to Paray.*

*From left to right, front row: Enrique Systermans, Superior General of the Congregation of the Sacred Hearts of Jesus and Mary; Bishop Chiriboga; Archbishop Mosquera; Archbishop Serrano; Father Gamboa, the Apostolic Vicar from Aguarico; and lastly, Father Luis Albisser.*

*Back row: Father Enrique Soria Madrid; Father Riou, Corazonist; the Chaplain priest from Paray; Father Bonadio, the Provincial from France. Lastly, Mrs. Teresa de Bonifaz and her husband, Mr. Cristobal Bonifaz Jijon.*

his voice to Christ in the Blessed Sacrament exposed on the altar. Let us hear some of his expressions:[49]

> O Divine Jesus! In return for Thy goodness, we men have wounded Thy most Holy Heart; and through our lukewarmness and coldness we have wrested bitter complaints from Thy lips. Here Thou hast us prostrate, in this place hallowed by the revelations of Thy inexhaustible love and unending mercy to Saint Margaret of Alacoque; here Thou hast us, the bishops of Ecuador, prostrate, in order to renew, in our capacity as pastors, the consecration of our lives to Thy holy service, and to offer Thee a homage of humble reparation...
> 
> We are here to proclaim before the world that our country, Ecuador, truly belongs to Thee as do all nations on earth, by Thy rights as God and as Redeemer; but particularly by having chosen Thee, for the first time in the entire world, as its King and Lord, by consecrating itself officially to Thy Most Holy Heart, ...
> 
> We implore Thee that our national flag may remain in this place, as a constant prayer of our country. May it entreat Thee, at every moment, that the rays of light which break forth from Thy Heart may reach Ecuador and never be extinguished... Deign to forgive our faults and those of our nation, especially the public crimes of nations...
> 
> May our flag continue fluttering gracefully, next to the flags of other nations, like a footstool for Thy Majesty, on this memorable day of Thy universal Feast...

The event was crowned with a final flourish by the little nuns of the Visitation chanting the hymn, *Christus vincit, Christus regnat, Christus imperat.*[50] The document was signed by Bishop Benigno Chiriboga in representation of the Cardinal Archbishop of Quito, His Grace Carlos Maria de la Torre; by His Grace Antonio Mosquera, Archbishop of Guayaquil; His Grace Manuel Serrano, Archbishop of Cuenca; and Father Higinio Gamboa, Apostolic Prefect of the Ecuadorian Mission of Aguarico.

Where was the precious document deposited? It was deposited together with a luxuriously bound volume and with the title of *Libro de Oro del Ecuador.*[51] It contained the names of the families who, by the hundreds, had consecrated themselves to the Heart of Jesus and had enthroned His sacred image in their homes. There were families from some thirty-eight years back, and they belonged to the dioceses of Chimborazo and Bolivar. The place where that book rested and continues resting cannot be more emotive: the little room, transformed into an oratory, where Saint Margaret Mary had lived and died.

Let us return to Ecuador. On June 1, 1967, there was a culminating homage to Christ Exposed in the Blessed Sacrament in Cuenca, and the finale of its National Eucharistic Congress. The President of the Republic, Doctor Otto Arosemena Gomez attended officially and gave an example by partaking of the Eucharistic Manna. We extract these paragraphs from his address to the multitude:

> The reinvigoration of spirituality takes on greater urgency every day. Let each person turn his gaze, through the prism of his respective religion, to the Almighty: and let us Catholics turn our eyes, tired of animosity, to the Eucharist, the permanent source of spiritual life. Either we spiritualize society or the hard battering ram of hate will destroy the bodies and souls of human beings...
> 
> The encyclicals have the value of being documents treated in the light of science, by people who, having renounced everything, can evaluate the social drama in its proper degree, and propose solutions that are free of passion. As the Head of State I should take this opportunity of addressing employers and landowners, workers and farmers, bankers and manufacturers, powerful and humble, women and men, and everyone involved in social dynamics, by quoting the encyclicals, in order not to be out of tune with this solemn Catholic moment, and of adopting a position with regard to serious human issues, for which we are all responsible from the social and economic level in which we find ourselves situated in society...

Omitting other religious activities on the part of civil and military authorities, one can at least be happy that State persecution of the Church has more or less disappeared for the benefit of sincere benevolence and mutual support. The introduction of the catechism into the public schools is still lacking. Such an absence continues corrupting Ecuadorian society with the increase of crimes and a weakening of character, which contrasts with the President-martyr's thesis, according to which each Ecuadorian group in particular had to adhere to the General Consecration, and moreover had to live it, by the practice of pure morals in accordance with the consecration to the God of purity. [52]

*Carlos Maria de la Torre,
Cardinal Archbishop of Quito.*

## The Return of the Heart of Jesus of Garcia Moreno

On September 8, 1967, his Eminence, Cardinal Archbishop Carlos Maria de la Torre, exhausted by old age and illnesses, left his pastoral charge with the permission of the reigning Supreme Pontiff, Pope Paul VI. These inspired clauses have been selected from his paternal farewell or testament:

> Since the momentous importance of the Official Act of the Consecration of the Republic, whose centenary is approaching; and the international status of the sanctuary of the apparitions in Paray le Monial, require that the Catholic hierarchy of Ecuador, faithful to its glorious traditions, perpetuate at the famous Sanctuary in a noble Document and officially endorse the great day of the National Consecration, an outstanding religious achievement in our republican history: we have gladly decided to ratify, once more, publicly and solemnly this our Official Consecration to the Sacred Heart of Jesus, consecrating to Him, therefore, this Quitonian Archdiocese, its public officials, its clergy and its people; and offering to Him, in its name, the loyal recognition of His Divine royalty and sovereign authority; and at the same time, submitting to His sweet vassalage all our glories, our interests and our destiny, since in reality we belong to Him entirely...
>
> We do not want to take leave of our beloved flock without delivering it, for the last time, as a fatherly gesture of love, into the arms and the Heart of our most sweet Lord and Father Jesus Christ, Immortal King of the ages; and into the most sweet lap of Mary our Mother; recommending to all our children, priests and faithful, that by doing honor to our official Consecration, they may work and fight so that Jesus Christ may be glorified and triumph in them, in their families, in childhood and youth, in workers, in magistrates, in laws and institutions, in the entire life of the Republic, the beloved daughter of his Divine Heart.[53]
>
> And in order that history may keep this testimony alive, as an example to future generations, we ask our beloved children to sign this Document, and in this way fulfill it by their pastors' command.
>
> Lastly it is our desire, and we ask the Most Excellent Bishops of Ecuador, to kindly adhere to our declaration, and consequently to sign many other Declaratory Acts of the Consecration to the Heart of Jesus in their respective dioceses: so that in this way the *Libro de Oro* of the National Consecration may serve

as a perpetual memory for the glory of God and honor of the Ecuadorian Nation...

Since Ecuador is now approaching the centenary of its Consecration, it is convenient that an international team of missionaries traverse, one by one, all the dioceses whose renewed consecration and general Communion should be presided over and received by the wonder-working image called "The Heart of Jesus of Garcia Moreno."[54]

On August 31, 1973, the episcopate renewed the Ecclesiastical Consecration. On October eighteenth[55] the Supreme Leader of the Republic renewed the consecration of the State; and finally on March 25, 1974, the consecration was renewed by the Church and the State, united in the Basilica or Church of the National Vow, in the area where at least the hearts of Archbishop Ignacio Checa and of Gabriel Garcia Moreno should repose. Let us recall these words of the President-martyr:

It is necessary to build a new and magnificent church in the capital to perpetuate the memory of our official Consecration for future generations. Let it also be the center of religious restoration, at least for the republics of Spanish America.[56]

Let us recall moreover the following dictum by Bishop Jose Felix Heredia:

God demands two things for the rehabilitation of Ecuador: that it promote as much as possible the glorification of Garcia Moreno and that it bring to completion the construction of the Basilica of the National Vow.

As to the former, let us disregard the calumnies and sophisms invented by evil sons of the nation; let us proudly make known the Hero's true character and achievements; let us increase the number of his statues and monuments; and finally, let us promote the establishment of the canonical process of his martyrdom, for there is abundant and praise-worthy material. As to the second, may what is transcribed below serve to motivate us. It is taken from the author's pamphlet whose title is *Abanderado del Corazón de Jesus*:[57]

# The Return of the Heart of Jesus of Garcia Moreno

Around the year 1942, the superior of *La Providencia School* in Ambato provided a goldsmith not only with precious metal, but also had paid in advance. Once the article was made, a sacred vessel, the artist pawned it in exchange for money lent, and disappeared from the superior's sight. She had recourse to a public investigation, but in vain. She entreated the favor from the Souls in Purgatory, paying them with a thousand prayers for the dead said by the numerous students: all in vain. Then the patronage of Garcia Moreno was invoked, to whom a donation was promised for the construction of the National Basilica. So typical of Garcia Moreno, without delay, that same day the goldsmith was captured in Ambato when setting his feet on the train to leave for another city. The article returned to the hands of the superior and the alms were given for the work on the Church of the National Vow.[58]

# Endnotes

[1] In the year 1941 Peru had invaded Ecuadorian territory. Faced with this emergency, the Archbishop of Quito ordered that Triduums in honor of several titles of the Most Holy Virgin be prayed in the various churches of Quito, imploring the cessation of hostilities. On July twenty-fourth, the Triduum in honor of Our Lady of Good Success began in the Church of the Immaculate Conception. Three days later, from seven o'clock in the morning on Sunday, July 27, 1941, until three o'clock in the morning on July 28, that is to say, for twenty hours, the statue of Our Lady of Good Success moved its eyes. Its face was changing alternately from a reddish tone to one similar to marble. A kind of mist was covering the statue. When it disappeared, the statue was surrounded by a supernatural radiance. The statue's eyes, which normally look downward, during the miracle turned upward little by little until they were looking towards heaven in an attitude of supplication; then they lowered towards the faithful, and repeatedly in this manner. When the news spread, thousands of faithful invaded the church to gaze at the miracle, leaving the international events of enormous magnitude relegated to the second place. The maternal blinking of the sacred image was seen by more than thirty thousand people. On the afternoon of the same day, July twenty-seventh, the newspapers announced the cessation of hostilities with Peru. The news relating the marvelous event came out starting the next day in the various newspapers throughout the country:
*Ultimas Noticias (Breaking News)*: July 28,1941; *El Telegrafo (The Telegraph)*: July 28, 1941; *El Universo (The Universe)*: July 28, 1941; *El Debate (The Debate)*: July 27, 28, & 29, 1941; *La Sociedad (Society)*: August 3, 1941; *La Voz Obrera (Voice of the Working Class)*: August 10, 1941; *La Voz Catolica de Loja (The Catholic Voice from Loja)*: October 5 & 12, 1941; and *El Comercio (Commerce)*: July 28 & 29, and August 3, 1941.

[2] "*Sucedio en la Frontera.*"

[3] A *cholo* is a *mestizo*, or a person of mixed race, e.g. of Spanish and Indian ethnicity. Thus *cholito* is a diminutive or affectionate form of the word, and so here would mean, "little half-breed."

[4] Cf. Gomezjurado, vol. 12, pp. 303-304.

[5] Doctor Julio Tobar Donoso, *Rio de Janeiro Protocol*, p. 10 ff. As Foreign Minister of Ecuador, he had to subscribe to that abominable Protocol. Leonardo Chiriboga Ordonez, *Sucedio en la Frontera, (It Happened at the Border)*, p. 3 ff.

[6] The monthly magazine, *Cristo Rey (Christ the King)*, under the direction of the religious of the Sacred Hearts in Riobamba, May, June, and July, 1942.

[7] Gomezjurado, vol. 12, p. 312 ff.

[8] *Idem.*

[9] Luke 2, 10.

[10] The Spanish Jesuit, Father Jose Urarte, on the occasion of the protocol which despoiled Ecuador of a large portion of the Amazonian eastern region, pub-

lished in his *Mensajero del Corazon de Jesus o Republica de Corazon de Jesus* (*Messenger of the Sacred Heart of Jesus or Republic of the Heart of Jesus*), the text of the protocol that came into the hands of the parish priest of Quinche, Father Felix Granja, and of Bishop Gonzalez Suarez, in the year 1910, and which was consigned to chapter fourteen, pages 274 and following of the author's volume eleven. Naturally, the reading of this text produced the impression that what was frustrated in 1910 took effect in 1941, in accordance with the Masonry of Lima. Cf. *supra* chapter twelve.

[11] Cf. Jeremias 2, 28.
[12] *Idem.* Also, the *Bulletin of the Archdiocese of Quito,* months of May and June.
[13] The Quitonian magazine *El Voto Nacional (The National Vow),* months of July and August.
[14] *Idem.*
[15] "Holy Heart / Thou shalt reign / Thou shalt ever be / King of my nation."
[16] Again, the magazine *Cristo Rey* (*Christ the King*), months of August and September.
[17] On a visit made around the year 1940 to Bishop Heredia in Guayaquil, the author heard from his lips this thesis expressed in the text.
[18] The construction of the *Basilica Sagrado Corazon de Jesus* in the city of Riobamba began in 1883, and it was consecrated to the Sacred Heart of Jesus by Bishop Machado on June 9, 1915. It took thirty-two years to complete and was the work of the Jesuit Fathers. In the main altar is the image of the Sacred Heart of Jesus, which is topped by a harmonious and beautiful dome. The inauguration is mentioned on page 308 of the eleventh volume of Father Gomezjurado's *Vida de Garcia Moreno.*
[19] Riobamba is the capital of the province of Chimborazo and is called "The Sultana of the Andes."
[20] The magazine, *Cristo Rey (Christ the King),* was founded by Mother María Isabel Busson at the instance of Sister Leticia de Jesús Carrasco on May 1, 1927. It was a very important means of communication in Ecuador for the formation of students, professors and fathers of families. (Taken from www.ssccecuador.org.)
[21] Regarding the mummy of Montalvo, let us listen to the following account, written in his own hand, of Father Carlos Ribadeneira, S. J., stationed in the community of the *Compania* in Quito: "August, 1942. In the Episcopal Palace we were speaking about the whereabouts of the body of Juan Montalvo. Among the Canons was Monsignor Felix Rousille, a model priest for his great abnegation; great preacher and professor of philosophy, etc. When Monsignor Barriga died, Monsignor Pio Vincente Corral was named Administrator Apostolic, who protested, saying: 'Why was ecclesiastical burial given to a wicked man [Montalvo] who died refusing the Sacraments?' Then Canon Felix Rousille answered: 'I will remedy this on this very day.' Late at night, with four laborers, he took out the body of Juan Montalvo from the Catholic cemetery, brought it to the Guayas River, and tying it to a large stone, sank it in the river... Those in Ambato claimed the body of Montalvo. So to avoid disputes, they took the

cadaver of a mulatto and sent it. Felix Roussille concluded our discussion thus: 'I personally threw it into the Guayas River.' About the year 1938, Bishop Alberto Ordonez of Riobamba said to Father Eudoro Ribadeneira: 'The cadaver of Juan Montalvo was thrown into the Guayas River. The very one who threw it in told it to me.'" (Taken from Gomezjurado, vol. 12, p. 320 and pp. 346-347).

[22] Again, the magazine *Cristo Rey,* months of December, 1942, and January, 1943. Also the monthly bulletin from Riobamba called *La Hojita Mensajera* (*The Messenger Leaflet*), month of January, 1943.

[23] *Crespon.* See endnote 16 in chapter 10 above.

[24] Again, the magazine *Cristo Rey*, months of April, May, June and July of 1943.

[25] This sentence was added from a parallel passage in Gomezjurado, vol. 12, p. 324.

[26] *Mercury.*

[27] *La Revista Catolica (Catholic Magazine),* organ of the diocese of Cuenca, months of April, May and June of 1943. [Azuay is the province in which Cuenca is located. Translator's note.]

[28] Original verses: ¡Bienvenido, Señor, a nuestros lares, a este dulce rincón de la floresta andina. Has retornado, por fin, de tan largo exilio, para la dicha de tus pobres hijos.

Impenetrables por demás son tus arcanos, y no puedo comprender, Señor, por qué te fuiste, cuando un mártir y sabio Magistrado de la naciente República Ecuatoriana, con ardiente fe y anhelo, te proclamó Soberano y Rey del Ecuador... Nos dejaste huérfanos y solos tanto tiempo. ¡Qué días de duelo, lágrimas y tragedia han venido sucediéndose año tras años, en tu larga ausencia, hasta el extremo de que hoy encuentras mutilada a tu Nación.

Pero ¡has vuelto, Señor, bendito seas! Con empeño y tesón, posa tus pies en el azuayo suelo.

Mas no te llegues como humilde peregrino, con trémula planta y ropaje desgarrado. No vengas con cayado de viajero, en busca de hospitalidad, como extranjero. No sangre más tus sienes, no mendigo de amor con tu mirada triste... No traigas esas cárdenas heridas que duelen tanto en tu costado abierto... Yo no quisiera verte así. Torna en corona de príncipe las espinas, y en cetro de monarca tu cayado. Ven como Rey a gobernarnos, como Padre a bendecirnos. Como amigo, ven a consolarnos, que aquí todos te esperan, con ternuras de rondador en las campiñas, con ternuras de amor dentro del pecho; y despetalando las mejores flores, los niños te darán su alma inocente.

¡Bien venido, Señor!; que los poetas templado han ya sus místicos laúdes, para rimar, con finuras de ensueño sus poemas.

¡Bien venido, Señor!; y los que nada para ofrecerte hemos tenido, de lágrimas hacemos presurosos los irisados prismas, para guindar el borde de tu palio.

¡Bien venido, Señor!; y como dueño y soberano de las almas y las cosas, asienta tu Realeza en tu ciudad amante.

¡No te vayas otra vez ya nunca, nunca!; que todos sabremos adorarte.

¡No nos dejes solos, Señor! Necesitamos tanto de ti, para ser buenos.

Tú que aprisionas las furias desgreñadas del infierno, y encadenas del mar y las nubes las tormentas: pliega por siempre de la maldad sus negras alas, y cúbrelas con el lábaro bendito de tu manto.

¡Bienvenido, Señor, y no nos dejes!

[29] *El Voto Nacional (The National Vow),* months of April, May and June.

[30] Original verses:
1. Ven, Jesús, a tu pueblo que un día / te aclamó por Monarca y Señor, / ven y reina en la Patria que ansía / ser tu trono perpetuo de amor.
2. Inebriada de gozo profundo / se ofrendó nuestra amada Nación,/ la primera entre todas del mundo, /para altar de tu Real Corazón.
3. Siempre fiel al feliz juramento, / por tu nombre sostuvo la lid,/ y en tus aras fue mártir sangriento / su más grande y más noble Adalid.

[31] "Song to the Consecration of Ecuador and to Garcia Moreno." Flyers with the verses composed by Doctor Luis Cordero Crespo were also thrown to the four winds.

[32] *Boletin de la Archidiocesis de Quito (Bulletin of the Archdiocese of Quito),* months of June, July and August. With express permission from The Reverend Father Correa, Most worthy General of the Oblate religious of the National Basilica, on one of the days in the month of September, 1972, the author thoroughly studied the material and ideological content of the magnificent frame.

[33] The monthly magazine from the diocese of Loja, entitled *Documentos Diocesanos (Diocesan Documents),* months of November and December. Besides, an entire book of 350 pages entitled *El Corazon de Jesus en Loja (The Heart of Jesus in Loja),* with illustrations, so that this city surpassed others.

[34] Original verses:
Lienzo sagrado y querido / en que el pincel del artista / hizo el ideal concebido / por el Hombre esclarecido / irradiar a nuestra vista: / de rodillas en ti adoro / la realeza de ese Rey / que dio a la Patria decoro / cuando ella cifró en su Ley / de la grandeza el tesoro.

[35] The Jivaros are South American Indians of eastern Ecuador and northeast Peru.

[36] The account about Brother Diego Navarrete is narrated on page 193 of the author's book *¿Martyr Garcia? (Is Garcia a Martyr?),* edited in the year 1952 in Cuenca.

[37] I.e. "some eight years later" (Gomezjurado, *Vida de Garcia Moreno,* vol. 13, p. 408).

[38] This paragraph has been expanded from a parallel passage in Gomezjurado, vol. 12, p. 333.

[39] Father Benigno Chiriboga's contribution in Buenos Aires, narrated in the *Hojita Mensajera (Messenger Leaflet)* of December 16 to 23, 1944, in Riobamba.

⁴⁰ In the author's presence, Father Chiriboga himself transmitted the part about the Ecuadorian flags in the procession.
⁴¹ *Boletin de la Arquidiocesis de Quito (Bulletin from the Archdiocese of Quito),* June and July, 1949.
⁴² "Five years pass by, and that same Vicar of Christ, speaking with Cardinal Dacosta, Archbishop of Florence, said to him: 'One of the causes of canonization that I would most willingly like to see in Rome is that of Garcia Moreno.'" Cf. Gomezjurado, vol. 12, pp. 406-407. "In 1954, the Jesuit priest, Father Julian Bravo, an Ecuadorian, was in Florence, and heard Pius XII's longing from the lips of Cardinal Dacosta himself. The aforesaid religious conveyed this fact to the author on various occasions." (*Ibid.* p. 409).
⁴³ Father Mateo Crawley was hospitalized at that time in the city of Trois-Rivieres. The author immediately took note of his cablegram, but out of carelessness, he did not write down the newspaper in which it was written.
⁴⁴ Again, the *Boletin Arquidiocesano (Archdiocesan Bulletin),* October and November of 1952. Also the pamphlet entitled *El Campeon de los Errores, (The Champion of Errors),* first page, Mexican edition.
⁴⁵ Velasco's words have been published in the pamphlet printed in Mexico under the name of *El Campeon de los Errors (The Champion of Errors),* August, 1960. Its author, the Ecuadorian Cesar Perez Moscoso, refuted the pamphlet entitled *El Santo del Patibulo (The Saint of the Scaffold)* written by Doctor Benjamin Carrion.
⁴⁶ The full text may be found in Gomezjurado, vol. 9, p. 153.
⁴⁷ "*La Dolorosa del Colegio.*"
⁴⁸ *Boletin Arquidiocesano,* June and July, 1954. *Idem.,* September and October, 1958. Cf. Gomezjurado, vol. 12, p. 407 & *Radiomensaje de Su Santidad Pío XII al III Congreso Eucarístico Nacional de Ecuador* (AAS 50 (1958), p. 747).
⁴⁹ Chronicles of the Visitation religious of Paray le Monial, translated into Spanish by Bishop Benigno Chiriboga, who had acted there in representation of the Archbishop of Quito.
⁵⁰ *Idem.* Also the trimestral French magazine *Horizons Blancs,* January of 1964.
⁵¹ *Book of Gold from Ecuador.*
⁵² Garcia Moreno spoke of this aspiration in his own home while a servant of his was present, by the name of Antonio Barriga, who transmitted it to his son Segundo Antonio Barriga. The latter put it in writing, along with other characteristics of this Great Man, and gave those documents to the author on August 11, 1959, when they were together in Cayambe.
⁵³ The composition and remitting of the cited *Libro de Oro (Book of Gold)* was the work of the Jesuit Father Francisco Villagomez, the longtime Director of the Apostolate of Prayer in the provinces of Chimborazo and Bolivar. Also, the weekly magazine from Guayaquil, *Catolicismo (Catholicism),* the first week of June, 1967. The Cardinal's leave-taking, according to the *Cronicas de las Religiosas Visitandinas (Chronicles of the Visitation Sisters).*

[54] De la Torre's farewell or testament has been taken from notes by Bishop Chiriboga consigned to the *Chronicles of Paray le Monial.*
[55] Garcia Moreno had signed the decree of the Consecration of Ecuador on October 18, 1873, as stated above in chapter 2.
[56] See chapter 4 above.
[57] "Standard-bearer of the Heart of Jesus."
[58] P. 78 of the author's booklet, *Abanderado del Corazon de Jesus.*

# Appendices

# Appendix I
# History of Garcia Moreno's Beatification Process[1]

There is, on page three hundred thirty-six of my book entitled, *La Consagracion*, a photograph of "Garcia Moreno's Eucharistic Crusade" in Riobamba, in the year 1935.[2] The upper part shows the portrait of the President-martyr with the initials for "God does not die" (*"Dios no muere"*), and beneath are the members of the Directory with myself, the Ecclesiastical Advisor, and two boys representing the Children's Section. The latter are in the uniform and armor of the Crusades in the Middle Ages.

It was a seed that bore fruit in a special manner three years later when one of those companions came to me holding a writing of his. "Are you bringing me more verses to be corrected?" I asked with a little displeasure, since on two previous occasions I had retouched his poetic compositions at the expense of some work. "There are no verses," he answered me, "but only this." And he put a paper into my hands. "You have really outdone yourself! ...You have written by the impulse of the Holy Ghost. The prayer that you have composed will easily be published in the press with the sole permission of the diocesan bishop, whereas if I had been the author, I would have had to obtain moreover permission from my Father Provincial, who would have denied it to me through fear of a Masonic reaction against the Jesuits."

In fact, at this same time, I was working on the edition of the biography of the President-martyr, ending with three prayers asking God for his beatification. Well then, the censure of my major superior was couched in the following terms, "Booklet approved with applause, but the prayers are suppressed."

After I had revised one or more grammatical expressions of the prayers composed by Mr. Muyrragui, he rushed to the Episcopal House, and was attended by the Very Reverend Vicar-General Virgilio Camacho, in the absence of His Excellency Bishop Alberto Ordonez. Having read the text with special circumspection, the Vicar-General granted his approval for its distribution by the press. Let us now hear its content in its entirety:

**Prayer asking God for the glorification of the Martyr of the faith, Gabriel Garcia Moreno.**

O Lord! God of goodness, who makes the virtues of Thy servants shine forth before the face of the world, grant, we humbly beseech Thee, by the virtues practiced during the mortal life of Thy faithful servant and martyr of the faith, Gabriel Garcia Moreno, that we may have the unspeakable joy of seeing him exalted to the honors of the altar, so that he may be held up and imitated in the world as the perfect model of those who govern, for Thy greater glory and the spiritual good and benefit of our souls. Amen.[3]

For the greater glory of God. A Franciscan Tertiary, Riobamba.
Ecclesiastical Government of the diocese. September 29, 1938. Imprimatur. The Vicar-General.

Note: We call Garcia Moreno a martyr with merely human criterion without trying to anticipate the judgment of the Church.

Concerning the manner in which the first prayer was officially approved by the Church, imploring the canonical glorification of Garcia Moreno, it took its beginning on the feast of the Archangel Saint Michael. "Who is like God!" said the latter. "Power of God," [i.e. Gabriel], was the name of the former, the author of the apothegm, "God does not die! (*Dios no muere!*)"

Four days passed, and the circulation began with two thousand holy cards having the portrait of Garcia Moreno on the front and the aforesaid prayer on the back. I gave a conference on the subject in the College of the Sisters of St. Mariana of Jesus, having obtained beforehand the permission of my rector, Father Luis Mancero; and the aforementioned holy cards were made available to the public at a low price, so that Mr. Muyrragui would not suffer economic loss, being poor of fortune.

Immediately my rector was besieged by individuals who branded this propaganda as a spark that would provoke a Masonic arson attack against the Jesuits. Consequently, the packages of the images had to be put "on ice" and hidden, even though their owner was a layman, who bore it with patience, convinced that alone he would not be able to utilize these holy cards, and strengthened by my words, "This opposition shows that the work is from God, and has to culminate in triumph."

# APPENDIX I

My aforesaid rector wrote to Quito, to the Reverend Father Provincial, informing him of the affair, and asking him for a higher decision. This decision came to Riobamba, and the contents were in substance the following: "The Fathers of higher authority having been consulted, all were in agreement that we ought not to take part in this propagation. God has to indicate the time in which we can honor, as is fitting, the Man who honors mankind."

Who was our dictator at this time? It was Doctor Manuel Maria Borrero, one of the arms of the Masonic pincers.[4]

A few days later, a letter arrived from Father Ricardo Vasquez in which he was saying to me, "I am annoyed with you. Have patience. Who is more devoted to Garcia Moreno than I, who even have received extraordinary favors through his patronage; and nevertheless I also consider that it is still not yet time to promote his beatification!"

Father Alfonso Escobar was another of those annoyed, since the bank account of the Apostolate of Prayer had been used up by printing some of those thousands of holy cards. He had with him the original approved by the Very Reverend Vicar Camacho, and he showed it to His Excellency, Bishop Alberto Ordonez, when he had just returned to the city. He added these words, "See what your Vicar approved in the absence of Your Excellency." The prelate read the prayer intently, took a pen and inscribed his approval next to that of the Very Reverend Vicar Camacho. Father Escobar enclosed the prayers approved by both ecclesiastical authorities of Riobamba in an envelope, and sent them to the aforesaid Father Ricardo Vasquez in Quito, who directed his steps to the Archiepiscopal Palace, asked for an audience, and put the prayer, doubly approved in the "Sultan of the Andes," into the hands of His Eminence Carlos Maria de la Torre.

Archbishop de la Torre, on his part, read it slowly, brandished his quill and adjoined his approbation. Moreover, at the bottom he wrote the following note: "Distribution is to be made in the religious associations and Catholic schools."

At once Father Ricardo Vasquez published thousands of Garcia Moreno's holy card and prayer, and distributed copies in Riobamba and throughout Ecuador. Muyrragui, Escobar and I were exulting with joy.

And the Masonic arson attack against the Jesuits? Not even a hint. The Quito newspaper entitled, *El Dia*, reacted at once, but took the matter in a humoristic point of view. Here is its article which appeared at the end of October. Unfortunately the collections which I am reviewing are incomplete; but I well remember the substance, which is as follows:[5]

After Garcia Moreno's holy card and prayer have been reproduced, it is said that General Elroy Alfaro also deserves to be raised to the altars, since he does not lag behind Garcia Moreno since he had been barbarously assassinated. Besides, Elroy Alfaro has performed a portentous miracle, which is the following:

A certain devotee of his, suffering from complete deafness, prayed before the portrait of Alfaro, and with a lit candle in his hand, was asking him to perform the miracle of taking away this ailment. Before he had finished the prayer, what an astounding miracle! The Alfarist devotee began to hear wonderfully with both ears in perfect condition. Even more, he began to perceive sounds with excessive intensity, like claps of thunder, even the buzzing of flies and the sputtering of the candle.

This was the whole of the Masonic arson attack against Father Gomezjurado and all the Jesuits.

Feeling more zealous, Father Ricardo Vasquez published thousands of leaflets with instructions on the matter. Let us listen to some of them:

What are the conditions that the Church requires for giving the title of martyr to a heroic Christian? The canonical conditions are three: real and voluntarily accepted death of the victim, unless God prevents it miraculously; that the tyrant or perpetrator of the death caused it unjustly; and that the reason for sacrificing the victim was hatred for God, the Church, the [true] religion, or some Christian virtue, or the rights and prerogatives of the Church.

Were these conditions verified in the death of Garcia Moreno? He knew very well that they were trying to kill him as a victim and he was preparing himself for the sacrifice: "The enemies of God and of the Church can kill me, but God does not die. I am going to be assassinated, I am happy to die for the faith."

Who killed Garcia Moreno? There can be no doubt that the [Masonic] lodges and other enemies of the [Catholic] religion [killed him].

Why did they assassinate him? Because they saw in him the model of a Catholic ruler.

How did Pius IX and Leo XIII judge the death of Garcia Moreno? Pius IX said, "Garcia Moreno fell under the steel of the assassin, a victim of his faith and of his Christian charity." And Leo XIII, "He fell under the steel of the wicked for the Church."

Does this mean to say that Garcia Moreno did not have any faults or defects? Not at all, since even great saints have their faults, and for this reason they do penance.

How do martyrs wash away their sins? By shedding their blood for the love of God; so much so that, perfectly purified, they immediately go up to paradise.

Who still hates Garcia Moreno? Freemasons, Socialists and enemies of the Church and of the homeland; also some badly influenced Catholics, imbued with prejudices, who do not know the hero.

Are there some people who reverence and love him very much? All Catholics and the best people of Ecuador; and likewise all good people outside of Ecuador, with rare exceptions.

Can one implore the Divine favor and ask for miracles through the intercession of Garcia Moreno, by making use of his image or of his relics? Yes, but only in private; and in the event of obtaining them, it is fitting to report them in detail to the ecclesiastical authorities for consequent purposes. God is accustomed to glorify His servants in this way.

Blessed soul of Garcia Moreno, pray for me![6]

His Excellency Bishop Heredia, Bishop of Guayaquil has said, "I have always maintained my opinion that God is asking two equally obligatory things of us: firstly, the construction of the National Basilica, so that national and perpetual worship may be given there; and secondly, the glorification, as far as possible on our part, of the Martyr of God and of country amongst us."

A few months later I left for Quito and all the Jesuits from there congratulated me for having taken the vanguard in the glorification of Garcia Moreno, and they added, "If we are waiting for politics to change first, nothing will ever be done." Father Ricardo Vasquez, with the emphasis of a deep and anxious desire which was engraved on my mind, added these words: "May God give you constancy."

Immediately I composed a prayer, the contents of which were the religious deeds of Garcia Moreno in concrete form. His Excellency Alberto Ordonez, an ardent devotee of the President-martyr, knowledgeable about his anecdotal features and even his unpublished feats, advised me. Let us listen to it:[7]

O Most Sacred Heart of Jesus! Remember the consecration that President Gabriel Garcia Moreno made to Thee of his Republic; the enthronement of Thy sacred image in his presidential home; and his blood shed to seal his unshakeable adherence to Thee and to Thy vicar, the Pope, and grant us the canonical glorification of such an exemplary ruler, that men powerful in deeds and words may rise up for the cause of religion and country, and finally the particular grace which we ask of Thee, in accord with Thy good pleasure. Amen.

The preceding prayer has been approved not only by the bishops of Ecuador, but moreover by the bishop of Pasto in Columbia, by the bishop of Santiago in Chile, by the bishop of Sao Paulo in Brazil, by one of the bishops in Argentina through the action of Father Herve Le Lay, and by a bishop of Scotland through the action of Hamish Fraser. As is obvious, it has been translated into Portuguese and English. I estimate that the number of Garcia Moreno holy cards with such prayers surpassed a hundred thousand, over the course of forty years.

I also promoted sending requests to His Eminence Carlos Maria de la Torre, begging him to begin the cause of beatification of the great man. Signatures abounded of gentlemen, artisans, ladies, religious men and women, seminarians and students, etc. The replies from the Metropolitan consisted in grateful acknowledgements for the requests and promises to fulfill them at an opportune time. The Tertiaries of St. Francis did more: being proud of having had the President-martyr as their member, four of them in person left for Quito: Arturo Salazar, Aurelio del Pozo, Javier Bustos and Alberto Muyrragui; the latter was the author of the first prayer, which had the glory of having been fought against at the beginning. They presented themselves to Archbishop Efren Forni, Apostolic Nuncio of the Holy See, and they placed the request into his hands. Going first to the aforesaid prelate was a mistake, when the right of introducing the Cause was incumbent upon His Eminence, Archbishop de la Torre of Quito, where Garcia Moreno had died. But this involuntary discourtesy contributed to stimulate the boldness of the prelate of the capital.[8]

In November of 1939 a reunion of all the bishops of Ecuador took place, and at it Archbishop Forni read out loud the petition brought by the Franciscan Tertiaries of Riobamba, and thereupon laid the written and signed document on the table in view of all. Immediately, and with energetic emphasis, Archbishop de la Torre said, "This matter is my concern, because Garcia Moreno died in Quito"; and right away he picked up the document for himself. A month passed, and he published the following decree, the contents of which are pure gold:

Inside and outside of the Republic, serious and prudent men well versed in Sacred Theology, who have studied with special care and diligence the death of Lord Doctor Don Gabriel Garcia Moreno and the cause which motivated it, believe that they have discovered in them the essential marks and characteristics of a true martyrdom.

It seems to them that the deaths of Saint Canute, Saint Wenceslaus, Saint Thomas of Canterbury and of the English Catholics sacrificed in the fateful days of Henry VIII and Elizabeth I, keep perfect consonance and analogy with the Ecuadorian President; and that, if the infallible decision of the Church has decorated them with the aureola [little golden crown] of martyrdom, she could well encircle the brow of this man with it also.

Such an assessment is far from negligible indeed, as is the interest that not only simple and devout faithful but even conspicuous members of the College of Cardinals have shown, so that within the canonical framework, it becomes possible for the very upright Magistrate to be placed upon the altars, who, notwithstanding the incredulity and apostasy of his century, has shown his faith and his unwavering adherence to the Church and to the Vicar of Christ, and of his innermost conviction, expressed by constant and superhuman efforts, that only the nation, which in its customs, its laws, and its constitution recognizes the sovereignty of Christ, will be happy. They have moved us to take the first steps for the clarification of such an important point.

How much glory we would give to God, with what new splendor the Church would be clothed, and what unfading honor would redound to our country, if with infallible lips the Roman Pontiff would declare that Garcia Moreno was and ought to be called a **martyr of Christ**![9]

No one is unaware of the protracted and delicate proceedings that have to be performed prior to the Church placing of one of her sons upon the altars, having first proved with unmistakable certitude the heroism of the virtues or the reality of martyrdom. Still more, the desired goal will not be reached unless God Himself, by means of wondrous deeds above all natural powers and wrought through the intercession of the Servant of God, does not put, so to say, His signature and His seal upon the Process and show that it is His will that this hero be honored and glorified as a saint or martyr of the faith.

The first inquiry about the heroism of the virtues or the reality of martyrdom pertains to the Ordinary in whose territory the Servant of God ended life's journey.

So that the Sacred Congregation of Rites, to which the Process has to be presented, may not brand it as null, it must adhere strictly to everything the sacred canons have treated concerning so delicate a matter.

The whole second part of the fourth book of the Code of Canon Law is put together to give these rules and regulations. And in regard to historical Causes, that is to say, those in which, due to so much time having passed since the death of the Servant of God, it is not possible to receive statements from eyewitnesses, Pius XI, of holy memory, in his *Motu Proprio* of February 6, 1930,[10] marked out the lines that the Sacred Congregation of Rites ought to follow in the processing of these causes.

Recently the same Sacred Congregation of Rites, dated January 4, 1939, published the "Norms to be Observed in the Formation of Ordinary Processes concerning Historical Causes."[11] The first of these norms prescribes that before beginning the Process, the Ordinary, the Promoter of the Faith or the Fiscal Promoter[12] will constitute a commission formed of three members whose expertise concerning historical methods and concerning the investigation of the archives are fully attested, and who are bound *in solidum*[13] "to gather all the historical sources about the life, virtues or martyrdom, the ancient fame of sanctity or of martyrdom, or the ancient veneration of the Servant of God."

Therefore, after invoking the light of the Holy Ghost, having heard the views of our Fiscal Promoter, fearful of incurring Divine indignation, if perchance we put forward some resistance to the designs which perhaps God may have upon the privileged soul of whom Pius IX said that "he had fallen victim of his faith and of his Christian charity," and Leo XIII that "he surrendered his life for the Church at the hands of the wicked": and the Congress of 1875, that "he shed his blood for the holy cause of religion, morality and order, peace and progress."

In compliance with what has been ordained by the Sacred Congregation of Rites in the document cited above: we deem it beneficial to constitute the Historical Commission which will have for its end to gather all the historical documents relating to the death of Doctor Gabriel Garcia Moreno, who died riddled with gun wounds in the Plaza of Independence of Quito, on the first Friday, August 6, 1875.

This commission will be composed of the Very Reverend Juan de Dios Navas, Magisterial Canon of our Metropolitan church and archivist of our Ecclesiastical Curia; of Reverend Father Joel Monroy, Provincial of the Order of Ransom; and of Reverend Father Jose Le Gohuir of the Company of Jesus.

Given in Quito, on the 20th of December of 1939. Carlos Maria Archbishop of Quito. Angel Humberto Jacome, Secretary.

Various religious associations of Riobamba sent letters to Archbishop de la Torre, this time to congratulate him for the introduction of the idolized Cause. The Metropolitan answered by thanking them, and at the same time asking for prayers. This correspondence of letters can be found in the *Boletin Franciscano* of Riobamba, August 6, 1941.[14]

Father Le Gohuir, a very competent man, as he had been the author of thick volumes about Garcia Moreno, such as *Un Gran Americano* and the second volume of *Historia de la Republica del Ecuador*, was writing his thesis about the Garcian Martyr, when he was surprised by death, just seven months after his appointment as a member of the Historical Commission. Unfortunately, it has not been possible to ascertain the whereabouts of that manuscript. Archbishop de la Torre appointed Father Jose Ricardo Vasquez as his replacement, who, a year before, in his journal entitled, "*La Republica del Corazon de Jesus*," had published his thesis of the martyrdom of Garcia Moreno, elaborated by the French Jesuit Jose Jouanen. The latter in turn finished by being appointed a member of the Commission, and being of such character, he gave greater breadth and depth to the aforementioned thesis, and he put it into the hands of Archbishop de la Torre.

Both this illustrious Archbishop and I, and all those who read the lucubration by Father Jouanen, affirm that his proofs of martyrdom are not apodictic or convincing. Why does it possess such defects? Because this religious, very praiseworthy in other activities, here only actually demonstrated that Garcia Moreno was a martyr of liberal doctrines. Well now, such a course gives leeway to the following objection:

The Ecuadorian and intellectual instigators of the Garcian assassination, such as Juan Montalvo, Alfonso Polanco, Avelardo Moncayo and Roberto Andrade, have declared that their mortal hatred was not only aimed at the anti-liberal regime of Garcia Moreno but also at his authoritarian and ruthless methods.

The reasons, therefore, would be political-religious. It is clear that even so, it is easy to demonstrate that hatred towards the religious aspect of Garcia Moreno predominated in them. Jouanen stresses the fact that these instigators, personally, had not received from him any notable inconvenience. Just by being insane, they hurled themselves to the assassination of a praiseworthy ruler in public deeds and beloved by his people. This approach is developed more fully in chapter XV of our ninth volume.

Meanwhile, back in the Old World, in Belgium, a spark was enkindled tending toward the canonical glorification of the Man who honors mankind. This took place in Mechelen, the primatial ecclesiastical city of the Belgian Kingdom, where a six page booklet was published in November of 1944, amidst the rubble and smoke of the dreadful conflagration [of the Second World War].

On the first page the portrait of Garcia Moreno is presented with the facsimile of his name and signature, taken from an original autograph.

On the second page begins the following literary work in French, which when put into English reads in these terms:

### Prayer for obtaining the beatification of Gabriel Garcia Moreno:

O God, Who has deigned to raise up in the person of Thy servant Gabriel Garcia Moreno the eminent virtues which enabled him to save his nation and lead it to Thee, by lifting it from material and moral prostration, and consecrating it to the Sacred Heart of Thy Divine Son: deign to glorify this Thy servant and grant us to see him soon placed upon the altars by the Church.

Saint Gabriel the Archangel, Strength of God, who has been chosen to be the patron of Gabriel Garcia Moreno on the day of his baptism, you who, without any doubt, obtained that strength by which he did not retreat before the enemies of God, but rather he longed for the favor of being judged worthy of shedding his blood for the Church: deign to grant us the happiness of seeing his name soon recorded on the list of the saints, and that Divine Providence may bestow upon us the graces which we request through his intercession.

Our Father, Hail Mary, and Glory Be.

Imprimatur. Mechelen, the 11th day of November of 1944. Jose Carton de Wiart, Vicar General...

# APPENDIX I

Then the well-known features of Garcian governance are presented, comparable with those of St. Louis, King of France, and with Charlemagne; and it finishes with three paragraphs which we transcribe here below:

Garcia Moreno was far from being a passing meteor without leaving a trail behind itself. Not to present his personality in all its glory would be not to give God glory for His works, and to this great man the immortality which is due to him even on earth. It would be, moreover, to deprive the human race of an enormous help; since the life of Garcia Moreno presents a providential lesson to ward off the cataclysm which he alone undertook to remedy.

What more beautiful example could be offered to our rulers, faced with almost superhuman difficulties which characterize these postwar years? In fact, the clearing of a heap of ruins, the bringing of prosperity, and above all the rectifying of the standards now so wrong, and the leading of nations according to the principles of the Christian life under the gaze of God and of His Church, did he not achieve all this in a splendid manner in a few years, within the sphere in which he had to act?

And in this century in which His Holiness Pius XI has called Christians to the practice of Catholic Action, who can compare with Gabriel Garcia Moreno, who for his piety, study, and activity has merited to be chosen as one of the patrons of Catholic Action?

It is a pity that there has not lived for a long time a prelate so determined in favor of the Cause of Garcia Moreno.

Finding myself in Cuenca, and especially for the centenary of the dogmatic definition of the Immaculate Conception of the Most Holy Virgin, I composed the prayer which follows and was approved by the illustrious bishop of that city:

O Most Holy Virgin of Lourdes! Remember that your servant Gabriel Garcia Moreno swore to defend the privilege of your Immaculate Conception. He was a member of your Congregation,[15] and assiduously recited the holy rosary. He expired at the foot of your sacred altar, and according to the testimony of Pope Pius IX, who defined your exemption from original sin, "died as a victim for the faith and because of his Christian charity for his country." Obtain for us the canonical glorification of such an exemplary ruler, that men powerful in deeds and words may rise up for the cause of the same faith and their country, and finally grant us the particular grace which we implore through your intercession and for his glory, if it be for the good of our souls. Amen.

*(Ask for a particular grace, and recite a Hail Mary and a Glory Be.)*

The preceding prayer was also approved by other venerable bishops, and was even enriched with an indulgence of three hundred days by His Eminence Maria de la Torre, Archbishop of Quito. Undoubtedly this has increased the power of the patronage of Garcia Moreno. Consider the following case:

Finding myself in Jiron, in a neighborhood near Cuenca, a woman said to me:

For several days I suffered interior anguish which was leading me to despair. When Saturday arrived, I entered a church and invoked the Most Holy Virgin, "My Mother! I do not ask you for riches, neither for honors, nor for a house, nor a job. I want to be a good Christian, fulfilling the Commandments of God's Law and of the Church. But deliver me from the terrible sadness that even tempts me with despair." Scarcely had I finished this prayer, when I felt in my soul that the Most Holy Virgin was answering me, "Invoke Garcia Moreno."– I replied to her, "My Mother, are you not infinitely more powerful than Garcia Moreno, and do you not love me like a daughter? I have heard that Garcia Moreno has worked miracles, but I do not know him well nor do I have faith in him."

The aforementioned woman continued suffering the diabolical temptation, and even more dreadfully, was gripped by a cruel melancholy. The next Saturday, she entered the church, knelt before the image of Our Lady, and repeated to her the same prayer as before, but this time with greater vehemence and bathing her rosary with tears. The Most Holy Virgin answered her the same way as she did eight days before, but with more energy, "Invoke Garcia Moreno." Then the poor little woman obeyed docilely, lifting her eyes to heaven, she exclaimed, "Garcia Moreno, have mercy on me! I do not ask you for riches, or for honors, or for a house, or a job. I want to be a good Christian, fulfilling the Commandments of God's Law and of the Church. But deliver me from the terrible despair that makes my life an insupportable torment..." She lowered her head and immediately felt an immense spiritual relief, as though a strong arm had lifted off her shoulders a crushing burden that was torturing her. She experienced a heavenly sweetness and an internal joy which she had never experienced before, even in moments of great devotion.[16]

She told me all the above in the church of Jiron, and added, "From that moment, Father, I have not suffered again even a trace of that despair; I have recourse in my works to the patronage of Garcia Moreno and he has not left me disappointed."

In the year 1952, when I was in Cuenca, I published a booklet entitled, *¿Martir Garcia Moreno?* I tried to show that the authorship of the crime of August sixth[17] was in the Masonic Lodges of Germany. It is true that Father Berthe had already said this sixty-five years ago; but my contribution consisted in reinforcing the thesis with new testimonies. Behold the cogency which demonstrates with certitude the martyrdom of Garcia Moreno, without significant objections. What jealousy about the borders or the economic and military power could the German Empire of those years have had towards the Garcian Ecuador? ... On the other hand the *Kulturkampf* viewed with disgust that, on the shores of the Pacific and on the equator, great progress was being shown, based on and influenced by a lofty and exuberant Catholicism. Hence its hatred, mixed with contempt, of the Protagonist of that progress.

When the distinguished Father Jouanen had died and I had been transferred to Quito, I was appointed a member of the aforesaid Commission on February 16, 1957. This note sent to me by Archbishop de la Torre on April 17, 1962, shows his concern for the advancement of the Cause:

> Would you be kind enough to inform me if you have something written about Garcia Moreno? I ask this in regard to what I have commissioned you, in view of the goodwill, erudition, and other qualities which adorn your person. I would be very grateful to you. Your trusted and affectionate servant in the Lord, who blesses you. Carlos Maria Cardinal de la Torre, Archbishop of Quito.

Immediately I presented myself before His Excellency, and told him that the material is not ready at present. In effect, I found myself at that time working on the sixth volume of my monumental work about the life of Garcia Moreno, and only in the ninth volume would I deal with the decisive influence of the Masonic Lodges of Germany in the assassination of the Hero. His Eminence also told me that it would not be necessary for me to present the evidence of martyrdom but only the documents from which the evidence could be drawn. This extraction would concern the judges of the Process, which would constitute the second canonical phase of the Cause.[18]

The year 1969 arrived, and having completed the composition of my ninth volume, I reckoned that I had not only compiled the materials but had also selected them and put them in strategic order, so that they could demonstrate the martyrdom. Thus the tasks of the Process would be easy and rapid.

Doctor Wilfrido Loor Moreira was working with me at the same time on the same thing, with the publication of his book entitled, *Garcia Moreno y sus Asesinos*, published in 1955, which was also the reason why he was appointed a member of the Historical Commission. Its first edition sold out, and the second was released in 1966. In my opinion, the chapters dedicated to the biographies of those involved in the crime of the sixth of August, such as Faustino Rayo and his minions, constitute its irreplaceable value. They are shown there to be wretches and great sinners, and not as they are presented by their ideological colleagues: innocent and heroes. Another of Wilfrido Loor's merits consists in his documentation taken from the criminal proceedings concerning the crime of the sixth of August, in which the testimonies are enhanced by the sanctity of the oath. May God grant that these three voluminous dossiers be published soon, for the greater prestige of Garcia Moreno.[19]

Jubilant, I then ran to His Eminence, and said to him, "Now I have the materials ready for the Process." "I am glad," he answered me. "Go to my secretary, Monsignor Angel Humberto Jacobe, and tell him on my behalf to write the decree establishing the Process, which I will approve with my signature." It should be noted that His Eminence, as a result of having suffered a stroke, could not write this document by himself. Moreover he did not see anyone in the Archiepiscopal Palace but in his residence in Ciudadela Mariscal Sucre. From there I emerged triumphant, heading for the aforesaid Palace, where I transmitted this notification to Monsignor Jacome. This Most Illustrious Secretary pointed out to me, "Since His Excellency Pablo Munoz Vega is the Coadjutor Bishop '*Sedi Datus*,' he must be informed of the matter. Let us wait for him to return from Bogota; it is a question of a few days."

But weeks and months passed by and such a decree was neither drafted nor written. What had happened? I did not know that a profound social change had taken place, unfavorable to Garcia Moreno's Cause.

Doubtlessly His Eminence Cardinal de la Torre did not know it either, owing to his illness, his isolation, and his ninety-five years.

I presented hundreds of signatures to the Archbishop, on behalf of Catholics from the capital city, begging that impetus be given to the Cause. In May of 1974 I returned from Spain, bringing with me also hundreds of signatures on the matter. Finally, a Scottish foreigner named Hamish Fraser sent a similar request, written by Catholics in France, Scotland, and Ireland. The reply of the then Cardinal Archbishop of Quito, His Eminence Pablo Munoz Vega, coincided with my pessimistic assessment of a profound unfavorable social change; the reply which Hamish Fraser enclosed in a letter to me, and which substantially read in these terms, was, "Unfortunately there is neither the religious nor the political environment."

In the hope of a favorable social change, my volumes ten, eleven, and twelve will contribute to my collection of numerous testimonies in favor of the fame of sanctity and martyrdom of Garcia Moreno. Likewise [it is so hoped] with [regards to] a declaration made by Mrs. Maria Mercedes Carpio, widow of Faustino Rayo, the ill-fated assassin of the Protagonist of our pages.

Finding myself in Latacunga in January of 1976, I spoke with Mrs. Rufina Granda, Mr. Ladd's widow, an elderly woman having reached 96 years. This lady told me the following account, which I write continuously, for greater ease to readers, although she was interrupted by me several times for the greater clarification of the passages:

> I was fourteen years old, in 1894, and I was in the parish of Guaytacama, whose pastor, Father Nicolas Silva, had an interview with my mother, whom I accompanied. Lustrums before, the aforesaid priest had been the godfather for one of the children of Faustino Rayo, to whom he gave the name of Nicholas, doubtlessly because of the sponsor.
>
> After the tragic sixth of August, Mrs. Maria Mercedes Carpio, Rayo's widow, conversed with her *compadre* Nicolas Silva and said to him, "My deceased spouse had been accustomed to sell many things to the Indians of the East, and received gold nuggets in payment, which they were washing in the rivers. Almost all of them had outstanding, old debts; hence my husband wanted to go back east to collect them, but he came up against the inexorable prohibition of Garcia Moreno.[20]

Three or four gentlemen were coming at night to the house, and were having talks with my husband behind closed doors, inciting him to kill Garcia Moreno. To induce him better, they were giving him gifts. I came to know this, and I frequently said to my husband, "Do not rush into such a great crime, and the worst thing is that they are going to kill you also." He answered me, "They are not going to kill me because I have a few people to defend me. We are going to enjoy a comfortable life."

"Rayo's wife was very virtuous," the above-mentioned pastor of Guaytacama finally said.

Mrs. Rufina Granda continued by giving information to Father Gomezjurado in these terms:

About the year 1896, when I was in Guaytacama, both of Rayo's sons turned up, in soldiers' uniforms, and took possession of two horses to use them in the Alfrarist campaign against the guerilla fighters of the province of Chimborazo. I and others, hoping to prevent the robbery from taking place, said to them, "These horses are the property of Father Nicholas Silva." No sooner had they heard this name, they were taken aback and returned the horses.[21]

# Endnotes

[1] This translation has been made from the book, *Vida de Garcia Moreno* (Quito, Imprenta ARPI, 1979) by Father Severo Gomezjurado, S. J., vol. 12 (Years 1921–1974), pp. 224-248.

[2] See page 265 above.

[3] "Garcia Moreno's Eucharistic Crusade," for the adult section. For the children's section, the patron and model was Guy de Fontgalland, whose life was at the height of its popularity during those years. The adult members of the Directory were Neptali Cisneros, President, in the middle; on his right, Pacifico Merino; on his left, Alberto Muyrragui, author of the first prayer requesting the beatification of Garcia Moreno. In the front row: myself; at my right, the child Alberto Pipa; at my left, the child Guillermo Anda.

[4] *La Consagración*, p. 336 ff.

[5] *Ibid.* page 338.

[6] The fliers by Father Ricardo Vasquez were published in the form of small sheets of paper under the title of "Leaflet Messenger."

[7] Father Jose Legohuir was another one of those who were very pleased with the first prayer, since he was the author of important books about Garcia Moreno which we have already mentioned on preceding pages.

[8] Cf. *La Consagración*, p. 340 ff.

[9] *Ibid.* p. 348, where endnote 25 [p. 277, endnote 60 of this edition in English] reads in these terms: "It was Bishop Ordonez, an eyewitness, who told me of the energetic expression and words of the Metropolitan, who always took pride in valiantly promoting the beatification of Garcia Moreno without taking notice of the Masons."

[10] Apostolic Letter *Gia da qualche tempo* (AAS 22 (1930), pp. 87-88).

[11] *Normae servandae in construendis processibus ordinariis super causis historicis* (AAS 31 (1939), pp. 174-175).

[12] "The fiscal promoter (*fiscus*, public treasury) — though perhaps, if we attend to the most important part of his office, a better title would be "promoter of justice" — is a person who, constituted by ecclesiastical authority, exercises in the ecclesiastical courts and in his own name the office of a public prosecutor, especially in criminal cases (*Instr. S. C. Episc. et Reg.*, January 11, 1880, art. 13). If we wish to include in the definition all that is comprehended in his office, he might be defined as a public person legitimately appointed to defend the rights of his church, especially in court. Peries, in his article "*Le procureur fiscal ou promoteur*" (*Revue des sciences ecclésiastiques*, April, 1897), rightly says that the whole office of the fiscal promoter may be summed up in three points: solicitude for the observance of discipline, particularly among the clergy; attendance at the processes of beatification and canonization in episcopal courts; and defense of the validity of marriage and of religious profession. All these functions, it is true, are not always carried out by one and the same person; they are all, however, included in the full idea of the *promoter fiscalis*, for it is this official's duty to

defend the rights of the Church, the decency of Divine service, the dignity of the clergy, the holiness of matrimony, and perseverance in the perfect state of life" ("Ecclesiastical Courts" (*The Catholic Encyclopedia* (1908 ed.), vol. 4., p. 450).

[13] "His competit 'in solidum' officium colligendi omnes fontes scriptos circa vitam, virtutes vel martyrium, antiquam famam sanctitatis vel martyrii, aut antiquum cultum Servi Dei. His competit 'in solidum' officium colligendi omnes fontes scriptos circa vitam, virtutes vel martyrium, antiquam famam sanctitatis vel martyrii, aut antiquum cultum Servi Dei."

[14] Cf. *La Consagración*, p. 343 ff.

[15] I.e. the Marian Congregation of Artisans in Quito directed by the Jesuit Fathers.

[16] The favor performed in Jiron has been previously published in my booklet entitled, "*Caballero de la Virgen*."

[17] President Garcia Moreno was assassinated on this day in 1875.

[18] The document by which the Cardinal Archbishop appointed me a member of the Historical Commission, is published in my third volume, page 7. A short time later Doctor Wilfrido Loor was included in the Commission, using more or less the same words.

[19] The first edition of *García Moreno y sus Asesinos* has 244 pages, and the second 328.

[20] In the baptismal registers of the parochial church of San Roque in Quito, I found the birth of Maria Rosa Antonia Sinforosa Rayo Carpio, baptized on August 9, 1870. That of Manuel Antonio Faustino Rayo Carpio, baptized on December 24, 1874. During various hours I searched for the one for Jose Maria Rayo Carpio, who was a pharmacist, and I did not find it either in San Roque or in the Sagrario. Doubtlessly this last one was the godson of Nicholas Silva Vaca and he took his name.

[21] The Alfarist abuse of taking possession of horses, to support the criminal war sustained by Masonry against the legitimate government and against the vote of the people, was called "the seizure by beasts."

# Appendix II
# Favors Attributed to Gabriel Garcia Moreno[1]

One should not expect to consider all the following favors to be first class miracles, but as all being, indeed, the testimony of so many Catholic faithful who think that Garcia Moreno was a true saint and martyr. In the year 1938 a renewal of faith and confidence in the intercession of the President-martyr took place. Until now only three [of the following] cases could be evaluated as having the character of first class miracles, following the examination and approval of Holy Church. All that is contained in these pages in this respect is a reproduction of what is already edited in my books, *Christian Hercules, Standard-bearer of the Heart of Jesus, Garcia Moreno, Is Garcia Moreno a Martyr?, Knight of the Virgin, Fourteen Machete Blows and Six Bullet Wounds, Champion and Martyr of Progress, The Consecration*, etc., which have all been published with ecclesiastical approval. Since these editions have sold out, it is fitting that these favors be recorded in the following pages.

**Patron of Travel**

Many travelers entrust their journeys to Garcia Moreno's soul, remembering how that great man traveled along roads at the edges of cliffs, or infested with robbers. He forded torrential rivers, or went on marches while in bad health. The travelers, above all those from the province of Bolivar and the canton of Guano, offered stipends for Masses to be offered for this intention, and they declared that they were helped in an extraordinary way. The news of such favors reached the ears of Father Escobar, S.J., my professor, who passed this on to me in the year 1938.

While I was in San Jose de Chimbo until the aforementioned year, they told me that Mariano Montenegro had to cross a river while walking on a plank of wood that was made to serve as a bridge. Being then middle-aged, he was afraid but he invoked Garcia Moreno by saying to him, "Give me a hand." He recovered his courage and walked on the board as though there were no danger.

The same Mariano Montenegro, knowing that a lady was in danger of death, with terrible pains of childbirth from being unable to give birth at the due time, directed his steps there and invoked Garcia Moreno. Thereupon, the sick woman gave birth to twins and recovered her strength and health to the surprise of all.

By the testimony of Monsignor Alberto Ordonez, Bishop of Riobamba, the illustrious Bishop of Portoviejo, Pedro Schumacher, was accustomed to commend his great apostolic enterprises to Garcia Moreno, and related that he had thereafter great success in them.

Reverend Father Virgilio Maldonado, Apostolic Administrator of Portoviejo, made a novena of prayers to Garcia Moreno, asking for the cure of a relative suffering from a chronic illness. Well, when the sixth of August arrived, the anniversary of the death of the President-martyr, the sick man recovered in a marvelous manner, and suddenly became completely cured. Upon hearing this, Archbishop Gonzalez Suarez said with wit, *"The sixth of August? But Faustino Rayo[2] also died on this day!"*

The venerable Doctor Virgilio Palomeque, pastor of Colimes for many years, did not cease to wonder how he had invoked Garcia Moreno when he had been called to give the sacraments to a woman in a desperate condition from childbirth, and immediately after that, the sick woman gave birth with admirable ease.

The eminent Jesuit Ricardo Vasquez, in the year 1938, sent a letter to me from Quito in which he said, *"I am a great admirer and devotee of Garcia Moreno, and have received notable favors through his intercession."*

In the year 1929, I received a letter written from Lima by one of my aunts, Sister Elisa Gomezjurado, a religious of the Sacred Hearts, in which she said to me, *"I heard that Garcia Moreno works miracles; I have received some, but I do not dare put them into a letter."*

### The Burned Bread

In Mr. Jaime Vincio Sosa's museum there exists the scarf which some orphan girls from Cuenca had given to Garcia Moreno. The chaplain of the orphanage was Canon Leon. The latter, who had scarcely heard the news of the assassination of the great man, spoke to those orphans exhorting them to consider his death as a true martyrdom and to commend themselves to him in trials and tribulations. The lesson had its effect:

When their oven had been overheated, the bread was burned. Mercedes Torres, who was responsible for the bread that week, was greatly alarmed. She knelt down and prayed, *"Blessed soul of Garcia Moreno, help in this disgrace. Restore the bread."* One of her companions and assistants, Ana Merchan, also knelt down and made the same prayer. Immediately the lifesaving idea came to them of going to the chaplain, so that he would intercede before the Directress, Carmen Maldonado, who was a strict disciplinarian, and who would deprive them of their supper and make them work the whole night making new bread.

The Canon verified that all the bread was almost completely burned and closed the bakery with a key. When taking his leave he said, *"You have invoked Garcia Moreno and so sleep tranquilly. If there is no miracle by the holy martyr, I will speak tomorrow with Miss Carmen so that she does not punish you."*

Minutes later the Directress asked them, *"How did the bread turn out? Let us go to see it." "Madam, the bakery is locked, and the Canon took the key." "What a strange thing for the Canon to do!"* replied the Directress.

On the following morning, Canon Leon came to the orphanage and said, *"Before celebrating Mass let us go and see the bread."* He opened the door and they entered. *"Miracle, miracle!"* they exclaimed. *"The bread has become completely better. Yesterday it was black, and now it is golden."* They tested some pieces and what an exquisite taste! The cleric shared their emotion and surprise, of course without tasting any, since he had to celebrate the Holy Sacrifice. In the chapel he congratulated the orphans and again extolled the patronage of Garcia Moreno and his martyrdom.

Half an hour later, the patrons who supported the orphanage also marveled at the special exquisiteness of the bread of that day.

Mercedes Torres, the one in charge for the week, gave this account to Sister Josefina Iniguez, and she finally passed it on to me, the author of these pages, in the year 1949. Moreover, she told me, *"After Garcia Moreno did this marvel for me, there is no favor that I have asked of him that I have not obtained."* Magdalena Chacon and Josefa Velez, companions of Mercedes Torres, also said to the aforesaid religious, *"The change in the bread is a certain fact."* Finally, Ana Merchan, along with Mercedes Torres, transmitted this account to her younger sister, Encarnacion Merchan, who was still alive in the year 1949, and passed it on to me in that same year.

## Cure of a Fistula

Pedro Aviles was a priest from Latacunga famous for his extraordinary devotion to Garcia Moreno, whose virtues he tried heroically to imitate. When he heard the name of the President-martyr, he invariably uncovered his head. An ulcer appeared on his foot, of a chronic type which is commonly called a fistula. The malady worsened to the point that the doctors judged it necessary to amputate his diseased foot. Then

Aviles earnestly besought the intercession of Garcia Moreno, spending whole hours in prayer during the night, without omitting to sprinkle some white powder on the fistula, <u>which had been used for some time with no success.</u> During the course of the night the foot seemed to be so much better that, in the morning, the surgeons determined that amputation was unnecessary. He improved in a few days to complete health. The grateful man did not cease to repeat emphatically, *"Garcia Moreno is the one who cured me."* One of the witnesses is a priest from Riobamba... Another person who told this same story is Sister Francisca Aviles, Pedro's sister.

**Advocate against Injustices**

Reverend Mother Sabina, Superior of a community of Marianites, was in serious danger of being dispossessed of some lands, due to criminal maneuvers by unscrupulous lawyers. She commended the matter to the Blessed Sacrament and to Garcia Moreno. She set out for Quito and requested an audience with the Dictator, Frederico Paez, who had begun his term by troubling the Church. Having already entered the Presidential Palace, her constant prayer was this, *"Garcia Moreno, do justice."* Well then, the dictator by public decree ordered the lands to be returned, under penalty of the swindlers being sent into exile to the Galapagos Islands if they did not comply.

**Increase of "Garcianism" since 1938**

Due to the prayers approved by the Church, the new biographies, and finally the introduction of the Cause of Beatification by Archbishop Carlos Maria de la Torre, we very solemnly relate favors of greater importance:

In Guayaquil, a sick man had to undergo surgery on the following day. He decided to invoke Garcia Moreno. *"I fear the operation. Make me healthy without too much trouble."* The fatal hour arrived. The surgeon examined the ailing man as a pure formality, and became perplexed. He examined the man more thoroughly, and being moved, he exclaimed, *"You have cured yourself without an operation."* That is what happened.

During the first days of July in 1940, in Ambato, a religious of the Providence Order was in bed with a temperature between one hundred and two and one hundred and four degrees Fahrenheit.[3] The Community besought the intercession of Garcia Moreno, *"If you are a saint, please let it not be typhoid, since the college mustn't close."* Moreover, a picture of the President-martyr was placed near the bed of the sick sister. The decision of Doctor Humberto Ordonez: *"Typhoid. The sick sister must go to the hospital and the College must be closed."*

Other doctors had a less pessimistic opinion, and declared, *"It is a very serious matter to close a college, precisely when there are only fifteen days until the final exams. It ought not to happen, since it is not absolutely certain that it is typhoid"* As a result of this, the confidence of the religious increased and they doubled their prayers to Garcia Moreno.

To eliminate all hesitation, blood was taken from the sick sister and was examined in the laboratory: typhoid! Then the sister infirmarian angrily snatched the picture of Garcia Moreno, crushed it, and threw it into the garbage.

Nevertheless, something extraordinary happened: the sick sister had a lower temperature: only one hundred degrees Fahrenheit; and she felt strong and brave. But the analysis did not give any room for doubt: the establishment was closed, and the sister with typhoid had to be brought to the hospital. She wanted to go on foot, but it was not allowed. In the meantime she was completely healed. The doctors were shocked. The little sisters, in fact, looked at each other with smiles, as though saying, *"Then Garcia Moreno is a saint."* As a precaution, the recently cured sister still remained in the hospital for five days, returned to her Community, and the College resumed its classes. It seems to be a first class miracle.

**Sudden Cure of Deafness**

At the end of November 1943, the historic oleograph of the Heart of Jesus of Garcia Moreno was exposed in the Cathedral of Loja receiving the homage of the crowds, when the Franciscan brother, Diego Navarrete, joined them and raised the following prayer:

> *"Oh Garcia Moreno, you who consecrated Ecuador to the Heart of Jesus before this picture, work a miracle, make me recover the use of my ears. I was given no hope in Quito, a cold climate; I was given no hope in Guayaquil, a hot climate; I was given no hope in Loja, a moderate climate. I want to be a missionary in Zamora, to teach the catechism to the Jivaros.*[4] *But how can I do it being deaf? You, who consecrated Ecuador to the Heart of Jesus before this picture, make me hear."* A few minutes passed, he paid attention and relates that he heard everything: the bell that rings, the people who pray. He exclaimed, *"Now I can go to Zamora."*

Some eight years later he spoke with me in Gualaceo and said to me, "*I was unable to hear for six months. I can swear that I was given no hope in Quito, in Guayaquil, and in Loja. The doctors who attended me can swear that they gave me no hope.*"

Here is a case that can be considered a first class miracle; an oath was signed by Brother Navarrete and by each one of these three doctors. But after some eight years had passed, I found myself in Cuenca, engaged in working on the edition of the first volume of my monumental work on Garcia Moreno. I am confirmed in the persuasion that the Cause did not fail for lack of first class miracles.

About this time, I found myself in the hospital of Gualaceo where they had brought me to administer Extreme Unction to a boy in agony. The child was nine years old and he had fallen from a high place upon a rock. His skull had been split about three centimeters. I examined inside the gap, and I noticed that it was black and dark. The child's mouth was half-opened; his eyelids were half-closed and trembling. His rasping breath or snoring was typical of the dying. The nurse injected him with blood serum and she covered the wound with a bandage. On my part, I anointed him and touched his neck with a relic of Garcia Moreno, asking the servant of God for a miracle. The nurse exclaimed, *"If he does not die, it will be a great miracle, because the meninges[5] are threatened."*

Upset from having seen an open skull for the first time, I went to the banks of the Gualaceo River to get a breath of fresh air. About twenty minutes later I returned to the hospital, and the boy whom I had left dying was found sitting up in bed, speaking with those around him, answering questions: *"Where is your house located; what is your father's name; how did you fall on the rock?"* I exclaimed, *"It is a miracle."* All agreed, including the sister who had injected the blood serum, who said, *"Without any doubt, this is a miracle."* It was six o'clock in the evening.

The following morning I spoke with the hospital doctor, hoping for an official confirmation. But the doctor decided, *"There is no certitude of a miracle, because it is not certain that the wound had been deep."* I objected to him, *"The state of agony did not indicate a deep cerebral disturbance?"* The doctor's answer was, *"The state of agony can be unreal and only apparent, and for the latter a superficial disturbance is enough."* I confirmed here the assertion of Reverend Father Molinari, Procurator in Rome of the Causes of

Beatification of the Jesuits, *"The Pope will have to make do with the proofs of heroic virtue or of martyrdom, since the doctors will easily find reasons for judging more or less instantaneous cures as not being miraculous."*[6]

**Incurable Baby**

In Tanicuchi, near Cotopaxi, a four month old baby became stricken with a violent whooping cough. One of the doctors declared himself defeated. Another also felt the matter to be hopeless and refused to prescribe anything. Only to placate the mother, he advised two drinks. But the sick child was unable to drink anything. He closed his eyes. The coldness of death had already come upon the child from his feet to his knees. His death that very night seemed inevitable. The parish priest suggested "a novena of prayers to Garcia Moreno," and he led the prayers in the presence of the parents and the servants. The following morning, to the admiration of all, the sick child became better. The novena continued and the improvement likewise continued. When the novena was finished, the child had completely recovered and his parents received Communion in thanksgiving.

**Other Favors Attributed to Garcia Moreno**

In Quito a young lady was near death, to judge from science and the services of three doctors, and in spite of prayers to different saints. Finally the three doctors gave the verdict: *"The invalid is going to pass away tonight."* Then the priest, Father Benitez, suggested, *"Let us entrust the matter to the intercession of Garcia Moreno."* But they objected, "We do not have faith in that intercession." "I certainly do," replied the priest, *"and if the invalid recovers her health, it ought to be attributed to him."* "Without any doubt," they answered. Father Benitez invoked Garcia Moreno, and the patient not only did not die that night but the next day she was out of danger, and was completely cured in a few days to the surprise of all.

A certain individual put the holiness of Garcia Moreno to the test, *"If the dignitary was a saint, may he make me get a house this very day, furnished in such a way, in such a neighborhood, and at such a price."* Others laughed at him. Nevertheless on this same day the speaker obtained the house with all the conditions that he had made. Since then he has absolute faith in the sanctity of Garcia Moreno.

A certain person was accustomed to invoke Garcia Moreno in all his difficulties. He did this with much fervor when he felt the vibrations of the earthquake on May 13, 1941. Because of this, his house was not affected except for a slender crack like a thread, while some of his neighbors' houses fell, and others were badly cracked or collapsed. And the prodigy was greater with respect to his nearby stable, which, without any need of an earthquake, was ready to collapse merely from its age and dilapidation. He went towards it before the sun had fully risen, and found it standing. He drove the animals outside. Then he felt a crash behind him. He turned around, and it was the stable that had fallen to the ground, as though it had been sustained by Garcia Moreno until the moment in which the animals left.

In the hospital of Ambato the aforementioned priest, Antonio Benitez, found an incurable woman, having within her womb a child which had been dead for three days. The priest invoked Garcia Moreno in the following words, *"President-martyr, save this woman's life: and so that I may know that you have performed the miracle, make that poor woman happily deliver, today, at one o'clock in the morning."* Four hours later he received news of the delivery of the dead child, partly corrupted. He asked, *"At what hour did it take place?"* — They answered him, *"At one o'clock this morning."*

In the canton of Milagro, Angela Quesada suffered very acute pains in one foot, caused by a fall. She was not able to take a step. She was unable to get to sleep the whole night. Just after daybreak she was able to invoke Garcia Moreno and applied his picture to the injured foot. At the cost of terrible discomfort and supported by other persons, she arrived at the church, where she began again to recommend herself to the President-martyr. When holy Mass was finished, she felt herself instantaneously cured and she returned to her house walking on her own feet without the least difficulty.

In the same Canton of Milagro, around the year 1959, a rich man asked his workman, *"What do you have in your hands?"* He answered, *"A picture of Garcia Moreno, who does miracles." "Ha, ha, ha...How can a tyrant work miracles?"* The workman remained silent. But the man, reflecting for a short while like one who has been keeping a sorrow in his heart, exclaimed, *"Good heavens! If it is true that Garcia Moreno is a saint and does miracles, then let him do one right now. For many years I have been searching for my mother and I have not found her. I have invoked St. Vincent, St. Joseph, and other saints, but to no avail. Let Garcia Moreno make me find my mother today and then I will believe that Garcia Moreno is a saint and I will promote his beatification."*

He said this and departed by car to Guayaquil. In this city he found a hotel and ordered lunch. A few moments later, a little old woman came in and begged, saying, *"Sir, give me alms, or if you prefer, that which is on your plate."* The rich man lifted up his eyes and took out a coin saying, *"Take a sucre, and who are you?" "I am so and so,"* and she said her first and last name. The rich man was struck, because a long time before he had heard that his mother was so named. *"And how is it that you have fallen into such misery?" "Oh, sir, many years ago my husband abandoned me, and bad luck followed me." "And what was your husband's name?" "His name was..."* and she mentioned his first and last name. The man felt his heart beat violently, as he knew well that such a first and last name matched that of his father. *"And did you have a son?" "I had only one small child, a little boy, but I had to give him away to a rich man, because I did not have the wherewithal to feed and clothe him." "How old would this boy now be and what was his name?" "Alas, this son of mine would now be about thirty years old and his name was..."* She said the name and both last names.

Then the speaker, weeping tears of tenderness, lunged toward her and embracing her exclaimed, *"You are my mother, and I am your son!" "How can you be my son for whom I have been looking so long?" "Yes, mother, I am he, and from now on I believe that Garcia Moreno is a saint and I am going to cooperate in his beatification."* He put his mother into a car and brought her to his house. Before then he used to carry a revolver in his hand to threaten his enemies. Now he took out a small box to give them a cigarette and shook their hands, saying to them, *"We are friends. Through Garcia Moreno and my mother, I can do this..."* (What is here related is recorded in a letter which I received in the year 1959, in accordance with what is on page 128 of my little work, *14 Machetazos y 6 Balazos*.)

I have in my possession a letter which Brother Clemente de Tulcan sent me on May 28, 1958, in which he related to me the extraordinary favor which we are going to record below. Months later I departed to Tulcan and I questioned the aforementioned religious, *"From what source did Your Reverence know of this event?" "Well, from a letter which the same person favored by the wonder sent me."* I had spoken about this to Brother Hilario Yerovi of the Christian Brothers of St. John Baptist de La Salle, who told me, *"The fact related by Brother Clemente de Tulcan is substantially the same as what I heard from Miss Mercedes Ribera Murillo in Tulcan."*

This lady, very advanced in years, was sleeping in her house in Pupiales, Columbia, accompanied only by a woman servant. In the silence of the middle of the night they realized that a few thieves were picking the lock or breaking the door of the reception room in which many valuable and easily portable objects were kept. (There was no avarice in the lady, who had made valuable donations to the La Salle School in Tulcan and to the minor seminary of Ibarra.) The miscreants were already inside, and the aforesaid lady had invoked Garcia Moreno, when in the same instant a horrendous crash, like an electric train and the collapse of a house produced by an earthquake, caused panic in the assailants who left the stately home in terror. Again there was deep silence.

When the day dawned, Miss Ribera and her servant were in the reception room and found the doors open and broken. They examined all that was contained in the chamber, and they noticed that everything was in its place and that not a thread was missing.

The letter by Brother Clement of Tulcan added a detail that can be more debatable: that a portrait of Garcia Moreno, which was not found hanging on a wall, was found high up on the opposite wall well fastened with strings and a nail; and that such a flight and change of place by the picture contributed to the terror of the bandits.

Again in the canton of Milagro, Mr. Rogerio Fernandez Ortiz, in the year 1964, spoke with me in these terms: *"A short time ago I left my house while invoking Garcia Moreno, the holy President, 'Allow me to catch the thieves who have gotten into my bedroom and have stolen my suit of clothes and a thousand sucres which I had inside.' As soon as I walked a short distance, I was met by a gentleman who asked me, 'Where are you going in such a hurry?'* – *'Sir, I am going to the police, because thieves have entered my house and have robbed some of my clothes and money.' The gentleman said to me, 'Do not be troubled: the man whom you suspect is the thief. Make him go to prison, and recover your clothes and your money. Good-bye.'"*

Fernandez Ortiz went a few steps more, and he thought to himself, "Why did I not ask this gentleman, what reason do you have to tell me, 'The man whom you suspect, that very man is the thief?'" In fact, this knowledge of Fernandez Ortiz's suspicion, a thought imperceptible to others, also made him suspect that such a gentleman was not from this world. In any case, the wronged man calmed himself thinking, *"The gentleman has to be around here; it has not been more than a moment since he went away."* He looked behind and he did not find him, nor was he ahead. *"It is a rare occurrence,"* he exclaimed. *"This road is long and straight. There are no doors where he could have entered or corners where he could have turned."*

When he arrived at the police station, he retold his story and spoke about the gentleman who had vanished into thin air. *"Here in this city,"* they answered, *"there are an immense number of thieves. Look at this long list. The matter is not going to be solved in a short time. Go back to your house, and we are going to investigate and search."* While walking down his road, the troubled man kept asking himself, *"Who can this mysterious man be?"* He had hardly entered his house, when he cast his eyes on a portrait of Garcia Moreno and exclaimed with joy, *"He is exactly the same... Identical... He is the same man who appeared to me on the road."*

Again he went to the police. He insisted so much that so-and-so was the thief that a group of three prison guards marched to the indicated address and obliged the householder to go outside for a moment. At the same time the one making the search entered into the rooms of the suspect, and immediately found Mr. Rogerio's new clothes and the thousand sucres.

The following year, 1965, that same man devoted to Garcia Moreno spoke with me and told me, *"I confirm that it was Garcia Moreno who appeared to me on the road: the figure, forehead, the eyes and all the features are identical to those in the portrait. Those thousand sucres that were recovered were to pay the bakery. I buy in bulk and sell retail. Take another five sucres for making our holy President known."*

I transcribe verbatim a narrative text published in *El Mensajero del Corazon de Jesus* of Santiago, Chile, September of 1953:

> *"La Serena, Chile. Mrs. Juana Rodriguez tells of the favor that she obtained from the Sacred Heart and the glorious martyr Garcia Moreno, President of Ecuador:*
> 
> *'I was seriously injured in my left leg, especially my knee, and had acute pains, and not finding any improvement for a long time, it occurred to me to invoke the glorious martyr Garcia Moreno, so that I might obtain improvement from the Sacred Heart, promising Him to put His portrait in a frame. The time was twelve midnight. I slept until two in the morning. I awoke completely cured. Being thankful, I publish the favor of my glorious intercessor and distinguished martyr of the Sacred Heart of Jesus...'"*

**Story related by Reverend Mother Prioress Luisa Maria Palacios:**

> *"In the month of May, 1975, kneeling before the mortal remains of the President-martyr, I said to him, 'Morenito, for ninety-three years we have had you in our church without charging you a centavo.*[7] *Now I ask you for the sum of thirty thousand sucres with which I need to pay a debt immediately.' This plea was made at three in the afternoon. An hour later, or at four o'clock of the same afternoon, I received an airmail envelope in which I found written, 'To the Mother Superior of the Convent of Saint Catherine.' I tore open the envelope and found a check for thirty thousand sucres to the bearer. I was not able to decipher the signature, try as I might. At once I sent the check to the bank, and they remitted thirty thousand sucres in currency, with which I then paid my debt."*

Father Aurelio Aulestia, S.J., at the advanced age of eighty-three years old, suffered from the following ailment: a kind of electric charge in his entire right arm, with discomforts that made him burst into prolonged cries. This affliction repeated itself about three times per week, for some three months. What did the doctors say? They said that such an ailment is the effect of insufficient circulation of the blood, caused by old age. How is it counteracted? By spraying the arm with certain liquids that have the power of invigorating circulation. But Father Aulestia was opposed to doctors and medicine.

When August 6, 1975, arrived, the cramp repeated itself five times. Such a turn for the worse, and on the exact centenary of the death of Garcia Moreno, impelled the aforesaid religious to take a fragment of the clothing of the President-martyr and to apply it to the infirm arm. Well, he never felt those pains again despite the advance of old age. Here is another case that, taking into account the doctors' report, could be considered as a first class miracle.

Letter written in Las Lajas, Columbia, with the date, June 13, 1976:

> *"Reverend Father Servero Gomezjurado, S.J.,*
> *Thank you for the holy cards, which I no longer have, since I had to give them away, along with the oil painting which Your Reverence blessed. Do you remember? I gave it to a niece of one of our Mothers, for whom it has worked many favors; among those that I*

*know, it freed her from death three times. She says, 'If it were not for my Gabrielito,⁸ I would not be alive now.' When she invoked him, she said to him with all confidence, 'Blessed soldier of Ecuador,⁹ help me with this!' and she always got out of the predicaments. And not only she, but also the persons who go to her house to pray to him.*

*She lives in Ipiales, Columbia. As the picture had been only on vellum, she put it into a beautiful gilt frame with glass. Another lady, for a great favor obtained, financed the permanent lighting of the picture with electric light. All kinds of people go there, even currently incredulous students, to ask him for them to pass their subjects during the year, and he helps them. The lady who has the picture has had Masses offered in thanksgiving...*

*Your affectionate and faithful servant in Christ and Mary, Sister Maria Luciana Proano"*

**Three Different Novena Prayers**
(With Ecclesiastical Approval)

O Sacred Heart of Jesus! Remember the consecration that President Gabriel Garcia Moreno made to Thee of his Republic; of the enthronement of Thy sacred image in his presidential home; and of his blood, shed to seal his unshakeable adherence to Thee and to Thy vicar, the Pope, and grant us the canonical glorification of such an exemplary ruler, that men powerful in deeds and words may rise up for the cause of religion and of country, and finally grant the particular grace which we ask of Thee, in accord with Thy good pleasure. Amen.¹⁰ (Ask for a particular grace and end with a Glory Be.)

oooooooOooooooo

Remember, O most holy Virgin of Sorrows, that your servant, Gabriel Garcia Moreno, swore to defend the privilege of your Immaculate Conception; he was a member of your Congregation;¹¹ an assiduous reciter of the holy rosary; he expired at the foot of your sacred altar, and according to the testimony of Pope Pius IX, who defined your exemption from original sin, "died as a victim for the faith and Christian charity for his country," and obtain for us the canonical glorification of such an exemplary ruler, that men powerful in deeds and words may rise up for the cause of the same faith and of country, and finally the particular grace which we ask through your intercession and for his glory, if it be for the good of our souls. Amen.¹² *(Ask for a particular grace, and recite a Hail Mary.)*

ooooooOoooooo

O Jesus, our God and Savior! Remember that His Grace Ignacio Checa,¹³ Archbishop of Quito, and Gabriel Garcia Moreno, President of Ecuador, whose hearts always remained united, consecrated their country to Thy Sacred Heart and fell victims for their Catholic faith; and grant us the canonical glorification of both so that men powerful in deeds and words may rise up for the advancement of the same faith and of country; and finally grant us the particular grace which we request, for their glory, in accord with Thy Divine good pleasure. Amen. *(Ask for a particular grace, and end with a Glory Be.)*

# Endnotes

[1] Translated from the monumental biography, *Vida Garcia Moreno* by Reverend Father Severo Gomezjurado, S. J., (Quito, 1981; vol. 13, pp. 403-418). On December 20, 1939, the Archbishop of Quito, Carlos Maria de la Torre, formed a Commission of historians in preparation for the establishment of the beatification process of Garcia Moreno, "Martyr of Christian Justice." Archbishop de la Torre was later elevated to the cardinalate in 1953 by Pope Pius XII, and thus became the first Ecuadorian to be admitted to the College of Cardinals. Father Gomezjurado had been the leading member of the aforementioned Commission, and this article is taken from the final volume of his thirteen volume work.

[2] Faustino Rayo, hired by the Freemasons, was President Garcia Moreno's assassin.

[3] I.e. 102-104° F.

[4] The Jivaros are South American Indians of eastern Ecuador and northeast Peru.

[5] The meninges is the system of membranes which envelops the central nervous system.

[6] An account of a woman in Jiron freed from temptations of despair has been omitted here as it is found above in Appendix I.

[7] A *centavo* is equivalent to a "penny."

[8] I.e. an affectionate form of Gabriel Garcia Moreno's first name.

[9] I.e. *Puendito bendito*, in Spanish. *Puendos* was the nickname given the Ecuadorian soldiers by the soldiers of Columbia during the Ecuadorian–Colombian War of 1863.

[10] This prayer has been approved not only by the bishops of Ecuador, but moreover by the bishops of Pasto in Columbia, of Santiago in Chile, of Sao Paulo in Brazil, by another in Argentina through the mediation of Father Herve Le Lay. It has been translated into Portuguese and English. More than 100,000 holy cards of Garcia Moreno with these prayers were distributed within forty years.

[11] I.e. the Marian Congregation of Artisans in Quito directed by the Jesuit Fathers.

[12] This prayer was approved by His Eminence Cardinal de La Torre, Archbishop of Quito, on November 10, 1959.

[13] Archbishop Ignacio Checa y Barba was poisoned with strychnine during the Mass of the Presanctified on Good Friday in the Cathedral of Quito on March 30, 1877, for his opposition to the liberal and anti-clerical demands of the liberal government which followed the assassination of Garcia Moreno. These two heads of Church and of State consecrated Ecuador to the Sacred Heart in the same Cathedral where the former died and the latter was poisoned, as it were, to seal their covenant with God in the same place with their own blood.

# Appendix III
# Discovery of Garcia Moreno's Mortal Remains[1]

With the passing of time, history is purged and examined more closely and acquires data and new documents. In our book entitled *The Consecration* Garcia Moreno's mortal remains were said to have been removed as a result of Alfaro's triumph in Gatazo, to guard them in a more hidden and secret place, and thereby to preserve them from profanation by Masonry. It is also said that Canon Terrazas intervened in this charitable act. There are two errors here.[2] From whom did the author hear them? From several persons authorized by their old age and affection for the President-martyr, especially from Sister Ana Maria Arroyo, whose dialogue with the author was recorded on tape and [being transcribed was] reproduced in Xerox copies, thanks to measures taken by Mr. Cristobal Bonifaz Jijon and the Reverend Father Soria, a Lazarist priest. Mr. Bonifaz gave one of the Xerox copies as a gift to Monsignor Juan Larrea Holguin. Such errors have been reprinted in the current volume, chapter 12.[3]

The follow text is taken from the note that was put into a bottle in Garcia Moreno's casket when his body was moved from the cathedral and hidden in the convent of the Sisters of St. Catherine of Siena:

Garcia Moreno's embalmed corpse, after a pompous and magnificent funeral in the Cathedral, was buried in that same church. There his remains lay until March twenty-seventh of the current year [1883], and were exhumed on that day by Canon Doctor Jose Maria Terrazas, under the pretext of repairing the church; and if there was no marked animosity in this toward Garcia Moreno's memory, at the least it is the work of a complete lack of common sense, Christian prudence and moral sensibility, by sending, as he did, the message to my sister Mariana, widow of the Hero-martyr, by a clumsy sacristan at a bad time, that she should dispose of her husband's remains, as though it were an insignificant thing.[4] Such news reopened the wound that had never ever healed, not only of that desolated widow but also of her entire family and of the author who writes this. And let the reader imagine the impression it caused in the minds of his relatives, family and friends."[5]

## Exhumation of Garcia Moreno's Body

*By the previous announcement of His Eminence Cardinal Doctor Pablo Munoz Vega, S. J., a commission came to our Saint Catherine's Monastery comprised of Reverend Father Rigoberto Correa, General of the Oblate Priests, Reverend Father Jose Maria Vargas, O.P., and the University graduate Francisco Salazar Alvarado on Monday, April 14, 1975, at nine o'clock in the morning.*[6]

The commission was given the responsibility of conducting the search for the remains of ex-President Garcia Moreno, assassinated on August 6, 1875, to be completed by the date of the centenary of his death.

Also present were the Prior of the Santo Domingo Convent, Friar Gonzalo Valdivieso, O.P., representing the Provincial Priest, Friar Manuel Freire, O.P., and the Monastery Chaplain, Friar Sebastian Acosta, O.P. Among those who served as witnesses are to be mentioned Mother Ana Maria Arroyo, O.P., Mother Luisa Maria Palacio, O.P., Mother Maria Magdalena Salazar, O.P., Father Domingo Soto, O.P. and Sister Cecilia de Jesus Almeida, O.P.; Sister Dominga del Rosario Guerrero, O.P., and Mother Juana de la Cruz Pozo, O.P., served as eyewitnesses.

The oral tradition of the location in which the remains of Garcia Moreno were interred was kept by the oldest religious; nevertheless, the exact place was not precisely specified; and so several excavations were made in the interior of the church for two consecutive days. Due to the unsuccessful results, the search was suspended in the church because of information obtained that the cadaver was in a different place.

At the insistence of Mother Luisa Maria Palacio, O.P., Prioress at that time, and of Mother Juana de la Cruz Pozo, O.P., one worker continued the excavation and at five o'clock in the afternoon on Wednesday, April 16, 1975, the remains of the ex-President were found in the place of "The Stairs."[7]

"The exhumation and identification of the body provided an opportunity for a public reading of the documents found together with it, signed by Mr. Ignacio del Alcazar, the ex-President's brother-in-law, and Rafael Varela, a friend of the family, who related the events that occurred regarding Garcia Moreno's assassination, and dated April 3, 1883, the date from which the remains rest in the church of the Dominican convent.

"The exhumation ceremony was enacted in the church of the convent of Saint Catherine and sealed with the proper affidavit in the presence of the ecclesiastical and civil authorities of the time, and it reports the transfer of the remains to the principal church, the Cathedral of Quito, on August 6, 1975, by decision of the prelates, and the leaving to the nuns, in commemoration of this event, Garcia Moreno's right arm bone, cap and shoes which the sisters preserve and display in the Monastic Museum of that same religious community."[8]

The location of the venerated remains of Garcia Moreno was indicated in a letter dated February 28, 1941, by Sister Maria Amada de Jesus Noboa, O.P, the superior of the Convent of Saint Catherine of Siena, which said, "Reverend Mother Teresa de Jesus Navarro [had]... indicated to me the location where they were put or where the stairs are today."[9]

# Endnotes

[1] Gomezjurado, *Vida de Garcia Moreno*, vol. 11, p. LIV.

[2] Cf. vol. 11, pp. 193-197. Firstly, the transfer of Garcia Moreno's remains was not in 1895, but in 1883; secondly, Canon Terrazas' motive was not to prevent their desecration by the Masons out of charity, but to vent his long held grudge against Garcia Moreno. For in 1867 he had been suspected, as mentioned in a letter by the Apostolic Delegate to the Secretary of State of Pope Pius IX, of being a supporter of "the enemies of Garcia Moreno," i. e. the Masons ("the Reds") or at least of the Liberals, and so had to go into hiding when Ecuador was being purged of the Liberal clergy at the prompting of Garcia Moreno. (*Ibid*. p. LVII.)

[3] Gomezjurado, vol. 11, p. LIV.

[4] Tabani's quoted letter to Rome against Terrazas and his colleagues who had hidden that Prebendary so he would not run the risk of falling prisoner, constitute an explanation. Theological studies before Garcia Moreno's time were very deficient and contaminated with Regalism and Liberalism. Therefore, Canon Terrazas might have suffered from doctrinal errors. As a result of the finding of Garcia Moreno's remains, our current Most Reverend Canons were astonished that Terrazas had not consulted with the Chapter before proceeding to the exhumation; but it is recorded in the archives that this Canon was in charge of the repair of the cathedral. If the remains were underground, how could that hinder any repairs? Perhaps they reposed close to the surface; perhaps he did not consult the Chapter, so that the secret would be better kept. The Most Illustrious Archbishop Ignacio Ordonez was very 'Garcian,' yet his intervention does not figure into the matter. His presence is not recorded in the archives at the end of March, 1883. Was he, perhaps, absent from Quito, on a pastoral visit?" (*Ibid*. p. LXII)

[5] *Ibid*. p. LIX.

[6] Taken from the Monastery Chronicle, vol. II, Archive section.

[7] Testimony furnished by Mother Mercedes Quintana, O.P., Directress of the Monastic Museum.

[8] Taken from the booklet, *Saint Catherine of Siena Monastery in Quito*, 1592-2009, pp. 36-37.

[9] Francisco Salazar Alvarado, *Encounter with History: Garcia Moreno, Catholic Leader of Latin America* (Oconomowac, Wisconsin, Apostolate of Our Lady of Good Success Editors, 2006), p. 23.

# Appendix IV

# Homage to Garcia Moreno by Louis Veuillot[1]

Let us pay homage to this noble figure, one worthy of history. The nations are bombarded with presentations of sumptuous but meager gadflies whose time never seems to end. Seditious men, intriguers, empty phantoms, who insolently line up to deceive the famished public. Ahead of each of them we hear: "This is the man Providence has sent!" He is weighed, but has no weight: there is no man there at all! Oblivion devours him, and if he has by chance left some trace, a similar speck of dust easily fills in this vile and arid furrow. Such is the common history of presidents of the republic: a few unremarkable crimes; an infinity of dull idiocies, sometimes just plain, honest vulgarity. [They have] nothing to offer for the present, nothing for the future. These colorless characters are loveless, lacking any ideas or flame. They carry on business, especially their own business; they get bored; they are boring. Clear off! That's how we speak to people whom we do not like very much. It's the worst of occupations. An occupation without fruits, without pride, without any strengths, whose most happy and successful outcome can only be the result one might expect of a competent trade: namely, bread, oblivion and, if one has any conscience, some remorse. Garcia Moreno was of quite a different order, and posterity will recognize it. He was admired by his people; he shunned criminal activity, vulgarity, remorse, oblivion, and would even have avoided hatred itself, if God had permitted it that virtue should not attract hatred. We might suggest that he was the most ancient of the moderns, "a man who gave honor to man." [He was] not just a character from Plutarch: that would not be sufficient. He did everything that Plutarch recounts of his very greatest heroes, which he did by applying what was natural in his character and by an unfailing adherence to the rules by which he lived. But it would be unworthy of him to see him just as a character from Plutarch. He had a conception much more vast in its greatness. By pursuing his great and holy duty, and by ceaselessly pushing himself on, he dared to attempt what this age considers to be impossible, and he achieved it. In the government of the people he we was a man of Jesus Christ.

This is the supreme and outstanding characteristic that makes him a man without equal: a man of Jesus Christ in public life – a man of God. A small southern republic has shown us this wonder: a man who was so noble, so strong and intelligent that he was able to persevere in his plan to be, as it is said, a "man of his time"; who studied contemporary sciences, who accepted contemporary ways and knew and followed modern customs and laws and yet did not cease to be a strict and faithful man of the Gospel; that is to say, a strict and faithful man of God; and, what is more, (once he had taken on their leadership) to make his people strict and faithful in their service of God. And throughout his administration, (perhaps it would be better call it his "reign") he acted in this way. One of his fellow citizens has left us a serene painting of him. Under him the young, wise republic of Ecuador lived through its golden age. He was obeyed, not without hard work on his part, but with no resistance or ill-will on the part of those he governed. His reign, quite contrary to current ideas, was as tranquil as it was fruitful. Led by his hand, which was happy to be guided by Heaven, the people of Ecuador allowed themselves to be formed so as to become a great people with a great destiny. They honored and loved the man who, in a mere ten years, and without depriving them of their liberty or oppressing them with taxes, and having taken them over in a scattered and tormented condition, had given them a magistrature, an army, a public fortune, many schools, scientific establishments, buildings, roads and agriculture and all good things; but honor also, which surpasses everything. The Ecuador of Garcia Moreno had become the envied model among the republics of the New World. What could such a hardworking, industrious and Christian people not achieve in the future when led by such a man?

Garcia Moreno had no enemies in Ecuador. He enjoyed a respectful and unparalleled popularity and a level of confidence and credit without limit. In general in that region, we are told by a southern republican, presidents amass their riches which they move to Europe and then they follow them; this is well known, and they are unable to borrow. Everyone was keen to lend to Garcia Moreno. They had his word. The stock exchanges were as open to him as their hearts, and he was able to do what he wanted. The rich called him "the Great"; the people called him "the Just." No one any longer tried to throw the slightest shadow over his virtue, which was as well recognized as his genius. Humble workmen stopped him in the street to get him to adjudicate on their differences; he managed to spread peace between neighbors and even into homes. His decisions were accepted by both parties who praised his wisdom and his fairness in equal measure. These are characteristics which make us recall the greatest times among the judges of Israel. Without doubt his memory will be invoked as a blessing, and the people of Ecuador will have to wait a long time for another Garcia Moreno! But what was the basis of this universal popularity, this power and this great glory? He regulated his whole conduct by the divine precept, *Quaerite primum regnum Dei,* and therein lies the great secret of how to rule.

The priest who had the honor of delivering his funeral oration limited himself to commenting simply on this text from the Holy Scriptures: "Because you have asked neither for riches, nor glory, nor the lives of those who hate you, nor a long life, and because you have asked for wisdom and knowledge to enable you to govern my people, wisdom and knowledge are given to you." *Da mihi sapientiam et intelligentiam ut ingrediar et egrediar coram populo tuo.* That is the prayer of the clergy, and that was the constant and fervent prayer of this great man. That is how he had prayed in Paris during his years of exile and study, because even then he was aware of his destiny and he wanted to fulfill his duty. That is how he continued to pray with still greater ardor when he came to power, not that he had sought it, but because he could not refuse it.

He was truly one of a great race of industrious and assiduous shepherds of people; resolute even to showing contempt for his own life; upright and, above all, a lover of justice. He believed that God had given him to the people to be all of that, and so as to make His law prevail. With that aim, he showed constancy in life and a disdain for comfort or fortune. He used to say, "I wish to leave power poorer that when I assumed it. I have not become leader so as to pursue my own business interests or my own leisure." When told that he was tiring himself too much, he would reply, "God is able to make Himself wait, but I do not have the right to require Him to do so. When He wants me to rest, He will send me an illness or death."

He worked without ceasing, whether on an inspection, or at council, or at his office, never conceding to human nature what it did not snatch from him with urgency. He required attentiveness from his employees, but there was not one employee in the republic of whom he asked more than he asked of himself. His great relaxation came from prayer. At home, among his household, with his guards and his servants he played the part of a good head of household. Every day: prayer and rosary; every Sunday and Feast day, according to the Spanish custom: Sunday rest. "It was a joy and an example to see him at prayer," said one of his relatives who was often a witness to such scenes, "his noble voice, deep and penetrating, read out to us a text which we knew, but at times his piety inspired in him new words that arose from the needs of the moment. He would ask for help for the pressing needs of the State, asking God to dictate to him what he must do, and how he should act when he felt himself to be helpless. Ah, what a man they have assassinated!"

With all this, he was mild, kind, joyful in himself and with friends; simple, hospitable, always ready to oblige and to please. He loved the little ones, and was compassionate towards the sick and afflicted. He was even known to warn evildoers of the justice he must otherwise employ against them. One such man, a dangerous and determined conspirator who was guilty of treason and other serious crimes, and whom he had to prosecute in the end, dared to enter into his private quarters secretly, with the intention of deceiving him once again. He said to him: "This is the end: I can no longer hold back justice, I cannot see you again. I have tried to warn you; you are being searched for. You must hide and save yourself. If you are caught, you know that I have proof of your crimes and you will be shot." This man could have hidden for a short while, but he allowed himself to be arrested and he was shot.

He was implacable towards conspirators and looters, who were the scourge of the country, so by bringing them to justice he thereby delivered his people. His last term as president was calm. Six years of peace! Ecuador was born during these fruitful years, and the peace did not end with his death.

His courage was known to be indomitable, and the whole of America spoke of the examples of courage which he showed. Nothing mattered to him less than putting his life at risk, because he sincerely believed that it did not belong to him. If his duty summoned him, he was always ready: he spoke immediately. We have spoken of how he put down the sedition of Urbina at Guayaquil. On another occasion, he left entirely on his own for a town that was in revolt at the instigation of the military chief. He arrived alone in the town, went into where the thwarted traitor was, and said to him: "I am here! Go to prison!" The good men were reassured; the evil trembled. Sedition was vanquished. The chief was the same conspirator whom the president later had shot, despite the intervention of foreign diplomats, and prayers from round the world. He replied, "I am doing this out of conscience!" The next day, the day of the execution, he left the town on his own. On the occasion of the man who was bribed by Peru, he stated by public proclamation: "Those who corrupt gold will be chastened by lead." *Aquellas que corrompe el oro reprimera el plomo.*

# APPENDIX IV

It was in these ways that Garcia Moreno was everywhere victorious, and by which he affirmed the laws which had previously been so debased. As soon as he heard of a crisis, whatever the obstacles or the distance involved, he would set off and arrive like a thunderbolt, saying, "I am here!"

Bossuet says "A warlike spirit is mistress of the body it animates." How much more so a righteous spirit!

From an early date he was a lover of justice. He knew the misfortune of his country, and from that sense of foresight which great spirits never lack, he was made aware that he would have a role to play. Early in life, so that God might be with him, he desired to be with God. In Paris, where he was for the second time, as a senator and an exile, he led the life of a student, working because that was what God wanted, and because his country had need of it. Shut up in a narrow room in the Rue de la Vieille Comedie he made a special study of the sciences of civilization. He had a particular fondness for chemistry and history, but he did not neglect the others: physics, mathematics, industry and commerce, legislation: his head, which was no less sound than passionate and persevering, took it all in, and extracted from it sound and wide-ranging ideas. Nor did he neglect literature and chant; later on he sent a professor to Rome with the mission to study sacred chant, since, like Charlemagne, he knew that sacred chant has a missionary function. As to literature: nature had made him a writer, and although his role as statesman did not allow him to devote himself to Letters, his communications are held up as models of their kind.

All week he would carry on with his studies, and extract from them what he needed to retain. He reserved Sundays to himself to rest, to serve God and to examine his heart. He would spend Sundays partly at his parish church of St. Sulpice, and partly walking in the outskirts of the city. He refused all other distractions, and throughout the time of his stay he never visited a theater. It was also on his free day of Sunday that, if he was ill, he permitted himself some degree of relaxation for the benefit of his health. On other days he had to pursue his studies; on those days he never had the time to be ill, and on Sundays he never omitted to perform his religious duties. *Da mihi sapientiam et intelligentiam ut ingrediar et egrediar coram populo tuo.* The Mass is essential to enter into the life of the people and to exit from it. By living this way, he learned to understand life and mankind, but not to love, or despise, either of them more than is required. The sciences are good; they are like the vases of the Egyptians, which have to be taken from them so they can then be filled with a wine far more precious.[2] But he who learns God's science knows how to live and how to die. And so Garcia Moreno, in a foreign land, alone, unknown, but sustained by his faith and his great heart, taught himself how to reign, should this be the will of God. He learned all he needed to know to govern a people which had once been Christian, but which had reverted to savagery, and which could no longer be brought back to the civilization of the cross otherwise than with a bridle adorned with the jewels of Europe. With this aim in mind Garcia Moreno had determined to become wise, and Paris, where Providence led him, was just the right workshop for this apprentice. Paris, which was also Christian, but at the same time barbaric and wild, offering the spectacle of combat between the two elements. There were schools, priests and martyrs; there was a vast factory of antichrists, of idols and of executioners. The future President and missionary of Ecuador had before his eyes good and evil, and indifference towards good and evil, all of which he saw in abundance, because in Paris even indifference is also an activity. When he was finally able to return to his distant homeland, his choice was made. He knew where true glory lay, where true strength and the true workers of God. If we had to choose the threshold from which he left, but the final place where his heart lay, and of which he treasured his fondest memory, it would be his dear church of St. Sulpice, or possibly a small missionary chapel where he was accustomed to go to pray for his homeland. At St. Sulpice several of us must often have seen him. We like to believe that perhaps, without knowing him, we have united our prayer with his. In any case, he belonged to us and we claim the honor of belonging to him.

He left France in 1857, and was at first professor of chemistry and rector of the University. In 1860 he was dictator and then President. No one needed to wait long to know what he was going to do.

He was the kind of Christian that the role of sovereign no longer seems to consist of; a leader of the kind that nations no longer seem worthy to have; a man of justice of the kind that the seditious and conspiratorial no longer seem to fear; a king of such a kind that nations have forgotten. There was in him something of the Medici, and of Ximenes: Medici without the deceit; Ximenes without the Roman crimson or the temper. He had the extensive genius of both of them, the magnificence and the love of his country. But in his makeup there were also those admirable characteristics of just and holy kings: goodness, mildness, justice and zeal for God's cause.

He asked a great deal of the clergy, which the revolutions had oppressed down to the earth. He asked nothing of the Church except that she should lead him and give him her laws. It is well known how much he did for her, and for the Holy See; it was always whatever he could, and much more than what seemed possible. He made a concordat in the form requested by the pope, founded monasteries, summoned teaching congregations for all the schools, and made the State pay the expenses of St. Peter. In all that concerned the Church, he sought to bravely obey in the same way as he commanded all others, and in this way he followed the great advice of Bossuet: "Kings: govern boldly."

As soon as he became known, he was condemned to death by that sect which is so powerful in America and which he boldly declared to be his enemy. He knew of this, as the numerous passages from his private letters bear witness. He knew that the death sentence, which had been pronounced in Europe, had been ratified in the American cells and would be carried out. He did not concern himself about this overmuch. He wanted it. The essential thing for him was not to be let off. He was Catholic, and he had resolved to remain so, everywhere and always: Catholic without remedy, from a race which these days is almost unknown among official leaders of nations, a race which turns, above all, towards our Father who is in Heaven, and which says to Him in a loud voice: "May Thy Kingdom come!"

This man of great goodness, this truly great man, whose enemies could only reproach for wanting to regenerate both them and their country through an unconquerable love for light and justice, was quite aware of the fact that he was being threatened by assassins. He used to say to his friends, "They will kill me when I am assured of public approval, then the dagger will no longer be able to wait." When people implored him to take precautions, he would reply, "How can one defend oneself against people who reproach you for being Christian? If I gave in to them, I would deserve to die. From the moment they ceased to fear God, they became masters of my life; I do not wish to be God's master, I do not wish to leave the path which he has marked out for me." He followed his straight and rugged road, which led to the death in this world, but to life eternal; he would repeat his usual saying, *Dios no se muere*; "God does not die."

The more honorable of his political opponents had been converted to his system of government, to his person and to his God. He had performed extraordinary and sublime acts of faith in the presence of his country and in his country; he had latterly been seen, the actual President of the republic, carrying the cross on his shoulders in procession through the streets of Quito; he had filled all the job posts and given every possible example of the most fervent patriotism, of the most enlightened genius, the most energetic soul and the most generous heart. He had been professor, rector of the University, dictator, general in chief and president. He had brought together for the first and up till now the only time, the functions of president of the republic, and those of the director of the hospital of Quito, not an honorific post but executive and unpaid, which hospital he reformed and furnished at his own expense. He also joined to his presidential role that of member of the congregation of the Poor, and he fulfilled all his duties there. Everywhere he showed himself to be hard on himself, sober and chaste. He did not increase, but on the contrary he reduced his personal fortune; he was economic with the public finances but liberal with his own resources; modest, great in all things. He had just been reelected for the third time. The moment of the dagger had arrived.

He was killed in the street by a man of no substance whom he had taken in and helped, but whom he had dismissed on account of his unworthiness or incompetence, the sort of man that sectarians regularly find to carry out this sort of attack.

This man struck him from behind with a bestial fury, attacking like a madman or a wild beast descending on his noble victim. He ran off, but was overcome by the people and subjected to their anger. He was from New Grenada, and on him were found Bank of Peru banknotes, the principal hideout of the Freemasons.

It was the sixth of August, the Feast of the Transfiguration of Our Lord. Garcia Moreno was coming out of the neighboring church where he had attended morning Mass, and was returning to his work in the Government offices. He was stabbed on the steps of the church and brought inside, to the chapel of Our Lady of the Seven Sorrows, an object of his special devotion. He died there a few moments later. His last words were: *Dios no se muere.*

We might dare to say that God owed him a death such as this. He deserved to die in his strength, in his virtue, in his prayer, at the feet of the Virgin of the Seven Sorrows, a martyr for his people and for his Faith, for both of which he had lived. Pius IX publicly honored this worthy son; his people were plunged into a long period of mourning and they cried for him like ancient Israel cried for her heroes and her just men. What glory did he lack? He had given an example that was unique in the world and in the times in which he had lived. He had been the honor of his country: his death was yet another service, perhaps the greatest service: he had shown the whole human race what kind of leaders God was able to give them, and to what miseries it exposes itself by its folly!

# Endnotes

[1] *L'Univers*, September 28, 1875.

[2] "Moreover, if those who are called philosophers, and especially the Platonists, have said aught that is true and in harmony with our faith, we are not only not to shrink from it, but to claim it for our own use from those who have unlawful possession of it. For, as the Egyptians had not only the idols and heavy burdens which the people of Israel hated and fled from, but also vessels and ornaments of gold and silver, and garments, which the same people when going out of Egypt appropriated to themselves, designing them for a better use, not doing this on their own authority, but by the command of God. The Egyptians themselves, in their ignorance, provided them with things which they themselves, were not making a good use of; in the same way all branches of heathen learning have not only false and superstitious fancies and heavy burdens of unnecessary toil, which every one of us, when going out under the leadership of Christ from the fellowship of the heathen, ought to abhor and avoid; but they contain also liberal instruction which is better adapted to the use of the truth, and some most excellent precepts of morality; and some truths in regard even to the worship of the One God are found among them. Now these are, so to speak, their gold and silver, which they did not create themselves, but dug out of the mines of God's providence which are everywhere scattered abroad, and are perversely and unlawfully prostituted to the worship of devils. These, therefore, the Christian, when he separates himself in spirit from the miserable fellowship of these men, ought to take away from them, and to devote to their proper use in preaching the gospel. Their garments, also,—that is, human institutions such as are adapted to that intercourse with men which is indispensable in this life,—we must take and turn to a Christian use." (St. Augustine, *On Christian Doctrine*, bk. 4, chap. 40, n.60)

www.ingramcontent.com/pod-product-compliance
Lightning Source LLC
Chambersburg PA
CBHW031230290426
44109CB00012B/229